DEALS

THE BIGGEST, THE BOLDEST, THE BEST

DEALS

The World's Shrewdest and Most Lucrative Deals from Business, Entertainment, Politics, and Sports

Cheryl Moch and Vincent Virga

Crown Publishers, Inc., New York

To the deals
that will bring world peace

Published by Crown Publishers, Inc., One Park Avenue, New York, New York 10016 and simultaneously in Canada by General Publishing Company Limited

Manufactured in the United States of America

Designed by Rhea Braunstein

LIBRARY OF CONGRESS CATALOGING IN PUBLICATION DATA

Moch, Cheryl.
Deals.

1. Deals. I. Virga, Vincent. II. Title.
AG243.M62 1984   031'.02   84-1786
ISBN 0-517-55039-3

10 9 8 7 6 5 4 3 2 1

First Edition

Contents

Let's Make a Deal

Since humanity first clambered down from the treetops, that dance of advantage known as the deal has oiled the gears of society. Deals are the barter of life and are even thought to bring access to heavenly realms. They were a prelude to the world's oldest profession: Before the act, the terms had to be settled. Dealmakers create social harmony; clearly deals, not love, make the world go round.

We have riffled through history, that record of expert dealmaking, and come up with some of the most instructive stories of the rich and famous and how they got away with it, of the wheeling and dealing that determines such matters as the boundaries of nations, which films are financed, and where our favorite athletes will play next season. These are the tales of back-room deals that have affected—and will affect—our daily lives on the most profound level, from the wars we fight to the price of bread at the market.

By observing some of the shrewdest and most spirited dealmakers of all time, we learned how they used what they had to get what they wanted, skills as useful in the bedroom or the war room as in the board room or the mail room. Everyone does it. Abraham did it with God and called it Israel; Jackie Kennedy allegedly did it with Onassis, then called it a marriage contract that covered every aspect of their conjugal life; J. P. Morgan did it with John D. Rockefeller and Andrew Carnegie, then called it United States Steel; Tom Selleck wanted to do it with *Raiders of the Lost Ark*, but "Magnum, P.I." wouldn't let him; Billie Jean King did it for Martina and all women athletes who followed her.

All of life's a deal, and each of us is a player. Whether our maneuvering results in averting a war, establishing a conglomerate, signing a book contract, or arranging a marriage, a mortgage, or a job, certain techniques are necessary, while particular rules always apply. Most of our deals are game plans from the masters and the winners. Take some tips and achieve your goals, as each of them has done!

And here's the deal we are offering you: For planned, subsequent volumes of *Deals*, we'd love to hear about your favorites. They can be deals of a personal, anecdotal nature—the ones you've participated in that might not have had wide-ranging results, but are of interest—or the historical deal, or dealmaker, that is your favorite. We can't promise you life after death, as one of our Dealmakers can, but if we use your material, we'll cut you in on the action. Is it a deal? Let's shake on it.

Our address is: DEALS
c/o The Elaine Markson Agency
44 Greenwich Avenue
New York, NY 10011

No man profiteth but by the loss of others.

MONTAIGNE

Do unto others as you would have them do unto you.

THE GOLDEN RULE

I

UNDER THE TABLE: BUSINESS

What is a man profited if he shall gain
the whole world and lose his own soul?

MATTHEW, 16:26

Ring Out the Old:
The Divestiture of A.T.&T.

BACKGROUND: Before the antitrust-suit solution of 1982, A.T.&T. made $11,000 a minute, or $16 million a day, more than GM, Ford, GE, Chrysler, and IBM all put together, and more than the gross national product of all but twenty of the world's nations. The reorganization of A.T.&T. ripped apart and rearranged an enterprise with more assets, shareholders, employees, and profits than any in the world.

THE OLD DEAL: In the early 1900s, Bell Telephone's legendary leader, Theodore Vail, worked out an arrangement with the government. The United States government would regulate the phone company, put a ceiling on its profits, protect its monopoly, and allow it to make a decent profit. Bell, in return, would put a telephone into every home and office in America.

RESULTS: This agreement attracted bankers who invested the money needed to accomplish Bell's manifest destiny. If the government had not allowed the monopoly, how could Bell have guaranteed that the phone lines would connect beyond local areas? And the monopoly assured the best service for the cheapest price—or so the arguments ran. Early on, people questioned whether this monopoly was good public policy, but its success put the phone into cities, towns, and hamlets alike, while its system of interstate networks grew to astoundingly complex proportions: The continent was tied up in Bell wires, the largest "spider web" of its kind on earth.

In 1956 (a technological century ago), in order to settle an antitrust suit, A.T.&T. (conglomerate Bell) agreed to limit itself to providing only telephone service. Thus, the monopoly stayed intact. In the late 1960s, when the MCI Communications Corporation developed a microwave circuit for long-distance business calls, Bell was not bothered. However, in the early 1970s when MCI, using new technology, asked to tie its system into the Bell system, Bell balked. MCI wanted to compete, but Bell already owned all the lines. Bell claimed

it was a "protected" monopoly; MCI argued that there was no such thing in the United States and sued A.T.&T. for restraining trade. After a battle that lasted over a decade, an FCC ruling opened the long-distance market to all comers and required Bell to allow the interconnection of competitors with its phone lines, though only Bell could provide local service on those lines. (MCI's record $1.8 billion judgment was overturned in 1983, but a new trial to set damages for A.T.&T.'s eight antitrust violations against MCI was ordered.)

At the same time, a virtual revolution in telecommunications technology was creating new markets (and mushrooming profits), which A.T.&T. was forbidden to enter because of its 1956 agreement with the government. A.T.&T. lobbied furiously for changes in the regulations. They announced: "We are having a difficult time responding to the new communication environment!" In 1981, the Senate passed a bill (by a vote of 90 to 4) to divide A.T.&T. into two subsidiaries: one for regulated services and one for competitive services. The House was preparing a similar bill that was even more restrictive. What the antitrust laws could not control, the legislature would dismember. A.T.&T. petitioned the government to drop its 1975 antitrust suit, pending this new legislation. The federal district judge refused, demanding A.T.&T. "refute the factual showing" of monopoly.

So with competition growing, the electronics era booming without them, the telephone's local service offering minimal profit growth, Congress working its own solutions that might impose layers and layers of regulations, and the judge on the antitrust suit seemingly unsympathetic, the new chairman of the A.T.&T. board, Charles L. Brown, decided "to try to come to some accommodation with public policy."

THE NEW DEAL: On Friday, January 8, 1982, in a consent decree with the Justice Department, A.T.&T. settled its seven-year antitrust suit by agreeing to spin off within the next eighteen months its twenty-two local-service phone companies (some two-thirds of its $155 billion assets), which provide the nation with 80 percent of its local telephone service. The twenty-two phone companies would be restructured into seven regional holding companies, each with about $17 billion in assets and restricted to providing local-monopoly phone service only. In return for A.T.&T.'s taking "the divestiture route," the Justice Department modified the 1956 consent decree that had limited A.T.&T. to the regulated phone business. A.T.&T. would be allowed to continue publishing the Yellow Pages, a $3-billion-a-year business, and would continue to sell or rent *all* its equipment.

RESULTS: Without government restraints, A.T.&T. was free to enter into any unregulated nontelephone field; that is, computer-to-computer communication services, cable television, data processing, or electronic publishing—the most lucrative growth areas in the world today, many of which are dependent upon transmitting information via existing telephone lines. Even after the largest divestiture in history, A.T.&T.'s assets were just under $44 billion. (Exxon was the only larger corporation, with $56.6 billion.) A.T.&T. retained its Long Lines Department (with its long-distance telephone network), Western Electric (its huge manufacturing subsidiary), Bell Laboratories (its research arm), all its equipment (thus depriving the local companies of an estimated $4 billion in rental and sales income), and all its licensing rights to its considerable inventions developed at Bell Labs using ratepayers' money. A.T.&T. set up a separate subsidiary to market its unregulated activities for as long as its long-distance service remains regulated: Telephone subscribers will not be paying for A.T.&T. computer development, they claimed.

But Timothy Wirth, chairman of the House subcommittee on telecommunications, questioned A.T.&T.'s new business freedom *and* old control over long-distance lines, which may automatically give them "a chance to discriminate against competing companies who wish to transmit data-processing information." A.T.&T. Chairman Brown disagreed: "I think freed of the restrictions imposed by the '56 decree, there's no question that the A.T.&T. part of the split will really thrive. I just think [A.T.&T.] has had the kind of shackles on it that were unfair and unreasonable under the current competitive conditions." Then a federal judge, required by the Tunney Act to approve settlement of federal antitrust cases, made some radical changes in the settlement.

THE NEWEST DEAL: The twenty-two local companies would keep control of the profitable Yellow Pages (to help prevent instability and skyrocketing rates) and they would be allowed to sell or rent, though not manufacture, telephones and terminal equipment. A.T.&T. is barred from electronic publishing until competition is firmly established.

RESULTS: While many newspapers, state regulators, specialized common carriers, and consumer groups were satisfied by the judge's adjustments, there were many dissatisfied by the absence of a more comprehensive telecommunications legislation. Congress has put the question aside, since A.T.&T. agreed to the settlement. Meanwhile, although Bell has sold its local companies, there is nothing in the agreement to prevent them from setting up a rival service by cable, or microwave, or cellular radio, or some new creation of Bell Laboratories. . . .

Dealmaker Financial Rewards: Perk Up

♦"Golden Parachutes" are the special termination agreements that protect chief executive officers (CEOs) from losing their shirts during takeover battles. The top executives win either way: if they keep their companies and their positions, *or* if they lose their jobs and gain huge compensations. Says Paul Meyer, a "compensation consulting firm" manager: "I truly believe that key executives need to be financially secure in order to strike the very best deal for their shareholders in takeover negotiations." Meanwhile Felix Rohatyn of Lazard Frères [see "Dealmaker as Savior: Felix Rohatyn," page 207], a prominent corporate matchmaker, suggests: "If an executive needs a multi-million-dollar contract to get his mind clear in a takeover situation, then maybe he should see a psychiatrist."

No two parachutes are alike. Some open easily (a 20 percent change of ownership triggers benefits); some operate only under the most dire circumstances. Many stipulate that the executive cannot bail out unless he suffers "diminution in compensation or position" in the reorganized company. Almost all are initiated by management to save corporate assets.

THE BIGGEST PARACHUTES

Company	CEO	Amount (in millions)
American Family	John Amos	$7.8
GK Technologies	Robert Jensen	7.3
Conoco	Robert Bailey	4.1
Bendix	William Agee	4.0
Thiokol	Robert Davis	4.0
Allied	Edward Hennessy	3.9
Penzoil	J. Hugh Liedtke	3.7

♦ *Signing Bonus:* This is a very civilized way to compensate a new employee for lost pension and profit sharing, a pleasant way to say Welcome Aboard! and a way to hire a desirable person who may be more expensive than the job category permits.

CEO	From	To	Signing Bonus (in millions)
Archie McCardell	Xerox	International Harvester	$1.5
Charles Acker	Air Florida	Pan American	.25
Tom Wyman	Pillsbury	CBS	1.0

◆ *Year-End Bonus:* These are usually tied to company profits, with a specific percentage of return on equity.

Company	Percentage Rate
Sears	17
NCR	6
Wang Labs	15

Company	CEO	1981 Salary	1981 Bonus
W. R. Grace	J. Peter Grace	$549,000	$265,000
Gulf and Western	C. Bludhorn	810,000	554,000
Union Oil	Fred Hartley	531,000	800,000
Sears	Edward Telling	650,000	350,000

◆ *Fire-Proof Systems:* As in sports contracts, the company agrees to pay a specific amount each year for a settled number of years *no matter what,* except in the event of a felony offense on the employee's part.

CEO	Company	Number of Years	Amount
James Kerr	Avco	until retired	$310,000 yearly plus pension plus 500,000 over 10 years
Robert Bauman	Avco	5	310,000 plus bonuses
Stanton Cook	Tribune	10	300,000 plus bonuses

Some CEOs have a termination clause that demands their option be picked up twelve months before expiration; if not they may spend their last year offering their services elsewhere, on company time.

◆ *Pension Plan:* The Tax Act of 1982 allows $90,000 in annual payments into a company pension plan. CEOs have their usual pension supplemented.

◆ *Miscellaneous:* Stock options + free legal assistance + free-lance options on free time + time off + education + health clubs + life insurance + IRA accounts + deferred compensation + company cars + club memberships + low-interest loans—and anything else an accountant can devise.

When You Wish upon a Network: The Birth of Disneyland

BACKGROUND: Walt Disney had already proven his ability to found a fortune on a mouse, but when it came to finding funding for a Magic Kingdom, staid bankers thought Disney had gone bonkers.

Mickey Mouse and his gang (Minnie, Pluto, Goofy, Donald, Daisy, et al.) had been a universal craze since they first began appearing in animated shorts in the late 1920s. The licensing of products bearing their irresistible likenesses (everything from Mickey Mouse watches to radiator caps emblazoned with mouse ears) made Disney a very rich man. Everyone seemed to love then except those notorious sourpusses, the Nazis, who banned Mickey, saying that he represented "the most miserable ideal ever revealed. Mice are dirty." In the 1940s, Disney proved with *Snow White* that full-length animated feature films could make millions.

However, in 1952, when Disney approached the banks asking for millions to fund his latest visionary project, everyone refused him: An amusement park named Disneyland with no ferris wheel? No roller coaster? No beer? Forget it!

Disney said that amusement parks were usually "dirty, phoney places run by tough-looking people." But this one, conforming to his unique vision, would be different—it would be a Magic Kingdom! He borrowed on his life insurance to raise the money to draw up detailed plans and models of what he had in mind. His researchers, looking for a site near the burgeoning population center of Southern California, found 160 acres of orange grove (later expanded to 185) in Anaheim, twenty-seven minutes on the new Santa Ana Freeway from Los Angeles. Even as the land was being purchased, Disney was still searching for the financing necessary to actually build his dreamland. Television, the newly popular mass medium, had been asking Disney to throw some of his pixie dust its way, but Disney had refused all offers to do TV programming—until it dawned on him: ABC, perennially number three in the ratings, needed Disney magic; and he needed their network bucks.

THE DEAL: Disney would provide, for seven years, a one-hour weekly show called "Disneyland"—later changed to "Walt Disney Presents." ABC would invest $500,000 in Disneyland Park, thereby becoming a 34.48 percent owner, and would guarantee bank loans of up to $4.5 million.

RESULTS: Excavation for Disneyland began in August 1954. The TV series premiered on October 27, 1954, with the "Disneyland Story," describing the coming attractions of the park. The show immediately became the number-one series on TV, and ABC was able to sell $15 million in sponsorships the first season. And TV proved to be the most persuasive barker an amusement park ever had: In the first full year of Disneyland's existence, more than three million people visited the park, with adults outnumbering children four to one. Disney considered Disneyland to be the crown of all his creations, his Versailles, and he made sure that the sparkle did not tarnish. The young staff was spiffy and ever smiling, the physical plant was kept in top shape; chewing gum was scraped off the sidewalk *every* night. Unfortunately for Disney, and to his everlasting regret, he was unable to control developments just outside the border of his Magic Kingdom. With millions of tourists flocking to the once-sleepy town of Anaheim (today, ten million come each year), the place exploded as developers moved in, building hotels and motels (today there are twelve thousand rooms there), gas stations, and restaurants. And none of these millions of tourist dollars, lured there by his park, went to Disney.

Disney made sure that this did not happen again when he was searching for the site for a new park, east of the Mississippi. This time he purchased 27,400 acres in Orlando, Florida (forty-three square miles, twice the size of Manhattan island). Although Disney died in 1966 before Walt Disney World and its far-out sisterland, EPCOT (Experimental Prototype Community of Tomorrow), opened, they both conform to his vision; and within this huge leisure-opolis, the Disney organization controls *everything*. The "Vacation Kingdom" in Orlando has proved so popular—an estimated twenty-three million people visit yearly—that it ranks as the sixth most visited "nation" in the world (behind Spain, Italy, France, Canada, and the United States). The two Disney kingdoms combined outrank all but Spain as tourist meccas. In 1982, the two parks generated nearly $700 million for the Disney corporation. In 1983, a new $450-million-dollar Disneyworld opened near Tokyo, the first Magic Kingdom outside the U.S. The Disney Corporation has no equity in the project, but receives 7.5 percent of all revenues as a licensing fee.

ABC revealed just how they managed to remain in last place all those years when they canceled the popular Disney shows (by then Disney had created "The Mickey Mouse Club," which was so popular that mouse ears sold at a rate of twenty-four thousand a day, and the unforgettable "Zorro") and sold their interest in Disneyland back to Disney in 1960, for $7.5 million.

> "I am corny; but millions of people eat corn. There must be a reason they like it so much."
>
> Walt Disney

When Disney died in 1966, Eric Sevaried eulogized him on the "CBS Evening News": "What Disney seemed to know was that while there is very little grown-up in a child, there is a lot of child in every grown-up. . . . By conventional wisdom, mighty mice, flying elephants, Snow White . . . all these were fantasy, escapism from reality. It's a question of whether they were any less real, any more fantastic than intercontinental missiles, poisoned air, defoliated forests. . . . This is an age of fantasy however you look at it, but Disney's fantasy wasn't lethal."

If You Have to Ask How Much It Costs, You Can't Afford It: J. P. Morgan Puts Together U.S. Steel

J. P. Morgan portrait by Edward Steichen, 1903.

BACKGROUND: By 1900, financial titan J. P. Morgan had finally gained control of America's rail lines, and he was looking around for a new industry to dominate when someone suggested steel. The notion of a giant steel company, controlling everything from ore to finished product, appealed to Morgan; no one had ever done anything that big before. But there was one hitch: American steel was already dominated by two of the most powerful masters of American industry—Andrew Carnegie, whose steelworks constituted the largest industrial unit in the world; and John D. Rockefeller, the "Lord of the Underground," who, in his vast Mesabi ore fields of Minnesota, controlled 60 percent of U.S. ore. Like Morgan, they were among the richest men in the world; like Morgan, each was a despot, used to total control of his own domain. Perhaps that's why Morgan took them on.

Morgan's first move in steel came when he "consolidated" the western steel producers into the Federal Steel Company. With assets of $56 million, Morgan capitalized the company at $200 million, easily selling that much inflated stock (known as "watered" stock) because America was, at that time, being swept by an investment craze. Promoters could make large amounts of money combining previously competing companies into "trusts" and selling stock in the new ventures to an avid public. The process of combining companies also appealed to industrialists because it eliminated costly and troublesome competition. Carnegie was unperturbed by Morgan's organization of Federal, commenting: "I think Federal's the greatest concern the world ever saw for the manufacturing of stock certificates, but they will fail sadly in steel." Morgan continued to bring about important consolidations in the steel industry, buying out companies that used steel to manufacture such items as pipes, nails, hoops, wire, fencing, and bridge parts. Joining forces with other important steel users, Morgan and his allies informed Carnegie, the nation's largest raw-steel producer, that they would no longer be buying his steel but would be making their own. To Carnegie, this was a declaration of war.

"In these days of trusts and swindles," Carnegie declared, "Carnegie Steel should keep a pure record . . . independent concerns will soon beat the trusts." Carnegie, backed by a personal fortune of $100 million, profits of $40 million a year from his company, and an agreement with John D. Rockefeller that gave him a fifty-year exclusive to the giant Mesabi ore fields, was not about to crumble. He told his partners: "After peace is gone, the worst policy is 'gentle war' . . . it is survival of the fittest. Go into making their products at once. Lose not a day . . . hoop, rod, wire, nails . . . spend freely." If Morgan and his cohorts would make their own steel, Carnegie would make finished products. His agents purchased a five-thousand-acre site and announced plans to construct the most modern pipe factory ever built. Morgan retaliated: the Pennsylvania Railroad suddenly announced that it was doubling its freight charges between Pittsburgh ("Steel City") and the East Coast. Carnegie was now furious: "A life and death struggle! . . . The Deliverance of Pittsburgh is my next great work!" He would, he announced, build his own railroad.

Now Morgan began to worry. He had spent many years "securing harmony" in the railroads, as he liked to describe the process of crushing competition, and here he was stirring up the tempest of industrial war. His new steel companies were vastly overcapitalized, and their stock prices completely depended on investor confidence. "It is not at all certain," a Morgan partner later recalled, "that Carnegie would not have driven entirely out of business every steel company in the U.S." There had to be a way out: If Carnegie could not be beaten, perhaps he could be bought. Morgan called for Charles Schwab, president of Carnegie Steel (and later president of U.S. Steel). "If Andy wants to sell," said Morgan, "I'll buy. Go and find his price."

Schwab told Carnegie about Morgan's offer over a game of golf. Carnegie slept on the idea and the next morning jotted down some figures on a slip of paper. It was that slip which Schwab showed Mor-

"I have done nothing except stop men fighting. I don't like to see men fighting. There is too much waste."

J. P. Morgan

gan, who never bargained. Glancing at the paper, he murmured, "I accept."

THE FIRST DEAL: Carnegie asked for a whopping $420 million. He demanded that his share ($213 million) be in first-mortgage, 5-percent bonds, so that he remained a creditor, not an investor, in the new venture; if it collapsed, Carnegie could repossess it.

RESULTS: Morgan now controlled the production and manufacture of steel, but without ore fields he was vulnerable in the most fundamental area. American ore was in the hands of the Rockefellers, who also controlled the most efficient fleet and railroad for shipping ore from the Great Lakes region. When Rockefeller acquired the Mesabi fields, it was rumored that he would be setting up steel mills to compete with Carnegie; but, in fact, in 1896, the two signed an agreement giving Carnegie exclusive rights to the ore. ("I was astonished that the steelmakers had not seen the necessity of controlling their ore supply," Rockefeller later said about his purchase of Mesabi.) Now that Carnegie was out of the business, Morgan was after the ore fields.

There was no love lost between Morgan and Rockefeller. Rockefeller said of Morgan: "I have never been able to see why any man should have such a high and mighty feeling about himself." Morgan thought that Rockefeller was an unscrupulous upstart. When Morgan asked Rockefeller to come to his office to discuss Mesabi, the imperious Rockefeller replied, "I never go downtown." Morgan then swallowed his pride and went uptown, where Rockefeller, with chilling courtesy, informed him that he was retired; business, he said, should be discussed with his son Junior, age twenty-seven. A few days later, when Junior came to see him, Morgan demanded, "What's your price?" Junior replied, "I think there must be some mistake. I did not come to sell. I understood you wished to buy." And with that, Junior left. "The whole thing," he told his father, "suggested the final sweep-up of the room, and we seemed to be the crumbs around the edge." The Rockefellers enjoyed tormenting Morgan but did intend to sell out; when Henry Frick, a former Carnegie partner, came to visit them with an offer from Morgan, John D. said, "I am not anxious to sell my own properties . . . but I never wish to stand in the way of a worthy enterprise." Rockefeller recognized that Morgan was doing for steel what he, himself, had done for oil—eliminating messy, inefficient competition.

THE SECOND DEAL: Rockefeller would receive $8.5 million in cash for his Great Lakes fleet, and $80 million for the Mesabi ore fields. Morgan would pay him half in common and half in preferred stock of the new venture. And he would get a seat on the board of the new company, a seat that one day would go to Junior.

RESULTS: Morgan incorporated the new venture, the U.S. Steel Corporation, in New Jersey, where the laws were so favorable to monopolies that the state was called the "Mother of Trusts." He capitalized the new venture at $1.4 billion (later a federal investigation would put the value of all tangible assets at $682 million). It was the first billion-dollar corporation, at a time when that amount represented one twenty-fifth of all industrial value in the United States. Annual appropriations of the United States government would not reach $1 billion for another ten years.

The syndicates underwriting the stock immediately made a profit of $57.5 million, including $11.5 million that went to the House of Morgan. Brokers, hired to manipulate the stock price, successfully created the illusion of a boom, and within two weeks the price of common stock rose from 38 to 55. Insiders, who suspected the true worth of the company, began quietly to sell out. When the bubble of speculative mania burst in 1903, the price of common stock sunk to eight dollars a share. U.S. Steel has been beset by problems ever since: explosive labor disputes, management problems, and ruinous competition from abroad. But Big Steel has hung in there: 141,623 people were employed by U.S. Steel in 1982, a year in which the corporation lost $361 million on sales of $18.9 million. In 1982, U.S.

Steel acquired the Marathon Oil Company, the seventeenth largest domestic oil company in the United States. They paid $6.6 billion in cash and notes for the company, which is expected to account for 40 percent of U.S. Steel revenues. Oil just might prove to be the silver lining in the cloud over Big Steel. Rockefelle knew that all along.

J. P. MORGAN AND LAWYERS

Junius Morgan's advice to his son, J. P.: "I hope that you will not be tempted into litigation. Life is too short for that."

When, in response to some outrageous Morgan proposal, his lawyer said, "I don't think you can legally do that," Morgan told him: "Well, I don't know as I want a lawyer to tell me what I cannot do. I hire him to tell me how to do what I want to do."

J. P. Morgan's lawyer commenting on the Sherman Antitrust Act of 1890: "What looks like a stone wall to a layman is a triumphal arch to a corporation lawyer."

Dealmaker as Financial Titan: John Pierpont Morgan

John Pierpont Morgan, who would become the most powerful financier that America, and quite possibly the world, had ever known, was born in 1837 in Hartford, Connecticut, of New England Brahmin heritage. His paternal grandfather founded the Aetna Insurance Company; his maternal grandfather was a well-known radical abolitionist preacher. Junius Spencer Morgan, J. P. Morgan's father, was a merchant turned London-based banker. He raised his son to follow in his footsteps, teaching him to "keep a correct account of the money you receive," and urging him "not to get intimate with any but as are of the right stamp."

Morgan succeeded because he was able to wed finance to industry just as agrarian America was being transformed by industrial development. His success came initially because, through his father's contacts in Europe, he was able to raise huge amounts of capital to finance American railroads. Having raised "venture" capital in the railroad industry, he then had a strong interest in ensuring the profitability of the industry: He used the resources of the House of Morgan to "secure harmony" in the railroads, which some called killing off competition. Through financial manipulations, he gained control over more than half the nation's railroad lines. He used the tremendous financial resources of the House of Morgan to gain control of other financial institutions: He dominated three great banks (Banker's Trust, Guaranty Trust, and the National Bank of Commerce) and three large insurance companies (New York, Equitable, and Mutual), and then used their tremendous assets to control other corporations (among them, International Harvester, General Electric, A.T.&T., and Western Union). He created the first billion-dollar corporation, U.S. Steel, giving him control over 60 percent of American steel. For one year he owned the London underground, and street peddlers there sold a "License to stay on Earth—signed, J. P. Morgan." In 1895, President Cleveland asked Morgan to stop a run on the nation's gold supply. He obliged. In 1907, President Roosevelt asked him to stop a run on the banks. He was able to do this. The grand total of all the financial and industrial resources of Morgan and the House of Morgan was, by 1912, approximately $22.5 billion.

The withdrawn and antagonistic Morgan was a domineering man of iron resolution. His personality has been likened to a force of nature, his piercing stare compared to looking into the headlights of an oncoming train. In his certainty, he inspired tremendous confidence, and, in the days before government regulation of financial institutions, the financial community looked to him for guidance, especially in times of crisis. An associate said, "He was absolutely certain that the money of the country was safer in his hands than if left lying around for others to take a whack at it." He never cheated his business associates, and many of them grew richer than he did himself; but he had no qualms about selling watered stock, cheating consumers, viciously oppressing workers (including the children laboring in his steel mills), and ruthlessly crushing unions.

Morgan was disfigured early in life by a chronic skin condition that worsened as he aged and caused his nose to resemble a swollen, lump-encrusted beet. He liked to surround himself by beauty: At work, he was known for a penchant for hiring associates so handsome that it was said on Wall Street, "when the Angels of God took unto themselves wives among the daughters of men, the result was the Morgan partners." At home, he was surrounded by his legendary art collection. Known as a "checkbook collector," Morgan spent over $50 million buying priceless art treasures from cash-poor European aristocrats.

When he died in 1913, his estate was valued, for tax purposes, at

"If we have done anything wrong, send your man to my man and they can fix it up."

J. P. Morgan to President Theodore Roosevelt

"This is a most illuminating illustration of the Wall Street point of view. Mr. Morgan could not help regarding me as a big rival operator, who either intended to ruin all of his interests or else could be induced to come to an agreement to ruin none."

President Theodore Roosevelt, commenting on a visit from J. P. Morgan

$77.5 million. Astonished, J. D. Rockefeller was heard to comment: "And to think, he wasn't even a rich man!"

Today, the Morgan Library in New York, housed in his former mansion, displays illuminated medieval manuscripts, Renaissance manuscripts, early printed books, and works by Old Masters [see "The Odor of Sanctity: The Lasting Results of Expert Dealmaking," page 311]. The House of Morgan merged with the Guaranty Trust Company in 1959, and as "wholesale" bankers, "meeting the specialized financial needs of business concerns, other banks, institutions and individuals of substantial means," the Morgan Guaranty Trust Company of New York still plays a significant role in world finance.

EAST SIDE, WEST SIDE

On January 28, 1975, Japan signed a general agreement with the Soviet Union concerning oil rights to Sakhalin, an island off the Siberian coast which Stalin grabbed for Russia at Yalta. Oil-poor, the Japanese agreed to supply all the equipment and expertise to explore Sakhalin—which is oil and natural-gas rich—in return for purchasing half the oil discovered at 8 percent below the market price in the Persian Gulf. The Japanese commitment is about $20 million a year and will make them dependent on the Soviet Union for oil.

Meanwhile, the Japanese are *totally* dependent on the United States for the technology and consultancies they need to drill on Sakhalin. For $2 million a year from Japan, the Reagan administration is enabling the general agreement to come to fruition. The Soviets have already successfully created energy dependencies in Europe with a pipeline financed by Germany and France, which will provide as much as 40 percent of the natural gas to those countries by the end of the decade; Reagan failed to stop it, and is now trying to prevent a second pipeline. East side, West side, the Soviets have their neighbors' oil needs sewn up.

Greasy Business: The Oil Companies Divide the World

BACKGROUND: Of course, no one in the oil business was pleased when the Bolsheviks seized control of Russian oil fields in 1917, but no one expected them to remain in power very long either. Walter Teagle, head of Standard Oil of New Jersey (now Exxon), the largest company of any sort in the world, and Sir Henri Deterding, the head of the British-Dutch company, Royal Dutch Shell (the second largest oil company), denounced the Bolsheviks publicly ("they repudiate the code of civilized ethics," said Teagle) and swore they would never buy even one drop of Russian oil. Secretly they scrambled to buy large quantities of the oil, cheap. But then Deterding married a White Russian and began to espouse anti-communism with a kind of religious zeal that ended with his later becoming a Nazi and moving to Germany. He insisted that Standard join him in a complete boycott of Russian oil and threatened to lower Shell Oil prices in India if Standard continued to buy from the Russians. A price war soon spread across the globe, driving smaller companies out of business and rocking industry profits.

Because the oil companies market a product which, to the consumer, is virtually identical, they are particularly vulnerable to price competition. Because the spread between the cost of production and the cost to the consumer is usually very generous, the temptation to slash prices in order to gain markets is very strong in an industry traditionally gorged by vast profits. But why should oil companies limp along with small profit margins when, with a little cooperation and planning, their profits could soar?

The 1920s were very critical times in the oil industry: Middle Eastern oil fields, the richest in the world, were just being discovered. Those huge deposits could serve to drive prices down to a rock-bottom level—or they could be developed and marketed slowly and sensibly. The behavior of the oil companies at this critical juncture would seal their fate for many years to come. Deterding, finally convinced that his price war had resulted in a stand-off that benefitted only the consumer, invited Teagle and Sir John Cadman, head of British Petroleum, the third largest oil company, to Achnacarry Castle in the remote Scottish Highlands. It was a "grouse-shooting party," they told the incredulous press, and that's all they told them until the full story was revealed in 1952.

THE DEAL: The "Achnacarry Agreement," or "As Is" (as it was called), began by stating that "excessive competition had resulted in the tremendous overproduction of today." To remedy the situation, the three majors agreed to "the acceptance by the units of their present volume of business and their proportion of any future increases in production." They would not compete with each other for new markets or resources but would maintain their market share according to

People of the same trade seldom meet together, even for merriment and diversion, but the conversation ends in a conspiracy against the public, or in some contrivance to raise prices.

Adam Smith, *Wealth of Nations*

the present status quo, sharing jointly in new fields and competing only with outsiders. New resources would be developed only as demand increased. The world price of oil would be set by the "Gulf Plus" system: Regardless of where oil was produced and shipped to, it would be priced as if it had been produced in Texas and shipped from the Gulf of Mexico. Therefore, companies selling Middle Eastern oil to nearby European markets would not have a price advantage over American producers.

RESULTS: The "As Is" agreement became the virtual constitution of the oil industry. The "Big Three" won the cooperation of the four other giant companies. (Together they are called the Seven Sisters; the others are Mobil, Texaco, Gulf, and Socal.) The seven companies formed the most powerful cartel in history, carving up the world's oil resources and markets into neat parcels. They became quite adept at forecasting the supply/demand environment and allocating to each company its share of the pie.

Although "Gulf Plus" was abandoned after 1948, the rest of the arrangement continued until the new leadership of the oil-producing nations (who received pennies per barrel) grew more militant. By 1960, the producing nations had their own cartel: OPEC—the Organization of Petroleum Exporting Countries [see "The Cartel as Dealmaker: OPEC," page 23]. As one representative explained: "OPEC couldn't have happened without the oil cartel. We just took a leaf from the oil companies' book. The victim had learned the lesson." (Often that lesson was learned by the sons of Arab sheiks sent to Western universities such as Harvard and Oxford, where they studied the history of Big Oil with interest.) Although sovereign states can seize control of their oil or reduce foreign or private oil companies to minority shareholders (or just plain contractors, exploring and producing oil for hire) the OPEC producers quickly realized that not only was it the majors who could provide them with assured markets, but that both cartels had the same objective: high prices. In 1973, the year of the notorious Arab oil boycott of the United States, the profits of Exxon shot up 103 percent. Shell did even better—up 138 percent. The ghosts of Achnacarry Castle would have been proud of them.

Dealmaker as Patriarch: John Davison Rockefeller

John D. Rockefeller was born in 1839 on a modest farm in upstate New York, the son of a flimflam man who peddled elixirs and billed himself as "Dr. William Rockefeller, the Celebrated Cancer Specialist." William, who was not a doctor, took a real interest in his sons: "I cheat my boys every chance I get. I skin 'em every time I can. I want to make 'em sharp." He insisted that they keep ledger books, accounting for every penny of their small allowances. In 1849, William was indicted for the rape of a family servant. In 1853, the family moved west to Cleveland.

John had distinguished himself in high school but decided to forgo college because he was eager to begin making money. He took his first full-time job at sixteen: Working with near religious diligence as a clerk-accountant, he tripled his yearly salary in three years to $600. In 1859, he went into business as a commodity merchant, and his profits grew from $4,400 the first year to $17,000 the following year. With the outbreak of the Civil War (he bought his way out of the draft), he made a small fortune selling provisions to the Union army.

With the drilling of the first successful oil well in 1859, an enormous market for kerosene lamps developed, and a whole new industry was born. Rockefeller watched with interest as refineries sprang up all over Cleveland. In 1863, he made a $3,000 investment as a silent partner in a refinery. By the following year, he was silent no longer but was diligently applying himself to becoming the Master of Oildom.

John D. Rockefeller at age ninety-five.

From the start, Rockefeller was fanatical when it came to small economies; if thirty-nine drops of solder would seal a can, why use forty? He developed strict cost-accounting procedures for keeping careful tabs on his growing empire. ("In his soul he was a bookkeeper," said one associate.) In the beginning, he believed in borrowing heavily for expansion; and then, when his company was large enough to demand a "quantity discount" from the railroads (shipping was a major item in the cost of the product), he parlayed the discounts and rebates he received into a strong competitive advantage he could use against smaller refiners. He set out to eliminate competition by a process he called "combination and concentration," asking his more talented competitors to sell out to Standard and join his management team; many did. His argument was logical: free-market competition served only the consumer by keeping prices low; monopoly was good for the producer. "The Standard was an angel of mercy," Rockefeller explained, "reaching down from the sky and saying, 'Get into the ark. . . . We will take the risks.'" Competitors who refused to amalgamate or who were deemed "sub-Standard" were driven out of business by the periodic price wars Standard could afford to indulge in.

By 1870, Standard was refining 10 percent of all U.S. crude; by 1873, 40 percent was in their hands; that mushroomed to 90 percent by 1880. By 1883, Rockefeller was worth $40 million; that grew to

> Two men have been supreme in creating the modern world: Rockefeller and Bismarck. One in economics, the other in politics, refuted the liberal dream of universal happiness through individual competition, substituting instead monopoly and the corporate state.
>
> Bertrand Russell

$200 million by 1897. By 1913, he was a billionaire (income tax was not instituted until 1913, so Rockefeller, in his lifetime, paid a mere $67 million in income tax). From 1899 to 1911, Standard made yearly profits of nearly $80 million.

"The ability to deal with people is as purchasable a commodity as sugar or coffee, and I pay more for that ability than for any other under the sun," said Rockefeller, who was not known to be Mr. Charm. Rockefeller was, in his day, easily the most hated man in America: He was contemptuous of workers (jobs, he felt, were "charity" to workers; and he mercilessly busted attempts to unionize his operations), and the monopoly nature of Standard aroused great hostility in the American public. Early attempts to "trust-bust" proved futile—Rockefeller carefully paid off the right government officials. After Rockefeller and his cohorts beat their first restraint-of-trade case, one journalist jibbed, "They have done everything to the Pennsylvania legislature except refine it." But although he was ruthless when it came to labor, and extortionist when it came to prices, he was fair with his investors, never selling watered stock. In those days, no one lost money investing in Standard Oil, and many people became very, very rich.

Although the Sherman Antitrust Act was passed in 1890, it wasn't until Teddy Roosevelt came to office (he was called "His Accidency" by industrialists) that federal action was brought against Standard. In 1911, the Supreme Court ruled to dissolve Standard, stating that Rockefeller's "very genius for commercial organization soon begat an intent and purpose to exclude others." Standard was divided into thirty-nine theoretically competing companies. Rockefeller sent notes to his associates, saying, with uncharacteristic wit: "Dearly beloved, we must obey the Supreme Court. Our splendid happy family must scatter." Some of the offshoots quickly proved to be more profitable than the parent and, today, three of them (Exxon, Mobil, and Socal) are among the most powerful oil companies in the world. And at nearly the same time, as though the gods themselves were protecting the Standard, just as electric light was replacing kerosene lamps the automobile was replacing the horse, and the market for petroleum grew even larger than it had been before.

"God gave me my money," Rockefeller was fond of saying. He spent the last third of his long life giving away his money—$500 million in all. The dynasty he founded has played an important role in both the political and economic life of the world. Grandson Winthrop was governor of Arkansas; grandson Nelson was long-time governor of New York and short-time vice-president of the United States; great-grandson Jay is governor of West Virginia; great-granddaughter Clare is active in New York City politics. Grandson David became head of the Chase Manhattan Bank, the cornerstone of family finances; by virtue of having Standard and Rockefeller family money deposited there, it was, by 1930, the largest bank in the United States.

When John Davison Rockefeller died in 1937, at ninety-eight, the role he had played as charitable benefactor of the human race had done much to remove the stain from the family name [see "The Odor of Sanctity: The Lasting Results of Expert Dealmaking," page 311]. His money had been called tainted: "Sure it's tainted," went the old joke—" 'Taint yours, and 'taint mine!"

> "His heart was pure seeing that he had never done wrong save in the way of business."
>
> Finley Peter Dunne on John D. Rockefeller

The Hostages Had a Friend at Chase Manhattan: U.S. Banks and Iran

BACKGROUND: American bankers loved the stable, anti-Communist Peacock throne of the Shah of Iran, especially David Rockefeller of Chase Manhattan Bank, who had a special understanding of the oil business. Price hikes after 1973 (led by the Shah) made the monarch even richer; and ever-growing billions from the National Iranian Oil Company and from the Shah were being deposited abroad for investment and safekeeping. World bankers competed furiously for the privilege of making profitable loans to the Shah and to other credit-rich members of the Pahlavi family, who preferred to spend borrowed money rather than tap their own invested capital. It was the largest banking bonanza in history. Spectacularly large sums were loaned to the lavishly spending Iranians; in 1977, Chase organized an international banking syndicate to raise a record $500 million to help the Shah balance a budget suffering from huge military expenditures. Heady from their profits, the bankers failed to notice the growing instability of the regime. ("It's not the role of the bank," Rockefeller explained, "to be in touch with the opposition parties.") Failing to extend military rule, the shah went into exile on January 16, 1979. American bankers panicked: Had they loaned money to the Shah or to Iran? The revolutionary government was quick to reassure them by scrupulously paying interest on all foreign loans even as foreign relations deteriorated. The deposed Shah traveled from Egypt to Morocco to Mexico, then applied for asylum in the United States. President Carter and the State Department vacillated: Iran had just tried the Shah in absentia and condemned him to death; they were demanding his return. Henry Kissinger, then employed by Chase Manhattan as the chairman of its advisory board, publicly decried U.S. hesitation, saying he was "protesting the conscience of American honor." David Rockefeller quietly lobbied on the Shah's behalf. Meanwhile, Rockefeller's personal physician, flown to the ailing Shah in Mexico, discovered that the monarch had lymph cancer. "Someone" told Carter that the Shah was "near death" and required immediate medical aid available *only* in the U.S. Carter acquiesced, but only if the Shah agreed to refrain from political activity. When word reached Teheran that the Shah was in New York, a furious mob stormed the United States embassy there, taking all the Americans hostage. Nine days later, Iran announced that it was withdrawing its vast deposits from all United States banks. Uncertain of what the repercussions might be on the world's money market, Carter quickly summoned his treasury officials. He announced that he was freezing all Iranian deposits held domestically and in United States banks abroad. This unprecedented action raised some serious legal questions: Foremost was, did the United States government have jurisdiction over United States banks abroad? The president of Citicorp said that the litigation arising from the case would provide "a guaranteed income for the legal profession, their children and grandchildren." As the hostage problem dragged on, it became clear that the frozen assets would become a crucial bargaining point. Iran had begun an expensive war with Iraq; moreover they wanted to break all ties with "the Great Satan" of American corporations. The Shah died. Citicorp's top counsel in West Germany secretly began negotiations with Iran's German lawyers in May 1980. As relations worsened between Washington and Teheran, even after the aborted rescue attempt, these talks continued. Finally, on January 15, 1981, both sides agreed to a plan.

THE DEAL: The hostages would be released to a hero's welcome in the United States as $5.5 billion of Iran's money was being transferred to a special Iranian account in the Bank of England. Over the next twelve months, $4 billion more, held in the United States, would be released. This $9.5 billion represented all Iranian money in U.S. banks—*minus* every penny ever loaned to them, *minus* a hefty 17 percent interest rate.

RESULTS: There were huge parades all over the United States when the hostages were released. Iran got money to pay for the ongoing war with Iraq. The banks got everything they wanted, including a last-minute addendum to the agreement which prevented the Iranians from making any additional claims *ever*. U.S. banks were not completely unscathed, however: Other large depositors, frightened by the specter of unilateral American action to freeze money hoarded abroad, began leaning toward the safety of European and Far Eastern banks. The chief executive of the Deutsche Bank quickly assured them in bank-speak: "For an international bank, the departure from the international stage in order to assume temporarily a purely national role, is not compatible with the degree of interdependence reached in the Eurocredit market."

The Cartel as Dealmaker: OPEC

If we stick together, they'll have to give in.

AN ANONYMOUS IRAQUI SHEIK

September 1960	Saudi Arabia, Iran, Iraq, Kuwait, and Venezuela meet in Baghdad to form Organization of Petroleum Exporting Countries (OPEC). They set price at $1.80 per barrel. The nonmember nations follow suit.
November 1964	OPEC negotiates greater share of oil-company profits. Price: $1.80 per barrel.
June 1967	After Six-Day war, Arabs call for boycott of Israel's Western supporters. Iran and Venezuela say no; end of Arab boycott. Price: $1.80 per barrel.
December 1969	Oil in North Sea adds to new discovery in Prudhoe Bay, Alaska. Price: $1.80 per barrel.
October 1970	Libya demands more money from oil companies, threatening nationalization. OPEC countries get more, too. Price: $1.80 per barrel.
February 1971	Twenty-three oil companies agree to price increases with the OPEC nations acting as an organization. Price: $2.18 per barrel.
October 1973	Yom Kippur war; no OPEC shipments to U.S. Then OPEC doubles price: $5.12 per barrel.
June 1974	OPEC resumes U.S. shipments. Price: $10.95 per barrel.

February 1979	Khomeini revolution cuts Iranian oil supply from 6 million barrels a day to .5 million. OPEC surcharges of $14.59 per barrel going up daily on sales of 30.6 million barrels a day.
May 1981	OPEC swells to twenty-three members. Price: $35 per barrel.
January 1983	OPEC members discounting oil due to glut and decrease in world demand (from conservation and other non–OPEC suppliers). Price: $33 per barrel.
February 1983	When Britain and Norway cut price to $30 per barrel, OPEC loses Nigeria as member. Coming apart, OPEC makes a statement to competitors: "We shall interfere with all our might to guarantee that others have to think twice before entering a price war with us." As OPEC crumbles, Wall Street trading reaches a new high, closing at 1121. Gas-pump prices fall. The prime lending rate at two major banks falls to 10.5, the lowest since November 1978.

Mother Russia Takes the Pepsi Challenge: Pepsico Wins a Cola Monopoly

BACKGROUND: No American consumer product had ever been made or marketed before in the USSR, so, in 1971, when Pepsi was granted a Soviet cola exclusive, the corporation readily agreed to a couple of unusual demands: First their slogan had to change: "Feelin' Free" did not go over big with the guys in the Kremlin. And Pepsi was forced to accept payment not in hard cash but in Russia's liquid asset: Stolichnaya, the legendary vodka.

Pepsi, and its larger and slightly older twin, Coke, had conquered nearly the entire globe, always leaving in their wake those ubiquitous red signs, monuments to their corporate genius. A Coke brochure once summed it up: "When you don't see a Coke sign, you have passed the borders of civilization." But until 1971, the East did not glow cola red: Both China and the USSR barred those bottled "essences of capitalism" from their shores.

In 1962, in an attempt to further boost their sales, the perennially number two Pepsi offered the presidency of their foreign division to a politically well connected but temporarily unemployed man named Richard Nixon. He turned them down, preferring instead to join a prestigious Wall Street law firm. Soon his friends at Pepsi gave him the lucrative Pepsi account, and Nixon spent the years before he ascended to the White House calling upon foreign leaders on behalf of Pepsi. Once president, he became the architect of détente, encouraging enhanced trade with the USSR; the Russians proved eager. It was expected that they would hunger for serious things, like machinery and grain. That they thirsted for soft drinks surprised everyone, even Pepsi chief Donald Kendall, who was approached by Premier Kosygin himself while in Moscow for a trade show. By the time he left town, the two had a very oral agreement.

THE DEAL: Pepsi would be granted exclusive cola rights to the USSR for a renewable ten-year period. Sales of Pepsi in the USSR would be linked, liter by liter, to United States sales of Russian vodka. Pepsi would send technical personnel to build a high-speed bottling plant near the Red Sea and would supply Pepsi concentrate. Payment would be made strictly in vodka.

RESULTS: Pepsi really hit the spot all over the USSR; Americans went wild for Stolichnaya. Within five years, five Pepsi bottling

While Soviet citizens lined up to join the Pepsi Generation, the Kremlin vetoed the slogan "Feelin' Free."

plants were working night and day to fill the huge demand. (The Russian thirst seems to be for consumer gratification through a tangible Western status symbol, as much as for the soft drink itself.)

The folks at Coke were furious and charged that Nixon had unduly used the majesty of his office to peddle Pepsi. At a Senate investigation, Pepsi chief Kendall admitted that Nixon "had created the climate of understanding without which such a transaction would have been impossible."

But the tides of soft-drink diplomacy flowed on: In 1976, a Coke man became president. (Jimmy Carter and Coke both hail from Georgia, and Coke, a traditionally Democratic company—as Pepsi is a traditionally Republican one—was an early and generous contributor to the Carter campaign.) In 1978, days *before* China and the U.S. announced the normalization of relations, Coke was granted exclusive cola rights to the huge China market for an indefinite period. And Coke would be paid in cash. Of course, the nine hundred million Chinese "consumers" (a quarter of the world's population) are mostly peasants with yearly incomes of $380—and no refrigeration. But Coke is sanguine about its Chinese future and pleased that, by chance, the literal translation of Coca-Cola in Chinese is "can mouth, can happy!"

And back in the USSR—the ad campaign that replaced the unintentionally subversive Pepsi slogan was: "A drink of cold Pepsi-Cola will create a good mood and will refresh you." The ten-year exclusive was renewed. Lift your glasses and toast: *Nosdrovia!*

NO WONDER THINGS GO BETTER WITH COKE

John Styth Pemberton, a fifty-three-year-old druggist, was eager to invent a medicinal tonic that, while alcohol-free, still packed a punch. In 1886, experimenting with extracts of the stimulants kola nuts and coca—including small amounts of cocaine—mixed with flavorings such as oil of nutmeg and sugar, he hit upon the formula of the soft drink he called Coca-Cola. Originally promoted as an "Intellectual Beverage and Temperance Drink," and as a cure "for all nervous afflictions—Sick Headache, Neuralgia, Hysteria, Melancholy, Etc.," Coke immediately proved popular. Syrup sales went from twenty-five gallons the first year to over one thousand the next. In 1890, nine thousand gallons were sold. The following year, Asa Candler, a prosperous Georgia druggist, bought all rights to Coke, including the still-secret formula, for $2,300. Thanks to Candler's aggressive marketing campaign, thirty-two thousand gallons were sold in 1892. Revenues that year were $49,600—and Candler sank one quarter of that back into advertising. By the turn of the century, the "Holy Water of the South" was selling nearly three hundred thousand gallons a year, and Candler was being pressured to remove the cocaine from his formula, a measure he was finally forced to accept in 1905. Coke's popularity survived.

In 1916, multimillionaire Candler retired from Coke, giving the business to his sons. Three years later, his sns, without telling dad, sold the company to Ernest Woodruff, president of the Trust Company of Georgia, and a consortium of banks, for $25 million.

Today, 250 million Cokes are imbibed every day.

Dial N for Nazi:
ITT and the Third Reich

BACKGROUND: What's more American than apple pie, Mickey Mouse, and ITT? All are perfect symbols of the American way. But during World War II, one of them played both sides, placing money *über alles*.

In 1941, ITT had an estimated investment of $30 million in Germany. After Pearl Harbor, America's business attitudes toward Germany publicly changed, but in 1943, ITT's American boss Sosthenes Benn met ITT's German boss Gerhardt Westrick in Madrid to decide what strategies should be used to prevent the company from going up in smoke.

THE DEAL: In return for German ITT's technical aid, Benn and National City Bank (an ITT backer) were guaranteed that *all* the European investments would be safe from seizure, not only by the Germans but also by their puppet governments.

RESULTS: ITT continued to produce (and perfect) the German communications system: telephones, teleprinters, aircraft intercoms (including the Focke-Wulf bomber that had killed thousands of Americans), and submarine and ship phones. When Hitler's postal minister wanted to seize ITT Germany, Benn's Gestapo allies created a secure and profitable protective arrangement whereby ITT formed a partnership with the Nazi government in time of war. ITT never stopped producing goods for the Nazis in their European plants; and with investments on both sides of the battlefield, ITT was guaranteed financial growth no matter what the outcome, though the Nazi promise of a new *world* order would have suited their accountants best. Meanwhile, the United States government and FDR were perfectly aware of their behavior.

THE NOT-SO-NEW DEAL: ITT knew that FDR could not survive if the corporation was not on the American side; and FDR knew that ITT's unmasking would devastate United States morale. Therefore, silence in Washington was the stance regarding ITT's policy of "business as usual" with the enemy.

RESULTS: The global domination by the immense corporations was finalized. When the war was over, there was no pursuit of Benn or his cohorts for war crimes against the United States government because Truman arrived with his "cold war." A Fascist supporter was by definition anti-Communist [see "The Fall from Grace: Klaus Barbie and U.S. Army Intelligence," page 254], and for Truman and his crew, the *worst* threat to America was communism. Former Fascists were on his side against the *real* enemy of his time. All was forgiven. Besides, we won the war, didn't we?

◆ ◆ ◆ ◆

Other Corporations with World War II Nazi Business Ties

RCA
Standard Oil of New Jersey
General Motors
E.I. du Pont de Nemours and Co.
GAF
Sterling Drug
W. R. Grace
Morgan Bank
Chase Manhattan Bank

CIVILIZATION AS WE KNOW IT

You must agree that formerly the diverse people of the world communicated very little among themselves, that there were no relations between states, that people came together only to make war, that is, to exterminate one another. It is to those past times that the author of *The Spirit of the Laws* traces "the mindless rights of escheat and shipwreck." "Men," he wrote, "thought that foreigners were not united to them by any bond of civil law; they owed them, on the one hand, nothing by way of justice; and, on the other, nothing by way of mercy." But commerce, in its development, has cured us of those barbaric and destructive prejudices. It has united and brought together men of all countries. The compass opened the universe. Commerce civilized it.

The Preliminary Discourse of
Code Napoléon, 1804

Otto Ambros's Fall to Grace: Chemist to the Third Reich and W. R. Grace

"If you want to win, you've
got to sin bravely."

Amory Houghton, Jr.,
Chairman, Corning Glass
Works

BACKGROUND: Finding cheap labor has always been a problem for
capitalists. The most recent solution is robots on the assembly line.
The most ruthless will always be the plan devised by a chemical company and the National Socialist government of Germany.

I. G. Farben is a multinational German chemical cartel. Otto Ambros was one of their stellar chemists at just about the time Hitler realized that his aggressions would eventually result in embargoes of raw
materials critical to any war effort. The Nazi high command contracted with I. G. Farben to invent synthetic rubber, oil, and gas. Ambros
was put in charge of the rubber; called "buna," it was to be produced
from coal, methanol, and other fuel distillates.

Even after the war had progressed, coal was plentiful, but reliable,
cheap labor was scarce. Ambros's solution was simple and tied in
nicely with a more famous Nazi solution to another problem facing
the Reich. As Ambros wrote to his I. G. Farben mentor, "Our new
friendship with the SS is proving very profitable."

THE DEAL BEFORE NUREMBERG: A buna plant was built at the joint expense of I. G. Farben and the government in the concentration camp
at Auschwitz. Controlled by Rudolf Höss for the Reich and Ambros
for I. G. Farben, Auschwitz was worked by the inmates.

RESULTS: The plant was enormous; it used more electricity than the
entire city of Berlin. It never managed to produce any buna. Auschwitz could hold 140,000 prisoners at a time. Until the camp was liber-

ated by the Allies, over 100 workers every day—more than 25,000 of the 35,000 workers sent there—died from exhaustion, beatings, starvation, illness, and rancid food. (The life expectancy of a Jenson worker was three to four months.) Over 10,000 people a day were murdered in its gas chamber. It was the largest extermination center of the Reich; at least four million perished there. Ambros and other Farben officials were found guilty at Nuremberg of mass murder and slavery. Ambros was given eight years in prison but served only three. In 1951, he came to terms with Peter Grace.

Grace had inherited W. R. Grace & Company from his grandfather in 1945. The vast American company was principally concerned with shipping, trading, real estate, and mines. In 1942, it was listed among "the worst" companies by United States military intelligence for its dealings with "suspected enemy agents." After the war, Grace wanted to diversify into superlucrative chemicals.

THE DEAL AFTER NUREMBERG: Peter Grace hired Otto Ambros as a "consultant" to W. R. Grace. Though, as a war criminal, Ambros was legally forbidden to enter the United States, Grace intervened with the United States authorities and managed a visa for him to visit on Grace business.

RESULTS: From 1951 to 1981, Ambros helped make W. R. Grace one of the largest chemical producers in the world. In 1958, Grace wrote to the State Department of Ambros, "we have developed a very deep admiration not only for his ability, but more important, for his character in terms of truth and integrity."

Grace, an arch-conservative and leader of the Catholic Knights of Malta, is a close friend and supporter of President Reagan. In the spring of 1982, he organized the President's Private Sector Survey on Cost Controls (PPSS) to save $60 billion in tax dollars and improve the working of government by suggesting cuts in social expenditures and domestic programs. When asked about his connection with Ambros, Grace said that it's "a good way for my enemies to get me." The White House dismissed it as unimportant. And Ambros, when asked about his past, said, laughing, "You Americans are funny."

"I believe that everybody has to suffer the consequences of their conduct in this world."

J. Peter Grace

◆ ◆ ◆ ◆

The Constituent Companies of the I. G. Farben Cartel

1. BASF   Badische Anilin und Soda-Fabrik of Ludwigshafen

2. Bayer   Farbenfabriken vorm. Friedrich Bayer & Co. of Lever-
              kusen
3. Hoechst   Farbenwerke vorm. Meister Lucius und Bruening of
              Hoechst am Main
4. Agfa   Aktiengesellschaft fuer Anilinfabrikaten of Berlin
5. Cassella   Leopold Cassella & Co. of Frankfurt
6. Kalle   Kalle & Co. of Biebrick

Selling Out for Beans:
Jack and the Beanstalk

BACKGROUND: Even Jack's own mother had to admit that her son was
a kind of good-natured dope, unable to keep a job because he was always gazing into the sky and daydreaming. She never would have sent
the boy off to market to sell the cow if her husband hadn't been so ill.
As it was, she made Jack swear that he would not accept a penny less
than £50—the cow was their only asset! Jack was leading the animal
to market when he was stopped by that funny man all done up in
chartreuse velvet, whose green eyes twinkled like the stars. Jack trusted him.

THE DEAL: The man gave Jack five beans "guaranteed to grow, by
morning, all the way to the very sky above." Jack gave him the cow.

RESULTS: "Idiot!" screamed Jack's mother. "Fool! Moron! Dumb-
dumbhead!" She shrieked. She raged. She sobbed. Then she threw
the beans out the window, put her head in her lap, and wept quietly.
Jack went to bed. When he awoke, his room glowed green. Sure
enough, there in the yard was a beanstalk growing clear into the very
sky. Quick as a wink, Jack climbed and climbed until the clouds were
far behind him. There stretched a road that led him to the ogre's
house. Luckily, the ogre was out, and his wife took a liking to young
Jack. As they chatted, the house began to shake. "Quick," she said,
motioning Jack to the pantry, "hide in there!" The ogre came in sniff-
ing: "Fee-fi-fo-fum, I smell the blood of an Englishman. Be he alive or
be he dead, I'll grind his bones to make my bread!" His wife giggled.
"There's no Englishman around here, sweetheart! Maybe it's that fish
I fried for dinner." Jack peeked out of the pantry door. The ogre was
counting gold coins and stuffing them into sacks. Soon he was overcome by drowsiness and fell asleep. Jack ran off with the biggest sack

he could carry down the beanstalk. His mother was overcome at the sight of all that gold—Jack had saved the family from certain ruin! Later, when another beanstalk grew, Jack climbed it, staked out the ogre, and stole the hen that laid the golden eggs. On his last trip, Jack was running off with the singing harp when the ogre started chasing him down the beanstalk. With the help of his mother, Jack chopped down the beanstalk as the ogre, midair, clung to it. No more ogre.

And Jack, having already seen beyond the very sky, turned his gaze earthward, where he used his wealth to do good deeds and became his mother's pride and joy.

Dealmaker as Industrialist: Andrew Carnegie

Carnegie spent his working life becoming the world's richest man, then gave it all away in retirement.

Andrew Carnegie was born in 1835, in a modest cottage in Dunfermline, Scotland, and moved to Allegheny, Pennsylvania, in 1848. As his son would be a master of the industrial revolution Carnegie's father was to be its victim. He had been a weaver of fine linens who was driven from business by machines that could do his work much quicker but, he felt, not nearly as well. He was so emotionally crushed that he was unable ever to support his family again. Carnegie's mother became a shoemaker to support the family. At the age of thirteen, Carnegie went to work full time in a textile mill, earning $1.20 a week as a bobbin boy. He worked twelve hours a day, and went to night school to learn bookkeeping. In 1849, through Scottish connections, he got a job as a messenger for a telegraph company. By working diligently and studying telegraphy at night, he was promoted to telegraph operator in 1851 and soon became one of the few people in the United States who could "read" the sound of telegraph clicks without looking at the readout. In 1852, Thomas Scott, superintendent of the western division of the Pennsylvania Railroad hired the seventeen-year-old Carnegie as his personal telegrapher and secretary, paying him $35 a month. For Carnegie, it was a golden opportunity. He worked at the side of the man who one day would head the Union Pacific Railroad and learned the intricacies of railroad management. He stayed with the Pennsylvania Railroad for twelve years, advancing with Scott and developing valuable personal contacts. At the age of twenty-one, he borrowed money from a bank to invest in the first sleeping-car company, then convinced Scott to buy sleeping cars for the railroad. By 1863, his yearly salary was $2,400; he was earning

Skibo Castle, the retreat Carnegie built near the small cottage where he was born in Scotland.

$40,000 a year in dividends on his investments, which were mostly in railroad-related companies.

In 1865, Carnegie left his job and went to Europe to sell securities in the new American railroad companies. Highly successful, Carnegie sold over $30 million worth of securities, earning himself high commissions. On his frequent visits to England, he was able to study the new steel industry there. Bessemer had just invented his process of steelmaking in 1856, and while the future of steel, which was more durable but more expensive than iron, was still controversial, Carnegie believed in it. When he returned to the U.S. in 1872, he gave up all his speculative businesses and concentrated on steel, opening his first mill in Pittsburgh. Through his extensive railroad contacts, he was able to persuade railroad managers to replace iron rails with steel rails, and throughout the 1870s, rails represented two-thirds of all Carnegie's business.

Carnegie was a master manager, the first to apply the modern cost-accounting systems he had learned in the railroads to the steel industry. He explained that "one of the chief sources of success s the introduction and strict maintenance of a perfect system of accounting so that responsibility for money and materials can be brought home to every man." Skillful managers were rewarded with small but profitable shares in the business, and they were paid extravagantly well. "There is no labor so cheap as the dearest in the mechanical field," Carnegie wrote. But he ruthlessly underpaid his workers, tying their salaries to the price of steel, forcing them to work twelve-hour shifts, seven days a week. His labor practices precipitated, at his plant at Homestead, Pennsylvania, one of the bloodiest strikes in labor history (14 people were killed, 163 seriously wounded).

In 1873, he produced twenty-one thousand tons of steel; by 1889, he was producing twenty-five times that. In 1880, his profits were $1.5 million; that increased to $5.3 million by 1890; $11.5 million in 1898. In 1900, Carnegie profits were $40 million. Twenty thousand people worked for Carnegie Steel at the turn of the century. It was the largest industrial concern the world had ever known. In 1901, when Carnegie sold the company to J. P. Morgan for $420 million, his personal share was $213 million. He was the richest man in the world.

Carnegie was fond of saying, "The man who dies rich, dies disgraced"; and once he was retired, he tried to give away his entire fortune—and came close. He distributed 90 percent of it—some $350 million. When he had given away $180 million and realized that his money was actually growing faster than he could distribute it, he set up his foundation, the Carnegie Corporation, and endowed it with $125 million. Of the money he gave away, 80 percent of it went for educational purposes. He endowed three thousand libraries [see "The Odor of Sanctity: The Lasting Results of Expert Dealmaking," page 311]. Carnegie himself had had only five years of formal education.

When he was a youth, Carnegie vowed to his mother that he would never marry while she was alive. She died when he was fifty-one, and Carnegie married the following year. His wife described his mother as "the most unpleasant person I have ever known." Their only child, a daughter named Margaret, was born when Carnegie was sixty-two.

When Carnegie died in 1919, he had $30 million left. Two-thirds of it went to the Carnegie Corporation. Another $10 million went to pensions for Scottish relatives, old friends, and the widows of Theodore Roosevelt and Grover Cleveland. Margaret was left "provided for."

A MEAL IN STEEL

I've been asked to have a meal
By a big tycoon in steel
If the meal includes a deal
Accept I may.
But I'm always true to you darling, in my fashion,
Yes, I'm always true to you, darling, in my way.

Cole Porter

Reviving a Wounded Warrior: Mazda's Comeback

"No one else can protect you from the weakness within yourself but yourself. Being able to survive by applying every bit of wisdom, determination, and resources eventually made us stronger than before. It gave us the confidence to face the future."

Yoshiki Yamasaki, president of Toyo Kogyo Co. Ltd., makers of Mazda

BACKGROUND: When Japan's fourth-largest automaker, the company producing Mazda autos, faced a setback, its lead bank set up a unique plan, binding all hands to cooperate in its fight for survival. Chrysler turned to Uncle Sam to guarantee bank loans in its time of similar trouble, but the Toyo Kogyo Company (TKK) went a route more in keeping with the old-fashioned notion of capitalism, where competition is not a parochial but a worldwide issue.

TKK was founded in 1920. A family business, it produced machine tools, then autos and trucks. In 1967, the company introduced the first rotary-engine car, selling them in the United States—along with piston and diesel engines—in 1969. Mazda was a *huge* success; dealerships were vying for their product. By 1973, sales in the U.S. alone reached 119,004 cars, and 81 percent of them were rotary powered. The engine was designed for superlative performance. *Road Test* magazine voted it Import Car of the Year—*not* for economy, as it averaged only ten miles per gallon in the city. Enter the oil embargo of October 1973. The price of gas skyrocketed and Mazda sales plummeted by 43,775 cars (although production still outstripped sales by 126,000 units). In 1976, Mazda sold 41,000 cars in the United States, and the company suffered a deficit of $75.3 million—an after-tax net income loss of $7.3 million. TKK was facing bankruptcy, a loss of a hundred thousand jobs, and a debt of $1.6 billion.

Banks in Japan have a symbiotic relationship with the major corporations. A company's lead bank often owns 3 to 4 percent of the company's voting stock, assuring the bank access to the inside information it needs to monitor its client's progress. Superbank Sumitomo was providing 16.2 percent of TKK's financing—reaching $234 million in 1977—and held 10.8 percent of its stock. It was also a joint-owner of Mazda's Central United States distribution arm. Sixty-two other banks and insurance companies collectively held another 42 percent of its stock. Unlike Chrysler's nearly four hundred banks, and its note and debenture subscribers, TKK's creditors had more to lose than their loans if the company collapsed. While Chrysler was forced to turn to the United States government to underwrite new loans up to $1.5 billion, Sumitomo took command of TKK and everyone joined hands.

THE DEAL: Sumitomo sent a "rescue team" of (ultimately) eleven bankers to take over TKK and invested an added $70.9 million. Two

36

other banks sent two executives each. In return for this financial assistance, TKK made radical management changes, labor changes, product changes, and underwent a complete financial realignment.

RESULTS: *Management.* TKK's third-generation president was "kicked upstairs" to chairman and retired in 1978. "Top-down," single-family management was replaced by a debating-forum executive committee, including the division chiefs, who were urged to make suggestions on other divisions rather than just report on their own.

Labor. Because of the tradition of lifetime employment, there were no layoffs, but attrition and bonuses for early retirement reduced the work force from thirty-seven thousand to twenty-seven thousand. Lacking production work for everyone, five thousand factory employees were allowed by the union to join the door-to-door sales force all over the country (few people visit showrooms in Japan). Leaving home, the salespeople went to live in dormitories owned by Mazda dealers and were paid TKK salaries, commissions, and expenses. They hit the streets, visiting up to fifty homes and offices a day, for from eight months to a year; some remained in the field for up to three years. The move sold cars—one man alone averaged six cars and trucks a month ("I cried when I sold that first car," he said)—and effectively converted TKK's corporate culture from a manufacturing to a marketing orientation. The union also agreed that two-thirds of the section chiefs would be shifted to new positions. The reshuffle changed their ways of looking at problems. A four-year assembly-line hiring freeze was instituted and time cards were abandoned to boost morale. Individual workers on the assembly lines were given the power to stop the entire line to correct faults, and everyone was required to say "good morning," because the simple greeting is the beginning of daily communication.

Product. Inventory of parts was reduced by 46 percent; parts are now made as needed, freeing workers to do other jobs. New machines and robots (all repairable by the line workers) were introduced to increase productivity: Each worker went from working on 19.3 cars a year to 43.3. More engineers were hired for research and development. Rotary engines dropped from 51.5 percent of production in 1973 to 8.4 percent in 1982, *but* mileage was increased to twenty-one miles per gallon in the city and thirty on the highway. Ten new models (piston and diesel) were introduced from 1977 to 1980. TKK cars won awards around the world, and in 1982, U.S. sales reached 165,000.

Financial. Sumitomo, as lead bank, agreed to share equally in repayment of old TKK loans, and new loans were made totaling $70.9 million. TKK sold its stock in Sumitomo. TKK dividends were cut by 20 percent for two years and held 10 percent below normal for one additional year. Managers with section-chief rank and above took 4 percent salary cuts. There were no raises or bonuses for four years for managers or board members. The union accepted lower pay raises than the industry standard until 1979. After-tax profits for 1982 were $68.4 million, or 88 percent above 1973. Debts of $1.6 billion were reduced to $943.5 million, or 21.5 percent of operating revenue.

In November 1979, the Ford Motor Company was allowed to purchase 25 percent of TKK stock as part of TKK's "global strategy" to cope with the "worldwide automobile war." TKK had been selling "Courier" pickup trucks to Ford since 1972. The linkup assured TKK a stabilized segment of business despite trade restraints, bringing in for 1983 an estimated $565 million, or more than 10 percent of total sales.

A new $150 million Mazda plant was recently completed in Hofu. Highly automated, state-of-the-art production has allowed two shifts of nine hundred workers to turn out twenty thousand complete and seven thousand partly assembled cars a month, *whereas* forty-seven hundred workers at Chrysler's Jefferson Avenue plant in Detroit turn out only twenty thousand cars a month. "Our dream," says Yoshiki Yamasaki, president of TKK, "was to build a plant where unnecessary noises are shut out, where plenty of natural light streams in, and where workers are stationed comfortably in a color-coordinated environment." Mazda workers seem content and motivated. In 1982, they made more than 2.6 million suggestions on how to make Mazda number one.

Aristotle Explains It All for You!

Of everything which we possess there are two uses: both belong to the thing as such, but not in the same manner, for one is the proper, and the other the improper or secondary use of it. For example, a shoe is used for wear, and is used for exchange; both are the uses of the shoe. He who gives a shoe in exchange for money or food to him who wants one, does indeed use the shoe as a shoe, but this is not its proper or primary purpose, for a shoe is not made to be an object of barter. The same may be said of all possessions, for the art of exchange extends to all of them and it arises at first from what is natural, from the circumstance that some have too little, others too much. Hence we may infer that retail trade is not a natural part of the art of getting wealth, had it been so, men would have ceased to exchange when they had enough. In the first community, indeed, which is the family, this art is obviously of no use, but it begins to be useful when the society increases. For the members of the family originally had all things in common; later, when the family divided into parts, the parts shared in many things, and different parts in different things, which they had to give in exchange for what they wanted, a kind of barter which is still practiced among barbarous nations who exchange with one another the necessaries of life and nothing more; giving and receiving wine, for example, in exchange for corn, and the like. This sort of barter is not part of the wealth-getting art and is not contrary to nature, but is needed for the satisfaction of men's natural wants. The other or more complex form of exchange grew, as might have been inferred, out of the simpler. When the inhabitants of one country became more dependent on those of another, and they imported what they needed, and exported what they had too much of, money necessarily came into use. For the various necessaries of life are not easily carried about, and hence men agreed to employ in their dealings with each other something which was intrinsically useful and easily applicable to the purposes of life, for example, iron, silver, and the like. Of this the value was at first measured simply by size and weight, but in process of time they put a stamp upon it, to save the trouble of weighing and to mark the value.

When the use of coin had once been discovered, out of the barter of necessary articles arose the art of wealth getting, namely, the retail trade; which was at first probably a simple matter, but became more complicated as soon as men learned by experience whence and by what exchanges the greatest profit might be made.

Aristotle, *Politics*

Aquinas Explains Aristotle

A tradesman is one whose business consists in the exchange of things. According to the Philosopher Aristotle, exchange of things is twofold: one, natural as it were, and necessary, whereby one commodity is exchanged for another, or money taken in exchange for a commodity, in order to satisfy the needs of life. Such like trading, properly speaking, does not belong to tradesman, but rather housekeepers or civil servants who have to provide the household or the state with the necessaries of life. The other kind of exchange is either that of money for money, or of any commodity for money, not on account of the necessaries of life, but for profit, and this kind of exchange, properly speaking, regards tradesmen. The former kind of exchange is commendable because it supplies a natural need; but the latter is justly deserving of blame, because, considered in itself, it satisfies the greed for gain, which knows no limit and tends to infinity. Hence trading, considered in itself, has a certain debasement attaching thereto, in so far as, by its very nature, it does not imply a virtuous or necessary end. Nevertheless gain which is the end of trading, though not implying, by its nature anything virtuous or necessary, does not, in itself, connote anything sinful or contrary to virtue: wherefore nothing prevents gain from being directed to some necessary or even virtuous end, and thus trading becomes lawful. Thus, for instance, a man may intend the moderate gain which he seeks to acquire by trading for the upkeep of his household, or for the assistance of the needy; or again, a man may take to trade for some public advantage, for instance lest his country lack the necessaries of life, and seek gain, not as an end, but as payment for his labor.

Aquinas, *Summa Theologica*

"We Were Schnookered": The United States—Soviet Grain Sale

BACKGROUND: In 1972, with their citizenry clamoring for more meat, a Russian purchasing delegation made a clever raid on the United States grain supply and treasury, leaving Americans baffled by enormous price hikes at the supermarket. Let them eat cake, said the greatly enriched grain companies.

All was not well in the Ukraine, the great grain basket of the USSR. A severe draught was dashing hopes of increasing the amount of meat available to Russians. It takes 17 pounds of grain to produce one pound of tender beef. Russians consume a paltry 97 pounds of meat per capita each year, as compared to the hearty 237 pounds eaten by an average American.

At the same time, the United States, the world's largest supplier of grain, was awash in a sea of wheat, rice, corn, soy, and other grains. The fertile plains and prairies of the United States produced what seemed to be a permanent surplus, stored in cathedral-size bins that, in 1972, were crammed full. American farmers were being paid *not* to grow wheat, and the United States government kept other countries from producing a glut that would depress prices by keeping the price at sixty dollars a ton on the world market. When the domestic price rose above the sixty-dollar mark, the international grain companies selling abroad were given the difference in the form of an export subsidy, which had existed since 1949.

But even with half of all U.S. wheat going abroad, as did one-third of the rice and one-fourth of the corn, America was still swimming in grain, and storage was beginning to be a problem. Because this giant surplus meant low prices to farmers, the Nixon administration was very concerned: In an election year, which it was, Washington could not bear the unhappiness of farmers. Secretary of Agriculture Earl Butz announced that he was increasing the wheat acreage to be taken out of production by 25 percent for 1973. The U.S. Department of Agriculture (USDA) would pay farmers up to $1 billion to "set aside" wheat fields.

On June 29, 1972, a specially trained purchasing delegation of Russian grain experts arrived in the United States, having asked the U.S. government to keep news of their arrival quiet: They were afraid that publicity about their presence in the United States would generate higher prices on the volatile commodity markets. Although nobody else knew it at the time, the Russians were planning to embark on the largest grain-buying spree in history. They would be making these purchases from the huge multinational grain companies who are the middlemen of the industry. They buy, sell, ship, and sometimes process grain, but never involve themselves in anything as chancy as actually growing it. The two largest of the six companies that dominate the world market, Cargill and Continental, together handle half of all United States grain exports (the other companies are Cook, Dreyfus, Garnac, and Bunge).

The first grain executive to be summoned by the Russians was Michael Fribourg, owner and president of Continental Grain, the largest family-owned business in the United States, with 1973 sales totaling $3 billion. The Russians asked him for his best price on a whopping four million tons of wheat—as much as all of America consumes in a hundred days—and three million tons of feed grains. Since this prospective sale represented the largest single transaction in the history of grain trading (it would take over a hundred thousand box cars to bring that much grain to port), Fribourg told the Russians that before giving them a price he'd have to check with the USDA. He wanted to make sure they would continue export subsidies on a sale of that magnitude, going to the Russians. Assistant Secretary of Agriculture for International Affairs Carroll Brunthaver immediately assured Fribourg that the subsidy would continue (Brunthaver, who later insisted that he did not consult with anyone else in the USDA about this decision, had been on the job for eleven days). Fribourg then told the Russians that they could have the wheat at the artificially low price of sixty dollars a ton, maybe even lower, because Fribourg was planning to take advantage of a federal rule that allowed grain companies to register for their subsidies any time between the sale of the wheat and the time it was actually shipped. ("The secret of success in the grain business is to sell cheaper than you buy and still make money," said one veteran trader.) Fribourg planned to begin buying quietly, for low prices, from desperate farmers; and later, as word of the size of the Russian purchases circulated and the price rose, Fribourg would register for his subsidies. Fribourg, who at the time thought the Russians were buying only from his company, had no idea of just how well this strategy would work: While Fribourg was negotiating the largest single purchase that the Russians would make, they were romancing his competitors as well.

THE DEAL: By the time their buying spree ended in August of 1972, the Russians had purchased nearly 20 million tons of grain for $1.2 billion from five multinational companies. That included 433 million bushels of wheat sold at an average of $1.61 to $1.63 a bushel, or 1 or 2 cents below the prevailing market price. The grain companies got U.S. government subsidies of up to 47 cents a bushel on the wheat, at a cost to United States taxpayers of $316 million. And to help pay for all this, the Russians obtained a U.S. government loan of $750 million, at only 6.125 percent interest.

RESULTS: It was the United States Budget Director Caspar Weinberger who ordered the USDA very abruptly to announce an end to the wheat-export subsidy: Selling wheat to the Russians was costing the treasury a fortune. The grain companies were given one week to register for all subsidies owed to them for sales already made. With other hungry countries competing for what was now a limited supply of wheat, the price, by 1973, spiraled from $60 a ton to $180. And because Secretary of Agriculture Butz had limited the size of the 1973 harvest by increasing the set-aside acreage, 1973 was a very lean year and severe shortages reigned. The shortage in feed grain led to astonishing increases in the price of meat and poultry. By January 1973, United States beef prices were increasing at an annual rate of 54 percent; chicken and pork prices escalated at an annual rate of 62 percent. Overall, by the end of 1973, Americans were spending 20 percent more for their food. Table talk in the USSR became far more satisfying, as Russians found food supplies considerably beefed-up.

The grain companies found the incident very easy to digest. Cargill's after-tax earnings for 1973 rose $120 million over the previous year. Cook's earnings jumped a hefty $36 million. Fribourg's company, Continental, being just a family affair, does not have to release its figures, but just before the Russian sale, Continental had borrowed $15 million to finance an acquisition; a year later, the company financed an $11 million acquisition out of "working capital."

During investigations of the wheat sale held later, Earl Butz insisted that, in spite of the billions the United States spends in gathering information about the Russians, he had no idea of how hard up they were for grain. This lends credibility to his insistence that he had no idea of the dimensions of the sales taking place in his own backyard until September 19, which is why he continued to push the set-aside program, even as the surplus was being sold. His assistant, Carroll Brunthaver, left office and went to work for Cook Industries.

Butz's boss, President Nixon, busy that summer organizing his successful reelection campaign and his unsuccessful attempts to squelch the just-budding rumors about Watergate, offered this succinct analysis about the clever maneuvering of the Russians: "We were schnookered," said the president.

BUY CHEAP

Rich bourgeois with others' money
Making a God of your paunch
You like to traffic in wheat
Buying cheap and selling dear

                          Anonymous thirteenth-century French poet

---

Sticktoittiveness:
Rewarding Workers' Inventiveness
at 3M

BACKGROUND: Bosses are always mouthing platitudes about encouraging creativity and inventiveness in their workers. The 3M Company has taken all the idealistic gibberish and made it a way of life.

More than fifty thousand products have been created by 3M. They did $6.1 billion worth of business in 1980, and each year, 25 percent of sales are derived from products that are less than five years old. There are more than forty divisions at 3M. The fun begins when you are hired by 3M—say in Division Number 1—and come up with an idea.

THE DEAL: If Division Number 1's manager rejects the idea, you, the Creative Individual (CI), can take the idea to any one of the other divisions. If Division Number 7's manager likes the idea, he or she will receive a percentage of the venture capital supplied by 3M to the CI and the CI's "venture team," made up by 3M of full-time assigned experts from the appropriate disciplines (marketing, finance, manufacturing, technical) and interested volunteers who believe in the CI. If the venture succeeds (for example, Scotch Tape), the CI gets a chance to manage the product as if it were the CI's own business. If it doesn't work, the CI returns to Division Number 1 with no demotion for time "lost," and with encouragement to try again. If no division manager "buys" the CI's dream, 3M supplies a New Business Venture Division, where nothing needs justification.

RESULTS: A 3M motto: "We tend to make market forecasts *after* we enter the market, not before." The company and its employees thrive on risk-taking, knowing that a CI's notion will probably take ten years from inception to marketing. As the venture team produces the goods, promotion across the board is forthcoming and titles change: The CI Engineer becomes "Product Engineer," and when the product sells $5 million, the CI becomes "Product Line Engineering Manager." When $20 million in sales are reached, an Independent Product Department is created, with the CI as manager.

Since all the executives at 3M are CIs who have triumphed with a venture team, they refuse to stifle an idea no matter how far out or limited it may seem in the beginning. Scotch Tape was originally intended by its CI for industrial packaging only, then a sales manager invented the dispenser with a built-in blade.

And there are no restrictions on the types of ideas. One CI created a "surgical drape," or bacterial skin barrier, that instigated 3M's $400-million-a-year health-care business.

Nine-to-five and assembly-line drudgery, for some, are a thing of the past.

Are Diamonds Valuable Forever?: The USSR and the Diamond Cartel

BACKGROUND: The difference between pricey gemstones and cheap semiprecious stones is scarcity. When huge diamond deposits found in the USSR threatened to crush world prices, the diamond cartel convinced the Russians that this was no way to treat a girl's best friend.

Until 1725, when diamonds were discovered in Brazil, the world supply was tiny, and came entirely from the rivers of India. The Brazilian lode was just running out when the largest deposit ever found was uncovered on the South African farm belonging to the De Beers brothers. The De Beers were quick to sell out and move on, leaving only their name behind, as swarms of miners came rushing in. Among them was Cecil Rhodes (as in "Rhodesia" and "Rhodes scholar") who, by 1890, had gained a monopoly—eventually known as "De Beers"—over most of the world's diamond supplies. Rhodes understood quite well that unless the number of diamonds reaching world markets was strictly controlled, they would become as cheap as other semiprecious gemstones. He therefore sold his diamonds to only one marketing syndicate, and together they controlled the world market and kept prices high. Ernest Oppenheimer, who ultimately took over De Beers after Rhodes died, took over the marketing syndicate as well, creating an even more powerful cartel. Oppenheimer said, "the only way to increase the value of diamonds is to make them scarce,"

"The danger to the security of the diamond industry is not the discovery of a new rich diamond field, but the irrational exploitation of it."

Sir Ernest Oppenheimer

and to increase the demand. By investing heavily in advertising ($23 million yearly by 1983 in the United States alone), De Beers created a "tradition" of diamond engagement rings that did not exist until fifty years ago. They inculcated the public with the notion that the proof of true, lasting love and honest intentions was the diamond engagement ring, and the bigger the better.

In the 1960s an unexpected challenge suddenly threatened to bring about the collapse of De Beers—huge deposits were discovered in the frozen earth of Siberia. Once the inhumanely harsh conditions at the site were overcome by the construction of an entirely enclosed mining town that stands on ten-foot-tall metal legs, the Soviet Union, using jet engines to pound the icy ground, began a crash mining program. It seemed as though a tidal wave of Soviet diamonds was about to drown the cartel, but Harry Oppenheimer, Ernest's son and successor, moved to bring the USSR into the cartel. Oppenheimer explained: "A single channel is in the interest of all diamond producers whatever the political differences between them may be." He offered to buy all the uncut diamonds the Russians wished to sell. The Russians understood the advantage of a cartel, but the international political situation made it difficult for them to become part of De Beers, since it was a South African corporation and the USSR, an ally of many Third World countries, was publicly sworn to the destruction of South Africa. That meant, among other things, a total trade embargo.

Even in Russia diamonds are a girl's best friend!

THE DEAL: The Russians, eager to preserve the "illusion" of diamond scarcity to keep prices high, agreed to sell all their uncut gems to De Beers, but only if the arrangements were kept absolutely secret. Corporate fronts, not traceable to De Beers or to South Africa, were established.

RESULTS: Business has been good for these strange bedfellows. By 1978, one-quarter of the world's diamond supply came from the USSR, and they were making more than half a billion dollars a year in desperately needed hard currency. The Russians have shown their willingness to protect the cartel when they can: In 1975, when the Portuguese withdrew from Angola, the new, left-leaning government quickly expelled De Beers from the Angolese diamond mines they had traditionally controlled. The new government was about to give the lease to an independent American firm, when word came from Moscow that the American independent was just a De Beers front. The Russians then shepherded their trusting ally to the Diamond Development Corporation in London—a true De Beers front.

But the joint forces of the most successful cartel in modern commerce and the mighty USSR cannot prevent the discovery of diamond deposits in areas of the world they cannot control (a possibility that now looms large with recent discoveries in China and Australia) or the possibility that one day diamond gemstones might be successfully produced in a laboratory. Oppenheimer is taking no chances; quietly taking the profits from those glittering bits of carbon, he has gained control of a third of the world's gold production, as well as much of its uranium mining and a good chunk of other strategic minerals. In 1980, his Anglo-American Corporation was the second largest foreign investor in the United States. The diamond cartel might not be forever, but De Beers will live on.

Sayonara, Almost, in Tennessee: Japan and the United Rubber Workers Union

BACKGROUND: A little bit of Japan—in Tennessee? That's the MO, though there's a little question of cultural differences.

Americans are growing touchy on the subject of imports [see "Toy-Chevies in 1985: General Motors and Toyota," page 48], and Japan's prestigious Bridgestone Tire Company is the fourth largest tire manufacturer in the world, with 50 percent of its $3.3 billion yearly sales in exports. Many of these tires ride United States roads on imported cars, but Bridgestone wanted a cut into the United States replacement tire market. Firestone, number three after Goodyear and Michelin, was eager to sell its small plant in LaVergne, Tennessee. The plant wasn't doing too well—why else would they sell it?—and the entire work force had dropped from 850 in 1980 to 260 in 1983. Bridgestone paid $52 million.

They planned to sink $35 million over the next five years into modern, efficient equipment that would increase production by 400 percent. First thing, their expert Japanese management team arrived and ran headlong into the perks and seniority systems of American unions, vociferously embodied in the president of Local 1055 of the United Rubber Workers Union, Tommy Powell. The Japanese, accustomed to shifting valuable workers from department to department (and job to job), questioned seniority's automatically granting power to someone over people who might be more competent. Enraged, Powell made references to Pearl Harbor and ordered the Japanese out

> He who wants a new world must first buy the old.
>
> **Dutch Proverb**

of his American domain. They returned to Japan. Firestone, unamused by Powell's style, threatened to close the failing plant. Powell apologized to Japan and they returned to negotiate an amicable settlement.

THE DEAL: Though terrified of automation, like most American unions, Local 1055 agreed to allow Bridgestone maximum automation in exchange for the seniority system, Firestone wage levels, and work guarantees for current employees.

RESULTS: Japanese management will try its best with the Tennessee plant despite the obstacles of a labor system in that industry which has proven to be outmoded: "American workers are used to doing what they are told by superiors. That's it; that's their job. We expect production people to think about how they can improve what they do. We want to tap their talents; we encourage them to utilize their dormant brains," said Norihiro Takeuchi, Bridgestone's U.S. corporate secretary. They invited Powell to make suggestions on "enhancing the working environment." Together they planted four tulip poplars, Tennessee's state tree, and the workers cheered the start of an "era of unity." Bridgestone rehired 170 laid-off workers, and the show was on the road.

Toy-Chevys in 1985: General Motors and Toyota

BACKGROUND: "An imported plant assembling mainly imported parts, with only the cheap, easy-to-make components procured locally"—sound like a developing nation hitching up with a technological leader? Yes, but not quite. . .

General Motors, the world's largest industrial corporation, needs a new subcompact car to replace their Chevette, and Japan needs to silence their American critics who are screaming for more price controls and restrictions to curb their incursion into the American market (every fourth car sold in the United States is made in Japan). The solution is simple.

THE DEAL: GM will spend $30 million, and supply the bulkiest, lowest-value parts that cannot be shipped from abroad: springs, seats, glass, trim, battery, body panels. Toyota will spend $150 million and import the engine, transmission, the mechanical systems (pumps, motors, carburetors, brakes, and so forth), the steel, and the robots.

RESULTS: GM plus Toyota equals California-built Japanese cars. Japan will establish an American manufacturing presence, supplying Americans with jobs while producing a front-wheel-drive version of the Toyota Corolla. With the less expensive Japanese parts, advanced production technology, and labor-management cooperation, an estimated $1,700 is saved per car, giving GM the edge on its American competitors. Rather than producing the American-Japanese superhybrid as promised, GM has let Toyota do all the work, further undermining this country's competitive position as a producer of cars. GM has bought the back seat and become an assembler of imported parts. Such an unbalanced contract is against the law in Mexico, Brazil, and South Korea.

INVOLVED CAPITALIST WORKERS = ESOP

ESOP: Employee Stock Ownership Plan. Under an ESOP, a trust is created, and banks make loans to the trust; the trust then buys the company's stock. The company makes payments to the trust to retire the debt, and as lenders are repaid, the trust allocates stock to employees. ESOPs provide extensive tax advantages (both the principal and the interest on the payment of loans used to set up ESOPs are tax-deductible), while they give workers a stake in their companies. There are more than 5,000 ESOPs in the United States; most are operated by small companies, but over 1,250 have more than a thousand employees. The idea is not to give workers "control," making them socialists, but to make them involved "capitalists." If a board of ten is formed for the new company, two would be from the plant's management, two from the workers' union, and six from the outside, selected by the company's lenders. (Pan Am is an ESOP; worker control is 13 percent.)

The most famous ESOPs are Rath Packing Company of Waterloo, Iowa, Katz Communications, Inc., of New York, and the South Bend Lathe Company, of South Bend, Indiana. (In 1980, workers of South Bend Lathe went out on strike because they felt they were being shut out of management decisions; in effect they were striking against themselves.) The largest is the Weirton Mills in West Virginia. When it became an ESOP, Weirton's eleven thousand workers had to accept a 32 percent reduction in wages and benefits, and stock was to be distributed equally to employees, regardless of wages earned. National Steel sold the company to the ESOP for $266 million in 1983.

The Return of the Circus: Mattel Sells Ringling Brothers

BACKGROUND: When Mattel Inc. sold the Ringling Brothers and Barnum & Bailey Circus *back* to the Feld Brothers after eleven years of ownership, Irvin Feld was pleased: "The good Lord never meant for a circus to be owned by a big corporation," he said, coolly pocketing a *huge* profit.

The Felds, successful theatrical booking agents, had originally purchased the circus in 1967, ending ninety-seven years of continuous Ringling family ownership. (The Felds had been managing the circus since 1955, turning around what had been a losing proposition by eliminating such traditional niceties as the canvas "Big Top"—too vulnerable to the weather—and installing the show in less romantic auditoriums instead.) In 1970, Mattel Inc., the billion-dollar manufacturer of toys and games, purchased the circus for $47 million in stock.

After eleven years of worrying about such things as transporting dancing elephants from coast to coast and finding talented dwarfs, Mattel decided it wanted to get back to basics. Besides, the circus and the other companies in Mattel's entertainment division (the Ice Follies, Holiday on Ice, and the Circus World Theme Park in Orlando) were losing money. In 1980, they hung a For Sale sign over the proverbial Big Top—and the Felds eagerly stepped right up.

THE DEAL: The Felds would purchase the Greatest Show on Earth (including twelve hundred performers and employees, five hundred circus animals, and ninety-eight specially constructed railway cars) *and* the Ice Follies *and* Holiday on Ice, for a total price of $22.8 million— $25 million *less* than they had been paid for just the circus eleven years before.

RESULTS: "We've wanted it back in our family for a long time," said two-time circus purchaser Irvin Feld. In 1983, Ringling Brothers traveled to eighty-five cities and was seen by seven million people.

And a cheer has gone up from the crowd on Wall Street: Mattel might have imprudently run off and joined the circus, but now the prodigal toymaker has returned to the cozy domestic pleasures of dollies—and Intellivision.

Up, Up, and Away:
McDonnell Douglas and Alitalia

BACKGROUND: There's nothing like throwing out the old and familiar and starting out "fresh." The Italians do it with their government all the time; now their airline is getting into the act, with the help of American ingenuity, of course.

Since the late 1960s when McDonnell took over Douglas Aircraft to become McDonnell Douglas (MD), it continued to make money on defense contracts but lost more than $500 million in the commercial market. DC–10s did not sell as well as was hoped, and airlines weren't buying new planes while the recession kept people grounded: 1982 produced the worst downturn in United States airline history— a loss of $2 billion. Then MD unveiled its new twin-engine, fuel-efficient DC–9 "Super 80," a 142-passenger number, and things turned around. In the fall of 1982, American Airlines and TWA leased—they couldn't afford to buy—thirty-five Super 80s at $200,000 a month, which is what the airlines will save by not flying the mammoth 727. Then MD hit the jackpot with Alitalia, Italy's national airline, and even solved the financing in these troubled times.

THE DEAL: Alitalia bought thirty Super 80s for $1 billion. In return, MD helped convince the United States Export-Import Bank to finance or guarantee roughly $700 to $800 million of the purchase price, and MD itself agreed to take Alitalia's used DC–8s, DC–9s, DC–10s, and Boeing 727s in trade to sell to the other airlines.

RESULTS: Alitalia got a whole new fleet and MD made the biggest sale in its history. But more important for MD, its Super 80 beat out Boeing and Europe's Airbus Industrie, EAI, who have plans for their own fuel-saver compact plane: A-320. (Boeing, however, managed to convince Delta in December 1982 to lease thirty-three of its 737–200s for fifteen years rather than MD's Super 80s; as partial payment, Boeing took eleven Lockheed TriStar widebodies to sell overseas.) Whatever happens in the sky wars, MD has won the first round and will probably turn a profit with the Super 80s. Like all successful enterprises these days, MD plans to do spin-offs: a whole family of Super 80s.

Made in the USA by Nissan: Japan and the United Auto Workers

BACKGROUND: A little bit more of Japan . . . in Tennessee, which very well might be a turn in the road on the American Way.

In 1983, the Nissan Motor Company of Japan bought an auto plant in Smyrna, Tennessee, for $660 million, the largest direct investment in the United States by a Japanese company. The president of the American plant is Marvin T. Runyon, a former vice-president with Ford. They have devised a plan to merge the East with the West.

THE DEAL: "We're transplanting Japanese techniques wherever we can, whenever they seem appropriate," explained Mr. Runyon. The plant is not unionized: "We think we can deal with each other without the need for a third party." If the workers wanted jobs, they had to have no experience in the United States car-making way or its labor-management traditions, be willing to try "participative management," become proficient in more than one job ("cross-training"), travel to Japan for orientation if necessary, and do calisthenics each morning in a company uniform.

RESULTS: There were 80,000 people who applied for 2,000 jobs; 375 employees, including 128 hourly workers, have been sent to Japan to observe and work with their Japanese counterparts, an exercise that has cost Nissan several million dollars. Since the notion of worker/slave versus boss is considered nonproductive and obsolete, there are bonus payments for *all* employees and there are no "line workers," but rather "production operators" and "technicians." There are two company cafeterias for everyone and no executive dining room. Nissan is developing close ties with individual American suppliers, as is the Japanese way, eliminating "stockpiling" of product and hoping to produce thirteen thousand light trucks by the end of 1984.

> "We're going to be very dependent on our suppliers and they on us. There has to be close cooperation and trust between us for both parties to stay in business."
>
> Marvin T. Runyon,
> head of Nissan Motor Manufacturing Corp. U.S.A.

Golden Arches: The Birth of McDonald's

BACKGROUND: Back in the 1950s, the McDonald brothers were happy owning the one and only McDonald's restaurant, but supersalesman Ray Kroc came along and convinced them to allow him to franchise their formula. Kroc's predictions about the palate of the people were correct; he soon McDonaldized the planet.

Kroc was a fifty-two-year-old malted-milk-machine salesman in 1954 when he first visited the San Bernardino, California, hamburger stand owned by the McDonald brothers; he immediately knew he had stumbled into a gold mine. The savvy Kroc had spent his entire professional life in the food-service industry, and he was impressed by more than just the steady stream of customers eager for the fifteen-cent burgers and the ten-cent fries already famous for their golden crispness: The McDonald's were doing for food what Ford had done for the car—by streamlining product and production methods they were able to quickly and inexpensively meet consumer demand. Patty and potato were measured and cooked with timing so precise that each meal was identical to the one before. Although nothing was made to order and no deviation from the formula was allowed ("I'll sell you a car in any color," Henry Ford was fond of saying, "as long as it's black"), customers seemed reassured by the predictable, standardized food, and they appreciated the meticulously clean surroundings they found beside the Golden Arches.

Drive-in burger joints had been around since the 1930s (born, of course, in Southern California, spiritual homeland of all drive-ins), but the mass marketing of fast food did not really come of age until the popularity of the investment concept of the franchise grew in the 1950s. The Colonel was already doing it with chicken, but the burger market was wide open. Kroc was convinced that brothers Mack and Dick had a formula which could spawn an empire, and that empire should be called "McDonald's." It was a familiar-sounding name, and Kroc felt that its friendly and wholesome overtones could not be improved upon. The aggressive Kroc was incredulous when the McDonald brothers expressed complete disinterest in establishing a burger empire. "See that big white house with the wide front porch?" Mack asked, pointing to the hill overlooking their drive-in: "That's our home and we love it. . . . We don't need any more problems than we have in keeping this place going. More places, more problems." Just the kind of problems Kroc loved; he sprang into action with all the skill of the supersalesman that he was. What about letting him create a franchise empire that would spread Golden Arches across the world? The brothers would only have to sit on their porch as Kroc did it all for them. Well, in that case . . .

THE DEAL: The brothers insisted that their formula be followed exact-

"It's ridiculous to call this an industry—it's not. This is rat eat rat, dog eat dog. I'll kill 'em, and I'm going to kill 'em before they kill me. You're talking about the American way of survival of the fittest."

Ray Kroc

ly, down to the smallest detail: Menu, architecture, decor, methods of food production, even the lettering on signs had to conform to their standard. Should Kroc wish to change anything, he would have to receive approval in writing from both brothers. Kroc would be privy to all "secret" formulas (most important was their trick for crisping the fries). The coveted name, known to legions of children through its nursery-rhyme fame, was Kroc's to franchise for a $950 fee and 1.4 percent of gross sales. The brothers would stay home and receive .5 percent of gross sales.

RESULTS: The empire of McDonald's spread across the globe with the speed of a prairie fire, as people everywhere embraced Big Mac ("creeping American cultural imperialism," grumbled foreign critics). In 1983, there were seventy-three hundred worldwide, including one in a five hundred-year-old building in Freiburg, West Germany, and a bustling McDonald's in downtown Hiroshima. Mack and Dick sold out to Kroc back in 1961 for $2.7 million, which, after taxes, was worth an even $1 million: By 1976, their original .5 percent of gross sales would have been yielding them an astonishing $15 million a year.

Tokyo lunchbreak.

Chairman Kroc, who died in 1984, leaving a personal fortune estimated at $500 million, said, "When you're green you're growing, when you're ripe you rot," and his company has continued to change. Indoor seating was introduced in 1966 (premiering in Huntsville, Alabama). Fish was introduced to bolster Friday sales in Catholic neighborhoods, and now McDonald's serves chicken, ribs, dessert, and breakfast.

Today, franchises cost from $275,000 to $340,000, depending on the size and design options selected by the owner. Franchises usually run for twenty years. "In business for yourself, but not by yourself," said Kroc, whose interest in teamwork led him to purchase the San Diego Padres.

"I believe in God, family, and McDonald's and in the office, that order is reversed," Kroc went on. His company has achieved a universal popularity sought after by many religions. There are now McDonald's in thirty countries, and in the United States every day, over seventeen million people, or more than 7 percent of the entire population, visit McDonald's.

Do you deserve a break today?

II

BETWEEN THE SHEETS: MARRIAGE AND OTHER ALLIANCES

You scratch my back, and I'll scratch yours.

ANONYMOUS

Hyde Wishes upon a Star:
Marilyn Monroe and Johnny Hyde

BACKGROUND: A star is a small fixed point of light in the night sky. When Johnny Hyde met Marilyn Monroe, he saw entire constellations. She lit up the screen as a walk-on with Groucho in *Monkey*

Johnny Hyde, superagent, with the young actress he helped make a legend.

Business. He knew she was the stuff that dreams are made of, and he had the power to turn her dreams into his reality.

Born out of wedlock on June 1, 1926, Norma Jean Baker Mortensen was placed in a foster home by her twice-married working mother, Gladys Baker Mortensen who soon dropped the Mortensen. Norma Jean's family was blasted by mental illness: her grandparents, mother, and uncle spent years in institutions. At sixteen she married: Her husband was soon drafted and she got a dead-end job in a defense plant. An army photographer, assigned to document women on the work force, spotted her and used her as a model. She was brought to a modeling agency's attention; they immediately got her a job, which paid her enrollment fee in their three-month course, and she was fast on her way, with a newly bleached blonde coif and a Vegas divorce. (A single woman, unlikely to get pregnant and ruin a studio's buildup, was a more bankable starlet.)

The modeling agency directed her to a talent agency that signed her and directed her to Ben Lyon, head of casting at Twentieth Century-Fox, in July 1946. Lyon named her—Marilyn (for Marilyn Miller, a famed stage star), and Monroe (for Norma Jean's grandfather)—and got her a contract: seventy-five dollars a week, renewable every six months with a twenty-five-dollar increase to a maximum of fifteen hundred dollars a week. Nearly one year and two bit-parts later, the option was not renewed. Enrolled in acting school, she modeled again, then went to Columbia Pictures in March 1948, but was dismissed in September after only one movie. (Sam Cohn, head of the studio, never forgave himself. He created Kim Novak as a consolation prize. Kim's real name was Marilyn.)

A free-lance actress, MM played her brief scene with Groucho in February 1949, then it was back to modeling and her most famous job—"Miss Golden Dreams." On her way to another assignment, she had been in a car accident and had borrowed five dollars from a passing friend for a cab. The friend was a photographer. He called her a few weeks later: Would she pose for a nude calendar? Figuring she owed him a favor—and that the fifty-dollar fee would come in handy—and having no compunction about showing off her body, honed to perfection by dieting and exercise, she said yes. Then, in the spring of 1950, *Monkey Business* hit the screen. Johnny Hyde, elegant, sophisticated, starmaker, superagent, and millionaire vice-president at the William Morris Agency, was dazzled by her luminous quality. He bought out her smaller agency's contract. No Svengali ever had a more eager pupil.

THE DEAL: *Together* they would perfect Norma Jean's Marilyn Monroe persona. She would obey his instructions and advice, thereby surrendering her life and obsessive ambition but not her will. He respected her demonstrated judgment. He would make her a great star, an emblem of her era, by using his formidable connections and her uncanny instincts. He would protect her. She would trust him, be at his beck and call, and give him the public prestige of her radiant beauty. And, in time, he hoped she would love him.

RESULTS: Hyde spent thousands of his dollars escorting her to all the right parties, premieres, restaurants, and buying her clothes and jewels. He paid for plastic surgery to clip her nose and strengthen her chin. Ceaselessly, he prodded the moguls, insisting she was neither a joke nor a cunning dumb blonde but a breathy original: innocent, sensitive, intelligent, and a damn good actress with the right director. Besides, the camera adored her. She shimmered with sensuality under light, creating an exquisite image, and her irregular features were transformed into an incandescent beauty. Her terrifying fragility, made abstract by her talent and grace and humor, could move a heart of stone.

Hyde loved her. Divorcing his wife, he proposed. She refused: "I love him but I'm not in love with him." Between 1949 and 1950 she made six films, four directly attributable to him. Though he had other star clients, he worked overtime for her, against his doctor's orders. His weak heart began to rebel. He worked harder to make certain she was settled before he died. In October 1950, she signed a contract with Fox that would bring her $750 a week. On December 17, Hyde died. She had been staying at his home and was ordered out by the bereaved family. Against their wishes, she attended the funeral and became hysterical, screaming his name.

She left the William Morris Agency in 1951, feeling ignored by them and believing that Hyde's colleagues blamed her for his death. Fox raced her from film to film. Her new agent at Famous Artists got her salary up to $1,500 a week. By 1953, she was Fox's biggest star. But without Hyde pulling the strings, she was locked into the dumb-blonde stereotype that the Fox hierarchy, lacking all imagination, knew would make money for them. One of the world's most famous women, she completed sixteen films before leaving Fox in 1954. With her mental balance demolished by addictions to alcohol and medically prescribed tranquilizers and sleeping pills, she starred in four more films. Marilyn died of a drug overdose in August 1962 at the age of thirty-six.

Dealmaker as Womanizer:
King Charles II

Perhaps it was because his reign followed the drab Puritan Revolution that the handsome King Charles II (1630–1685) so indulged his taste for pretty women, keeping his mistresses at court and granting dukedoms to their sons. He sired over a dozen illegitimate children by the most glamorous women of his day, but his wife, who dearly loved him, was unable to produce an heir.

Charles had been forced to flee England when his father was beheaded and the Cromwellian Commonwealth took over. He lived in poverty-stricken exile until the Restoration. Assuming the throne, he cast about for a way of raising funds, and discovered the Portuguese infanta, Catherine. Her dowry included nearly a million dollars, the Mediterranean port of Tangiers in North Africa, and the town of Bombay, including trading privileges in India (this was the beginning of England's long involvement there). The two were wed in 1662.

The king was already a father. His son James had been raised in Paris, where his mother, Lucy Walter, the woman who followed the king into exile, had died. James came to England the same year his father was married and immediately caused a sensation. Never, witnesses said, had a more beautiful thirteen-year-old boy been seen. His father was so enchanted by the youth that it was rumored he would be made his lawful heir, but this never happened. King Charles arranged a very advantageous match for him, to the twelve-year-old Anna Scott, Countess of Buccleuch. She had vast estates and an income of nearly $50,000 a year. On the day they were wed, the king made his son the Duke of Monmouth. Monmouth, as he was known, grew up to be quite a despicable character, but his father continued to dote on him, forgiving him even after he participated in an assassination plot against him. But when Monmouth attempted to seize the throne from his uncle, his father's lawful successor, his uncle proved less forgiving. Monmouth was beheaded.

At the time of his wedding to Catherine, Charles was already involved with the magnificent and willful Barbara Villiers, described by an observer as "the finest woman of her age" (Sir Winston Churchill was a descendant of her great-grandfather). Barbara, who was nineteen at the time, was already married when she met the king. But in spite of her marital situation, she bore the king six children. So that his mistress would have a respectable title, Charles made her husband the Earl of Castlemaine. She demanded jewels and luxurious clothes and servants, and the king, completely smitten, complied. One of their sons, Henry, was "wedded" at the age of nine to the five-year-old Isabella, heiress of the Earl of Arlington, owner of Euston Hall, a splendid estate in the area now surrounding the Bloomsbury section of London. She also owned the manor of Tottenham Court, from which Tottenham Court Road derives its name. Since the legal age of marriage in Restoration England was fourteen for boys and twelve for girls, the official wedding could not be held until the bride was twelve years old. To please Barbara, the boy was made the Duke of Grafton. The eleventh Duke of Grafton still lives in Euston Hall, although the tenth duke demolished two-thirds of it in 1950, when the costs of maintaining a huge ancestral home became exorbitant.

The young Duke of Grafton was only five when the king became smitten with Nell Gwyn, the cockney woman who was the most celebrated actress of her day. "Pretty witty Nell," Pepys described her. She was earthy, lively, and fun, and the king adored her. He gave her a house (Bestwood Park—it stayed in her family until 1940) and an income; and unlike Barbara, she did not demand more. She was pregnant with one of their two sons when the king fell in love with a beautiful French woman named Louise de Kérouaille. The rivalry between the king's two mistresses captivated London for years. Louise gave birth to a son exactly nine months after beginning her affair with the king. He made her the Duchess of Portsmouth, and, when the boy was a mere three years old, the king made him the Duke of Richmond—the youngest person to be so honored in the history of England. Nell was so vexed by the honor bestowed on her rival's son that when the king next visited her, she held her six-year-old out of the window, threatening to drop him if the king did not give him a title. "Stop, Nelly," the king cried, "God save the Earl of Burford." At twelve, the earl was "promoted" to Duke of St. Albans, and at thirteen he was made the Hereditary Grand Falconer of England. In 1953, the twelfth Duke of St. Albans insisted on attending the coronation of Elizabeth II with a live falcon, to remind everyone of his title. When permission was denied, the duke boycotted the event.

The extravagance of Louise was even worse than that of Barbara Villiers. In 1674, the king settled an annuity of $30,000 on her. She agitated for a duchy in France, where the king controlled some territory, until he finally gave her the Duchy of Aubigny, making her the Duchess d'Aubigny in 1684. Her son was naturalized a French citizen so he could succeed her, and to this day the Duke of Richmond is also the Duc d'Aubigny in France.

Ironically, the Infanta Catherine, Charles's only legal consort, who

"This Duchess acts the fine lady ... as soon as any great nobleman dies she goes into deep mourning. If she is of such nobility, why is she a whore? She ought to die of shame. As for me, it's my trade. I don't set myself up as anything better."

Nell Gwynne commenting on Louise de Kérouaille, quoted by Madame de Sévigné loved her husband and suffered the presence of his fecund mistresses and their children at court, could not bear children. The throne passed to Charles's brother, James II.

The High-priced Baby Market: Rumpelstiltskin

BACKGROUND: Manners are important. The fate of a child once hung in the balance because polite introductions were not promptly made. But what can you expect from those engaging in a black-market baby swap?

In a quiet kingdom by the sea, a poor miller lives with his daughter. One summer morning, he is summoned by the king to report on the mill's productivity. Dressed in his finest, he hastens to the palace. It rests upon dunes and so startles the miller with its fairy-tale beauty that he nearly falls from his saddle; and when three silver knights in filigreed armor appear in order to escort him to the king, he is overwhelmed by shyness and low self-esteem.

Who is he to approach such splendor? "Who am *I*?" he asks himself. "I am the miller. If it were not for me, they would have no bread!" But as he draws closer to the Royal Presence, he grows more and more apprehensive, and by the time he reaches the throne room he is desperate to make a good impression, to seem worthy of the majesty surrounding him. "My daughter can weave common straw into gold!" he boasts, causing quite a stir. The young king, ever in need of gold to wage wars or to refurbish his finery, commands: "Bring her here *immediately*!"

When the trembling, bewildered girl is brought before her sovereign, he sends her to a straw-filled tower where a spinning wheel awaits. "You will make gold for me or I will cut off your head! See you in the morning." Alone, she weeps for herself and for her pitiful father. She does not notice the sudden appearance of a very ugly dwarf. "Mistress Miller?" he whispers, "why are you carrying on like this?" She quickly explains. "Is that *all*?" he asks, laughing: "What will you give me if I weave for you?" She offers her shell necklace. Within three hours, all the straw is woven into braided gold. Bowing to his Mistress Miller, the dwarf disappears. "I am saved!" she says, sighing and falling into a restful sleep.

The next morning, with the crowing cock, the king arrives.

Thrilled, he shouts for more straw and demands an encore. "But—" she objects, only to receive another death threat. Alone, she sinks into despair, then is lifted to her feet by the same ugly dwarf of the night before. "What will you give me if I weave for you?" She offers her birthstone ring. Within three hours, all the straw is chains of gold. Again, the king is deliriously happy but far from satisfied. "One more time," he commands, "then you will be my queen." "One more time?" she asks, moaning—"How can this be?" "Have you forgot about little old me?" the ugly dwarf whispers in her ear. "But I have nothing left to give you, sir," she tells him. "Hmmmmmmmm," says the dwarf, "let me think for a jot."

THE DEAL: "When you become queen," the dwarf quickly decides, "I want your firstborn child." "Me, the queen?" the miller's daughter muses. "Never happen." Glancing out the tower window at the rippling sea, she longs for freedom. "This is too much," she sighs. "When I become queen," she says, suppressing a smile, "you may have my first child if you weave this ton of straw into glistering gold."

RESULTS: The following morning, the king officially announces his engagement to the miller's daughter. Astonished, she never gives the dwarf a thought, after the king promises she won't have to work again. The marriage proves a great success. In due time, the queen gives birth to a princess. One night soon after, the dwarf appears and joyfully jigs around the room: "I've come for what's mine!" he sings. "At last a child of my own—no longer will I live alone!" Approaching the queen, he extends his pudgy little arms. "No!" she shrieks, bursting into a torrent of grief. "No, no!" she begs. She pleads. She makes a scene. She offers everything to keep her treasured child. Confused, the dwarf is moved by her distress. Had she not given him her word? He does not have a clue about how to behave. "The child belongs to me," he reasons, "but I'll play yet one more game. If you can guess my name within the next three days, I'll never visit you again to press my legal claim." Agreed!

The next night when the dwarf appears, the queen is ready with human names from Algenon to Zeke. "*Wrong!*" he yodels, twirling around the room. "Tomorrow try again!" The second day, she dispatches every knight to search and seize each proper name her kingdom owns. The second night, when the dwarf appears, the queen is ready with a list as long as threads of braided gold. "*Wrong! Wrong!*" he cheers, twirling round and round as she recites as many names as there are stars in Summer's skies. At dawn he wags a finger. "Time is running out, dear queen. Guess my name or lose our game!" "Game?"

she mutters, swooning in horror. The following dusk a knight appears at her room's door. He tells a curious tale. While riding through the densest wood, he spied a twirling dwarf singing in a shrill loud voice:

> At last a child of my own
> No longer will I live alone.
> The queen will never win my game.
> Rumpelstiltskin is my name!

"Rumpelstiltskin?" the queen repeats aloud. "What kind of name is *that*?" She grants the knight his fondest wish then waits for her nocturnal guest. "Come, come! In vain do try to guess my special name," he says to her.

"Celery?" "*Wrong!*" "Budgerigar?" "*Wrong!*" "Then how about . . . Rumpelstiltskin?"

The air seems sucked from the royal room as the raging dwarf becomes its still, hot center.

"*Rumpelstiltskin is your name!*"

With a bellow so loud it tilts the queen's crown, the dwarf stomps his left foot right through the floor, up to his knee. With another bellow that deafens her for two days, the dwarf yanks on his leg to pull it free and violently tears himself in half. Once the queen recovers from the shock, she lives happily ever after.

AND—*VOILA!*—BABY MAKES THREE

At thirty-one years of age, Christine X loved her twin sister very much. She and her twin, Magali, both lived in Paris. Both were married. Christine had two children; Magali had none. "For me, happiness is impossible without a child," Magali told her devoted sister. She could not have one, and adoption would not do. She begged Christine: "If you love me, give me a child!" Magali proposed that her own husband artificially inseminate Christine. They argued about it constantly. Christine was not too keen on the idea, and her husband was adamantly against it. Magali persisted: "If you love me ..." Soon, Christine's marriage was shaken by arguments with her husband over her sister's pleading for assistance at making a baby. Hadn't they helped each other with everything else? Christine mused: "My husband didn't understand. He was dark and handsome and I wasn't unhappy—but I pushed him into another woman's arms to be able to be with my sister again." To free herself from the emotional demands of her sister, Christine agreed to have the baby. Her husband agreed to a divorce. When the baby was born she moved away from Paris, and away from Magali forever. With French logic, she shrugged against her fate: "It's terrible to be a twin!"

The Lady Is a Bastard: Lady Sackville Sued for Title and 365-Room House

To become Lady Sackville, she had to prove her illegitimacy.

BACKGROUND: She was just a Spanish dancer, up from the squalid slum of Malaga, where her mom peddled old clothes, and her dad, long dead, had been a barber. He was an English aristocrat, the fifth son of the fifth Earl De La Warr. One day, he'd be Lord Sackville. But in 1852, twenty-five-year-old Lionel gazed upon twenty-two-year-old Pepita, and he knew he'd be willing to risk his budding diplomatic career just to have her. She was already famous throughout Europe: Crowds thronged to see the graceful dancer with the supremely voluptuous figure and the "face divine." She adored all the attention but was willing to exchange her career for domestic bliss with Lionel. He would have married her—he wanted to marry her. But she had made that unfortunate marital mistake back in Spain when she was a mere eighteen; Juan Antonia de la Olivia was also a dancer—and also a Catholic. Pepita could never marry again, not as long as Olivia lived, and he outlived her by many years. With Victorian society looking on askance, the couple settled in together. He rose through diplomatic ranks; she had seven children (five survived her). Never acknowledged by proper society, Pepita went by the made-up title of Countess West. She lived with the children in France, in a back-street twilight. But the couple stayed happily together for twenty years, separating only when Pepita died at forty-two, while giving birth to her seventh child. Lionel, his heart broken, packed the kids off to boarding schools and disappeared across the globe, going to Buenos Aires as British minister.

Seven years later, in 1879, their eldest daughter, Victoria, arrived in London from her convent school in France. No one had ever mentioned the fact of her illegitimacy to her, so she was quite shocked when her aunt, the Duchess of Bedford, refused to receive her. Happily, her other quite formidable relations were more cordial. One aunt, the Countess of Derby, was so taken by the girl that she wrote to Lionel, by then British minister to Washington (and still a bachelor), and urged him to invite Victoria to the United States to act as his official hostess. This girl, she said, is extremely beautiful and very charming. Lionel rather liked the idea, and he managed to surmount the diplomatic difficulties involved in introducing his illegitimate daughter to official circles. She quickly became her father's favorite companion and a huge hit on the social scene in America.

In 1888 they returned to England: Lionel had just become Lord Sackville, heir to Knole, a 365-room home. Victoria, with the help of sixty outdoor and indoor servants, took charge of the "huge house, with its tapestry-lined galleries, its silver, its romantically named bedrooms with beds draped like carafalques, its family portraits and its secret staircases."

In England, as in America, suiters flocked round the lovely Victoria. Finally she chose one—her first cousin Lionel, son of the aunt who had snubbed her. Victoria was less moved by love than by other considerations: Cousin Lionel was heir to her father's title and to Knole. By marrying him, Victoria would one day have the title, money, and influence that fate had denied her mother. Lionel's family was not cheered by the prospect of this match—"their English caution shrank from foreign blood of so incalculable quality." But the determined couple was married in the chapel at Knole in 1890. Two years later, their only child, Vita Sackville-West was born.

Lord Sackville died in 1908, and by the laws of English peerage, his title and estate passed to his nephew Lionel. But, most unexpectedly, a long forgotten voice yelled, *Hold Everything!* Henry, son of Lionel and Pepita, had been shipped off to South Africa years before, where he was expected to earn his living as a farmer and never, ever trouble his father's family. Henry claimed he had startling information: investigators he'd hired had discovered that Pepita's marriage to Olivia had been annulled, and he had evidence that his parents had been married in Germany. He triumphantly proclaimed his legitimacy and that of his siblings: Therefore, *he* was Lord Sackville. Victoria was shaken. If it was true that she was legitimate, she'd lose Knole and the title. As a bastard, she'd be the rich and richly respected Lady Sackville. The courts, sufficiently impressed by Henry's evidence, ordered that Knole be shut down and all revenues from the estate be placed in the hands of trustees until the right of succession was determined.

THE DEAL: The High Court of Justice (Probate, Divorce, and Admiralty Division) ruled that if Victoria could prove she and her siblings were illegitimate, the title and the estate would pass to her husband. If Pepita and Lionel had truly wed, then Henry would be made Lord Sackville, and Knole would be his.

RESULTS: The press adored the spectacle of high aristocrats embroiled in a legitimacy battle stemming from a passionate love affair begun sixty years before. Victoria and Lionel spent nearly a hundred thousand dollars on private investigators, on transporting witnesses from Spain (shabby Spanish relatives who completely mortified the snobbish Victoria), and on lawyers' fees. Ultimately, the court decided that Henry's witnesses were bribed, his evidence forged: The lady, being a bastard, was a Lady. She returned to Knole, in great triumph and extreme embarrassment.

Vita, the daughter of Lord and Lady Sackville, became a highly respected writer and landscape gardener. She married the writer Harold Nicolson but created quite a stir when, in 1920, she ran off with her lover and childhood friend, Violet Trefusis (daughter of the long-time mistress of King Edward). Vita was ultimately reconciled with her husband, with whom she lived until her death in 1962, but they had an understanding by which they were free to take other lovers. Vita had an affair with Virginia Woolf, for whom she served as the model of her book *Orlando*.

Knole, home of the Sackvilles since 1566, was given up as a private residence in 1947. It is now maintained by the English preservation society, the National Trust, and is open to the public.

> ....she had an almost morbid shrinking from the fact of her own illegitimacy, and now here she was placed in the position of hearing her illegitimacy and that of her brothers and sisters insisted upon by the very men who were working to gain a superb inheritance for her husband.
>
> Vita Sackville-West commenting on her mother

The Case of the Hollow Leg: Alcoholism

BACKGROUND: Disease is an absolute. It knows no distinctions, and it lights upon victims regardless of race, religion, or the size of the bank account. It is tacky and shameless, cunning and baffling. And, sometimes, it needs a drink to kill.

Alcoholism is a terminal, progressive disease. It has no cure but it can be arrested one day at a time. Though its etiology has not yet been discovered, doctors and professionals can diagnose it based on a host of physiological symptoms: a high tolerance for alcohol ("High tolerance is not a talent; it's a symptom"); impaired nutrition due to poor eating habits; inflammation of the liver; and confusing, troubling behavior—prevarication, loss of memory, tension, anxiety, depression, and so forth.

There is a difference in the way alcoholics and nonalcoholics metabolize alcohol. After two drinks, the nonalcoholic tends toward feelings of nausea, dizziness, headache, and a sense of "being out of control." The alcoholic frequently will feel more in control, more clearly focused until his or her higher tolerance level is reached, then a "blackout" occurs in which incidents are forgotten. Since alcoholics have no idea what drinking is like for "normal" people, it is impossible for them to understand, in the beginning, that they are having a different response to this socially acceptable drug. Insidiously, the disease and the drug join forces.

THE DEAL: The disease is virulent only when the compulsive craving for the drug is being fed. Since alcohol is mind-altering, it deadens inhibition and depresses resistance; then, upon intake, instead of quelling the compulsion, it further activates it. The more the victim drinks, the more the victim needs to drink. One drink starts the cycle.

RESULTS: Death is one, unless the drug is kept away from the disease; and the "alcoholic personality" is another, which is not the cause but, rather the outcome of the disease. If the victim stops drinking, then the disease can be forestalled. If the victim resumes drinking, the disease and the drug again join forces; and no matter what length of time they've been apart, the two resume where they left off, because the progression never stops. The victim does not return to square one if he or she stopped in square fourteen; the disease is alive and deadly, waiting on square fourteen for the drug.

Pass the Honeydew:
The Caterpillar, the Ant, and
Symbiosis

BACKGROUND: Insects do various things besides forage for food. There is one species of ant that farms its own mold by gathering leaf bits and creating a compost. Another has a relationship with a species of caterpillar that nicely serves them both. Coming together for mutual benefit, they enjoy what scientists call "symbiosis."

Butterflies go through three stages of existence. The first is as an egg; the second is as a larva or caterpillar; the third is as a pupa. The first and third are periods of transformation—from egg to caterpillar, from pupa to butterfly. They are stages when the creature does not feed. In its second stage, the larva or caterpillar manifestation, it does nothing *but* eat, storing up fat for its incarnation as pupa. Solitary feeders, each caterpillar grows in fits and starts, bursting its skin to allow a larger, sometimes twice as large, self to emerge from within to continue eating. This growth process is known as molting.

After a caterpillar's third molt, winter approaches. The vulnerable caterpillar is in need of a home. Enter its ally, a species of dairying ant known as *Myrmica rubra*. If these two don't join forces, the caterpillar perishes.

THE DEAL: Many caterpillars produce a sweet sap that is secreted through their "honeydew" glands. Worker ants "milk" the caterpillar of this secretion for up to an hour. The caterpillar then makes itself as small as possible and the ants carry it back to their nest, where in exchange for its nutritious nectar, the caterpillar is given a safe home for the winter and all the ant larvae it needs to survive.

RESULTS: The caterpillar feeds moderately, not disturbing the balance of the nest but taking in enough protein to produce honeydew for its busy, accommodating hosts. Then, when it enters the pupa state, it is allowed to rest undisturbed by the ants, who do not cart it out into the snow once the supply of nectar ends.

In the spring, a blue butterfly emerges from the ant's nest. It remains earthbound, clinging to a blade of grass until the sun warms its body to eighty degrees. Then, with enough solar heat in its wing muscles, the butterfly can fly to forage for food. When the sun begins to set, the butterfly roosts and sleeps until sunrise. Most species, if they survive predators, live only about a month.

BIRDS OF A FEATHER

The giant cowbird lays its eggs in the nests of oropendolas birds. The cowbird is spared the rigor of making its own nests and in "payment" eats the larvae of the deadly botfly, which kills the oropendolas.

A Deal Is a Deal Is a Deal:
Gertrude Stein and Alice B. Toklas

BACKGROUND: Sometimes, a chance meeting over a glass of *vin ordinaire* can lead to a *mariage extraordinaire;* in the case of Gertrude Stein and Alice B. Toklas, it was to last forty years.

Gertrude, having abandoned her aspirations to become a doctor after nearly completing medical school at Johns Hopkins, joined her brother, Leo, in Paris in 1903. The pair, nearly inseparable since childhood, set up house in a Left Bank atelier, living off the income from the small inheritance that had been left them by their father and wisely invested for them by an older brother. Leo had been intro-

Alice (left) and Gertrude at home in Paris.

duced to the avant-garde art scene by his friend, the art historian Bernard Berenson. At a time when there was almost no interest in the works of the great modernists, Leo and Gertrude began to purchase their works. Soon the walls of their atelier were crowded with paintings now recognized as great masterpieces—Cezannes, Matisses, Bracques, and Picassos—but available, at that time, for the price of a decent meal. The artists too gathered around the home of the Steins, and with them came the outstanding writers and poets of the day. Picasso and Gertrude became close and lifelong friends. When he painted her portrait (now at the Metropolitan Museum of Art in New York), her friends complained that she did not look like the portrait. "She will," Picasso assured them. The Stein salon became central to the life of the modern-art movement in Paris.

Gertrude was writing then, but in the absence of any strong encouragement (her brother's response to her work was decidedly lukewarm), she was not very clear about her goals. In 1907, when Gertrude met Alice B. Toklas, a twenty-nine-year-old Californian who was touring Europe, it was as though the two had been looking for each other all their lives. "Might be love," mused Gertrude, "might even be love."

THE DEAL: Alice would provide Gertrude with the inspiration, stability, physical nurturing, and the intense emotional support which would allow Gertrude to write the innovative literary works that would establish her enduring reputation. Alice would see to all domestic details; Gertrude would pay all the bills.

RESULTS: Alice believed that Gertrude was a great genius and, moving into the atelier, set about making herself indispensable to her. Brother Leo felt increasingly squeezed out of the ménage and finally left in 1913 with some bad feeling and half the legendary art collection. "Some trees," he commented, "are strangled by vines like that"; but his sister was not complaining. "Pet me tenderly and save me from alarm," she asked Alice, promising, "I am going to conquer." Alice became her secretary and literary critic, typing and helping to shape Gertrude's difficult manuscripts. When publishers failed to show much enthusiasm for Gertrude's writings (critics liked her work, but it was rather difficult to understand), Alice became Gertrude's publisher and publicist, but Plain Edition, their own imprint, also failed to attract a general audience. Alice pushed her mate to write a more popular book—a memoir about her years of friendship with some of the great artistic geniuses of the twentieth century. When Alice proved unrelenting, Gertrude gave in: "Shove," she wrote, "is a

> "If you listen, really listen, you will hear people repeating themselves. You will hear their pleading nature or their attacking nature or their asserting nature. People who say that I repeat too much do not really listen; they cannot hear that every moment of life is full of repeating."
>
> Gertrude Stein

proof of love." *The Autobiography of Alice B. Toklas* was written in six weeks in 1932 and became a best-seller. Gertrude was an internationally known star, Alice her impresario. They toured America and crowds gathered round. "Fame is a pleasure," wrote Gertrude, "to the beholder."

They shared their lives for forty years, until Gertrude's death in 1947. Alice lived on another twenty-one years, wrote her famous cookbook (marijuana is used as an ingredient), and awaited reunion with Gertrude. When she died in 1967, nearly ninety years old, she was buried in the same tomb as her love; characteristically, she had her name carved on the *back* of the tombstone.

"If one loves another, by that means they do not perish," Gertrude had assured Alice.

FIFTY-NINE CENTS ON THE DOLLAR

They marry young. *He* is in medical school—a very expensive place— *she* is in the work force supporting *them*. When they married, they promised to love, honor, and trade off future comforts for present labors.

But he, upon graduation, wants and gets a divorce. (A very common story.) He goes on to overabundance; she goes on and on in the underpaid work force: A woman earns fifty-nine cents on every dollar earned by a man. End of story.

But not for Loretta O'Brien, who may have found the fortitude and the right judge to change that scenario for good. When he, Michael, requested the divorce, she said okay, but she wanted a return on her investment—a decent share of his doctors' fees. Three days in court won her 40 percent of his earnings for the next ten years, or approximately $188,000. The judge ruled: "When a spouse finances another's education . . . it is unfair to deny her a share of this asset which would not exist but for her efforts." A precedent was set. *He* promptly appealed. His lawyer declared: "The court felt sorry for Mrs. O'Brien and wanted to do something for her. But the decision is too speculative. You can't evaluate what he doesn't have." *She* can evaluate what she has: no home of her own at thirty-seven, and a job teaching nursery school at $11,000 a year.

The case is still pending . . .

Seven Is Her Lucky Number: Snow White

BACKGROUND: Some marriages are made in heaven. Some in the bedroom. Some in the kitchen. And some all over the house! When a little beauty needed a roof over her endangered head, seven shrewd souls invented a way to make it all work for their mutual benefit.

She was the answer to her mama's prayers, a child as perfectly formed as a snowflake; but her mother died soon after her birth and her father married a narcissistic queen who valued only beauty and her magical mirror. Each day began with a tête-à-tête: "Mirror, mirror, true and tall, who's the fairest one of *all*?" The mirror always reassured: "Why you are, my queen!" Or, it *did* until Snow White turned seven. Then the aging queen got the scary news: "Why you, my queen, *were*," it said very softly, "but are no longer. Snow White is now fairest of 'em all. Sorry." The queen howled like a fishwife, envy glazing her steel gray eyes. "I'll teach that slut a thing or two," she vowed.

Without a qualm, she sent her stepchild on a picnic with an ax-wielding huntsman instructed to lop off the gorgeous tot's head, then bring home proof of the deed well done. In the woods, the clever child changed the killer's plan by promising to disappear from sight. He let her flee. Killing a boar for its heart and lungs, he gave them to the queen, who gleefully ate them lightly sautéed.

Meanwhile, Snow White wandered over seven mountains. In a clearing she found a tiny deserted house. It had seven of everything, and everything was just the right size for a child of seven. Falling into one of the beds, she slept soundly and did not hear the return of the owners: seven dwarfs who worked in a nearby silver mine. Touched by her beauty, they guarded her sleep. At dawn, when she awoke, they listened to her tale and came up with a plan.

THE DEAL: The dwarf family needed a cook, housekeeper, laundress, scullery maid, gardener, seamstress, and serving maid—in short, a mother. If Snow White took the job, they promised to feed, clothe, love, honor, obey, house, and protect her from harm.

RESULTS: Snow White officially moved into the attic, safe from all but that loudmouth of a mirror. When the queen asked for acknowledgment of her supremacy, it spilled the beans: "Why you, my queen, are *here*, but *there* across the seven mountains, dear Snow White has no peer." "Across the seven mountains?" she muttered. "Yes, my queen, in the home of the seven midgets." "*Dwarfs*, fool!" she shrieked. "*Everybody* knows they're dwarfs!" The mirror clouded over in the face of her rage.

The next day she slipped into crone drag and sped over those seven mountains. Pressing lace on the unsuspecting child, she pulled it tightly around her windpipe, leaving her for dead. The dwarfs arrived in the nick of time. They cut her free, applying artificial respiration before Envy claimed her life. All was well until that mirror passed the word of her survival. The crone reappeared with a poisoned comb that seduced the vain child; only its quick removal by the trusty dwarfs saved the day. Yet again the mirror blabbed; yet again Snow White accepted a gift—the child *was* only seven—and this final gift was a poisoned apple. One bite and the kid was finished: It literally stuck in her throat. Unaware of the Heimlich maneuver, the dwarfs could not revive her.

For seven days they sat by her body. When it failed to decompose, they placed her in a crystal coffin on a hill under a seven-story elm for the world's adoration. For fourteen years she lay, mysteriously growing to full maturity within her jewel box. Then, in springtime, a handsome prince, questing for perfection, found it in her face. He convinced the sentimental dwarfs that he would die without the sight of her. Hoisting the body into a gilded wagon, they stumbled on a tree root. The case fell to the flowering earth, and the tumble dislodged the cursed apple. Snow White awoke. The prince proposed eternal felicity. She joyfully accepted—"How many beds do I have to make?"—and off they went to the many-servanted castle with the seven dwarfs in tow: one for each day of each week of wedded bliss.

And as for the wrinkled, envious queen, she and her mirror were still at it. After receiving the invitation to the royals' winter wedding, she dressed in sables and had the usual chat with her glass: "Why you, my queen, are *here*! But *there* at the wedding, the dear new queen has no peer!" Enraged that her pal had not kept her *au courant*—a beauty doesn't suddenly appear—she cracked it end to end. Unable *not* to attend the wedding, she arrived and went numb at the sight of Snow White. Envy caused her scorched heart to implode. Her scalding blood etched a chute to the earth's core, where she and her envy burned miserably evermore.

What Was in That Coffee?:
The Lee Marvin "Palimony" Case

BACKGROUND: "Why should they buy the cow if they can get the milk for free?" asked many a canny granny; but now, thanks to a former torch singer, free can still cost you plenty.

Michelle Triola was a beautiful thirty-one-year-old singer when, back in 1964, she gave up her promising career to tend to the domestic needs of the obstreperous tough-guy actor Lee Marvin. In the six years they lived the good life together in a swell Malibu, California, beach house, Lee earned $3.2 million and an Academy Award for *Cat Ballou*. He has explained his financial philosophy as a determination to "spend all my money while I'm living so there'll be nothing to fight over when I go." In 1970, just after Michelle had her last name legally changed to Marvin, she found herself unexpectedly expelled from her seaside Eden when Lee suddenly married his high-school sweetheart. The "legal" Mrs. Marvin revealed that the two had "kept in touch and about every ten years he'd drop by for a cup of coffee. I always knew I had him on hold. I don't think Lee had a clue." Left to her own resources, Michelle proved resourceful: She took her tale of woe to famed Los Angeles divorce lawyer Marvin Mitchelson, who was eager for a case that would test the reciprocal property rights of unmarried couples. "I've always been fascinated by the question of why the existence or nonexistence of a marriage license should alter people's rights," Mitchelson explained. "Any two idiots can get a marriage license."

Michele Marvin, former "pal" of Lee Marvin, leaving court with her lawyer Marvin Mitchelson.

THE DEAL: Michelle claimed that only after Lee said he loved her and would look after her *forever* did she abandon her stage career to look after him and share his life. Since community-property laws in California dictate that worldly goods be equally divided when a couple splits up, Michelle claimed that Lee owed her over $1 million.

RESULTS: Look after her forever? "Idle male promises," Lee said, dismissing his promise as mere pillow talk. All male movie stars use phrases such as "I love you" as a matter of course, he explained. He owed her nothing, and the courts have traditionally agreed: Any woman living in an unmarried state with a man was per se engaging in what the legal system viewed as a meretricious or "whorelike" relationship. In the view of the courts, sexual services were being immorally (and in some states, illegally) exchanged for support, so that women in these situations had no legal claims. On this basis, the two lower courts in California refused even to hear the case, but Mitchelson appealed to the California Supreme Court. On December 17, 1976, it handed down a landmark decision in *Marvin* v. *Marvin*.

The Supreme Court began by informing the public: "The joining of man and woman in marriage is at once the most socially productive and individually fulfilling relationship that one can enjoy in the course of a lifetime"; but, nevertheless, "the mores of society have indeed changed so radically in regard to cohabitation that we cannot impose a standard based on alleged moral considerations that have apparently been so widely abandoned by so many." Therefore, "adults who voluntarily live together and engage in sexual relations may agree to pool their earnings and hold all property acquired during the relationship in accord with the law governing community property."

It was now up to Michelle to establish that a contract, implied or other, to share in all property acquired in the years she was with Lee, had existed between them. The case was heard in the California Superior Court, in an eleven-week, star-studded courtroom drama involving sixty-three witnesses and eight thousand pages of testimony. Both Marvins won, and both lost: The court decided that no contract did, in fact, exist between them, but that Lee still had to fork over $104,000 to Michelle under the legal principle of "equitable remedy" since Michelle had been tossed from the Hollywood heights, her chances of reviving her singing career appraised by the judge as "doubtful." The settlement, soon dubbed "palimony," was based on two years of Michelle's pre-Marvin salary of $1,000 a week. She was to use the money for "rehabilitative purposes . . . to re-educate herself and to learn new employable skills."

Lee refused to pay and appealed the decision. A year later the decision was overturned. Undaunted, Lawyer Mitchelson and groundbreaking client Michelle immediately began an appeal to the California Supreme Court.

Although Michelle might never collect, *Marvin* v. *Marvin* is a landmark case that invalidates the doctrine of meretricious relationships, at least in California. Very soon after the decision, six other states decided that reciprocal property rights might exist between the unmarried, and thousands of cases have been filed. And since the case recognizes that rights might exist beyond traditional marital law, it has raised questions about the legal rights of those living in other "nonconventional" arrangements—gay people and ménage à trois-niks, for example.

Lawyer Mitchelson, ever litigous, proudly asks: "Don't you love all the ramifications my one case has?"

Three's Company: Freud's Structural Theory of the Mind

BACKGROUND: As the human being evolved from the ape, the human psyche also evolved. But this merger of "blind" animal needs and "seeing" human wants created a dilemma: How was the poor human creature to cope with a complex, dualistic world of experience (stimuli)?

Human behavior is essentially the result of the organism dealing with stimuli. When the human organism is engaged by any stimulus, its response arises from twooppositional instincts, or drives. Psychologists call them Sexual (or Creative) and Aggressive (or Hostile). Moralists call them Good and Bad. The "healthy" personality is an amalgam of the two drives—with one usually dominant—which creates a sense of peace and serenity for the individual. The two drives are "married" by a complex ritual enacted for every stimulus/response and negotiated by the psyche from both its stations: the conscious mind and the unconscious mind.

Freud postulated the existence of an unconscious mind. He had observed that his patients' "hysterical" physical disorders (blindness, paralysis, false pregnancies) vanished after forgotten experiences were remembered or recalled via free association. Boldly, he ventured into this unchartered territory to explore the lay of the psyche's land. He discovered the system of checks and balances that manages the drives and oversees stimulus/response.

THE DEAL: In order for the psyche to function in a world of boundless stimulus/response situations and fuse the two oppositional drives to achieve peace and create social interaction, nature evolved three agencies for the management of the human mind: the Id (The Outlaw), the Ego (Reason), and the Superego (The Law). The Id and Superego are in constant opposition, like the drives they represent, with the Ego functioning as marriage counselor, seeking a fused stimulus/response pattern that will enhance self-esteem. The Id always has its way; the other two agencies must mold the demands of the Id into socially acceptable behavior. If the Ego is weak, the other two must battle it out.

RESULTS: The human being evolved (somewhat) successfully from the ape. If the Ego completes negotiations, the external factors of reality are accepted and the stimulation will be dealt with in a manner that is peaceful, leaving the person content [see "The Ego as Mediator: From Sadist to Surgeon," page 79]. There are various routes for impulses to take. However, once these are established in infancy—often, or always, in relation to the mother and her psychic patterns—they remain fixed unless intervention changes them [see "The Cure Is in Understanding: Psychoanalysis," page 79]. Most, or perhaps all, of these set-up patterns are congenital, passed down from generation to generation.

If the Ego is overpowered, the demands of the Superego and Id will create a chaotic result because objective, reasoned fact will be missing. The solution will therefore be forced and the human being will become irrational and unreasonable without nowing it. Dreams are the result of the Ego's abdication of responsibility during sleep.

The Three Agencies

Id (The Outlaw): Home of the instinctual drives, always totally unconscious. It has no sense of morality, time, or space. It is polymorphously perverse; that is, like an infant, it has no object sense, and instant gratification is all it knows. Gratification for the Id is to be stimuli-free, in a state known as *homeostasis*. Therefore, in a human being, the Id is never gratified. But the Id always deals with its stimuli, and gets what it wants.

Superego (The Law): Home of the conscience. It originates in response to social pressures from the parents or other authority figures. It is an internal censor that is both conscious and unconscious. The Superego is the home of negative thinking: "It can't be done."

Ego (Reason): The mind's emissary to the outside world. It is the reasoning agent, juggling reality's demands, the Id's cries for instant gratification, and the Superego's learned-by-rote dictates. It finds a way of balancing things which is acceptable to self-esteem. The Ego is never punitive. It knows only self-respect and appreciation of self.

The Ego as Mediator: From Sadist to Surgeon

The Id's sadistic impulses to hurt another person are forbidden by the Superego. The sadistic drive is powerful but so is the resistance to sadism. Somehow the Id must be satisfied. By sublimation, or "going underground," the Ego transforms the sadistic impulse into a socially acceptable, Ego-gratifying impulse; for instance, the sadistic impulse to cut and wound another human being is sublimated, and the surgeon is born. The more unconscious the impulse, the better the surgeon. If the Id's sadistic impulse overpowers the Ego and Superego, the result is *Psycho's* Norman Bates.

Other Examples of the Ego as Mediator

Socially Unacceptable Impulses	=	Socially Acceptable Sublimation
Exhibitionism	=	Actor
Domination/Power	=	Lawyer
Voyeurism	=	Therapist or photographer
Aggression/Violence	=	Organized sports
Homoeroticism	=	Football player

The Cure Is in Understanding: Psychoanalysis

Every psychoanalyst worth his or her hefty fee strikes a bargain with the patient's unconscious and the rational portion of the mind (Ego) that sought help in the first place. The name of the magical, lifesaving game is transference and countertransference. This heightened emotional reaction of the patient to the analyst (and vice versa) results in the reactivation of the patient's infantile feelings toward the authority figures of early life, such as parents, siblings, or nannies. The "repetition compulsion," as Freud named it, makes clear to the analyst the destructive ways in which the patient responds to the outside world (stimuli). For instance, though the patient does not remember that he or she was defiant as a child, the patient will be defiant to the analyst, generating destructive internal tensions rather than the serenity that comes from cooperation. The analyst also agrees to listen to *everything* the patient says. The way in which the patient resists and reneges on this contract reveals to the analyst the patterns of the patient's behavior.

The cure for these negative patterns of behavior is in the countertransference: First the analyst must understand the patient and feel what the patient feels, then the patient will understand himself or herself. The result of this interaction is not perfection of self, but the understanding and acceptance of self and the ability to make conscious choices about impulses. This can only be achieved when the patient believes he or she is understood. The analyst understands; the patient trusts. In the long run—a good analyst is not a quick-change artist—in terms of human experience, the real issue of therapy is for the patient to evolve into his or her own person. The patient then regains a zest for living and puts all energies into getting the most out of life without being destructive to self or others.

CIVILIZATION AND ITS DISCONTENTS

A good part of the struggles of mankind center round the single task of finding an expedient accommodation—one, that is, that will bring happiness—between this claim of the individual and the cultural claims of the group; and one of the problems that touches the fate of humanity is whether such an accommodation can be reached by means of some particular form of civilization or whether this conflict is irreconcilable.

Sigmund Freud

High Stakes: Joan of Arc

BACKGROUND: Of all the alliances in history, the one between the peasant maid and the heir to the French throne is possibly the most beloved. There are songs, plays, movies, and over twelve thousand books in France alone about Joan of Lorraine.

France's Charles VI (1368–1422) was recurrently insane. His cousin, the Duke of Burgundy—heir to the greatest duchy in France and Europe—was allied with England and fought to gain control of Charles's crown. After much slaughter, the fiercely powerful Burgundians won the upper hand over the rival factions and negotiated the Peace of Troyes (1420) making England's Henry V (1387–1422) successor to the throne of France. Henry married Charles's daughter, Catherine of Valois; Charles's son, the dauphin, was disinherited. When Henry V and Charles VI died in the same year, Henry VI (1421–1471) was proclaimed in England to be King of France, while the French people recognized Charles's son, Charles VII, as king; he lived at Chinon because the mighty Burgundians and the English controlled Paris and much of France.

Enter Joan of Arc. Born a French peasant in Domremy—a region controlled by Charles VII—Jeanne d'Arc was instructed by the voices of Saint Margaret, Saint Catherine, and Saint Michael to go to the aid of the dauphin. She went to the principal royal representative in her region, convinced him of her mission, and, dressed in male attire—a major symbolic gesture in feudal Europe—she journeyed to the castle at Chinon to strike a bargain with "the true heir" to the crown of France.

THE DEAL: If the dauphin would give Joan his kingdom of France, she would put it in the hands of the all-powerful God. Then, acting in the name of God, she would invest Charles with the kingdom of France, free of English domination. Along with the kingdom, Joan requested troops, the authority to lead them, and the opportunity to fulfill her destiny.

RESULTS: The dauphin handed the kingdom over, on paper. Joan was examined by theologians, found sound, and furnished with armor and troops. In May 1429, she lay siege to Orléans, trouncing the English, not so much by military prowess but by inspiring the French troops and raising their morale. She then took Jargeau, Beaugency, and Patay. Charles journeyed (through her persuasion) to Reims to be anointed and crowned King of France in the great Gothic cathedral, legitimizing his claim to the crown with her by his side. On the way, she took Troyes—a great symbolic victory—and afterward attempted Paris but was defeated.

The following March, she was captured by Burgundians at Compiègne and sold to the English who were so eager to have her that

> The woman shall not wear that which pertaineth unto a man, neither shall a man put on a woman's garment; for all that do so are abomination unto the Lord thy God.
>
> Deuteronomy 12: 5

Henry VI paid in cash from his privy purse, breaking the rules that demanded the English dominions in France pay their own way. Charles did nothing to assist her; he reverted to earlier inactivity. In order to avoid responsibility for her death—she was considered a miraculous presence by the people—Henry turned her over to the Catholic church's ecclesiastical court at Rouen, where she was tried for heresy and witchcraft before French clerics who supported the English but appeared defenders of the Faith. (It was claiming direct inspiration from God, ignoring the church hierarchy, that was her heresy.) On May 24, 1431, she made a public abjuration of her "sins"; four days later she recanted by once again assuming male attire; the next day she was burned at the stake in front of an estimated ten thousand people.

Instead of ending the career of Joan of Arc, the English and their clerical allies created one of the most enduring of heroines. In 1435, the Treaty of Arras reconciled Charles with the Burgundians, and he recovered Paris, destroying England's hopes of joining the two kingdoms. Joan was given a "rehabilitation trial" in 1456 by Charles, annulling the findings of the original trial. She was beatified by the Catholic church in 1909 and canonized in 1920 during its fight against Modernism, "the synthesis of all heresies." Ironically, she who was burned for a heretic was called upon to fight heresy nearly five hundred years after her death.

Down at the End of Lonely Street: Elvis and Priscilla

BACKGROUND: If you're the king of France or the king of rock 'n roll, arranged marriages can be the way to go. But if you're American royalty and fancy nymphets, there *is* no other way unless you want your career blasted like Jerry Lee Lewis's was when he married his fourteen-year-old cousin in 1958, or unless you want imprisonment on the Mann Act like Chuck Berry, who got three years in 1961. However, if you're a recluse and a zonked-out junky, and your queen-to-be's parents are consenting adults . . .

Elvis Aaron Presley was born in Tupelo, Mississippi, on January 8, 1935. His parents, Vernon and Gladys, impoverished and barely literate, lived in a two-room cabin. His mother's family saga was one of alcohol and drug addiction. When Elvis was two and a half, his father planned for broader appeal. Uncommitted to anything but his idea of Priscilla, Elvis went along for the lucrative ride. Surrounding himself with bodyguards (the "Memphis Mafia"), his drug abuse began to escalate; aided and abetted by the new goon squad and local doctors, his orgiastic life began to resemble the Hell-fire Club. Out on the blue horizon of his fading mind, Priscilla lurked, a virginal madonna who would rise from the sea and save his soul. They talked for hours via long distance. She was allowed to visit for Christmas of 1961. A visit wasn't enough. He devised a plan with the parents of his doll.

THE DEAL: Priscilla, sweet sixteen, would be allowed to live on permanent loan nearby with Elvis's father in Memphis, would finish her education in a Catholic school at Elvis's expense, and would have a stipend settled upon her by Elvis to make her financially independent, a sum not unlike an allowance. Elvis would *eventually* make her his Mrs., though no date was set.

RESULTS: Priscilla, having flown her parents' coop, moved in with Elvis at Graceland in May 1962. He transformed her fragile beauty into his hillbilly notion of heavily made-up, patent-leather-dyed, and teased-up feminine fabulosity. To his devoted fans and her classmates

Though married in Las Vegas in 1967, their involvement began in 1959 when Priscilla had just turned fourteen.

went to prison for forgery, then worked in Memphis, commuting to his family on weekends. Gladys turned her whole mind on her only child and isolated the two of them in a private world where blond Elvis fell in love with music on the radio. He started attending local radio broadcasts to watch pros and semipros perform. Though he never studied an instrument and never mastered one, he won second prize singing at a county fair when he was eleven.

In 1948, the Presleys moved to Memphis, where Elvis majored in shop. He was morbidly shy around girls and at parties would withdraw into his songs. But in 1951, at the age sixteen, the extrovert performer in him got the "Tony Curtis cut," or D.A. He bought pomade and became a laughingstock to his redneck classmates until a home room teacher encouraged him to sing in the annual variety show. He won first prize. Girls started checking him out. He decided to become a famous gospel singer and consciously mimicked the sounds of the great spiritual stylists. In 1953 he cut a demo at Sun Records to hear what he sounded like. Sam Phillips, owner of the company, heard him, liked his "black" sound, and recorded "That's All Right Mama." It became a local hit; when he performed it live, the house caved in at the sight of Elvis shaking and jerking his left leg. He earned a place on radio's "Hayride." Girls were all over him. He plucked them like berries, and the search for the perfect girl/woman (virgin) to have and to hold and to love and to wed was on.

Enter Colonel Parker. If Elvis was a young backwoods Faust willing to trade his soul for fame and glory and cash, Parker was a shrewd and greedy devil. He bound Elvis legally and sold him to the highest bidder (RCA), gilding his own pockets while compulsively gambling it away. "Heartbreak Hotel" was the first record to hit number one on all three music charts: R&B, C&W, and pops; it was his first time at bat in the big leagues. *Love Me Tender* made him a movie star. In 1957 he bought his mansion, Graceland, in Memphis, and on December 20, at the height of his wildcat success, he was drafted into the army. On top of that, his beloved mother died, allegedly of diet-pill and alcohol abuse.

In Germany for two years, he was forbidden by Parker to perform. Instead, he fell in love with Priscilla Ann Beaulieu. He met her in August 1959; she'd just turned fourteen. Her stepfather was a career soldier who objected to the famed "Pelvis" but changed his tune when marriage was bandied about. When Elvis was discharged and went stateside again, he immediately fell into the clutches of Parker, who, with Art Lastfogel of the William Morris Agency, sold him to Hal Wallis at Paramount with a desexed, laundered-by-the-army image

A man who has been the indisputable favorite of his mother keeps for life the feeling of a conqueror, that confidence of success that often induces real success.

Sigmund Freud,
The Letters of Sigmund Freud

she was his "protégée," his geisha being trained to serve the lord. She scooted around in a Corvair and didn't take part in extracurricular activities with the nuns because she was pooped from partying at Graceland. After high school she studied modeling. With Papa Beaulieu's prodding, Elvis finally agreed to marry. He went on a compulsive eating and spending binge and had to be starved for weeks to come down from 210 pounds. Parker staged the event in Vegas on April 29, 1967. In February 1968, Priscilla had a baby girl, Lisa Marie, and soon discovered that her husband wanted no part of her sexual maturity.

Elvis's sagging career got a high-voltage boost from TV and Vegas; but between shows, paranoid from drugs and overeating, he locked his retinue in Graceland. He was now injecting demerol and dilaudid as well as swallowing Quaaludes, dexadrine, biphetamine, and percodan around the clock. Frightened and alone, Priscilla took a lover. For three and a half years she maintained the clandestine affair while Elvis cavorted, a junky satrap. In February 1972 she took Lisa Marie and went to her lover. Elvis called her daily, threatening murder. In July, she asked for a divorce. Devastated by what he considered abandonment, he did not fight her, though the threatening calls continued for over a year. They had joint custody of Lisa Marie. She asked for a tiny settlement: $100,000 in cash, $1,000 a month for five years, and $500 monthly in child support. Elvis replaced her immediately with a new angelic virgin—procured by one of the boys—Linda Thompson, 1972's Miss Tennessee. Still crazed about Priscilla, he had another one of his boys arrange a Mafia hit on her lover. At the last moment, he came to his senses and canceled the contract.

In the spring of 1973, Priscilla requested a more realistic divorce settlement—after all, Elvis was earning $7 million a year! Stunned, outraged, drugged senseless, he agreed, terrified of seeing the truth of his habits in the headlines. She received $750,000 in cash, $1.2 million in payments of $6,000 monthly, alimony of $1,200 monthly to drop to $1,000 after five years, child support of $4,000 monthly, 50 percent of a house valued at $500,000, and 5 percent of two publishing outfits that Elvis owned. He shot up, charged on, and in 1974 was booked by Parker to play 152 dates around the country, sometimes so zonked he could barely stand or could not finish the show, and sometimes so fat his costumes split on stage.

The year Elvis turned forty, though he'd earned over $100 million, he was in debt. Most of his fortune had gone for taxes—there were no shelters for Elvis because Parker could not manipulate them—and to Parker, who took *50 percent* of Elvis's earnings in commissions while bleeding him dry by reverting various rights to himself. Drug-induced

He who likes cherries soon learns to climb.

German Proverb

85

extravagances ate up what was left: Elvis bought planes and limos and jewels as if they were hot dogs. Priscilla's career had begun to flourish; she eventually achieved her own success as a regular on "Dallas." Heartsick for Elvis, she sent Lisa Marie to comfort him. On August 15, 1977, Elvis died of an overdose of drugs, all legally prescribed by his doctor.

In the first three years after his death, Elvis earned $20 million. The estate is controlled by Lisa Marie. Parker is under investigation for criminal negligence, fraud, conflict of interest, and mismanagement of his only client's funds. Over one million people yearly visit the two-room cabin where Elvis was born; it has been refurbished into a serviceable shrine. His face is the second most reproduced icon in the world. The most adored face belongs to Mickey Mouse.

Killer to Killer: Eve Harrington versus Addison DeWitt

BACKGROUND: For some, ambition is like a racing car that can easily spin out of control. Eve Harrington is a perfect example of a dangerous and reckless driver; but Addison DeWitt is a master at playing traffic cop.

Margo Channing is a legendary star of the American theater. She is involved in a complex love relationship with the great stage director Bill Sampson and is currently performing in Lloyd Richard's latest smash hit, *Aged in Wood*. One night, Lloyd's wife Karen brings a poor but hugely devoted "fan," Eve Harrington, backstage to meet Margo. Eve is an aspiring actress. She snakes her way into Margo's life, becomes her understudy, makes a pass at Bill, seduces Lloyd, and manipulates Karen into waylaying Margo so that she, Eve, can go on for one performance of *Wood* to prove her abilities. One of the people most impressed by her performance is the powerful columnist Addison DeWitt. Eve then tries to blackmail Karen into pressing Lloyd to cast her in the lead role of his new play, *Footsteps on the Ceiling*, written for Margo. (Karen muses: "You'd do all *that* for a part in a play?" Eve informs her: "I'd do a lot more for a part *that* good!") But Margo marries Bill and forgoes *Footsteps*, so Eve wins the role without Karen's help.

On the brink of her theatrical triumph, Eve announces to starmaker Addison that she intends to marry Lloyd as soon as he divorces Karen for her. But Addison has other plans. He wants to talk.

"Champion to champion?" Eve queries. "Killer to killer," he corrects. Swiftly, he unmasks the cunning but desirable Eve by tripping her up on careless lies about her past ("There is no Shubert Theater in San Francisco!"). He traps her in a New Haven hotel room on the opening night of *Footsteps on the Ceiling*.

THE DEAL: Addison DeWitt will not publicly disgrace her in his column, demolishing her soaring career by revealing how she lied, cheated, and connived her way into *Footsteps*, if Eve agrees to "belong" to him. She refuses: "I can't believe my ears!" He convinces her by means of a few short words: "I'm nobody's fool, least of all yours!" and a well-placed slap. She accepts.

RESULTS: She can't go on. She goes on. She triumphs, winning the 1950 Sarah Siddons Award as well as a Hollywood contract. At Margo Channing Sampson's suggestion, she puts the award where her heart ought to be.

◆ ◆ ◆ ◆

All About Eve, a film written and directed by Joseph Mankiewicz, released by Twentieth Century-Fox, 1950. Margo Channing (Bette Davis); Bill Sampson (Gary Merrill); Lloyd Richards (Hugh Marlowe); Karen Richards (Celeste Holm); Eve Harrington (Anne Baxter); Addison DeWitt (George Sanders).

A Ring! A Ring! My Kingdom for a Ring!: Elizabeth and Essex

BACKGROUND: History frequently disappoints storytellers. Too often, because of romantic complications or for dramatic shape, adjustments must be made to deliver the goods to the paying customers. The long, eventful life of Elizabeth I, England's Virgin Queen, is a prime example [see "Dealmaker as Monarch," page 154]. Undoubtedly, Good Queen Bess, the epitome of the Baroque, would have scheduled an appointment with Mary Stuart had she known how essential the meeting was to become to future novelists, playwrights, and moviemakers. The same holds true for the delivery of her famous gift to Robert Devereux, the Earl of Essex.

Elizabeth loved the splendidly handsome, impetuous (though impecunious) Essex. Born in 1567, he lost his father at age nine. As the stepson of Robert Dudley, Earl of Leicester and a favorite of the queen, he had immediate access to her royal presence. By 1587, when he was not yet twenty and she was fifty-three, the two of them were never apart. She doted upon him and his youthful virility; he publicly worshipped the Divine Gloriana, eclipsing every other "suitor" at the court. They walked and talked and rode together; they played cards or one game or another through the night. He was a symbol to her of the Young England eager for independence from absolute monarchy; she was exhilarated to have him kneeling at her feet and endlessly proclaiming her sublime beauty.

THE DEAL: Perhaps during these halcyon days, Elizabeth gave Essex the apocryphal ring. With it went a promise: Whenever he sent it back to her, *no matter the circumstance*, even high treason—the gravest offence known to the law—it would bring instant forgiveness. Essex lavishly swore eternal fealty to his queen.

RESULTS: Elizabeth made Essex rich by granting him estates and a share of customs duties on imported goods, gifts common to court favorites. To her anxiety, he insisted upon actively defending her glory abroad in Portugal with Sir Francis Drake, and fighting for Henry of Navarre [see "Paris Is Surely Worth a Mass!: Henry of Navarre," page 239]. Politically, Essex aligned himself with Francis Bacon, whose genius guided him in his swift and successful ascension to the position of trusted minister and informed statesman. By 1593 he was a powerful member of the queen's Privy Council, who made suggestions while she alone governed. In 1596, with the support of the capture of Cádiz, he became a national hero; but no matter how much glory he achieved, he could never force his will upon the queen. Wisely, Bacon advised him to seek civil posts, not military ones, "for Her Majesty loveth peace." Essex dreamed of combat and was filled with ambitious projects for violent solutions to England's problems, solutions that the queen constantly rejected. In 1597 he was appointed Earl Marshall, and one year later Ireland became a cause for serious alarm. Hugh O'Neill, Lord of Tyrone, aspired to become Lord of Ireland; he formed a national league against England and created a full rebellion. Essex led sixteen thousand men to quell the rebels. Due to bad management, he squandered his forces and offered conditions of peace. When Elizabeth disavowed his actions, he returned to England in disgrace, having disregarded her orders, having acted as if he had independent authority, and having presumed upon her personal favor. She saw his behavior as a portent of the future when the Royals would be mere figureheads. She was determined to hold her ground.

After eight months' confinement, he was tried by a special commission and deprived of his offices in 1600. Unable to accept his fate, he recklessly made a bid for a restoration to power. He sent messengers to Tyrone and to Scotland's king asking for support. He planned to rouse London to his cause, and with the support of the city to force his way into the presence of the queen to demand she appoint him Lord Protector of the Realm. With three hundred men he rode through the streets shouting: "For the Queen! For the Queen! A plot is laid against my life!" Nary a citizen budged. The coup was a disaster. He was arrested, tried for high treason, and sentenced to death. On February 25, 1601, Essex was beheaded, a mercy extended by Elizabeth since high treason demanded he be strung up, cut down while life was still in him, castrated, gutted, and drawn and quartered. Two years later, Elizabeth was dead at age seventy.

The first reference to the ring appeared in 1620 in *The Devil's Law Case* by John Webster. The full-blown tale appeared in 1695 in *The Secret History of the Most Renowned Queen Elizabeth and the Earl of Essex,* by a Person of Quality. According to legend, Essex sent the ring. He dropped it from a window in the Tower of London into the palm of a boy instructed to deliver the treasure to one Lady Scropes, who was to bring it to the queen. The boy gave it to Lady Nottingham, Lady Scropes's sister and the wife of Essex's fiercest enemy. She kept it. Upon her deathbed, she confessed and Elizabeth exclaimed: "God may forgive you, madam, but I never can!" *Curtain.*

Three hundred and thirty-eight years later, supermacho Errol Flynn, as Essex in Michael Curtiz's *The Private Lives of Elizabeth and Essex,* keeps the ring, accepting death rather than beg forgiveness from a mere woman who won't give him complete control over her kingdom, while Bette Davis flamboyantly cries her eyes out: "My heart goes to the grave with him!" *The End.* Even legends must change to suit the needs of the times.

How Do I Love Thee? Let Me Count the Ways: Jackie and Ari

BACKGROUND: When the world's richest man married the world's most famous woman, it is claimed that crucial odds and ends of life had to be set down in writing.

Aristotle Onassis, with a personal fortune of nearly $1 billion, was

Ari described his bride: "Like a diamond, cool and sharp at the edges, fiery and hot beneath the surface."

described by an associate as the Sun King. After building the largest shipping concern in global history, he desired to enhance his glory by a marriage to the renowned Jacqueline Bouvier Kennedy. Ari described his newest passion as "like a diamond, cool and sharp at the edges, fiery and hot beneath the surface."

THE DEAL: According to the book published in France by a steward on the Onassis yacht, *Christina*, there was a marriage contract of 170 clauses signed by both Jackie and Ari. They agreed to apartments in Paris, Greece, and New York City, with separate bedrooms in each, an allowance of $580,000 annually for Jackie, and not more than three connubial visits a week. If divorced, she was to receive a settlement of $20 million.

RESULTS: The alleged contract made headlines around the world. Jackie strenuously denied that such a document existed. She told her then-confidante Truman Capote (not renowned for keeping secrets) that although such a legal formality was commonplace among the rich, she had refused to sign such a paper because it reeked of vulgar bartering. She swore she had nothing to show for her marriage but a few personal belongings, a savings account of $5,200, and an open charge account with Olympic Airlines.

Soon after the wedding, she and her interior decorator ordered $280,000 in new decor for her new homes. While Truman spread the news of her pecuniary plight, Ari grew to hate her legendary extravagance. (She is reported to have spent $1.5 million during their first year of marriage and to have removed his favorite allegorical friezes from the *Christina,* which she and her friends had openly mocked.) Soon he was describing her as "coldhearted and shallow." "My God!" he eventually exclaimed. "What a fool I have made of myself!" Changing his will, he reduced to the legal minimum her share of his estate, adding a codicil in case she challenged his decision: "I command my executors and the rest of my heirs that they deny her such a right through all legal means, costs and expenses charged to my inheritance." He brought in Roy Cohn, infamous colleague of McCarthy during the 1950s House Un-American Activities Committee hearings, as his legal representative [see "America's Inquisition: HUAC versus 'The Tinseltown Pinks,' " page 252].

Onassis died before opening official divorce proceedings. His widow, Jacqueline, was left the minimum allowed by law, $250,000. She contested this amount and negotiated a more acceptable $20 million settlement—a haunting echo of the divorce settlement promised in the alleged marriage contract. She took a job as an editor at Doubleday, the New York publishers. Arguing successfully for a zoning variance on Martha's Vineyard, she then built the tallest house on the island to guarantee her privacy. Truman Capote has nothing further to say.

"Of all the deals I ever made, Nanny-Poo, you were one of the smartest."

III

AROUND THE BLOCK: REAL ESTATE

A horse! A horse! My kingdom for a horse!

SHAKESPEARE, *RICHARD III,*
ACT V, SCENE IV

Go West, Young Men: Christopher Columbus and the New World

BACKGROUND: In 1484, King John II of Portugal was deeply committed to finding an African sea route to the treasures of India and Asia, but he rejected the eccentric proposal of Christopher Columbus, an Italian mariner who wished to sail west into the vast Oceanic Sea (the Atlantic). Columbus was convinced that it offered an unimpeded path to Japan's back door. Though the theory that the earth was round was controversial in the fifteenth century, it was not unique to Columbus; nor was he alone in believing that only the Atlantic prevented Eurasia from banding the globe. Sailors' yarns of land sightings and floating debris found beyond the Azores had convinced him of Asia's proximity; it was inconceivable that another continent existed between Europe and Asia.

Undaunted by King John's refusal, the persistent Columbus unsuccessfully brought his "Enterprise of the Indies," as he called the project, to other royal courts. After eight years of supplication, he triumphed when Spain's recapturing of Granada from the Moors after seven hundred years created an expansive and celebratory atmosphere at the home of the Spanish monarchs, Ferdinand and Isabella. They agreed to finance his daring journey west and commanded him to "discover islands and mainland in the Oceanic Sea." The two royals must have been feeling quite giddy, because nothing in the annals of exploration resembles the package they offered to him.

THE DEAL: Christopher Columbus was given three small ships lightly armed for self-defense, not for war, the standard trade goods (knives, brightly colored cloth, glass beads, hawk belts, and other trinkets) for barter on the coasts, and letters of credence to any and all sovereigns, including Marco Polo's "Great Khan." He was made viceroy of all new lands discovered, was given the right to nominate their governors, as well as 10 percent of the whole commerce of such lands. All this was granted in perpetuity with hereditary rights. Spain, in turn, would receive absolute sovereignty over everything he found.

RESULTS: The expedition sailed from Spain on August 3, 1492. After nearly ten weeks out on uncharted seas, there was a small mutiny against the abrasive and obsessive Columbus by his frightened and unhappy men. Luckily, two days later, on October 12, land was sighted—the island of San Salvador in the Bahamas. It was joyously claimed for Spain. The sailors were met by the curious, peaceful inhabitants who were named Indians by Columbus, believing himself in the Indies. With some natives impressed into service, he continued to discover other islands in the area. When one of his ships was wrecked off the coast of Hispaniola, he left thirty-nine gold-hungry men there to found a colony; driven by avarice, they brutalized the Indians until the colony was destroyed.

On March 15, Columbus returned to Spain. Surrounded by six Indians, gold, plants, and flowers, his reception at court was all he could wish. The king and queen rose to greet him, then sat him at their right. The Enterprise of the Indies was an astounding success for Spain, establishing an empire that would stretch to include nearly all of South America, Central America, southern North America, and the Philippines. Vast wealth would be pillaged by the violent conquistadores [see "Tears Wept by the Sun: Pizarro and the Incas," page 250] who would destroy whatever they touched. Sixteenth-century Spain would be the first European empire on which the sun never set.

Columbus, however, did not fare so well. The greed of the first colonists made his attempts at governing into disastrous failures. Then prisoners were transported on his third exploration, adding to the chaos while he went off exploring the other islands. In 1500, the monarchs dispatched an independent governor to investigate conditions on the lands ruled by Columbus. The governor was horrified and carted Columbus back to Spain in chains. The admiral was immediately released, but his favor at court was declining along with the novelty value of the "New World." His last expedition was a marooned mess; he had to be rescued from Jamaica. He died in 1506, neglected and forgotten. Even his reputation as a skilled navigator was debated for years among historians, who have only recently reestablished through his logs and papers that he was unsurpassed in charting unknown waters solely with dead reckoning. Though the Vikings and the Celts had discovered America before him, it was Columbus's voyage that marked the beginning of American history for the Europeans.

Damn Colonies: Napoleon Sells the Louisiana Territory

BACKGROUND: Thirty-four-year-old Napoleon Bonaparte was a brilliant general, but sometimes he seemed more like a schoolboy, trading countries like a kid swaps baseball cards. You give me the 520-million-acre New World territory called Louisiana, he told King Carlos of Spain, and I'll give you the Italian kingdom of Parma. He then turned around and immediately sold Louisiana. You could do that if you were Napoleon.

Napoleon had been eager to establish a New World empire. His enemy, the British, had quite a large one, even with the recent loss of the thirteen rebellious colonies. Spain's empire was enormous, but she was unable to control all she had—Montesquieu had condescendingly said, "They possess a great empire with insignificance." Playing on Spanish fears of losing Mexico, their mineral-rich colony, to the British or the Americans, the French convinced King Carlos that French possession of the Louisiana Territory would form a "wall of brass forever impenetrable." King Carlos liked the idea of a barrier stretching from the east bank of the Mississippi to the Rocky Mountains and from the Gulf of Mexico all the way to Canada. He would trade this wilderness for Parma, but Napoleon had to agree never to give or otherwise dispose of the territory to any third country. Both sides agreed to keep word of the swap secret until France could amass a New World military force sufficient to repel the Anglo-American invasion Napoleon expected, once they learned that France had taken over. Napoleon was planning to use the Caribbean island of Santo Domingo as a springboard for his occupation of Louisiana—that is, once the slave rebellion there, led by Toussaint L'Ouverture, was suppressed. An inconsequential skirmish, Napoleon believed it to be, and he sent his brother-in-law off to attend to it.

Just across the border from the Louisiana Territory, that feisty newborn, the United States, was bursting at the seams of the original states. Pushing through the Cumberland Gap, Americans, in large numbers, were settling the fertile lands west of the Appalachians. Spanish rule of western lands was regarded as ineffectual and temporary. But when rumors concerning Napoleon's plans to take over the territory began to circulate in the international diplomatic community, Americans were quick to voice their objections. The empire-hungry French, led by the aggressive Napoleon, were not the kind of neighbors America wanted in her own backyard. Of particular con-

Napoleon *by David.*

cern to the Americans was control over the port of New Orleans: It was through this conduit that American traders shipped their cargoes of skins, ginseng, and lumber out to the rest of the world. President Jefferson asked James Monroe to travel to Paris as special emissary to negotiate the purchase of New Orleans—no one even dreamed of asking for the whole territory. If Monroe's mission failed, he was to go straight to London to coordinate war plans with the English against the French.

Down in the Caribbean, Napoleon's plan to quickly crush the revolution was dissolving as the unexpected military skill of the slaves, the inspired leadership of Toussaint L'Ouverture, and yellow fever combined to claim the lives of nearly fifty thousand French soldiers, including Napoleon's brother-in-law. Napoleon, exasperated, was heard to mutter: "Damn sugar, damn coffee, damn colonies." Faced with the expense of the war he was planning against the British, Napoleon decided to concentrate his imperial efforts in Europe; he would raise the money he needed for his army by selling Louisiana. On the day Monroe arrived in France, Napoleon instructed his foreign minister, Talleyrand, to ask for 125 million francs.

THE DEAL: Monroe was astonished to hear that the French were willing to sell the entire territory. "Not interested," he responded, playing it cool—everyone knows that the United States is already too big and that big republics don't work. Ultimately, in the course of a sixteen-day bargaining session, he agreed to a purchase price of 60 million francs ($11,250,000) immediately, in cash, and up to an additional 20 million frances ($3,750,000) to settle claims Americans had against the French. Where the boundaries were, exactly, no one was sure. That didn't bother the Americans, who hoped thereby to encroach upon the Spanish borders to the south and west; and the French, eager to start trouble between the Americans and the English by leaving the northern border vague, were delighted. Napoleon insisted that the U.S. promise to protect the political rights of the people of the region and to make them American citizens as soon as possible.

RESULTS: The Louisiana Purchase was more than four times the size of the thirteen original colonies—it was more than seven times as large as Great Britian and Ireland together. In spite of some opposition ("We are to give money, of which we have too little, for land, of which we already have too much," wrote one critic), Congress recognized the staggering prize that had fallen into its hands and quickly ratified the treaty. Spain immediately protested that France had no right to sell the territory. Take that up with Napoleon, Jefferson told them—their complaints were "private questions between France and

Spain which they must solve together." The ego of the French, offended by this diminishment of their empire, was assuaged when Napoleon explained: "I have given England a rival who sooner or later will humble her pride."

In 1804, Creole natives of the territory sent a delegation to Washington requesting statehood—and therefore political status within the United States. Congress denied their request, President Jefferson explaining that "the principles of popular government are utterly beyond their comprehension." Congress established a form of territorial government of appointed officials, strangely reminiscent of English colonial government. But eventually, the territory yielded the states of Louisiana, Arkansas, Missouri, Nebraska, North and South Dakota, and much of Kansas, Minnesota, Colorado, Montana, and Wyoming. America's destiny as an imperial power had become manifest.

GOD'S GREEN ACRES:

How the Thirteen Original States Multiplied for an Average of Thirteen Cents an Acre

Date	Acquisition	Size (in thousands of acres)	Total Cost (in thousands of dollars)	Price per Acre (in cents)
1781–1802	State cessions	236,826	6,200	Free and .11
1789–1850	Indian "treaties"	450,000	90,000	.20
1803	Louisiana Purchase	520,000	15,000	.04
1819	Florida Territory, "ceded" from Spain	46,145	6,674	.14
1846	Oregon Compromise with Great Britain, dividing the Pacific Northwest	183,386	0	0
1848	Mexican "cession" (result of Mexico's defeat in the Mexican War)	338,681	16,295	.05
1850	Purchased from Texas	78,927	15,496	.19
1853	Gadsden Purchase (from Mexico: southern Arizona)	18,989	10,000	.53
1867	"Seward's Folly"—Alaska Purchase from Russia	375,300	7,200	.02

Magnificent Intentions:
Locating the United States Capital in Dixieland

BACKGROUND: After the American Revolution, federal officials were tired of moving from place to place, living out of suitcases. Everyone agreed that the newly independent United States needed a capital, but no one could agree about where it should be built until Jefferson and Hamilton got to drinking with some of the boys.

Alexander Hamilton, secretary of the treasury, was a worried man when he ran into Thomas Jefferson, secretary of state, coming from President Washington's home in New York. For months, the Congress of the new nation had been balking at passage of a critical part of Hamilton's economic program, the federal assumption of debts incurred by the states during the Revolution. Hamilton was convinced that to forge the powerful central government he favored, the allegiance of the commercial elite must be won. As it stood, the loyalties of this plutocracy were to the individual states that owed them money; Hamilton hoped that by switching those financial ties to a central power, the "enlightened self-interest" of the moneymen would dictate their support of the new national government. And besides, by eliminating state debt, the need for most state taxes would vanish, giving the national government a near monopoly in the collection of taxes. But some members of Congress opposed the establishment of a strong central government, equating it with tyranny; others opposed assumption because their states had either paid off their debts already or had not incurred any. And with four-fifths of the debt in the hands of the pro-assumption North, the issue broke down along North/South lines. When representatives from Massachusetts (heavily in debt) started grumbling about dissolving the infant union over this issue, Senator Richard Henry Lee of Virginia (they'd paid off their debt) answered that he'd prefer this to "the rule of a fixed, insolent Northern majority."

The newly formed Congress was bitterly divided on other issues as well. Where, for example, should the national capital be located? The Founding Fathers had mandated in the Constitution that a federally controlled capital be established, "not exceeding 10 square miles, as may, by cession of particular states and by acceptance of Congress, become the seat of the government of the U.S." [Article 1, Section 8], but the intense debate over where to place this federal city was stalemated. In the meantime, the governing body of the United States was itinerant: Since the end of the Revolution, Congress had been on the move, meeting in Philadelphia, Princeton, Annapolis, Trenton, and New York. Unable to control its own working environment, the government was forced to share offices with state and local officials (and, at Princeton, with faculty). Everyone agreed that this was an undignified way to run a country. The *New York Advertiser* lamented: "We pity the poor Congressmen, thus kicked and cuffed about from post to pillar—where can they find a home?" It wasn't that there were no offers—Congress was barraged by bids from scores of localities. But states were terribly jealous of one another, sectional antagonism was rampant, national consciousness was still inchoate—and people were convinced that wherever the federal city was built, there would arise a great center of population, commerce, and culture. Congress had, in principle, agreed that the capital should be centrally located, then quickly discovered that southerners took that to mean near the geographic center (their turf), while northerners insisted fairness dictated locating the capital in the center of the populace (their turf).

To the coolly rational Hamilton, a supreme realist, the question of where to locate the seat of government was one of extreme indifference. It was mere vanity, he figured, and an associate of his summed it up: "I would not find fault with Ft. Pitt, if we could assume the debts and proceed in peace and quietness." Jefferson, a Virginian, had been out of the country for years (as minister to France), and on the day he encountered Hamilton he was not yet familiar with all the details of Hamilton's financial plan. But what the Treasury secretary told Jefferson struck terror into the heart of the secretary of state: Because of assumption, people were seriously discussing the dissolution of the union that Jefferson had worked so arduously to establish. Jefferson, agitated, spontaneously used the diplomatic technique that had served him well in Paris: Come for dinner, he told Hamilton. I'll invite the boys.

THE DEAL: With the Madeira flowing freely at Jefferson's table, his guests, Virginia Congressmen Richard Bland Lee and Alexander White, agreed to throw their support over to Hamilton's assumption bill. In return, Hamilton would align northern votes to place the national capital on the gently sloping banks of the Potomac, in Virginia.

RESULTS: With southern support, the assumption bill easily passed. Combined with the rest of Hamilton's financial schemes, capitalist al-

It was originally chosen for the seat of government as a means of averting the conflicting jealousies and interests of the different States; and very probably, too, as being remote from mobs—a consideration not to be slighted, even in America.

Charles Dickens, 1842

legiance to the federal government has been unquestioned ever since. Hamilton has been called "the prophet of industrial America, a man who dwelled in the midst of a race of agrarians and dared to tell them that their future was bound up in ships, counting houses, banks, highways, canals and above all, factories." Jefferson, the exemplar of the pro-states-rights agrarian gentleman, soon came to realize the implications of Hamilton's financial plans, and the two became the bitterest of enemies. Later he would write that on the day he ran into Hamilton and arranged the fateful dinner, he was "a stranger to the ground, a stranger to the actors in it, so long absent as to have lost all familiarity with the subject."

The national capital was christened Washington, the District of Columbia, and was carved from one hundred square miles of Virginia and Maryland. President Washington, who had been a surveyor in his youth, personally chose the site, which was as close to his estate at Mount Vernon as possible. French engineer Pierre L'Enfant was commissioned to design the city; his grandiose plans for the remote region of fields, woods, and marshes were considered ridiculously pretentious. The government moved there in 1800 (after spending ten years in Philadelphia while some government buildings were being built), but very little of L'Enfant's plan was yet realized and the capital was primitive and dreary. It was a city "which so many are willing to come to and all are so anxious to leave," said one observer; and from 1797 to 1829, more senators resigned than failed to be reelected. The English poet Thomas Moore gibed: "This embryo Capital where fancy sees, squares in morasses, obelisks in trees." Congress expected the anticipated boom in real estate to pay for improvements, but the first public auction of ten thousand government-owned lots unloaded a mere thirty-five of them. The popular George Washington personally conducted successive auctions, but they fared even worse. The expected "Emporium of the Continent" failed to materialize, and even the federal government provided little employment: By 1802 only 291 people in Washington (including the president) were federally employed. Charles Dickens, visiting in 1842, reported: "It is sometimes called the City of Magnificent Distances, but it might with greater propriety be called the City of Magnificent Intentions. . . . Spacious avenues, that begin in nothing and lead nowhere; streets, miles long, that only want houses, roads and inhabitants; public buildings that need but a public to be complete. . . . One might fancy the season over, and most of the houses gone out of town forever, with their masters."

INDIAN GIVING

In the beginning, the Indians owned it all, every inch of the 2.3 billion acres that comprise the United States. Today, their holdings are reduced to the 52 million acres—2.4 percent of the continental United States—held in trust for them by the federal government (plus another 40 million acres in Alaska). Most tribes, having encountered U.S. military might, decided that it would be in their self-interest to compromise with the whites (it is now estimated that the United States spent $1 million for every Indian killed by the U.S. Army). Between 1789 and 1850, the United States ratified 245 treaties with Native American tribes, whittling away at Indian holdings. Through these treaties the United States obtained 450 million acres of Indian land for $90 million—twenty cents an acre. Each treaty "solemnly promised" that no further demands for tribal land would ever be made. Even though the United States kept breaking the treaties, the Indians, desperate, kept negotiating new ones. George Washington, the man who could not tell a lie, said of one treaty: "I can never look upon that proclamation other than as a temporary expedient to quiet the minds of Indians." When Andrew Jackson became president, he said, "I have long viewed treaties with the Indians as an absurdity"; one American general described treaties with the Indians as "a sardonic joke." Indians kept falling for these jokes because they had no choice. Ultimately, the land they got to keep was the land the whites didn't want: arid, desolate, isolated. But it seems that the Native Americans just might be having the last laugh: Indian lands contain vast mineral deposits—over $1 trillion worth of coal, vast quantities of oil, and about half the nation's uranium.

Forked Tongues:
Bamboozling the Cherokees West

At the time of the first treaty between whites and Cherokees, the Cherokee Nation possessed much of Kentucky and Tennessee and a good deal of Virginia, North and South Carolina, Alabama, and Georgia. Thirty-eight treaties later, the Cherokees were forced out of all 20 million of these eastern acres and forced to an 800,000-acre allotment in Indian Territory, several hundred miles west. Each of the treaties had promised that in the future, no further cessions of land would be requested. Each treaty promised that the United States would remove white encroachers upon Cherokee territory (this was never done). These treaties, which ended in Cherokee expulsion and the death of nearly one-quarter of the tribe, always promised "perpetual peace and friendship between the citizens of the U.S. and the Cherokee Indians." Here are the highlights of that "diplomatic" history.

1721	Cherokee land is ceded to the colony of South Carolina in exchange for a promise of protection and perpetual friendship.
1763	The English issue the Royal Order of 1763, stating that all land west of the crest of the Appalachians belongs to Native Americans. Whites are forbidden to cross the line without special permission. Colonists, reaping huge profits in the fur trade, are outraged.

Burial of the dead at the Battle of Wounded Knee, 1881.

1777	Because of the Royal Order of 1763, the Cherokees are loyal to England in the Revolutionary War. Because of their support of the enemy, most Cherokee land in South Carolina and large areas in Virginia and North Carolina are seized by Americans.
1785	In exchange for Cherokee acceptance of the boundaries forced on them in 1777, and permission for white traders to peddle their goods on tribal lands, the United States "solemnly" agrees to remove all white settlers encroaching on Cherokee land and grants the Cherokees the right to send a representative to Congress. The Cherokees later discover that Congress will not actually allow their representative in; nor will the United States remove white settlers.
1791	All Cherokee land in Kentucky and considerable land in Tennessee is ceded for a $1,500 annual payment. The treaty also promises that four whites will be sent to Cherokee land to establish "model" farms for the Cherokees to emulate. (The Cherokees had successfully farmed their land for generations before the whites arrived.)
1794	The $1,500 in cash promised in the Treaty of 1791 is changed to $5,000 in merchandise, annually. These items are to be chosen by the whites to help "civilize" the Cherokees. And, although this treaty promises that white encroachers will be removed, it also states that the Cherokees will be fined fifty dollars for every horse they steal from whites living on their land. The fines are to be deducted from the settlement.
1798	A large area of desirable farmland in Georgia is ceded for $5,000 in merchandise, plus an annual payment of $1,000 in merchandise.
1801–1819	Nine treaties are negotiated, in which the Cherokees hand over four million acres of land in exchange for $240,700. In 1817, a dangerous precedent is established when the Cherokees are forced to exchange large holdings in Alabama, Georgia, and Tennessee for land in the Arkansas Territory.
1828	Much to the great misfortune of the Cherokees, gold is discovered on tribal land in Georgia. As hoards of prospectors sweep through, the state of Georgia announces that it is nullifying all Cherokee law and all

federal law concerning the Cherokees: The laws of the state of Georgia will now prevail. Georgia forcibly seizes tribal land, forbids the Indians from mining for gold, bans their tribal council from meeting, except to *ratify* land cessions, and sends the brutal Georgia Guards to harass and terrorize the Cherokees.

1830   Congress passes the Indian Removal Act. Now, according to Federal mandate, the Cherokees can be forced to exchange their eastern lands for land west of the Mississippi. President Jackson announces that the removal of the Indians will "place a dense and civilized population in large tracts of country now occupied by a few savage hunters."

1831   The Cherokees win a decisive victory over the state of Georgia in the Supreme Court. In the *Cherokee Nation* v. *Georgia,* the Court decides that only the federal government has sovereignty over the Indians.

1832   Cherokee rights are further strengthened when the Supreme Court decides, in *Wincester* v. *Georgia,* that the Cherokee Nation is a legitimate political community, where "the laws of Georgia can have no force and which the citizens of Georgia have no right to enter"— without tribal consent. Unfortunately, the man in the White House hates Indians as much as he loves states' rights; Andrew Jackson sneers at the decision, saying "John Marshall has made his decision, now let him enforce it."

1835   The Cherokees, facing brutal repression and harassment, are completely split over what to do next. Some want to sell their remaining eastern lands and move west. Others want to stick it out. Their chief, John Ross, is a strong proponent of remaining on their ancestral land until he is convinced, in 1835, that this is no longer an option. He then suggests that the Cherokees sell out for $20 million and move to Mexican Territory. While Ross is in Washington trying to negotiate his price, federal agents are sent to negotiate with more compliant Cherokees. The Treaty of Echota, never officially ratified by the tribe, calls for the Cherokees to hand over their remaining 10 million acres of land in eastern states in exchange for $5.4 million and

800,000 acres in Indian Territory (Oklahoma). The United States promises to pay for all expenses involved in the move west, provide an adequate number of carriages, steamships, and physicians en route, and pay for subsistence for one full year after the Cherokee arrival in Indian Territory.

1838 The Cherokees are not eager to leave their homeland; finally the federal government takes action. The Cherokees are told to assemble at processing points for the trip west. When most of them fail to show up, seven thousand army troops swoop down on them, rounding them up without even giving them a chance to pack. A soldier reported: "I saw the helpless Cherokees arrested and dragged from their homes, and driven by bayonet into the stockades. . . . I saw them loaded like cattle or sheep into wagons and started toward the west." From October 1838 to the spring of 1839 (the harshest time of year), eighteen thousand Cherokees follow the "Trail of Tears." Four thousand people die along the way—with transportation facilities totally inadequate and none of the promised physicians.

1893 The federally appointed Dawes Commission recommends that the tribal claim to Indian Territory be extinquished and the land subdivided into individual plots. With individuals free to sell their land, many Cherokee soon give in to white pressure and sell out.

Present Even the full force of American military might was unable to kill the Cherokee Nation. During removal, several hundred Cherokees fled to caves in the Smoky Mountains, foraging for food until a trusted white friend was able to buy them a farmstead. Today, over forty-five hundred Cherokee live on their ancestral land, bearing witness to the tenacity of the human spirit.

LAND GRAB: RAILROADS CRISSCROSS AMERICA

The arrangement was fairly simple: The federal government would give land, of which it had much, to railroad companies, who could then use it as collateral to raise the funds needed to finance the building of railroads across the United States. The "national impulse" during the nineteenth century was to populate the West; the quickest way to spur migration seemed to be by building railroads; the quickest way to get them built seemed to be by giving land away to businessmen who would then finance the roads. But things got out of hand: Between

1850 and 1871 a total of 131 million acres were given away to sixteen railroad companies in what can only be called a spree, finally stopped by public outcry. The railroads knew who their friends were: Legislators, lawmakers, bankers, journalists, presidents, even a chief justice of the Supreme Court, all shared in this lavish bonanza. Collis Huntington of the Central Pacific Railroad spent $500,000 in bribes at every congressional session and was nearly outbribed by his competitors. Congressman Oakes Ames distributed free stock in the Crédit Mobilier, a railroad construction company, to his colleagues in the House—it paid 625 percent in dividends in one year—and siphoned off $23 million from the federal treasury. Jay Cooke, America's leading banker, masterminded the Northern Pacific Railroad scheme—ending up with 22,000 acres for every mile of rail they built. Chief Justice Salmon Chase hankered after the presidency of the Northern Pacific, but Cooke felt he was more useful where he was. Chase wrote: "Hurray for the Northern Pacific! I wish I was able to take four times as much bonds as you've assigned to me."

Today, those glory days are gone, along with most of the 131 million acres. But there are reminders: the Penn Central still owns most of Park Avenue in New York; in 178, the Southern Pacific Railroad earned over $52 million from its 3.7 million acres.

RAIL ON

Mr. Huntington is not altogether bad. Though severe he is merciful. He tempers invective with falsehood. He says ugly things of his enemy, but he has the tenderness to be careful that they are mostly lies.

He knows himself an outmate of every penal institution in the world; he deserves to hang from every branch of every tree of every state and territory penetrated by his railroads, with the sole exception of Nevada, which has no trees.

Ambrose Bierce

Love Me, Love My Wives: The Mormons Exchange Polygamy for Utah

BACKGROUND: Nineteenth-century America found the Mormon practice of polygamy unconscionable and revolting. Mormons were hunted and hounded and jailed until they gave in, divorcing all but one lawfully wedded wife. Only then could Utah become a state.

Back in 1838, when the governor of Missouri, home of the largest Mormon settlement, declared that "Mormons must be treated as enemies, and must be exterminated or driven from the State for the public peace," Joseph Smith, founder of the church and husband to forty-seven, led the faithful to Illinois. They quickly wore out their welcome there too: In 1844 Smith was imprisoned, then dragged from his cell by a hostile mob and murdered. His successor, Brigham Young (husband to twenty-seven) decided that the time had come for the Mormons to leave the United States. Hoping to establish a theocracy in the desert, thousands of the faithful followed Young to the remote, arid Salt Lake Valley, then part of Mexican Territory.

But if the Mormons would quit the United States, the United States would not quit the Mormons. The Utah Territory was ceded to the United States by Mexico in 1848 at the end of the Mexican War. This time the Mormons were determined to stay put, although they knew that as residents of an American territory they would have few independent political rights. The path to independence lay in establishing a state dominated by Mormons (only 10 percent of Utah was non-Mormon). Their first petition for statehood was denied, but the Mormons were encouraged when President Millard Fillmore appointed Young to be governor of the territory. Lulled by this into a false sense of security, Young, in 1852, officially brought the Mormon practice of polygamy out of the closet; previously there had been no official confirmation of the practice.

The press went wild, indulging in a sensationalist spree, as lurid accounts of Mormon family life filled the papers. America was both titillated and outraged. Politicians quickly entangled the issue of polygamy with that of slavery. Republicans insisted that Congress "prohibit in the Territories those twin relics of barbarism, Polygamy and Slavery," while the proslavery Democrats were even more vehement in their denunciations. In 1857, Democratic President James Buchanan removed Young as governor ("I am and will be governor," thundered Young, "and no power can hinder it until the Lord Almighty says, 'Brigham, you need not be Governor any longer' "), and in an attempt to unify a nation rent by slavery, Buchanan sent troops to impose martial law in Utah. The odd and ineffectual "Mormon War" was a stand-off between thirty-seven hundred federal troops and the Mormons, who met them peacefully and delighted in selling them provisions at exorbitant prices. When Congress realized how much this venture was costing, the troops were withdrawn and the fight against polygamy moved to legislative halls. Congress outlawed polygamy in 1862, disincorporated the church, and limited its assets to $50,000. But with the Civil War raging, the feds had no time to police bedrooms a thousand miles away. "You tell Brigham Young if he will leave me alone, I will leave him alone," President Lincoln told church officials in Washington.

With the war's end, the reformist zeal of the abolitionists turned to

"Polygamy imposes upon Congress and the Executive the duty of arraying against the barbarous system all the power which under the Constitution and the law they can wield for its destruction."

President Chester Arthur, 1881

"freeing" Mormon women. Harriet Beecher Stowe implored: "Let every happy wife and mother who reads these lines give her sympathy, prayers, and efforts to free her sisters from this degrading bondage." But Mormon women were vigorous in their defense of polygamy, contending that it presented an honorable alternative to the often wretched fate of poor unmarried women (then, as now, there was a glut of them) who, denied equality, were barred from most professions and miserably paid at the jobs open to them. Most Mormon men who had more than one wife had only two, and women on isolated prairie homesteads often welcomed the company of another woman. Brigham Young had insisted that polygamy was not a sensual pleasure, but rather a grim duty: "We must gird up our loins," he said, "and fulfill this, just as we would any other duty." Still, the Supreme Court ruled in 1879 that polygamy was *not* protected by the First Amendment, stating that "laws are made for the government of action and while they cannot interfere with mere religious belief and opinions, they can with practice." In 1882, Congress made polygamy a felony, disenfranchised all polygamists, and disqualified for jury duty all those who practiced or even believed in the practice of polygamy. And, more important, Congress made available abundant funds for federal marshals to be sent to Utah to investigate and prosecute offenders. If you abandon this barbarism, federal officials quietly told church leaders, Utah will be made a state (five petitions had already been denied). John Taylor, Young's successor, answered defiantly: "We are no craven serfs, and have not learned to lick the feet of the oppressor." Federal marshals swarmed across Utah, vigorously flushing out "cohabs" and giving them sentences of up to three and a half years in the federal penitentiary. Taylor told his followers that the United States was "no longer a land of liberty," and he, along with church leaders and other Mormon men, went "underground," moving from hide-out to hide-out in an attempt to elude the marshals. More anti-Mormon legislation was passed in 1884, making the prosecution of polygamists easier; the jails filled with over thirteen hundred Mormons.

In 1890, the Supreme Court dealt the final blow: All Mormons were disenfranchised and all church property was seized. The Mormon church faced utter destruction, its leadership underground, its farms and businesses crumbling from neglect as women and children suffered unrelenting harassment from federal marshals. "I have arrived at a point in the history of my life as President of the Church where I am under the necessity of acting for the temporal salvation of the Church," the Mormon leader wrote in his journal. "I have done my duty and the nation must be held responsible."

THE DEAL: In 1890, the Mormon president issued a manifesto which stated: "Inasmuch as laws have been enacted by Congress forbidding plural marriages, which laws have been pronounced Constitutional by the Court of last resort, I hereby declare my intention to submit to those laws, and to use my influence with the members of the Church over which I preside to do likewise." The church never again performed a plural marriage. A statewide convention was called, and the constitution they wrote stated: "Polygamous marriages are forever prohibited." Satisfied, the United States Congress ratified this state constitution, and on January 4, 1896, Utah became the forty-fifth state—"on an equal footing with the original states," said President Grover Cleveland.

RESULTS: With the ban on polygamy, some plural wives and their children found themselves abandoned without support, while other former husbands continued to act responsibly toward their dependents. Some "cohabs" continued exactly as before, and as long as there were no new recruits to polygamy, participants, aging and producing fewer children, were tolerated. In the twentieth century, a sociological survey conducted by a grandson of Brigham Young found that 53 percent of all participants in plural marriages deemed them successful, 25 percent moderately successful, and 22 percent gross failures leading to severe conflict, separation, or divorce.

Its assets were ultimately restored by the government, and today the Mormon church controls a billion-dollar financial empire that includes ownership of: Beneficial Life Insurance; the Utah-Idaho Sugar Company (1977 assets of $50 million); six large department stores in Utah with $60 million in yearly sales; a large number of banks; huge real-estate holdings both in and out of Utah (including a 220,000-acre site near Orlando, Florida); and a media fiefdom that controls many book, magazine, and newspaper publishers (including a chunk of the *Los Angeles Times*) and thirteen commercial radio and TV stations throughout the United States.

Utah is still dominated by Mormons, who today comprise 70 percent of the state. And in spite of the ban on polygamy, the Mormons have been fruitful, multiplying today to 5.2 million worldwide—3.6 million of them in the United States.

WHO OWNS AMERICA?

There are 2.3 billion acres of land in the United States, enough for 10 acres of land for every citizen. This land is distributed as follows:
♦ 58 percent, about 1.3 billion acres, is in private hands.
♦ 34 percent, about 762 million acres, is owned by the federal government.

- 6 percent, about 136 million acres, is owned by state and local governments.
- 2 percent, about 52 million acres, is held in Indian Trust lands.

Because of huge holdings of agricultural, ranching, and timber land, a mere 3 percent of the population (7 to 8 million people) own 55 percent of all United States land; taking into account only land in private hands, 95 percent of all United States land is owned by that 3 percent. Privately held land is distributed as follows:
- 63 percent of the 1.3 billion acres in private hands are farm, ranch, or timber land.
- 44 million acres are used for commercial, industrial, and recreational purposes, including 1.2 million acres in golf courses.
- Little more than 1 percent of the total United States land, about 25 million acres, is used for private homes.
- 568 large corporations control, through ownership or leasing, more than 300 million acres—23 percent of all land held privately.
- Eight oil companies own 65 million acres.
- More than 70 percent of the United States population lives on just 1.5 percent of the land.

Land is not the only monopoly, but it is by far the greatest of all monopolies—it is a perpetual monopoly, and it is the mother of all forms of monopoly.

Winston Churchill

We Took the Isthmus!: The Panama Canal

BACKGROUND: The United States, a bicoastal nation since 1848, was eager to establish a quick sea route linking the east and west coasts: The voyage around the Cape took over two months. The United States government was partial to a canal route across Nicaragua. A French syndicate had been forced to abandon ten years of work on a canal across the narrow Panama Isthmus in Columbia, defeated not by densely matted jungle, intense rainfall of up to ten feet a year, sweltering heat, swamps filled with putrid vegetation, giant rats, huge insects, scorpions, and hostile natives armed with poisonous arrows, but by the tiny, ever-present killer mosquitoes carrying malaria and yellow fever. Twenty thousand workers died, and over $287 million had been lost. In an attempt to recoup some of that, the French syndicate sent representatives to Washington to convince the United States to buy out French rights and property in Panama. They hired

William Nelson Cromwell, America's first professional influence-peddler ("He talks fast, and when he wishes to, never to the point," wrote one newspaper), and they sent Phillipe Bunau-Varilla, a Frenchman who'd begun his career as an engineer in Panama and who had risen to the top of the syndicate. With millions at stake, he was frantically devoted to resurrecting the project. After much politicking, a $60,000 contribution to the Republican campaign chest, and a volcanic eruption in Nicaragua at a propitious moment in May 1902, Congress voted in June for the building of the canal in Panama. The sum of $40 million was to go to the French; the Republic of Columbia was to receive $10 million in cash and a rental fee of $250,000 a year on a renewable ninety-nine-year lease. When the Columbian Senate refused to ratify the treaty, hoping for better terms, President Teddy Roosevelt became so infuriated that he wrote to his secretary of state: "We may have to give a lesson to those jackrabbits!" Instead, the eager Bunau-Varilla took matters into his own hands. Inviting some prominent Panamanians to his Waldorf suite in New York, he persuaded them to revolt against Columbia and to declare Panama an independent republic. (Later, the Waldorf was called the "birthplace" of Panama). With $100,000 given to them by Bunau-Varilla, they bribed the appropriate garrison commanders into a submission that was bolstered by the offshore presence of U.S. warships. The independent Republic of Panama was declared and recognized instantly by the United States (some thought with "undignified haste"). The new republic was more cooperative than the Columbians had been.

THE DEAL: Seven days after the birth of Panama, Bunau-Varilla, acting as agent for the new government, concluded negotiations for them. The Canal Zone, a 553-square-mile area, was signed away "in perpetuity," in exchange for $10 million in cash, $250,000 a year in rent, and United States protection (from Columbia). When the provisional government hesitated in ratifying the treaty, Bunau-Varilla cabled them, indicating that the United States would abandon them to the vengeance of Columbia. The treaty was formally approved, unanimously, with no modifications. The French syndicate got $40 million for rights and properties in the zone.

RESULTS: The $50 million purchase was the largest real-estate transaction in history. Work began in 1904 with the largest public-health program ever undertaken—the eradication of the disease-bearing mosquitoes, discovered by then to be deadly. Fifty thousand workers drawn from ninety-seven countries took ten years to excavate over 232,400,000 cubic yards of earth. Tiffany & Company designed the

"I took the Isthmus, started the Canal, and then left Congress—not to debate the Canal, but to debate me."

Theodore Roosevelt

official Canal Zone seal, which bears the motto: "The land divided—the world united."

The irate Columbians, after many years of legal proceedings, finally won a $25 million settlement against the United States for the loss of Panama. By 1970, $100 million a year in tolls were being collected. "In perpetuity" ended in 1978 when President Carter, succumbing to intense pressure from the Panamanians, signed a treaty returning control of the Canal Zone to Panama by the year 2000.

Seventy-six years after taking the Isthmus, we gave it back.

SAFE AS HOUSES?

John D. Rockefeller was a devout Baptist with "a horror of extravagance." The Vanderbilts built themselves opulent chateaus on Fifth Avenue during the 1850s, making the New York City avenue the hot address. Rockefeller, with his Standard Oil fortune, had more money than all of them; but when he decided to leave Cleveland he wasn't interested in joining the Havemeyers, Millses, Schieffelins, or even his partner Henry Flagler or brother William in a specially built palace on Fifth. Instead, he settled for a twenty-year-old brownstone on Fifty-fourth Street (4 West, just *off* Fifth). The house belonged to Arabella Worsham who married Collis P. Huntington, robber baron supreme and master builder of the first transcontinental railroad in 1869; she longed for Fifth Avenue.

Rockefeller, aware of the real-estate boom, had bought chunks of mid-Manhattan, including a lot on the northeast corner of Fifth at Seventy-second Street. In exchange for that lot, Arabella gave J. D. her house and its one hundred-foot garden.

John D., Jr., made up for his father's restraint; he built the largest private house ever constructed in New York City, right down the block: 10 West Fifty-fourth stood ten stories high. The house of John D., Sr., was his first piece of real estate in the Fifty-fourth Street area; it eventually became a hub for the six million dollars' worth of surrounding purchases—which became the land given to the Museum of Modern Art—as well as an enclave for his family. In 1928, the Rockefellers vigorously opposed and defeated an attempt to rezone West Fifty-third and Fifty-fourth streets for business. But, gradually, the side street was demolished for apartment buildings as the family dispersed, although Nelson (grandson of John D., Sr.) died hard at work in his office at 13 West Fifty-fourth in 1979.

Go West, Old Men: The Dodgers Leave Brooklyn

BACKGROUND: Few events have broken as many hearts as the Brooklyn Dodgers packing their bags and moving to Los Angeles. The trading of coasts was done by one man who had no time for hearts but who knew a good thing when he saw it.

In 1945, Walter O'Malley became part owner of the Brooklyn Dodgers with Branch Rickey [see "Can You Turn Your Cheek, Bite Your Tongue, and Run for Home?: Jackie Robinson Integrates Major-League Baseball," page 138]. The team was a great success, adored by its fans, but the two owners were not compatible. Five years later, O'Malley bought out Rickey.

O'Malley was certain from the beginning that a first-rate ball team like his Dodgers would clean up in sports-starved California. Ebbets Field was a beloved monument, but it was small and rundown and right in the heart of Brooklyn, where there was no room for expansion. Besides, in California they could practice and train all year round. In 1956, he went on a scouting trip to Los Angeles. Schooled in politics by the Brooklyn Democratic machine in the 1940s, he had made some contacts on the West Coast that proved helpful. Then the other National League owners balked: Unless O'Malley could get another major-league team to go with him so the others would have *two* opponents *out there* to make the airfare worthwhile, they would not allow it.

THE DEAL: O'Malley introduced San Francisco's mayor to Horace Stoneham, owner of the New York Giants—a team that had seen better days and was eager to flee New York. National League owners were happy. Then O'Malley swapped his own minor-league team in Fort Worth for Phil Wrigley's minor-league Angels in Los Angeles plus Wrigley Stadium, a nine-acre site at Wrigley Field. This stadium O'Malley deeded to the city of Los Angeles in return for 315 acres in Chavez Ravine and $4.7 million to build a 56,000-seat stadium. Enter the Los Angeles Dodgers.

> "I'm going to build my own park because I like the free enterprise system."
>
> Walter O'Malley

RESULTS: Eighteen hundred Mexican-American families were evicted, their homes bulldozed, as a referendum campaign was unsuccessfully mounted to revoke O'Malley's arrangement with the city council. In 1958, the team played its first game to 78,672 fans in the Los Angeles Coliseum. The big stars were Pee Wee Reese, Duke Snider, and Gil Hodges—old men in the baseball world but great draws and true stars. The team finished next to last in the league, twenty-one games out of first place. The next year, the "Brooklyn relics" won the World Series, and Los Angeles was on the map as baseball's sunny heaven.

Dodger Stadium opened in 1962. (They lost the pennant by a hair that year to the Giants.) It is the sole privately financed and single-sport stadium built in the past sixty years. Sandy Koufax pitched 25–5 during the 1963 season and struck out fifteen batters in that year's World Series victory, setting a record. With him was Maury Wills, who stole his 104th base in 1962, giving Los Angeles a whole new set of its own indigenous Dodger idols, including Don Drysdale. They again won the series in 1966, then finished eighth in 1967, and again were twenty-one games out of first in 1968.

In 1970, O'Malley made his son, Peter, president of the franchise. O'Malley himself became chairman of the board. Baseball was changing from the manager-controlled business into a corporate enterprise dominated by high-priced players. (In 1966 Koufax and Drysdale had successfully refused to play unless their salary demands were met, presaging the end of the "reserve clause" that forbade players from selling themselves to another team.) And football had triumphed on TV, endangering baseball's first place in the heart of the nation. But the Dodgers were more than a team; they were an institution and a *family*: The "Homegrown Dodgers" Cey, Russell, Lopes, and Garvey had become the longest-lived infield in history, with ten years together and four World Series.

Son Peter modernized the management (introducing computers) and hired a new front-office crew who devised new strategies to draw the crowds—"think blue" was a public-relations home run—and in 1978 the Dodgers became the only team *ever* to draw three million in one season. (They did it again in 1980, and in 1982 drew 3,608,881.) In 1983, they limited season tickets to 27,000—a figure higher than the daily attendance of most teams—to prevent the stadium from being sold out at lower prices by subscription and making it possible for the average fan to get in . . . maybe.

Walter O'Malley died August 9, 1979. His personal estate was valued at $20 million, in addition to a multimillion-dollar trust fund, and the Dodger franchise valued at over $60 million.

INDIAN GETTING

Native Americans hailed it as their greatest victory since Little Big Horn—an $18.5 million settlement of a land claim the Penobscot and Passamaquoddy tribes of Maine brought against the federal government. The tribes successfully argued that they had never been compensated for the 12.5 million acres (virtually two-thirds of Maine) that were seized from their ancestors. The 1981 settlement was split evenly between the two tribes. They immediately put $12.5 million into a general trust fund and set up a $1 million special fund for the elderly. The trust is invested in certificates of deposit, and in the first quarter, the Penobscots distributed $340 in interest to each of their fifteen hundred members. Most of the money is going into purchasing the land that once was theirs; the Penobscots immediately purchased a 120,000-acre tract of forest, and the Passamaquoddy started negotiating for another 100,000 acres.

With this much money in hand, both tribes have been heavily wooed by Wall Street, but they prefer to invest in Maine woodland. "They kept feeding me caviar," said Penobscot Governor Tim Love about one investment firm, "and I hate caviar."

SNAP!® CRACKLE!® POP!®:
Kellogg versus Battle Creek

BACKGROUND: In 1907, when William Keith Kellogg founded a breakfast-cereal company in Battle Creek, Michigan, the town was lovely and pristine—the site, in fact, of a well-known health spa run by Kellogg's physician brother. Until that time, Kellogg was just his

Kellogg's threatened to leave the impoverished Battle Creek, Michigan, unless some changes were made.

brother's helper, a "backroom bookkeeper," when, at the age of forty-five, he invented cornflakes and revealed a previously unknown but rather astonishing talent for promotion and mass merchandising. He built a huge breakfast-cereal empire.

However, by the early 1980s, Battle Creek was riddled with urban decay, plagued by the blight common to cities where the wealthier tax base has fled to outlying suburbs. Battle Creek was no longer the kind of town fit to be the international headquarters of a large corporation (1981 sales were approximately $2.3 billion). Corporation Chairman William LaMothe complained that "it has become more and more difficult for us to attract professional and technical personnel willing to relocate to this area."

THE DEAL: Unless the impoverished city of Battle Creek (population 35,724) and the wealthier suburban township of Battle Creek (population 20,589) agreed to merge (thereby providing the city with a richer source of funds for civic projects), Kellogg's was moving its headquarters elsewhere. The issue of merger was placed before the voters. The ballot read: "Shall all of the Township of Battle Creek be annexed to the City of Battle Creek?"

RESULTS: City voters said yes, 12 to 1; in the suburbs, they endorsed the measure 2 to 1. Seven hundred jobs and an annual payroll of $28 million were saved. Kellogg, committed to staying, immediately announced plans to build a new $30 million headquarters in Battle Creek. Moreover, the corporation has organized an $8 million fund to help launch new businesses in the city. Chairman LaMothe is counting on genetic engineering, one of the "great growth areas that will have a tremendous impact on agriculture and the food we eat," to rejuvenate the area. Senior Vice-President Gary Costley says he envisions turning Battle Creek into a "baby Silicon Valley" for biogenetic research in high-yield nutritional grains that might help to alleviate world hunger with a SNAPCRACKLEPOP!

SILVER ROLLS INTO CO-OP

New York City co-op owner Harold Lynn had twelve apartments to sell, ranging from $582,500 to $1.2 million. To encourage buyers, he offered a free 1983 Rolls-Royce Silver Spirit valued at $100,000 with every sale. "If you already own a Rolls, we can discuss alternative options."

Don't Leave Home without It:
American Express Buys New
Headquarters

BACKGROUND: When Mark Twain said, "Invest in land because they've stopped making it," he hadn't envisioned Battery Park City, 7.5 million square feet of commercial space that New York City created on Lower Manhattan by landfill, with the excavated earth from the World Trade Center. But Twain would not have been surprised by the way the men who make the rules change the rules when it suits their needs.

Olympia & York (O&Y), a privately owned, Toronto-based outfit, won a ninety-nine-year lease on the entire landfill property from the Battery Park City Authority (BPCA) in 1981. For this privilege, they committed themselves to buildin and leasing by the end of 1984 one huge four-tower complex, to be called the World Financial Center. (Other contractors had wanted to divide the area into small lots.) A property-tax abatement and yearly rental for the site was negotiated

— 119

with a clause forbidding O&Y to break up the complex for fifteen years.

Meanwhile, AMEX—the parent company of American Express, et al.—was making noises and sworn statements about moving its headquarters out of New York City. The immense conglomerate then expressed interest in relocating into one of O&Y's towers, *but* they preferred to own rather than rent the new fifty-one-story building. But what about O&Y's 1981 legal bind to keep the towers in the family?

THE DEAL: If the BPCA would drop the clause forbidding O&Y to sell off any of its four towers, AMEX would buy one for its glamorous new headquarters. Their presence in the site's flagship building would guarantee the success of the World Financial Center for O&Y and New York City. The city agreed to do whatever was necessary to encourage "growth," while discouraging corporate relocation to other states.

RESULTS: With Mayor Koch's endorsement and BPCA approval—their chairman, Richard Kahan, had a private financial investment in AMEX—the clause was deleted. O&Y bought AMEX's old headquarters for $240 million, giving AMEX a capital gain of $180 million. But in March 1982, Koch had persuaded the state legislature to repeal the state's 10 percent capital-gains tax on large real-estate transactions, saving AMEX $18 million. This action occurred just prior to AMEX's announcement that it was buying the new tower for $478 million from O&Y.

AMEX was also allowed to participate in O&Y's previously awarded tax abatement, saving another $85 million, from a formula in which half the building will get a 75 percent, ten-year write-off and the other half will get a 50 percent reduction for the same period. Though it was owner of a building on leased land, AMEX was also excused from paying full rental fees on the land, saving additional millions.

Then, on top of everything else, AMEX received $61 million in ten-year tax credits in May and June 1983, on corporate-profit taxes from New York City's Job Incentive Board, because the move will create 1,694 new jobs in the company and in four of its subsidiaries—all of whom will be occupying the new building. (The credit is actually for a fixed percentage of whatever corporate-profit tax they owe and assumes no increase in profits, which is highly unlikely; it means in dollars that they will get the same percentage break on higher profit taxes due over the years.)

Dealmaker as Corporate Leader: Peter A. Cohen

Peter A. Cohen became at thirty-eight the president and chief executive of Shearson/American Express in January 1983. In 1982, the corporation's earnings were $124 million, with revenues of $1.32 billion. One of his first bits of business was to take over an overseas banking network for $550 million, placing American Express "in the front ranks of foreign banking."

Cohen began at Shearson (then CBWL—or Cogan, Berlind, Weill, and Levitt—affectionately known on Wall Street as "Corned Beef With Lettuce") in 1971, when it was a small, six-year-old securities firm that was $1.2 million in the red. He started at $12,000 a year, leaving a job that offered $24,000 because, he said, "I perceived an opportunity to grow" [see "Dealmaker as Savior: Felix Rohatyn," page 207]. Two years later, with his share of the company's profits on securities transactions, he earned $81,000 and became assistant to CBWL's chairman, Weill. Again, he took a salary cut to $40,000: Weill, he said, "wanted me to help him, to be an extension of him." A series of major mergers were engineered with Cohen helping to run the show. By 1975, he was executive vice-president and director of "Shearson."

Three years later, he quit to work with Edmond J. Safra, a renowned banking *meister*, and became a millionaire while learning the ins and outs of international banking: "I was thirty-one and had the opportunity to go to work for a man I considered one of the most extraordinary men I ever met. I couldn't afford not to take advantage of an opportunity to learn from a guy like this." (It was Safra's banking network that Cohen eventually bought, making his former boss American Express's biggest shareholder, with 2 percent of the stock.) After one year, he returned to Shearson as senior executive vice-president and chief administrative officer to oversee the biggest brokerage-house merger on Wall Street: Shearson (150 offices and 5,000 employees) merged with Loeb Rhoades Hornblower & Company (180 offices and 7,000 employees). Promoted to vice-chairman, chief operating officer, Cohen was earning $310,000, and Shearson had one million clients. In 1981, they were taken over by American Express, "in one of the friendliest corporate mergers in Wall Street history."

"What might not be in your best short-term interest might be in your best long-term interest."

Peter A. Cohen

UNITED STATES REAL-ESTATE BARONS

	Controls	Estimated worth (in millions)
Harry Brakmann Helmsley, New York	Buildings	$750
William Walter Caruth, Jr., Texas	Land	600
A. Alfred Taubman, Michigan	Shopping centers	525
Edward J. DeBartolo, Ohio	Shopping centers	500
Trammell Crow, Texas	Buildings	500

New York City Plays Its Trump: A Tax Program

"When I walk down the street with Donald, people come up and just touch him, hoping that his good fortune will rub off."

Blanche Sprague, sales director, Trump Plaza— *New York Times*

BACKGROUND: What do you do to revive a corpse? Offer a fabulous tax exemption! But once the municipal corpse is up and about, the tax exemption may become a vampire, legally sucking the taxpayers dry; or it may cause choking on pieces of the Big Apple.

In 1971, real-estate development in New York City was nearly kaput. To stimulate action, a unique tax incentive was devised.

THE DEAL: The 421-A tax program. A real-estate developer can claim a ten-year adjustable tax exemption, with the first two years on the project 100 percent tax free, dropping by 20 percent every two years thereafter. Full taxes on the site and profits from the building are not paid for twelve years. The new building must replace a "functionally obsolete" one, and it must involve a "marginal neighborhood" with low and middle-income housing.

RESULTS: When Ed Koch took office as mayor in 1977, there were seven construction sites in the city. By 1982, the boom was on for many economic reasons, and there were over three hundred sites. The 421-A program was a critical factor. It was not without complications.

In 1975, Donald Trump began negotiations to build a monumental structure on Fifty-sixth Street and Fifth Avenue, next door to Tiffany's, not quite your basic marginal neighborhood.

THE TRUMP TOWER DEAL: Donald Trump (DT) bought Bonwit Teller's twenty-nine-year lease on its building, plus two small adjoining units on East Fifty-seventh Street and the air rights to neighboring Tiffany's, which granted the zoning change needed to build a high-rise apartment house in the area. Chase Manhattan lent $24 million and a bank-formed syndicate supplied the remaining $150 million with a construction loan. DT went fifty-fifty with Equitable Life Assurance Society, owner of the plot where Bonwit's stood. Trump's organization was to manage the building and name it. The partnership would qualify for the New York City residential tax abatement, or 421-A, for an estimated $30 million.

RESULTS: Trump put up practically none of his own money and, in all modesty, named his $200 million, sixty-eight-story skyscraper the "Trump Tower." It contains 263 condominium units worth $260 million (one-bedroom condos start at $407,000; 91 are priced above $1 million; and the triplex penthouse, which Trump took, is $10 million) and a vast rentable shopping mall dressed in salmon-pink marble, and thirteen floors of office space—yielding $28 million per year to the partnership. (There are forty shops, some paying $1 million a year in rent.) This structure replaced the nine-story art-deco treasure made "functionally obsolete" only because Bonwit Teller no longer occupied it. Trump had promised to donate the art-deco bas reliefs on the façade to a museum, then reneged and bulldozed them under.

Even though the New York City Planning Board opposed the immense tower, it granted the permits, and Trump never doubted that he deserved 421-A status. He was disappointed. The $30- to $40-million tax exemption was denied by the New York City Commissioner for Housing Preservation and Development, Tony Gliedman. Trump

"I am a very rich and powerful person in this town and there is a reason I got that way."

Donald Trump

Donald Trump flashes his Fifth Avenue tower: "You sell them a fantasy."

called the mayor, claiming he never would have built without the 421-A. Koch backed Gliedman: "If I ever told a commissioner to give or not give an exemption based on my position as opposed to the commissioner doing what he felt was right they should throw me out of office."

Trump and his barrage of lawyers went to court. They won the exemption, but in January 1984 the appellate division of the state supreme court overturned the lower court's decision. Mr. Trump planned to appeal. In July he won his appeal.

By February 1983, 90 percent of the Trump Tower had been sold, 50 percent to foreign investors, most of whom paid completely in cash. The construction loan has been effectively paid off, leaving the tower mortgage-free. If Trump had lost his case, he would have had difficulty pleading a capital loss.

In mid-May 1982, the Koch administration had presented a proposal to the Board of Estimate to limit tax breaks (particularly 421-A) to real-estate developers and to control exploitation-by-skyscrapers (via new zoning laws) on the east side of Manhattan's Midtown section. To the horror of the master builders, the board approved the mayor's plan. They quickly got a grip and looked for new horizons. No one can keep a good builder down.

Dealmaker as Master Builder: Donald J. Trump

The father of Donald Trump (DT) had to have his mother sign the checks when he started building in 1923 because he was a minor. He created an empire of middle-class housing in Brooklyn, Queens, and Staten Island worth $40 million. His son invaded Manhattan and increased the family's worth to $1 billion in holdings and a personal fortune estimated at $200 million (DT claims $500 million).

While still working on his B.A. at the Wharton School, DT started buying "little real-estate pieces" in Philadelphia, fixing them up and selling them for a profit. He joined his father's business in 1968 and soon began to "trump his father," as real-estate values soared. Fiscally conservative when building, DT likes to find a fifty-fifty partner in a gilt-edged financial institution or hotel chain: The $220 million Harrah's hotel/casino in Atlantic City was built by Holiday Inn on DT's land, bought cheaply by him *before* the New Jersey gaming laws went into effect; it may provide him with from $40 to $50 million annually. His now-inactive gold company made him a profit of $32 million.

"A record of successes has made it very easy to do deals. People want to invest with you."

Donald Trump

The $100 million Grand Hyatt Hotel sits on DT's Commodore Hotel property. It was bought for $10 million (minus $2 million from a furniture and fittings sale), then sold to the New York City Urban Development Corporation for $1 and leased back from them for forty years *in lieu of taxes* for $200,000 yearly (a fraction of its tax worth). The Hyatt Corporation manages the building, and the Chase Manhattan Bank and Manufacturers Hanover Trust financed it with $30 million and $70 million respectively. Trump got the largest tax abatement in New York City history, and the first for a commercial building by successfully claiming he was doing the city a favor—upgrading the neighborhood around Grand Central Station, giving people work, and saving hotel jobs. (His critics claim this was a political gift to his father, who had helped elect Mayor Abraham Beame.) Then he capped his recent work with the Trump Tower. "I want to bring a little showmanship to real estate," he explains. He is also the owner of the New Jersey Generals, bought for $1 million [see "Fastest-running Walker: Herschel Walker Turns Pro," page 129].

In 1980, he bought the Barbizon Plaza Hotel for $13 million; today it's worth $124 million. He received an option on vacant rail yards in Manhattan's West Thirties by guaranteeing to develop the site; then he lobbied to have the New York City Convention Center built there, won, and sold the city the land for $12 million, taking a commission of $800,000. But he lost the bid to build the center for $200 million—he wanted it named after his family—and the project is now two years late and $125 million over budget, something he feels he would have avoided. He offered to finish the job without a fee. Having conquered the city in 1975/1976, the low point in its economic history, in 1983 he can well afford the grand gesture of a pharaoh. "What sets Trump apart is his ability to . . . get things done," sums up Ben V. Lambert, a real-estate investment banker. "He gets projects literally off the ground while others are having meetings and doing feasibility studies. But his real skill is putting together complex pieces of the puzzles: financing, zoning parcels of land and such. This ethereal part of building is perhaps more important than the brick and mortar."

> "Those with the gold make the rules."
>
> Samuel J. LeFrak, real-estate mogul (new worth: $500 million)

> "Donald Trump is the Michael Jackson of real estate. We've been dealing with him since he was 16. He was an old trouper at age 25."
>
> Irving Fischer, HRH Construction, *New York Times*

The Trump Domain

DT Exclusives: Trump Enterprises, Inc.
Trump Corporation
Trump Development Company
Wembly Realty, Inc.
Park South Company

Land Corporation of California
Gold Company
New Jersey Generals, USFL

DT Near-Exclusives: Trump Plaza, The East Sixty-first Street Company (90 percent DT; 5 percent Robert Trump plus 5 percent Louise Sunshine)

DT Fifty-Fifties: Regency-Lexington Partners (with Hyatt Corporation)
Trump-Equitable Fifth Avenue Company (with Equitable Life Assurance Society of Trump Tower)
Seashore Corporation of Atlantic City: Harrah's (with Holiday Inn)

DT and Trump Family: Trump Equities, Inc.
Trump Management, Inc.
Trump Construction Company

RICHEST INDIANS IN HOT WATER

After kicking the Aqua Caliente tribe of Southern California off most of their tribal land, the whites took pity on them and allowed the tribe to hold on to a strip of desert, apparently worthless, that included their sacred hot springs, used in religious rituals. When the area, because of the springs, became desirable to whites as a resort, the Aqua Caliente held on to the land, renting it out at profitable rates on long-term leases.

Today, it is the pricey resort town of Palm Springs, California, and the Aqua Caliente is the richest Indian tribe, per capita, in the country. Descendants of the tribe—defined as anyone with at least one-eighth Aqua Caliente blood—all share in the bonanza; today, there are only 190 voting members in the tribe. Income figures remain private; but if any tribal members wish to reside in Palm Springs, they can afford to.

IV

OUT OF LEFT FIELD: SPORTS

When the One Great Scorer comes to write against your name,
He marks—not that you won or lost—but how you played the game.

GRANTLAND RICE

They Do It All for TV: The United States Football League

BACKGROUND: When the founders of America's new springtime football league, the United States Football League (USFL), started out to fill a seasonal "vacuum" that some claim did not exist, and to make some money along the way, they realized that their only hope of success lay in being successful on television. Big-time sports are money-makers only insofar as they make it on TV, and football is considered to be the perfect TV ball game. The ball is large enough to be easily seen, the field is large enough for interesting and varied camera angles, and league officials have been flexible enough to change the rules to accommodate television: "Official's" time out and the two-minute warning, one for each half, were created to provide more time for commercials. The National Football League (NFL), the traditional boys of autumn, was rewarded for this flexibility by a recent television package that gives each of its twenty-eight clubs approximately $14.2 million a year. The newly born USFL knows that the NFL arrangement is out of its league, but it has worked out two television arrangements, one with ABC and one with the cable network, the Eastern Sports Network (ESPN).

THE DEAL: ABC gets to televise all of the league's Sunday games, plus the play-offs and the championships, for which it pays the USFL $18 million for a two-year contract. For the same period, ESPN pays $12 million and gets to televise the league's Saturday and Monday-night games. The USFL schedule runs for eighteen weeks.

RESULTS: Although the NFL games attract 15 percent of the ratings, and the USFL, in its first season, attracted only 5 percent, thereby allowing ABC to charge a mere $30,000 for a thirty-second advertising spot (as compared to $165,000 for thirty seconds on ABC's "Monday Night Football," which is NFL), ABC has still expressed satisfaction with what it calls a "reasonable profit" from the USFL games. The USFL has announced plans to expand from twelve to eighteen teams, expressly to add regional television markets, and thereby to boost its national ratings.

Fastest-running Walker:
Herschel Walker Turns Pro

BACKGROUND: Early in 1983, the United States Football League (USFL), an organization of professional football franchises, announced that it would expand its playing season from March into July, disingenuously claiming to fill a "seasonal vacuum" in American sports by providing spring football. In some other respects, the new league did not differ from the National Football League (NFL), the established, autumnal organization: In its charter was a policy provision that no club would sign up a college football player who was still eligible to play college ball. In this way, the venerated system of using America's institutions of higher learning as the minor leagues for professional football was not interfered with.

Over the previous three seasons, a young man named Herschel Walker had played football for the University of Georgia. He had so distinguished himself as the best collegiate running back of his day that some said he was the best of all time. It was clear that Walker would one day turn pro. In 1982, Walker had threatened to sue the NFL over its provision forbidding the recruiting of college players, on the grounds that the provision restricted his employment opportunities. He did not sue, however, announcing instead that he preferred to earn his college degree and to compete in the 1984 Olympics, where he could reasonably expect to do well in the hundred-meter dash. But with only one year left until he finished college, Walker dramatically surprised the world of sports by announcing that he was turning pro.

THE DEAL: The USFL would not deny Walker an employment opportunity; in fact, the league would pay him an estimated $1.5 million per year for a three-year contract. Walker had requested a New York–area franchise and was signed to play with the New Jersey Generals.

RESULTS: In addition to achieving instant notoriety as a case of professional infringement on the (some say, nominally) "amateur" football scene, the contract made Walker the highest-paid football player ever, even before his first game. The benefits for the Generals and the new league may be suggested by the fact that after signing Walker, the Generals immediately sold thirty-two hundred season tickets, and by the fact that the league's first telecast, Walker's first game, achieved a rating of more than five times what was estimated.

Although Walker starred in his first professional season, he was not dominant, as had been expected in some quarters. He led the league in number of carries and in yards gained, but the Generals, with a record of six wins and twelve losses, finished third in a four-team division.

At the University of Georgia, where Walker was star running back no longer, fans wore black arm bands.

BIG BUCKS: FOOTBALL

The average salary for National Football League (NFL) players in the 1982 season was $90,412. Average salaries including bonuses and deferred payments raised this figure to $104,800. The average salary for quarterbacks was $272,247. Under the labor contract between the players and the teams, an NFL rookie must be paid a minimum of $30,000, a sum which increases $10,000 with each year of play, to a minimum of $200,000 for players with eighteen years of experience or more.

Herschel Walker caused an uproar when he quit the University of Georgia to join the New Jersey Generals of the U.S. Football League as the highest paid football player: He earns approximately $1.5 million a year.

Walton Payton of the Chicago Bears (NFL), a running back, earns $700,000 a year.

Dealmaker as Champion: Muhammad Ali

Muhammad Ali, née Cassius Clay, was three times heavyweight boxing champion of the world. He was a very public convert to a controversial religion and a wel-known draft resister during the Vietnam war. "Ali created a new relationship between the boxers, the press, and the spectators," said former middle-weight champion Nino Benvenuti. "He went beyond the borders of boxing."

Ali's career earnings are estimated at an astonishing $60 million. A full third of that went to managers. The champ was managed, for the first six years of his professional career, by the Louisville Sponsoring Group, a syndicate of wealthy Kentuckians. After 1966, Herbert Muhammad, the son of Elijah Muhammad, leader of Ali's religious group, the Nation of Islam, became his manager. Half or more of Ali's earnings went to the IRS, and he himself spent a great deal, what with professional expenses, divorce settlements, the maintenance, at times, of a considerable entourage, and his famous openhanded charity. Today, estimates of Ali's net worth range between $2 and $6 million.

Heavyweight contender Cassius Clay, 1964.

Born in 1942, Cassius Clay began boxing at the age of twelve. His amateur career reached a climax with an Olympic Gold Medal at Rome in 1960. He turned professional that year and won nineteen consecutive bouts before fighting for the championship. Along the way, Clay became one of America's most prominent sports personalities, famous for the showmanship and braggadocio with which he approached his fights, boasting in rhymes that he could predict the round of the fight in which he would fell his opponent. "They all fall/in the round I call," he said; often, he was right. After winning the championship in February of 1964, Clay announced his adherence to the Nation of Islam and the change of his name to Muhammad Ali. His career continued to flourish into 1967, as he took on and defeated all challenges. But when he refused induction into the

United States military, then deeply embroiled in the Vietnam war, he was stripped of his title and sentenced to jail. He had claimed status as a conscientious objector, citing his faith and stating: "I ain't got no quarrel with those Vietcong. They never called me nigger." Free pending appeal, but effectively prohibited from professional boxing, Ali, the "banished" champion, became a folk hero, lecturing and appearing across the country. His fame now transcended the world of sports.

He was vindicated when the United States Supreme Court reversed his conviction in 1970, and he returned to boxing that year, getting a title fight against champion Joe Frazier in May of 1971. For this fight, Ali received his first huge purse, $2.5 million, nearly the equivalent of all his previous earnings; he failed to win the title, however, suffering the first of only four losses in his career. In the next three years, Ali fought thirteen times, losing once (to a fighter who broke his jaw, but who lost in an immediate rematch). He beat Frazier in their second bout, for which Ali received his second seven-figure purse. Finally, he won the championship again, becoming only the second man ever to win the title twice, defeating George Foreman in a fight held in Kinshasa, Zaire ("the rumble in the jungle," Ali called it). For this fight, Ali was paid almost $5.5 million, the largest purse ever offered at the time. He defended the title a number of times in the next few years, and among these bouts was a third encounter with Joe Frazier. This fight was surely the climax of Ali's career, both financially (a $6 million purse) and in boxing terms. He barely won the bloody brawl, which fight aficionados have acclaimed was one of the greatest bouts of all time; it ended in a TKO after fourteen rounds. Ali proudly refers to it as "the Thrilla from Manila."

After that, the champ fought less often and against less worthy opponents. He lost the title to a young boxer, Leon Spinks, who was supposed to be easy pickings. He regained it in a rematch, becoming the only man ever to win the heavyweight crown three times. Then he retired. Two comeback attempts, one a difficult victory and one a defeat at the hands of a middling opponent, convinced him that, at forty, he was too old for the game. His last fight was in December of 1981.

Ali says that he wishes to evangelize for the Nation of Islam now that he is retired. He still makes considerable money from endorsements and appearances. In 1983, at the World Boxing Council's twentieth-anniversary dinner, Ali was named Champion of Champions—by the assembled world champions. "I float like a butterfly," Ali would say, "and I sting like a bee."

Frazee, Rhymes with Crazy:
Babe Ruth Gets Traded to New York

BACKGROUND: When Harry Frazee, dapper theatrical producer and Boston Red Sox owner, cavalierly traded the incredible Babe Ruth to the New York Yankees, Red Sox fans went wild: Frazee hadn't sold a mere record-breaking slugger for crass cash (and plenty of it), he'd willingly parted with a national treasure. They're still talking about it in Boston.

The Babe had only been playing pro ball for one year, when, in 1914, he joined the Red Sox (he was traded there along with two others for $8,500). He was a pitcher then, and a fine one, but pitchers can only play every four or five days, and by 1918, he was already revealing his legendary batting ability; the "Boston Terror" was switched to the outfield so that he could swing his potent bat at every game. The Red Sox won the series that year and the twenty-three-year-old Babe was declared "the greatest batsman the game has ever

"The Sultan of Swat" surrounded by young fans, 1922.

known." In 1919, he outdid himself and every record on the books by hitting twenty-nine home runs—his batting average was .322, and he led the league in runs scored (103) and runs batted in (112). Overflow crowds paid to see him hit those "glorious smashes," and he didn't disappoint them. The "Sultan of Swat" hit at least one homer in every stadium in the American league, and his homers traveled farther than anyone else's (into "an adjacent voting district," wrote one reporter). He was larger than life; he didn't talk, he growled; and when that full-moon face flashed a smile, an entire stadium would "blaze into hysteria."

Frazee, the Red Sox owner, was a theatrical producer with a taste for showgirls and an expensive habit—he produced flops. He regarded the Red Sox as a profitable plaything (they'd won the series in 1915, 1916, and 1918), but his heart was on Broadway. Colonel Jacob Ruppert, the owner of the third-placed Yankees, had a real interest in the future of his team. When he asked his manager how they could win the pennant, the reply was "get Ruth from Boston." Ruppert, the millionaire son of a brewery owner, approached the profligate Frazee about selling the Babe; Frazee named a sum that was so outrageously high he didn't dream it would be taken seriously. It was.

THE DEAL: Ruppert paid a whopping $125,000 for Ruth (the previous record was $50,000), and he loaned Frazee an additional $350,000 as a mortgage on Fenway Park. The Yankees got a twenty-four-year-old slugger who was about to break all batting records—records he himself had set.

RESULTS: "Boston," said one wag, "was shocked out of a year's growth and half a century of dignity." Ruth, who had been getting $9,000 a year playing for Boston, demanded and got a Yankee contract that paid him $40,000 for two years. Frazee, ever strapped for cash, continued to sell valuable players to New York—the Red Sox were dubbed "New York's best farm club." The Red Sox sank to last place in 1922 and stayed there for eight of the next nine years. The Yankees rose to the top, winning the pennant in 1921 through 1923 and 1926 through 1928. In 1923, the first year they won the series, eleven of their twenty-four players came from the Red Sox.

Frazee finally hit it big on Broadway with the 1925 smash *No, No, Nanette* (from whence comes the song "Tea for Two"), the biggest musical-comedy hit of the Roaring Twenties. (The 1927 sequel, *Yes, Yes, Yvette*, was a more typical Frazee production—it flopped.)

Yankee attendance more than doubled the first year the Babe played for them, and his fans were not disappointed: He broke his previous record of twenty-nine homers by hitting fifty-four (his batting average that year was .376). "To see the immortal Ruth make a home run is the ultimate hope and desire of all normal Americans," wrote one journalist. In 1927, he hit sixty homers—a record unsurpassed until 1961. In 1923, when the magnificent new Yankee Stadium opened, the massive structure was called "the House that Ruth Built."

The Babe retired from baseball in 1935. During World War II, marines reported that Japanese soldiers came at them screaming, "To hell with Babe Ruth!" The Babe died in 1948 at the age of fifty-three, and seventy-five thousand mourners filed passed his coffin in Yankee Stadium. And some of the records set by the Babe have yet to be broken.

SAT IN THE CORNER EATING *WHAT*?

Bob Horner, the home-run-hitting outfielder for the Atlanta Braves doesn't have to worry about money: His four-year contract is for $5.1 million. But Horner does have a figure problem, and the Brave's management thought they could help him deal with it by offering him a $100,000 bonus if he could keep his weight under 215 pounds for the season. He is weighed every two weeks.

BIG BUCKS: BASEBALL

The minimum salary, established by labor agreement, is $33,500. The average 1982 salary was $241,497. The median salary (as many players above as below) was $170,900. The average for 1981 was $185,651; for 1980 it was $143,756; for 1979 it was $113,558. With the advent of the free-agent system, each player contract includes all sorts of idiosyncratic perks and scams. The California Angels (owned by Gene Autry) pay the highest player salaries; the Minnesota Twins, the lowest.

George Foster of the New York Mets: $2 million a year plus an escalator clause keyed to the price-of-living index.

Dave Winfield of the New York Yankees: $2 million a year.

Can You Turn Your Cheek, Bite Your Tongue, and Run for Home?: Jackie Robinson Integrates Major-League Baseball

BACKGROUND: Branch Rickey, Brooklyn Dodger general manager, felt that the time had come to integrate major-league baseball. His scouts spent three years scouring the playing fields of North and South America looking for a black player who conformed to Rickey's notion of the perfect pioneer. In 1945, they thought they'd found their man. Twenty-six-year-old Jackie Robinson, a shortstop in the Negro Leagues, was not only a superb athlete, he was well educated and articulate as well. But Rickey had one hesitation: Could Robinson, known as an outspoken fighter against racism, calmly turn the other cheek when confronted by the vile abuse he was certain to confront?

Robinson had been a star college athlete, and UCLA's first four-letter man. During World War II, while in basic training, he applied for officer candidate school at Fort Riley, only to be told that blacks were not eligible. (The armed forces were so segregated that when

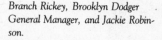

Branch Rickey, Brooklyn Dodger General Manager, and Jackie Robinson.

Lena Horne entertained the troops, only blacks were allowed to watch her.) Fortuitously, superstar Joe Louis happened to be stationed at Fort Riley as well. He pulled a few strings, and Robinson got into OCS—and rose to lieutenant. Robinson was the star of the Fort Riley football team until he realized that he was benched every time they played a segregated team. He quit—only to be told that he could be forced to play. "You can order me to play," he told his commanding officer, "but you can't control the quality of my performance." When he was transferred to Camp Hood, Texas, a base bus driver, in violation of federal regulations, ordered Robinson to move to the back of the bus. His refusal led to his being court-martialed; he was ultimately acquitted. When he was discharged, he joined a Negro League team, earning a salary of four hundred dollars a month. The major leagues were completely white—and in some cases, even the stadiums were segregated.

Sixty-seven-year-old Branch Rickey wanted to make history. Segregated baseball had been the target of progressive protest for many years—"good enough to die for his country . . . not good enough for organized baseball," read one leaflet—and the postwar years seemed right for ending Jim Crow baseball. The 1945 Yankee opening game had been picketed by blacks shouting, "If we can pay, why can't we play?" Moreover, the Dodgers desperately needed new talent, and there was plenty of that in the Negro Leagues; and in New York, an integrated team couldn't hurt the gate.

So, in 1945, the unsuspecting Robinson was summoned for an interview with Rickey. "I know you're a good ball player," Rickey said. "What I don't know is whether you have the guts." Robinson later wrote that Rickey was looking for a black who "could take abuse, name-calling, rejection by fans and sports writers and by fellow players not only on opposing teams but on his own. He had to be able to stand up in the face of merciless persecution and not retaliate." Robinson wondered, "Could I take all of this and control my temper? . . . I was twenty-six years old and all my life . . . I had believed in payback, in retaliation." He fired at Rickey: "Are you looking for a Negro who is afraid to fight back?" Rickey exploded, saying, "I am looking for a player with guts *not* to fight back."

THE DEAL: If Robinson, starting off as the first black to play with the Dodger farm team in Montreal, could demonstrate an ability to calmly withstand booing and racist jeers from the stands, name-calling and physical abuse from the players (including his own teammates), hostility from the press, threats to his family—and still play excellent ball

"As a batter he, Robinson, was thrown at almost daily. Verbally, he was assaulted with terminology proceeding from 'nigger' up to the most raw, sexually disturbing vulgarity that raw, sexually disturbed men could conceive. In the face of this, Robinson was sworn to passivity and silence. He had promised that he would encase his natural volatility in lead."

Roger Kahn,
The Boys of Summer

—— 139

while turning the other cheek, then he could join the Dodgers as the first black in major-league baseball.

RESULTS: Black fans turned out in unprecedented numbers to watch Robinson play. "Their presence, their cheers, their pride in me, all came through to me and I knew they were counting on me to make it. It put a heavy burden of responsibility on me, but it was a glorious challenge." Sometimes, especially when he was playing badly, he found the torrent of hatred pouring down on him to be even worse than he expected. But with truly amazing restraint, he reserved his fury for power swings, finishing the season in Montreal with a .349 batting average and a .985 fielding average. At the end of the season, when Rickey announced that Robinson would be coming to the Dodgers, protests erupted. Some Dodgers asked to be traded, while others circulated a petition against having blacks on the team. The St. Louis Cardinals announced that they would strike but retreated when the commissioner said they would be suspended. But with National League attendance rising to record levels as people packed in to see Robinson (and other black players, as Rickey signed the second, third, fourth, and fifth black), other teams quickly scrambled for black talent. Robinson scored more runs and stole more bases than any other Dodger and finished his first year with a batting average of .297. The Dodgers won the pennant.

Robinson's 1947 salary was $5,000; in 1950, he was earning $35,000, the top Dodger salary. He retired in 1957 and was elected to the Hall of Fame in 1962. In 1972, his number—42—was ritually retired, and five months later, at the age of fifty-three, he died. At his funeral, attended by twenty-five hundred people including a forty-person presidential delegation, the Reverend Jesse Jackson eulogized: "When Jackie took the field, something reminded us of our birthright to be free."

"I was a black man in a white world," Robinson wrote in his autobiography. "I never had it made."

CAN'T WIN WITH HIM, CAN'T WIN WITHOUT HIM

When the Montreal Expos first considered signing Gary Carter to a long-term, $15 million contract, they "thought they couldn't win without him," according to club chairman Charles Bronfman. But even before they signed the all-star catcher to the biggest contract in the Expos' history, they were having second thoughts: "Two months before Carter signed the contract, we were perfectly aware we were making a mistake. The next day, and a month later, we still knew we were wrong. I'll know it until my dying day, and I'm not saying that because Carter had a bad year," Bronfman insisted.

Carter's batting average went from .293 in 1982 to .270 in 1983.

Tom Terrific Becomes the Cincinnati Kid: The Trading of Tom Seaver

BACKGROUND: Early in 1976, Tom Seaver—the shining symbol of the New York Mets, "the franchise" to his fans, and the all-American hero of the sports media—balked at signing his new contract. He wanted more money. Mets board chairman M. Donald Grant labeled him an "ingrate," made noises about a trade, and accused him of being short on team spirit. Seaver, who had almost single-handedly carried the team from the basement to the 1969 World Series championship, explained: "My first loyalty is to my family." It seemed only fair to him that as one of baseball's greats, he deserved a bigger piece of the pie, even if he wasn't a free agent but an old-fashioned "contract player," committed to the team he'd played with for eleven years. He resented being treated like an indentured servant: "For me to say 'my *owner*' is the most ridiculous thing in the world. Does somebody *own* you?" But Grant behaved with old-school ownership pride.

Eventually, Seaver signed a three-year contract for $225,000 per year, with elaborate performance clauses that could raise it to $260,000 annually. But his bitterness and disillusionment were made known, and he later said, "I was never happy with my contract. I signed it out of loyalty." For the Mets, 1976 was a bad year. Seaver pitched a fine season but the team batting average of .246 was the lowest in the major leagues. The Mets were becoming a bad joke again. When spring training began in 1977, Dave Kingman—the Mets' only power hitter—decided not to sign his new contract but to gamble and become a purchasable free agent at the end of the season. Furious, Seaver openly criticized Grant's refusal to bid for the desperately needed batting power on the free-agent market. Grant told him to mind his own business and pitch. Seaver asked to be traded.

As a ten-year veteran, he could approve the trade. He chose Cincinnati, Philly, Los Angeles, or Pittsburgh—the best in the league. Grant would not appease him and publicly scolded him through leaks to Dick Young's column in the *New York Daily News*. Young ridiculed "Tom Tewwiffic," and Seaver's anger mounted. Suddenly, Joe Torre was appointed the new manager of the Mets. He quickly lifted the disheveled team's morale and gave the unhappy superstar much-needed understanding. As the trade deadline approached, Seaver wavered. Pitching against the Cincinnati Reds, he chalked up his forty-second shutout by striking out ten batters, which brought his lifetime total to 2,400, breaking the all-time record of 2,396 set by Sandy Koufax. The fans gave him a three-minute standing ovation—"a sound of respect and love," he said, deciding on the spot to stay with his team.

Feeling he "deserved a gesture of good faith," Seaver asked to renegotiate his 1976 contract. Grant wouldn't hear of it: "The contract is the fundamental cornerstone of our country and baseball as well." (This was before player "holdouts" made mockeries of fundamental cornerstones.) The night before the trade, Seaver spoke to the Mets president, Lorinda de Roulet, and everyone was informed that an agreement had been reached: Seaver was staying with the Mets. But the very next morning, Young wrote in his column that Seaver's wife, Nancy, was the cause of his wanting more money: She was envious of the wives of the better-paid players. Stunned and outraged, Seaver announced: "Everything is off! I want out! I've got to go!" Before team manager Torre was informed by the Mets' front office, Grant gave the "clubhouse confidential" scoop to Young. Readers of the *News* early edition were the first to know the story of "the most outstanding star to change teams since the Boston Red Sox sold the young slugger Babe Ruth to the Yankees in 1920" [see "Frazee, Rhymes with Crazy: Babe Ruth Gets Traded to New York," page 134].

THE DEAL: Tom Seaver, age thirty-two, at the peak of his powers, winner of 182 games and two pennants for the Mets, three-time winner of the Cy Young Award, and the best pitcher in the National

League, was traded to the Cincinnati Reds for one utility infielder (Doug Flynn), one young pitcher (Pat Zachry), and two minor-league outfielders (Steve Henderson and Dan Norman). Kingman also was traded after a terrible season. He went to San Diego in trade for two minor players. Grant proved his point: No one would tell him how to run a team.

RESULTS: Some sportscasters believed the Mets weren't adding new talent but "ridding themselves of old problems." It was the end of the "contract player" with loyalty to his team. With Seaver's departure, baseball joined the corporate ranks with players (like executives) for sale to the highest bidder. Tom Seaver cried when he cleaned out his Met locker at Shea Stadium, and the fans will never again be able to assume that a beloved superstar, no matter how valuable to the team, holds the franchise.

He immediately pitched a masterly three-hit shutout for the Reds in Montreal. He finished his 1977 season with a 21–6 record and an earned-run average of 2.59. The Mets finished *last* in their division that year, thirty-seven games behind the winning Phillies.

AT THE FAR END OF THE RESERVE CLAUSE: THE RESULTS IN YANKEE SALARIES

"We just don't have any easy ones. We never cruise. We never coast."

Dave Winfield

George Steinbrenner, owner of the Yankees, says his main goal "is to put the best team on the field for our fans." In 1973, he and a group of partners bought the team for $10 million. Ten years later, the team was the highest paid in baseball history: $72.5 million worth of the player contracts for the opening-day roster of twenty-seven players. In yearly wages that's $15 million—the average salary being $558,754. Of the twenty-seven players, twenty-one have contracts with a total guaranteed value of $1 million. Of the twenty-six teams in the major leagues, the Yankees have 10 percent of all players who have contracts valued at over $1 million a year: Dave Winfield, Steve Kemp, and Ken Griffey. The infield's Winfield earned $1,531,600 in 1983 (not including bonuses) on a ten-year contract of $21 million plus increases based on the consumer price index, which made him the highest paid player in baseball. The lowest paid member was rookie Don Mattingly, at the major-league minimum of $37,500.

Dealmaker as Trailblazer:
Billie Jean King

Tennis in the United States had traditionally been a country-club sport for the upper crust who could afford to value amateurism above financial rewards. Therefore both male and female competitors received very minimal stakes. When the sport opened to professionals in 1968, things changed: Only the women remained undercompensated. Billie Jean King, a fireman's daughter, fought for parity for all women players—and won.

As the number-one-ranked women's tennis champion in the world, King had publicly denounced "shamateurism," the system whereby players retained their amateur rank but received healthy per diems, generous "perks," even under-the-table payments. King was delighted when the International Lawn Tennis Association opened the game to competition between pros and nonpros alike, but she quickly became wary when she discovered that, in the first open tournament, the first-place men's winner got $2,400, while the women's winner took home a slender $720. The disparity grew worse; in United States tournaments, the ratio was four to one, sometimes five to one. Billie, playing with the National Tennis League for $40,000 a year plus expenses, began to reject the argument that supported much higher prize money for men: The crowds came to see the men play because the women's game was not as exciting. King, suspecting that her own superstar status and charismatic personality were a draw, and that there was indeed an audience for women's tennis, began agitating—

The winner of the Battle of the Sexes, 1973.

not for parity, but for a more equitable ratio of prize money. But in 1971, when she discovered that not only were women players getting far less than men but also that the United States Lawn Tennis Association had organized far fewer tournaments for women for the upcoming year, Billie began to feel "shut out cold." When the ratio rose (or sank) to twelve and a half to one for the Pacific Coast Championship in 1970 ($25,000 for men; $2,000 for women), King started talking boycott. With Gladys Heldman, the publisher of *World Tennis* magazine, King arranged a women's tournament to be held in Houston. Although the tournament was meant to represent nothing more than a protest against disparity in prize money, it became a revolution when the U.S. Lawn Tennis Association suspended all the participants. By then, Philip Morris had agreed to sponsor the tournament, and the Virginia Slims circuit was born. With King leading the way, top women tennis players began blazing their own trail, and they were soon earning a minimum of $10,000 per tournament as crowds and corporate sponsors rallied round them. King soon became the first woman athlete to earn over $100,000 in one sport in one year. *Sports Illustrated*, for the first time in the history of the magazine, named a sportswoman of the year in 1972: King. She stated that while they did so because of the extent of her money-making, it was still "a step in the right direction because it meant that the most prestigious sports magazine in the world had finally accepted women as a legitimate part of the sports world." Still not satisfied by the media coverage of women's sports events, King founded (and poured a large amount of her money into) *WomenSports* magazine. In 1973, she founded the Women's Tennis Association, which began with $1 million in prize money and today dispenses over $11 million. That same year, forty million TV viewers saw her whip Bobby Riggs in a tennis match that was billed as the "Battle of the Sexes."

In 1981, King's former secretary sued her for a share of her assets, claiming that King, who acknowledged they'd had a long affair, had promised to support her. Although King ultimately won the lawsuit, many of her lucrative corporate endorsements were lost as sponsors declined to have their products in any way identified with a lesbian love affair. Murjani jeans canceled a contract that would have been worth $300,000 to King. A line of tennis clothing for Illingworth-Morris was canceled—she lost $500,000 on that one. She also lost $150,000 in coaching and training jobs, $150,000 in corporate appearances, and $225,000 in TV commercials. With lawyer's fees thrown in, she suffered over $1.5 million in losses because of the suit. One company that kept King on as a sponsor expected piles of protest

> "She's a woman who goes for it. She's progressive, hard-driving and has definite goals she'd kill to achieve. She's the type of person who prompts some feeling from everyone."
>
> Jerry Diamond, Women's Tennis Association Executive Director

Martina Navratilova and the Lion Cup trophy, 1981.

letters, but received only half a dozen—a number equaled by letters of support. NBC continued to use her to broadcast tennis coverage, officially stating: "We feel that the relationship revealed last week has no bearing on her tennis expertise." King speculated that while "Yonex and Nike and Achilles and Power Grip also continued to use me for their products . . . I have no illusions that, as my contracts run out, some sponsors may choose to quietly drop me. And will any new product ever dare to sign me?"

In 1975, King, who had won twenty championships at Wimbledon (six singles, ten doubles, and four mixed doubles), threatened to call a boycott of the tournament unless the sponsors agreed to parity in prize money. They did. Today, all of the fifteen top-ranked women's players earn over $100,000 a year, and everyone in the top fifty earns over $60,000. King has written that "making women's sports acceptable, and making women's tennis, particularly, into a legitimate big-league game was a crusade for me, and I threw my whole self into it in ways that exhausted me emotionally as much as they did physically." She explains her motivation: "The main thing is not a matter of wanting to win; the main thing is being scared to lose."

YOU'VE COME A LONG WAY, MARTINA

Martina Navratilova was growing up in her native Czechoslovakia while Billie Jean King was fighting for parity in prize money for women tennis players. Navratilova, who was born in 1956, defected to the United States when she came to play at the 1975 U.S. Open at Forest Hills. She has become the number-one women's player in the world, dominating the game in the way that King did in her time. She has followed in King's footsteps by taking over as the head of the Women's Tennis Association. When she won the 1983 U.S. Open championship, her prize, for that game alone, was $120,000. By 1983, her career earnings topped $6 million, more than any other tennis player in history, including Jimmy Connors, who by 1983 lead the male players with earnings of $4.8 million. Asked in 1983 if there was anyone on the scene who could beat her, Navratilova said, "It doesn't look like it now." But she mused, "I know my time is running out. I know the sand is running through the hourglass."

◆ ◆ ◆

"Staying on top requires giving up almost everything. Bjorn, that's all he thought about. It's like Martina now where you have to go to extremes. She's No. 1 and wants to get to zero where there's no competition. Your dream is to get there. I dreamed about being No. 1, but in the back of my mind, I didn't think I'd ever get there. But, I did, and that's when it caught me by surprise. That's why it's a whole mental thing to deal with. It requires a lot more dedication."

John McEnroe

BIG BUCKS: BASKETBALL

In 1983, a players' strike was averted by an innovative four-year pact that has been described as a "statesmanlike settlement." The National Basketball Association (NBA) and the players' union agreed to a revenue-sharing plan, the first in pro sports. Under the terms of the agreement, there is to be a ceiling on players' salaries of 53 percent of gross revenues (gate receipts, television, cable, and radio). Players now have more incentive for pulling in the fans and encouraging increased media interest. Rookie salaries are $40,000 for the 1983–1984 season; $65,000 for 1984–1985; $70,000 in 1985–1986; and $75,000 in 1986–1987. In 1983, the average salary was $246,000 plus $20,000 in benefits.

"Of course no one is worth that kind of money but if Moses Malone is going to get $2 million a year, then Larry certainly should."—Former Celtic Bob Cousy on Larry Bird's $14 million-plus contract

Moses Malone (*left*) of the Philadelphia 76ers signed a six-year $13.2 million contract, plus bonuses, in 1982. Larry Bird of the Boston Celtics signed a seven-year contract in 1983 that is expected to bring him more than $2 million a year. He signed just as his five-year, $650,000-a-year contract was expiring.

When is a bargain a deal? When it turns out to be the most profitable horse in racing history. Sam and Dottie Rubin paid $25,000 for John Henry (JH) in 1979. By 1983, the eight-year-old gelding had earned $3.8 million. Secretariat, the world's most famous horse and a triple crown winner, earned only $1.5 million on the course, though his son, Canadian Bound, had a price tag of $1.5 million and turned out to be too slow to run a race. JH has earned, and will earn, all his money with his legs alone.

The odds against a thoroughbred horse winning a major-stakes race are more than sixty thousand to one. JH was sold as a yearling in 1975 for $1,100. His mother, Once Double, was sold for $5,000; his dad, Ole Bob Bowers, for $900. Old Bob had a fierce temper and had once tied the world record for a mile-and-an-eighth in 1968, but it was considered a wild fluke and he was sold as a stud horse. (His fee was $500 in 1977; since his son's success, his fee has risen to $1,200 a piece. In 1981 he sired seventy-nine mares, a nice return on $900.)

In 1976, JH was sold again for $2,200. Around this time, his own temper emerged and he gained a reputation for biting and kicking, but another buyer was found for $7,500. The new owner's vet said JH could never be trained; JH was gelded and sold for $10,000 to two women with a racing stable. First time out, he won the race, plus $1,200. In 1977, he won three and lost three. In 1978, he lost the first six, was placed in a claiming race with a $20,000 to $25,000 price tag, and no one bit.

Enter the Rubins. He, a bicycle importer, never owned a horse in his life, and JH was considered a second-rate three-year-old with an unimpressive speed. First time out for his new owners, JH won at Aqueduct in 1978. Then he won by fourteen lengths at Belmont Park on the grass. It was a claiming race again—this time the tag was $35,000—and no one took him off the Rubins' hands. Since then, he is not for sale. He has done nothing but win. He's now considered the finest grass horse in America. The Rubins haven't bought another horse. John Henry keeps their hands full.

Move Over, Big Boy:
Magic Johnson

BACKGROUND: Since signed contracts don't mean a thing to the players who "hold out" when they no longer like what they agreed to accept, maneuvers by managers to hold onto a valued player take many forms.

In his sophomore year at Michigan State, six-foot, nine-inch Earvin Johnson was voted the most valuable player after leading his basketball team to a triumph in the 1979 NCAA tournament. Rather than finish school, Johnson was drafted by the Los Angeles Lakers for five years and immediately proved himself invaluable. Though theoretically too tall for the guard position, he managed it flawlessly, until an injury to the legendary center Karem Abdul Jabbar required Johnson to take over Jabbar's position in the last round of NBA playoffs against the Philadelphia 76ers. Johnson wiped the floor with everyone.

Terrified of losing this magician when his contract expired in 1984, Jerry Buss, the owner of the Lakers, came up with a spiffy new safety valve.

THE DEAL: "Magic" Johnson signed a twenty-five-year contract in 1981 for $25 million, *to take effect in 1984*. The money will be paid in cash with no deferrals.

RESULTS: In 1984, Magic will earn $2,739.73 daily, not including endorsements. He is expected to play for ten to twelve years, then become a coach or general manager to finish the run of his contract. Buss is certain Magic's PR value is worth every cent.

Dealmaker as Hockey Superstar: Wayne Gretzky

Wayne Gretzky (WG) is twenty-three years old. At seventeen, he was a first-year professional hockey player with the Indianapolis Racers of the World Hockey Association, today a defunct league. He received $500 a month. On his first road trip, he was given $250 for ten days' expenses, and he couldn't believe they had given him so much money to spend. Times changed fast. Before he turned twenty-one, he signed a twenty-one-year lifetime agreement with the Edmonton Oilers that gave him $100,000 a year. But in 1982 he scored more goals and got more assists than anyone in the history of hockey. His contract was renegotiated at his insistence: $21 million Canadian or $16.5 U.S. million for twenty years. That's a raise of $900,000 a year. His agent, Gus Badali of Sierra Sports Representatives, Inc., gets 5 percent of the salary plus 20 percent of all endorsement money, which, it turns out, is an astounding piece of change.

In 1983, WG earned nearly $2 million in endorsements, tripling his salary. He's done a 7-Up commercial, appeared on several TV soaps, and negotiated a TV animated-cartoon series based on himself. There's a Gretzky doll that comes with uniform, sweatsuit, and tuxedo, a Gretzky chocolate bar, Gretzky jeans, a video game, wallpaper, sportswear, lunch boxes, bedspreads, drapes, mattresses, and his face on every kind of hockey equipment. The Gretzky watch in Canada outsold the E.T. watch. He also posed for a poster wearing a tuxedo out on the ice; he collects revenues from that best-seller on five different fronts: the manufacturer, the distributor, the wholesaler, royalties on its sale, and personal-appearance boosts in stores or an endorsement of a store. There's no ice on his pucks.

PÉLÉ PAYS OFF

Professional soccer leagues have existed in the United States since the 1930s, but they have existed on a grand, national scale only since the 1969 creation of the North American Soccer League (NASL). The league was founded on the premise that it would devote itself to the promotion of American soccer and the development of American soccer players, but all the teams continued to rely on foreign players. American interest in the sport remained, at best, lackluster.

In 1975, the New York Cosmos announced that they had lured out of retirement the fabled Pélé, who, in the course of his long career with the Santos Club of Brazil and various Brazilian all-star teams, had come to be regarded as the game's premier player. The Cosmos would pay Pélé $4.7 million a year for three years (or about $7 million, in all, after taxes). As a New York star, he stood to make much more in promotional fees. The Cosmos expected a tremendous increase in attendance and a much better shot at the championship.

The Cosmos got the championship only in Pélé's third (and final) year with the club, but began to profit immediately from what came to be known as the "Pélé Phenomenon": Wherever Pélé played, attendance figures leaped to new highs. All the clubs in the league therefore made more money because of Pélé. Moreover, other teams began to go after foreign superstars. NASL attendance increased, as did media coverage of the game, the teams, and the players. Pro soccer had reached the big time in American sports.

Olympic Marketing Race: Financing the 1984 Los Angeles Games

BACKGROUND: Hosting the Olympics has proved to be the financial ruin of many a town. It was feared that asking Los Angeles, with its reputation for extravagance, to be the host, would spell financial disaster not just for L.A., but possibly for the entire state of California. But a financial genius named Peter Ueberroth came up with a plan that not only keeps Los Angeles out of trouble, but possibly makes the Olympics the most profitable game in town.

Ueberroth, a self-made millionaire, began his job as head of the Los Angeles Olympic Organizing Committee (LAOOC) by examining the books of all previous Olympics back to 1932—all of them were losers. The Montreal Games (1976) left the city $1 billion in debt. Moscow (1980) was said to have cost $9 billion. For the Lake Placid Games, over 350 corporations had contributed an average of $50,000, but those games lost money, too. And the Los Angeles Olympics were expected to be the biggest ever, with the most athletes (14,000), coming from the most countries (150), competing in a record number of events. Ueberroth, who said, "We just don't plan to make any financial mistakes," came up with a Tom Sawyer–like approach to financing.

THE DEAL: The LAOOC strictly limited the number of corporate sponsors to thirty. This select circle had to prove their "commercial integrity" and their "long-term commitment to youth and sports" before they were allowed to pay a $4 million minimum. This chosen corporate elite is allowed to use the closely guarded trademarks of the Los Angeles Olympics (the Disney-created "Sam, the Olympic Eagle" and the stars in motion) in their ad campaigns, but they are prohibited from displaying ads in the stadia or in the open air above these structures—a departure from earlier Olympiads.

RESULTS: This "hard-to-get" approach worked perfectly. Soon the LAOOC had to turn down four sponsors for every one they accepted. "Contributions" ranged from $4 million to $13 million and, says Ueberroth, "they also have to provide their services, if they have a service we can use. IBM is going to do the computerization of the games. A.T.&T. is helping with communications." Atlantic Richfield spent $5 million refurbishing the Los Angeles Coliseum and built six new tracks around the city. McDonald's built an 11,000-seat swimming

stadium and forked over another $5 million for the fast-food conces-
sion. The 7-Eleven stores built a $4 million cycling velodrome. Other
corporate sponsors include Coca-Cola ($13 million), Levi Strauss ($8
million), and Anheuser-Busch ($11 million). Although American
firms were given preference, Fuji became the "official film of the L.A.
Olympics" when Kodak balked at the large financial requirement.

Of course, crafty Ueberroth took special care in negotiating the
broadcast rights to the games, which he expected would be watched
by 2.5 billion people, or half the people on earth. Leaving nothing to
chance, he commissioned two separate studies of what the networks
might expect to make in sales of advertising time, and then he asked
for double of what had previously been expected. ABC, in the largest
TV transaction ever, paid $225 million for the right to broadcast and
sell the available three thousand minutes of commercial air time. At a
fabulous $260,000 for a thirty-second time slot (thirty seconds on
"Dynasty" brings in $180,000), ABC quickly sold out. Moreover, the
network had to make $70 million in broadcast equipment available to
the LAOOC, enabling them to sell foreign broadcast rights. European
rights sold for $19.2 million, Australian rights for $10.6 million, but
broadcast rights to the Soviet Union went for a mere $3 million.
"They're tough bargainers," said a vice-president of the LAOOC.

V

BEHIND CLOSED DOORS: POLITICS

First, all means to conciliate;
failing that, all means to crush.

RICHELIEU

Dealmaker as Monarch: Elizabeth I

When Elizabeth I reached the throne of England and Ireland in 1558, the country of four million subjects was in total chaos. The confused last years of her father, Henry VIII, the faction-ridden reign of her brother Edward, and the divisive behavior of her inflexibly papist sister Mary resulted in the empire facing near bankruptcy, depleted military strength in the face of wars in France and Scotland, enormous inflation, and anarchy at home. Elizabeth's superb education at the hands of Cambridge scholars, and her selection of qualified advisors with diverse opinions who acknowledged and respected her genius, enabled her to see that what England needed most was stability and public order. She knew she could not marry a Catholic without alienating the Protestants still reeling from Mary's persecutions, and marriage to a Protestant would cause chaos among her Catholic aristocracy, offering a focus for discontent. Marriage to a foreigner would be unpopular with the people for whom union with a more powerful country would mean domination; marriage to an Englishman would rent her court asunder, since there was no unanimous favorite.

So she kept procrastinating and negotiating with possible suitors while using them brilliantly. Their hopes became a safeguard for her throne. By October 1559, there were ten to twelve qualified men competing for her favor. While they were wooing, they could not be warring. For example: Philip II of Spain, her sister's widower, wanted her hand. He was convinced she would convert to Catholicism for him, and England would be saved for God and the pope. Elizabeth had no intention of marrying him, but she was negotiating a peace with France, and to have Philip on her side gave her a stronger bargaining position. Archduke Charles, son of the Austrian emperor and scion of the House of Hapsburg was offered by his father. The Hapsburg connection was one of the foundations of English foreign policy. Elizabeth welcomed the offer, but she would not marry *anyone* sight unseen, and the offer was politely withdrawn because it would have been undignified for Charles to arrive for inspection. What if she rejected him?

Such was her nature—to float, when it was calm, in a sea of indecision, and, when the wind rose, to tack hectically from side to side.

Lytton Strachey,
Elizabeth and Essex

In 1566, when pressed by her parliament on the question of succession—the most polite method of discussing her marriage—she flew into a tirade, assuring them that she had the country's interest at heart and she would determine the succession at "a convenient time." If she remained a spinster, she would settle the succession on a worthy heir. She was "the best match in her parish"—all of Europe—in the words of Sir Francis Walsingham, her principal secretary for nearly two decades; and she used that position to display her will, her abilities, her resourcefulness, and her power to lead the country.

She created and encouraged the cult of the Virgin Queen, inspiring iconographic homage as complex in its symbolism as any devised for the Blessed Virgin Mary [see "BVM and the Immaculate Insemination: Mary, the Mother of God," page 228]. Throughout her reign, more time was spent pondering the question of her marriage than any other aspect of state policy. Even Pope Sextus V, her ideological enemy and staunch admirer, made jokes about a papal union with the Crown of England and the extraordinary children they would produce. She wanted her courtiers to be handsome and of good lineage, not necessarily rich since money was easily granted, but, most important, she demanded the gift of leadership: Their promotions came only when they had demonstrated ability. Christopher Hatton, Walter Raleigh, Robert Dudley, Philip Sidney, and Robert Devereux [see "A Ring! A Ring! My Kingdom for a Ring!: Elizabeth and Essex," page 87] are but a few of the men who achieved firm places in English history by her patronage. Of all the monarchs in this period, only she gave her name to the age. Never marrying, she passed her crown on her deathbed to James, son of her arch-enemy, Mary Queen of Scots. No longer able to speak, she affirmed his succession wordlessly.

IF YOU'RE GOING TO DO IT, DO IT RIGHT

He who would enter the profession of diplomacy must examine himself to see whether he was born with the qualities necessary for success. These qualities are an observant mind, a spirit of application which refuses to be distracted by pleasures or frivolous amusements, a sound judgment which takes the measure of things as they are, and which goes straight to its goal by the shortest and most natural paths without wandering into useless refinements and subtleties which as a rule only succeed in repelling those with whom one is dealing. The negotiator must further possess that penetration which enables him to discover the thoughts of men and to know by the least movement of their countenances what passions are stirring within, for such movements are often betrayed even by the most practised negotiator. He must also have a mind so fertile in expedients as easily to smooth away the difficulties which he meets in the course of his duty; he must have presence of mind to find a quick and pregnant reply even to unforeseen surprises, and by such judicious replies he must be able to recover himself when his foot has slipped. An equable humor, a tranquil and patient nature, always ready to listen with attention to those whom he meets; an address always open, genial, civil, agreeable, with easy and ingratiating manners which assist largely in making a favorable impression upon those around him—these things are the indispensable adjuncts to the negotiator's profession. . . .

A good negotiator must not only be courageous in danger but firm in debate. There are many men who are naturally brave, but cannot maintain an opinion in dispute. The kind of firmness that is needed is that which, having carefully and fully examined the matter, consents to no compromise but pursues with constancy a resolution once adopted till it is carried into effect. Compromise is the easy refuge of the irresolute spirit. . . .

An ancient philosopher once said that friendship between men is nothing but a commerce in which each seeks his own interest. The same is true or even truer of the liaisons and treaties which bind one sovereign to another, for there is no durable treaty which is not founded on reciprocal advantage, and indeed a treaty which does not satisfy this condition is no treaty at all, and is apt to contain the seeds of its own dissolution. Thus the great secret of negotiation is to bring out prominently the common advantage to both parties of any proposal, and so to link these advantages that they may appear equally balanced to both parties. . . .

One of the most necessary qualities in a good negotiator is to be an apt listener; to find a skillful yet trivial reply to all questions put to him, and to be in no hurry to declare either his own policy, still less his own feelings; and on opening negotiations he should be careful not to reveal the full extent of his design except in so far as it is necessary to explore the ground; and he should govern his own conduct as much by what he observes in the faces of others as by what he hears from their lips. One of the great secrets of diplomacy is to sift the real from the trivial, and so to speak, to distill, drop by drop into the minds of your competitors those causes and arguments which you wish them to adopt. By this means your influence will spread gradually through their minds almost unawares.

François de Callières (1645–1717),
On the Manner of Negotiating with Princes

Everybody's Hour: The Woman's Rights Movement versus Black Male Suffrage

BACKGROUND: Women had traditionally been asked to be helpmates; during the Civil War, the woman's rights movement was asked to drop its demands and help the Union. They were promised huge political rewards; they were cheated.

Nineteenth-century white women had few political, legal, or economic rights (until the Civil War, black women had none). They were denied the right to vote, barred from higher education, and prevented from entering most professions. In most states, a husband had legal control over his wife's property and wages. "Experts" debated whether women had mental capacities equal to men, and popular male opinion was that women were childish, feeble, and in need of every sort of protection. Even the progressives in the American Anti-Slavery Society were in conflict over woman's rights, and when William Lloyd Garrison, the leader of the organization, allowed women to attend meetings and serve as officers, the group split into two factions, with dissenting members declaring that to include women was an "insane innovation." When the Garrison-led group sent a woman delegate, Lucretia Mott, to the World Anti-Slavery Convention held in London in 1840, all hell broke loose. The convention refused to seat her or any other woman, insisting that the Bible proved that women were "constitutionally unfit for public or business meetings." Banished to a curtained-off gallery with other women, Mott was joined by Garrison, who refused to take his seat. It was in this balcony that Mott met Elizabeth Cady Stanton, and the seeds of the American woman's rights movement were planted.

In 1848, Stanton and Mott called the first Woman's Rights Convention. Held in Seneca Falls, New York, the widely publicized meeting issued a "Declaration of Sentiments and Resolutions," around which the newly born movement organized its efforts. With the leadership of the movement continuously touring the nation and popularizing the notion of woman's rights, including the right to vote, states began passing "Married Woman's Property Acts," which gave some measure of legal control to married women.

With the coming of the Civil War, the campaign for woman's rights came to a halt, the moderate leadership deciding to cancel the national conventions which had been held annually. They ceased agi-

> A woman, especially if she has the misfortune of knowing anything, should conceal it as well as she can.
>
> Jane Austen,
> *Northanger Abbey*

tating for woman's rights. Radicals like Susan B. Anthony decried this decision, but others were persuaded by their "fellow" progressives.

THE DEAL: The women would drop their demands for legal, political, and social rights, and devote themselves to the Union cause. After the slaves had been freed, and the war was over, the patriotic efforts of women would be rewarded with the right to vote.

RESULTS: Women poured their energies into the Union war effort, organizing hospitals and nursing facilities for the military. With the men gone, women went to work in factories, farms, schools, and offices. With the war's end, women were asked, once again, to postpone agitating for their own civil rights: The Thirteenth Amendment had merely freed the slaves, it did not grant them political rights. Women were now asked to extend their efforts in favor of black male suffrage. When the Fourteenth Amendment was written, women were shocked to discover that for the first time the word "male" was introduced into the Constitution, and it was being used in an exclusionary way: Any state that denied males, blacks or whites alike, the right to vote would be penalized by having its representation in Congress reduced in the same proportion that those deprived of the vote bore to the "whole number of male citizens twenty-one years of age in such State." Women would not be allowed to vote and progressives denounced the women who agitated for the vote because, they argued, two suffrage movements "would lose for the Negro far more

They were derided in their time, but a century later the U.S. Postal Service issued this commemorative stamp, purple in color, honoring their struggle.

than we should gain for women." Anthony founded the American Equal Rights Association which called for universal suffrage, arguing that two movements were inefficient, "since to do so must be at double cost of time, energy and money." The publisher Horace Greeley wrote: "I conjure you to remember this is 'the Negro's hour' and your first duty now is to go through the States and plead his claim." Stanton countered with "Now's the hour—Not the 'Negro's Hour' alone, but everybody's hour." *The Revolution*, the women's suffrage newspaper run by Anthony and Stanton, had as its motto: "Men, their rights, and nothing more; Women, their rights, and nothing less."

The Fourteenth Amendment, which penalized states which deprived black men of the right to vote, was ratified in 1868. The Fifteenth Amendment which unconditionally gave all citizens (interpreted as all male citizens) the right to vote was ratified in 1870. It was not until 1920 that American women finally won the right to vote, seventy-two years after the first woman's rights convention was held. By then, only one woman who had been in attendance at that convention was still alive. Charlotte Woodward and millions of other American women proudly cast their ballots as a new era of struggle was born.

Swinging Election: The Compromise of 1877

BACKGROUND: In February of 1877, with Inauguration Day less than one week away, no one knew who the next president of the United States would be. Democrats claimed the office for their candidate, Samuel J. Tilden, while Republicans insisted it go to Rutherford B. Hayes. With the election bitterly contested, and firebrands on both sides calling for armed insurrection, the dispute was reminiscent of the recent Civil War, in which it was rooted.

When the war ended in 1865, Republicans, holding a three to one majority in both houses of Congress, attempted to impose military rule on the rebellious states of the defeated Confederacy. Along with the army, and equally odious to white southerners, came new legislation designed to give civil rights to former slaves—including the Fifteenth Amendment, which gave black men the right to vote. Naturally, blacks flocked to the Republican party—Lincoln's party—and, together with northern carpetbaggers, controlled state governments in the South (20 percent of the white population had been disenfranchised due to their war involvement). White resistance to reconstruction found political expression in the Democratic party; and to enforce their will, the shadow army, the Ku Klux Klan, was born. KKK terrorism combined with economic coercion to keep blacks from the polls. The federal government responded with strict legislative measures, military force—even martial law—but the popularly supported terrorism was impossible to combat. In Louisiana, in 1868 alone, over a thousand Republicans, most of them black, were murdered by the KKK. "Who is to blame?" asked a Louisiana paper in 1868: "Assuredly not we people of the South who have suffered wrongs beyond endurance. Radicalism and negroism . . . are alone to blame. . . . These northern emissaries of advanced political ideas, and of progressive social reforms . . . have met the fate they deserved."

By the mid 1870s, northern Republicans, worn down by the virulence of the southern response to reconstruction, a raging depression, and an administration (Grant's) rife with scandals, found the plight of the blacks of decreasing concern. Carpetbagging Republicans still controlled the state governments of South Carolina, Louisiana, and Florida; and candidate Hayes had, in accepting the nomination, stated: "There can be no enduring peace if the constitutional rights of any portion of the people are permanently disregarded." But his concern was self-serving: White coercion of blacks was costing the Republican party upward of a quarter of a million votes.

With the American people anxious for reform, most observers expected the election of 1876 to go to Tilden. On election night, November 7, with results from around the country indicating a Tilden victory, *someone* in Hayes headquarters in New York calculated that if the three southern states still controlled by Republicans went for Hayes, he would win by exactly one vote. (That someone is believed to have been John Reid, managing editor of the *New York Times.*) Telegrams (signed by the head of the Republican party but charged to the *Times'* account) were sent to the three governors: They read, "With your state sure for Hayes, he is elected. Hold your state." The governors swung into action. The next day, the governor of South Carolina wired back: "All right, South Carolina is for Hayes. Need more troops. Communication with interior cut off by mobs . . ." With newspapers all over the country (but not the *Times*) declaring Tilden the winner, and even Hayes admitting defeat, the Republicans fought on. Canvassing boards, originally established to ensure fair voting practices for blacks (and entirely controlled by Republicans)

Power is always gradually stealing away from the many to the few, because the few are more vigilant and consistent.

Samuel Johnson

seized the ballots in the three disputed states and certified that not only had Hayes won but that Louisiana and South Carolina had elected a Republican governor and legislature as well. Democrats cried foul play, inaugurated their own state governments, and reported their own election results to Washington. The 19 disputed electoral votes, plus 1 disputed vote in Oregon, would determine who would be president. Tilden, with 184 certain votes, needed only 1; Hayes needed them all. Congress faced a grave and unprecedented dilemma: The Constitution provided no mechanism for determining the validity of dual returns, but merely stated that, "the President of the Senate shall, in the presence of the Senate and the House . . . open all certificates and the votes shall then be counted." The question was, which set of votes? And *who*, exactly, should count them? The Republicans controlled the Senate, the Democrats the House—chaos threatened. The controversy dragged on until, finally, in the last days of January, Congress created a special electoral commission to rule on the disputed votes. The fifteen members included five Supreme Court justices—they were supposed to be impartial—but the commission quickly divided on party lines. With the Republicans holding a majority, Hayes was declared the winner. But the catch was that their findings were not official until approved by Congress, leaving the Democrats with one powerful weapon: filibuster. With one week left to Inauguration Day, the only thing certain about the presidency was that Grant was leaving office. Anarchy might reign.

THE DEAL: Southerners, meeting with Hayes, agreed to end their filibuster before Inauguration Day and accept the findings of the electoral commission. In return, Hayes agreed to end federal occupation of the South immediately, withdrawing troops and carpetbagger governments; appoint a southerner to a cabinet-level post such as that of patronage-rich postmaster general; commit more money to public works in the South (since the war's end they were receiving a scant 10 percent of federal monies); and support the passage of the Texas & Pacific Railroad bill, linking the South with the Southwest.

RESULTS: Hayes became president on March 5, and by the end of April, federal troops were gone from the South and the carpetbagger governments with them. Reconstruction was over and so was any chance blacks had for civil rights. Jim Crow laws, upheld by the Supreme Court, eliminated blacks as a factor in southern politics until the rise of the civil rights movement in the 1950s and 1960s. For the next seventy-five years (with the exception of 1928) the "solid South" could be relied upon to deliver its votes to the Democrats.

Tilden, rebuffing supporters who urged him to fight for the presidency, remarked: "I think I can retire to private life with the consciousness that I shall·receive from posterity the credit of having been elected to the highest possible position . . . without any of the cares and responsibilities of the office."

A Brief Survey of Political Patronage

♦ The first recorded example of political patronage occurred in China. In 243 .., donors who contributed a certain amount of grain to the state received a job in the national hierarchy. China can claim not only the first patronage system, but the first merit system as well. The summit of their civil service was Mandarin status, a rank that could not be purchased, but could only be achieved by passing an arduous examination, requiring years and years of demanding preparation.

♦ The Catholic church sanctioned patronage by law: A patron who financed the building of a church could appoint the lower clergy and assign others, lay and clergy, to officiate in church services.

The church was also involved with nepotism—literally, favoritism shown to "nephews"—whereby the popes transferred their office, or other important jobs, to men who were actually their natural sons or even their lovers.

♦ In the fourteenth century, the sultans of the Ottoman Empire auctioned off the governorships of Syria and Egypt. The offices cost sixty thousand gold ducats, but yielded a return of one million gold ducats in annual tributes.

♦ Patronage really reached its apex in seventeenth- and eighteenth-century France. To nourish the badly depleted treasury, nearly all government offices were put up for sale; in fact, new job titles were created just to be sold, without any regard for their actual pertinence (they were called *offices imaginaires*). To make matters worse, these jobs were not only hereditary, they were transferable and could be traded, like stock, on the open market. The French bureaucracy was so lumbered by these useless salaried officials that the treasury was nearly bankrupt, which led to a revolution that cleaned out government service—often by decapitation.

♦ Patronage took root in the United States early on, despite George Washington's admonishment to fill government jobs with "those who seem to have the greatest fitness for public office." "Nonsense," said William Learned Marcy, governor of New York: "To the victor belong the spoils of the enemy." Men who had proved their

> "I said to the governor, 'Let's wheel and deal and do some trading. Tell them you're going to put that roll call behind your desk, and when they come looking for jobs and roads and contracts, you'll be looking at the roll call.' I said, 'Governor, this is nut cutting time. They're going to try to cut your nuts off, and you've got to try to cut theirs.'"
>
> George. E. Bagby, former Georgia Commissioner of Fish and Game, to Lester Maddox

dedication to the winning party through large donations or the delivery of substantial blocks of votes were given coveted government jobs and contracts. In the absence of a civil-service system of merit, the president controlled large numbers of appointments, creating a rather unstable situation. In 1860, Lincoln replaced 1,195 of the 1,520 jobs controlled by the president. A national reform movement, the National Civil Service League, pressed for reform. In 1883, the Pendleton Act was passed, calling for the creation of a civil-service commission. Although the establishment of a statewide merit system was left to each state, by 1939, states could be eligible for federally funded programs only if state workers were selected through merit systems.

Comrade Kaiser:
Lenin and the Sealed Train

BACKGROUND: Vladimir Ilich Lenin, Bolshevik party leader, found himself trapped in Switzerland when the Russian Revolution unexpectedly erupted in 1917, toppling the tsar. With World War I raging throughout Europe, Lenin had no way of getting home, until a most unlikely savior appeared, offering not only to safely transport him home, but to finance his radical party as well: Kaiser Wilhelm II, the tsar's own cousin.

With one million Germans fighting with Russia on the vast eastern front, and America about to enter the war against them, Germany was desperate to conclude a separate peace with Russia. The Allies were just as desperate to keep this huge fighting force exactly where it was. They weren't about to allow Lenin, a well-known, outspoken antiwar critic, to travel home through *their* territory. They would just as soon arrest him. Germany was, of course, willing to do just about anything to end hostilities with Russia. They had been disappointed when the new Russian government, a coalition of leftist groups (mostly Mensheviks and Socialist Revolutionaries—with Lenin's party, the Bolsheviks, representing a small, very far left minority) simply changed traditional war slogans ("For Tsar and Fatherland") into revolutionary slogans ("Soldiers to the trenches, Workers to the Factory Benches") and continued fighting. In fact, in the weeks following the Revolution, anti-German feeling seemed to have intensified. Even the Bolsheviks, headed, in the absence of Lenin, by Stalin and other comrades, printed an editorial in *Pravda,* their party paper, opposing a separate peace. Lenin was horrified. It was his opinion that "the military monarchy in Russia has been followed by a militant republic of capitalists who want to continue the imperialist war and who adhere to the robber treaties of the Tsarist monarchy." And he was even more horrified to learn that his party was talking of reconciliation with the more moderate Marxist party, the Mensheviks. Lenin's view on cooperating with moderates was also clear: They should be supported "the way a noose supports a hanging man." Here was an intransigent revolutionary the Germans could count on to stir things up! They never really dreamed that he could actually seize power, but these archconservative autocrats aimed at "creating the greatest possible degree of chaos in Russia," thereby disrupting the war effort. Lenin, watching from exile as the revolution he'd worked for all his life took root without him—seeing his own party subvert his goals—was aching to get home. He'd been in exile for ten years. Hesitating when the Germans first approached him, Lenin had to weigh the effects of being vulnerable, once back home, to his political foes smearing him as an agent of the Kaiser's (accepting enemy aid was treason and the Germans had just slaughtered two and a half million Russians) against the possibility of losing this great historical moment. He decided he had no choice but to accept the Kaiser's help; but Lenin, who had been trained as a lawyer, imposed certain conditions.

THE DEAL: Lenin and a party of thirty-two fellow Russians (all of them exiled leftists, but not all Bolsheviks) would travel through Germany on a "sealed train." (It was actually one carriage with three second-class and five third-class compartments.) The doors were sealed shut for the duration of the trip through enemy territory, and the Russians would not step foot outside of it. Nor would they even speak with any Germans—they brought with them a Swiss Social Democrat to act as intermediary. The Germans conferred on this sealed train the extraterritorial status of a foreign embassy. Lenin even insisted on paying his own fare. The Germans, counting on Lenin's special talent to shake things up, got him safely home.

RESULTS: The Kaiser's investment in Lenin succeeded beyond his wildest dreams. With strong-man Lenin once again running the party, the Bolsheviks quickly began antiwar agitation. At a time when other parties were strapped for funds, the Kaiser made millions of marks available to the Bolsheviks, who were therefore able to spend freely on propaganda (*Pravda* was distributed widely, at no charge), pay full-time agitators, and generously arm the Red Guard, their pri-

The Bolsheviks have subjected Russia to the kind of experiments I would not try on a frog.

Ivan Pavlov, Russian scientist

vate army. Party membership grew from a paltry ten thousand at the time the tsar was overthrown in March, to three hundred thousand in October when the Bolsheviks overthrew the shaky democratic coalition, the Provisional Government. Even before the Russian generals at the front were sure that the Bolsheviks had actually seized power, they received instructions to begin peace negotiations. In November 1917, less than seven months after Lenin crossed Germany, a Russian delegation crossed German lines to formally request an armistice. "We no longer wish to take part in this purely imperialist war in which the claims of the possessing classes are openly paid in human blood," said Trotsky, who headed the negotiating team. The Germans dealt with the Russians as a defeated foe, the German foreign minister announcing, "The only choice they have is as to what sauce they shall be eaten with." In the Brest-Litovsk Treaty ending hostilities, Russia lost a third of her population, a quarter of her land, and over half of her industry.

Before his death in 1924, Lenin had firmly established "the dictatorship of the proletariat," actually, the dictatorship of the Communist party. Germany lost World War I in spite of its separate peace with Russia, and in 1918 the Kaiser was forced to abdicate and flee to Holland, where he died in 1941. It was Winston Churchill, no friend of the Communists, who later wrote, "They transported Lenin in a Sealed Train like a plague bacillus from Switzerland to Russia."

Lenin sharing a quiet moment with his eventual successor, Joseph Stalin.

"Who Still Talks Nowadays of the Extermination of the Armenians?": Turkey 1915

BACKGROUND: From Herod's slaughter of the innocents in the Bible to the slaughter of two and a half million Cambodians by the Khmer Rouge in the 1980s, politically motivated mass extermination has been one of the horrific blights of human civilization. The eradication of the Armenians by the Turks was the first of this century and one of the least memorialized.

Today the region of the earth once known as Armenia is composed of northeast Turkey, the Armenian Soviet Socialist Republic, and parts of Iranian Azerbaijan. Set southeast of the Black Sea, south of Soviet Georgia, and west of the Caspian Sea, the area is a plateau of mountains and fertile valleys that rises up from the deserts of Syria and Iran. Its language evolved in mountainous isolation, independent of the main language systems; today the Armenian tongue is unique, with no connection to any other living language. Armenia was a thriving trade route, or pass, through the mountains that joined the Mediterranean and Greek world with the eastern empires. By A.D. 70, it was a full empire—one of the most powerful in western Asia—until Rome and the Parthians joined forces to defeat it. Through the missionary work of Saint Gregory it became the first nation of people to officially adopt Christianity as its "state" religion.

By the sixteenth century, all of Armenia was firmly in the grip of the Turkish Ottoman Empire. The Turks tolerated other religions in their Islamic midst as separate communities (*millets*), with appointed patriarchs of their own faiths. These "infidels" had no rights. The Christian *millet* of Armenia was divided into six manageable *vlayets*, and the inhabitants proved themselves invaluable servants as merchants and traders and bankers. Until the nineteenth century, the Turks and the Armenians lived together peacefully.

In 1828, Christian Russia, the northern neighbor, took the eastern part of Armenia after a war that won the Greeks independence from the Turks. The French Revolution had inspired a sense of nationalism throughout Europe. Yet the Turkish-Armenians remained *millet sadika,* the "loyal community," in the language of the Turks. In 1876, Abd al-Hamid became the thirty-fourth successive ruler of the Ottoman Empire. Russia again invaded Turkey in 1877, claiming to be "protecting Christians" in Turkish-Armenia. England sent warships and made a peace that enlarged Russian-Armenia and stipulated that Turkey make improvements and reforms in Armenia. The treaty brought the "Armenian Question" to world attention.

Hamid was enraged. Some Turkish-Armenians had actually welcomed the Russians, and others were talking about equality and freedom of opportunity. The sultan made severe reprisals against these "dangerous revolutionaries." The Armenian language could no longer be spoken in public and no mention of Armenians was to appear in print anywhere in his empire. A special cavalry of fierce, primitive Kurdish tribesmen was formed and honored with the name *Hamidiyeh.* Their garrisons were built near the major Armenian villages. The Armenians were then told to surrender all weapons by order of Sultan Hamid. In the summer of 1894, the massacre began. In two years, three hundred thousand were murdered, one-eighth of the Armenian population within the Ottoman Empire. News eventually reached the outside world. The sultan refused to comment on "internal matters," except to say that reports were grossly exaggerated. On August 26,

1896, a group of young Armenians seized a bank in order to draw attention to their plight. A bank, they knew, would be of concern to the world. The Turks, after easily routing them, went on a three-day frenzied rampage, clubbing over eight thousand Armenians to death in the streets. The city was literally bathed in human blood. A telegram signed by all the major European powers demanded that the killing "cease immediately . . . continuance means danger to throne and dynasty." The massacre was over. But not for long.

In 1908, a revolution led by the "Young Turks" ended "the long night of Hamidian despotism," and Armenians freely took service for the state in the cause of reform; but in 1909, at Adena, there was another massacre. The culprits escaped. The warning was not heeded, as imperialistic, territorial, and economic rivalries flared all over Europe into war in 1914. The European powers took sides, and Germany hesitated before accepting Turkey as an ally: The Turkish army was an ill-equipped, disorganized mess.

On October 29, German ships attacked a Russian ship. Russia declared war on Turkey. In April 1915, France and England, aided by Australia and New Zealand, invaded Turkey at Gallipoli in Churchill's disastrous attempt to seize the Dardanelles and Constantinople. Turkey's triumph, led by Germany, made them look to their borders for an attack from Russia. Armenia was the passage and the buffer. Both Turkey and Russia needed Armenian allegiance. Both approached their Armenian communities at the same time.

THE DEAL: Turkey offered its *millet sadika* full autonomy in a Turkish protectorate that would include some of the six existing provinces and the Russian-Armenian area. In return, Armenians had to give the Turks undivided allegiance and help in influencing the hostile Russian-Armenians to join the Turks. The Turkish-Armenians, always loyal to their government and to the Turks with whom they had been bravely fighting side-by-side since 1912 when they were allowed in the army, swore allegiance to Turkey and the Ottoman Empire.

RESULTS: The Turks immediately formed a Turkish-Armenian detachment to fight against the border Russians and to "liberate" the Russian-Armenians. The Turkish-Armenians refused to cooperate. They were eager to fight any enemy of Turkey but refused to fight with the Christian neighbors who had aided them during the Hamidian massacres. The Turks tried to infiltrate that area, but a small group of Russian-Armenians, calling themselves "the Armenian Vol-

"We have been reproached for making no distinction between the innocent Armenians and the guilty; but that was utterly impossible, in view of the facts that those who were innocent today might be guilty tomorrow. We have already disposed of 3/4 of the Armenians ... we have to finish them. If we don't, they will plan their revenge."

Minister Talaat, Turkish Minister of the Interior, to U.S. Ambassador Henry Morganthau

—— 167

unteers," was impeding their progress by using mountain-guerrilla techniques.

In September 1915, the official paper of Turkey, *Tanine*, openly advocated the extermination or forcible conversion of all Armenian women as "the only means of saving the empire." The Armenians were declared the sworn enemies of the Turkish people. In Van, they were attacked for being "traitors," and the surrounding Armenian villages were destroyed. All Armenians were removed from the Turkish army. They were barred from carrying weapons. They were formed into special battalions to be road laborers and pack animals, then were murdered *en masse*. Others were tortured, beaten, and shot, under the pretense that they were hiding guns. Talaat, the powerful minister of the interior, planned a systematic extermination by murder and deportation to the desolate and barren Syrian desert.

The deportees, mostly women and children and older men, were sent south to Aleppo, a central converging depot, on foot or crammed into cattle cars. Those on foot rarely reached their destination. The Muslim peasants and Kurds mobbed the "infidel traitors" in order to plunder and savage them. Most of those who reached Aleppo were corralled into concentration camps and starved to death or sold to passing Bedouins. A few survived to be marched naked into the Syrian desert to die. During 1915–1916, over one million Armenians were annihilated. On August 31, 1915, Talaat wired Germany: "The Armenian Question no longer exists." Turkish-Armenia was practically devoid of life. Approximately five hundred thousand had fled across the Russian border. In 1916, rescue and relief forces found another eight hundred thousand in prison camps or hiding throughout Turkey.

The Treaty of Sèvres (1920) liquidated the defeated Ottoman Empire and officially reunited Turkish-Armenia with Russian-Armenia as Greater Armenia, a republic. It remained so for less than a year. Russia snatched its portion back, proclaiming it a Soviet Socialist Republic, and allowed Turkey to absorb the rest. America and Europe, preoccupied with peace in their own lands, let the Middle East settle its own business. No one talked about the extermination of the Armenians. The massacre of 1915–1916 was the first example in this century of the systematic slaughter of a large group of people by a political enemy. When Goering questioned whether they could actually get away with "the final solution" to the Jewish Question, Hitler replied: "Who still talks nowadays of the extermination of the Armenians?"

Red Herrings:
Norway Expels Trotsky

BACKGROUND: Even exile was too good for Trotsky, as far as Stalin was concerned. From afar, the Soviet dictator did everything in his power to harass his defeated foe: He stopped at nothing.

With the death of Communist party deity Vladimi Lenin [see "Comrade Kaiser: Lenin and the Sealed Train," page 169] in 1924, the path was nearly clear for the ascent to power of the party's general secretary, Joseph Stalin. Only one man stood in his way: the brilliant Communist theorist, organizer of the Red Army, outstanding orator—and Jew—Leon Trotsky. Both men had been close to Lenin, who, toward the end, favored Trotsky as his successor and was beginning to suggest Stalin's removal from power. Trotsky and Stalin had been at odds for years; Trotsky, a more orthodox Marxist, believed in fomenting worldwide revolution, while Stalin was content with "socialism in one country"—as long as he could dominate that country. Trotsky's brilliance found expression in political theorizing; Stalin was brilliant at manipulating party in-fighting for his own ends. Trotsky never stood a chance. In 1926, he was expelled from the Politburo; in 1927, he was thrown out of the party; in 1928, he was exiled to Alma-Ata in Turkestan; and in 1929, he was permanently thrown out of the USSR. He settled unhappily in Turkey until 1933, when his followers were able to win him asylum, under terribly strict conditions, in France. He had to live incognito, was forbidden to visit Paris, and had to agree to constant police surveillance. In 1935, when the Labor party came to power in Norway and offered Trotsky asylum there, he thought it might make a nice change.

As Trotsky was packing his bags and moving to Norway, Stalin was consolidating his power in the USSR and his famous purges were at their height: One in twenty citizens was arrested and many thousands perished in his infamous camps. Trotsky said of Stalin: "That savage fears ideas, since he knows their explosive power and knows his weakness in the face of them." That savage was still out to get him.

THE DEAL: With Trotsky comfortably settled in Norway, the Soviet Union announced that it would purchase the entire Norwegian herring catch at a very good price. But in return the government had to expel Trotsky. The Labor government, desperate for money to pay for its progressive social programs, agreed.

> Like a packet of dynamite, wrapped in asbestos, he was again shunted from country to country; gingerly he was forked across frontiers as if the very elements of his person might spontaneously explode.
>
> John Gunther,
> *Harper's,* April 1933

RESULTS: Mexican artist Diego Rivera [see "Fooling a Rockefeller in Oils: Diego Rivera and Rockefeller Center," page 319] and his wife, Frida Kahlo, arranged for Trotsky to be given asylum in Mexico. He lived there until 1940, when a Spanish assassin pierced his brain with an ice pick. Although the murderer denied that he'd been sent by the Russians, he was officially made a Hero of the Soviet Union by Stalin, who went even a step further and gave the man's mother the Order of Lenin. When he was released from Mexican prison after twenty years, he moved to the USSR, but didn't like it and resettled in Czechoslovakia. In March of 1953, Stalin died of a brain hemorrhage.

LBJ Buys the House: The 1937 Election

BACKGROUND: In theory, a congressperson represents a majority of his or her constituents. However, a minority rules when the elected official owes the seat to a "specialized interest." When that official is a shameless aggressor on his rise to the top, a pattern is set that can (and did) win the approval of a president's seal.

Lyndon Baines Johnson (LBJ), born in 1908, was familiar with both wealth and Depression poverty, but his roots firmly established him as political gentry. His father and grandfather were both in the Texas legislature. LBJ arrived in Washington, D.C., as a secretary to a Texas congressman in 1931. His education was shoddy, but no one matched his eighteen-hour days, his seven-day-week schedule, or his cunning, commonsensical ability to get things done *fast*. To his astounding memory for facts and details was added an audacious genius for the bureaucratic political process, for ferreting out who had what connection with whom, and for shamelessly ingratiating himself with the individual and corporate sources of power. (He preached a democracy of small businesses, but he played knowing the United States was the corporations.) Every one of his boss's constituents got the help they asked for, and every one knew *he* was responsible for the favors.

By unethical means—he packed the house with people not legally entitled to vote—he gained control of the Little Congress, a moribund organization formed for congressional secretaries to debate current issues, then he turned it into a flashy showcase for his own ruthless ambition. His bustling determination and "spunk" made him a minor celeb in the "old boy's club" on Capitol Hill. At twenty-six,

"If Lyndon found out somebody really wanted something very badly, he would hold it up until he could trade it off for something he really wanted."

Stewart Udall, secretary of the interior under JFK and LBJ

he was offered a major job as a General Electric lobbyist that would have tripled his secretarial salary. But, he had other plans in mind.

In 1935, with the direct intervention of his mentor Sam Rayburn—a friend of his father's who was famous for never seeking favors—FDR appointed him the Texas director of the National Youth Administration. The NYA was created by executive order to make jobs for the masses without work in the Great Depression. LBJ was the youngest director in the program. He was also the most successful: Within six months, eighteen thousand were working across Texas. His fourteenth district had the best loan-repayment record of the 435 congressional districts, and the first check for plowed-up cotton went there. All those constituents who had received his Washington attentions were called on to help as he trekked across the entire state hustling jobs and materials and setting up the grassroots political foundation that would soon neatly serve his own ends. This was the era of the New Deal and he rode along on the crest of the wave, assiduously earning his way. His chief goal was to get back to the action in Washington with his own congressional seat. He didn't have long to wait. In February 1937, Congressman James Buchanan, from LBJ's Burnet County district, died. But how could a twenty-eight-year-old who had never even voted in the district, who had no actual political experience, and who had no campaign money win an election?

For years, an unscrupulous lawyer *extraordinaire*, counsel to the great oil companies, and ex-Texan Senator Alvin Wirtz saw a financial empire for the taking: The huge Hamilton Dam in Burnet County had been left uncompleted when its builders went bankrupt in 1932. The dam was intended for hydropower, but since all the hydro and most of the Texas politicians were controlled by the mammoth Texas utilities, the idea of getting federal monies and inviting federal influence to complete it was not attractive to the power brokers, even though it was the height of the Depression with local funds very scarce. So the dam sat unfinished. Then FDR created the Public Works Administration (PWA) to *give* monies to public authorities. Wirtz and his cronies boondoggled the Texas legislature into believing the dam was actually for flood control. In 1934, the legislature created the Lower Colorado River Authority (LCRA) and applied to the PWA for funds.

In 1934, Buchanan was head of the House Appropriations Committee. The dam's name was quickly changed to Buchanan Dam to goose him into getting the money from the PWA for his district. However, since the Buchanan Dam was no good for flood control, another *bigger* dam—the Marshall Ford Dam—was proposed farther down the river, at a cost of $10 million. The second dam would be financed by the Bureau of Reclamation, a part of the Department of the Interior. It would be built by Wirtz's clients, Brown & Root, Inc.

FDR approved the whole scheme. Everything seemed divinely ordained—until it was discovered that the Bureau of Reclamation did not have the authority to okay the allocated $10 million. Only Congress had the power to approve public works under FDR's new setup. *And* the bureau could not build on public land, only on government land. In Texas, a river was public land.

Congress recessed for 1936. Buchanan guaranteed Wirtz and Brown & Root that there would be no problems with Congress. He'd work it all out. Brown & Root began construction, sinking $1.2 million, their entire worth, into this project which, if successful, would net them an immense profit and great power in the state; but if it failed it would wipe them out. Everything seemed a shoo-in until Buchanan dropped dead.

One of the older men LBJ had cultivated in Texas was Alvin Wirtz. When he found out about Buchanan's death, he sped to Wirtz and offered his boundless energies, his proven skills, his contacts on Capitol Hill, and his soul for a crack at the seat for Burnet County. True, he was only twenty-eight and a political nonentity. But, boy, hadn't he proven he could get jobs done *fast*?

THE DEAL: Wirtz and Brown & Root would back and bankroll LBJ if he promised to get the dam certified and authorized and legalized, pronto. They bought the best campaign managers. LBJ would use his National Youth Administration setup and align himself tightly with the idolized FDR, *no matter what the issue*. He would remind everyone

"He worked with Brown & Root as if he was one of the firm's employees."

Robert A. Caro,
The Path to Power

Immediately after buying his seat in the House of Representatives, LBJ caught the eye of FDR. (Texas Governor James Allred, center*)*

172 ——

everywhere that his father and grandfather were legislators and would play down his age.

RESULTS: Seven other men threw their hats into the ring but none had LBJ's grassroots organization or the pots of money to buy posters, brochures, newspaper ads and editorial space, radio time, district political leaders, barbecues, and so forth. LBJ's backers spent enough bucks—nearly a hundred thousand dollars—to make this race one of the most expensive in Texas history. He tirelessly campaigned the back roads of eight thousand square miles, knowing that if he won the outlying districts he wouldn't have to worry about the cities where his opponents were well-known. He knew how to move people, how to inspire them, and how to use them. When the polls had him losing, he boosted his speeches by using an eight-year-old to warm up the crowd with Edgar Guest's "It Couldn't Be Done": "Just start in to sing as you tackle the thing/That 'cannot be done,' and you'll do it."

He did it. In the doing, he lost forty pounds and was hospitalized with appendicitis, but he won by 3,000 votes. This was 28 percent of the 29,948 votes cast, or 8,280, which was the smallest consensus in Congress.

The president took a special interest in "this remarkable young man." He was immediately appointed to the Naval Affairs Committee and he exploited the powerful, prestigious connections, including his mentor Rayburn, now House majority leader, who he humbly asked to stand beside him during his House swearing in. In eleven days he had the dam approved. Then he got an additional $17 million for a *higher* Marshall Ford Dam. Brown & Root had raised him to power and they openly, legally supplied him with enormous sums of money, much of it distributed to other needy, grateful congressmen for their campaign funds, to be returned in congressional support for LBJ. With the direct assistance of Congress—and in 1944 FDR himself killed an IRS fraud rap against them—Brown & Root became a multi-billion-dollar corporation and one of the largest construction companies in the world with dams, the $100 million Corpus Christi Naval base, oil equipment, and $375 million in war work. With infinite sums at his disposal from the new super industries of the Southwest—oil, sulphur, gas, aerospace—LBJ bought votes on a scale undreamed of before his time. He parlayed his sublime abilities of political diplomacy and compromise into a great American political career from Speaker of the House to vice-president—one oil company testified to giving him $50,000 in cash when he was vice-president—to the president of the United States.

> "I'm a compromiser and a maneuverer. I try to get something. That's the way our system works."
>
> Lyndon B. Johnson

Dealmaker Salaries and Honoraria

At the end of 1982, House members gave themselves a pay raise from $60,662.50 to $69,800.00 and accepted a ceiling on honoraria, or public-speaking fees, of $18,200.00 per year. Senators passed the pay raise with the understanding that they could keep their unlimited extra income, which for some tripled their salaries.

But public opinion was too strong for them. In recent years, these honoraria have been perceived by many as bribes, or direct cash payments from special interest groups in the public sector trying to sway legislators; and unlike political contributions, these fees go directly into a senator's pocket to be used as he or she sees fit. Honoraria payments went from $1.7 million in 1981 to $2.4 million in 1982. In June 1983 the senators adopted a compromise. Instead of eliminating the honoraria, they took a pay raise to $69,800 and limited their outside income from speaking and writing to 30 percent of wages, or $20,940. (There is no limit on a member's access to unearned income: stocks, bonds, investments.) Passed into law, it took effect on January 1, 1984. Since they have exempted themselves from the Social Security Act, they are not required to pay FICA (Federal Insurance Contribution Act) payroll taxes, even though they can draw benefits when they retire. They have a special pension system, as well as health and life insurance. (Carl Albert, ex-Speaker of the House, gets $85,000 a year, which is more than the current Speaker earns.)

The question of wages has become a heated political issue, because many rich senators have voted to keep down salaries for the sake of public appearance. Some 18,350 federal workers earn more than senators. At the Pentagon, some 8,200 military personnel have higher salaries, too. So do cabinet officers ($80,100), the vice-president ($91,000), Supreme Court justices ($96,700), and federal district court judges ($73,300). According to the Joint Economic Committee of Congress, since 1969 the Consumer Price Index has risen 168 percent, while members' salaries increased by just 43 percent, making the honoraria for some a necessity.

◆ ◆ ◆ ◆

The Top-Grossing Speakers

Robert Dole (R–Kan): $135,750 ($51,500 to charity)
Ernest Hollings (D–S.C.): $92,270 (none to charity)
Pete Domenici (R–N.M.): $84,450 ($27,000 to charity)
Richard Lugar (R–Ind.): $66,875 ($3,175 to charity)
Jake Garn (R–Utah): $60,799 (none to charity)

David Durenberger (R–Minn.): $60,700 (none to charity)
Paul Laxalt (R–Nev.): $60,000 (none to charity)
Howard Baker (R–Tenn.): $60,000 ($4,000 to charity)
James McClure (R–Idaho): $59,950 (none to charity)
Orrin Hatch (R–Utah): $59,400 ($9,500 to charity)

Sources of Honoraria Payments for 1982 (total: $2,461,245)

Business Groups: $1,530,195
   Financial (banks, securities firms, etc.): $250,100
   Food and restaurant industries: $156,888
   Real-estate industry: $143,950
   Communications industry: $132,600
   Energy industry: $125,200
   Insurance industry: $110,250
Ideological groups (religious and political): $553,399
Professionals: $174,906
Health groups: $86,000
Agriculture interests: $70,484
Labor: $44,261

The Second Frankenstein Monster: Hitler Becomes Chancellor

BACKGROUND: It all seemed harmless in the beginning. Just a few old-fashioned conservatives looking for a man to do their bidding. The one they chose gave no warning that he had a genius for evil and destruction unmatched in modern history.

In 1933, Germany needed a strong, decisive leader. There had been a string of weak chancellors, including the conservative Franz von Papen, who had held the office for a few weeks in 1932. All the various political parties were without a hero. The National Socialists were the single largest party, but they and their leader, Adolf Hitler—who had served a term in prison for an attempted coup on the republican government—were disreputable, extremist, and out of the governing fold. However, many major capitalists—including Jews undisturbed by Hitler's anti-Semitism—had formed a Nazi "slush" fund known as the Keppler Circle. (The famous Flick conglomerate had donated nearly one million deutsche marks. When Hitler rose to power, Flick bought out many Jewish coal and steel families for a marching song.)

Egged on by the capitalists and by his conservative friends, von Papen approached Hitler with a proposition to help stem the rising civil violence between Nazis and Communists, and to prop up the collapsing parliamentary government.

THE DEAL FOR CHANCELLOR: Von Papen and his allies would swing their support to Hitler, allowing him to become chancellor of Germany. *But* he would be surrounded by them in various offices. The Foreign Ministry and the Ministry of Defense would remain in conservative hands. Hitler would meet with Germany's president only with von Papen present. In short, Hitler would be a puppet of the capitalists and the conservatives. He agreed to the terms.

RESULTS: On January 30, 1933, Adolf Hitler became chancellor of Germany. That night, the Nazi Brown Shirts roared through the streets. Since he had been appointed without an absolute majority, the Reichstag (parliament) was dissolved and a general election was called for March 5. On February 27, the Reichstag building was set on fire, and Hitler, as chancellor, blamed and banned the Communist party, increasing the Nazi majority. But to win the election with a firm lead, the Center (Roman Catholic) party was essential. Without von Papen's knowledge, Hitler made them an offer they could not refuse.

THE DEAL FOR DICTATOR: The Center party agreed to vote for Hitler if he promised to respect the Catholic schools and not interfere with them. He agreed, winning their vote.

RESULTS: On March 5, the National Socialists won a majority of seats. On March 23, the Reichstag passed the Enabling Act, which gave the government (i.e., Hitler) dictatorial powers. Only the Social Democrats dissented; their party was dissolved. In a matter of months, the puppet was pulling the strings. When the president died in 1934, Hitler confiscated his powers. In a year, he ruled supreme and Germany was quickly becoming a complete Fascist state, with hatred and persecution of all "non-Aryans," dissidents, and homosexuals the accepted policy. In 1938, a carefully orchestrated scandal led to the dismissal of the top military commanders, and their power was taken by Hitler and given to his closest aides. In less than five years, civilized Germany had descended to violent barbarism.

Terror without End: Chamberlain Attempts to Appease Hitler

BACKGROUND: By bending over backward before Hitler, British Prime Minister Chamberlain hoped to avoid another world war. Even though he got bent out of shape, Chamberlain learned there's just no appeasing some people.

Until Hitler attempted to subjugate Europe, commit genocide, and otherwise sink to depths of moral turpitude previously unknown, people didn't realize he absolutely could not be trusted. Neville Chamberlain feared that Hitler was a madman and hoped that he was not: Hitler was, after all, the legaly appointed chancellor of Europe's largest, richest, and potentially most powerful country. Germany, in the 1930s, still felt the humiliating sting of their defeat in World War I; under Hitler, they were determined to abnegate those provisions of the Versailles Treaty which, having been forced upon them in defeat, curtailed their power. Even Chamberlain believed that the more virulent aspects of Nazism would disappear once reasonable German grievances were "appeased." He looked forward to a prosperous alliance with a Germany newly restored to her rightful place in the West. (Secondarily, Chamberlain hoped that a strong Germany would provide a natural geographic bulwark to hold the dreaded Bolsheviks in check.)

Therefore, when, in 1936, Hitler sent his army to re-occupy the Rhineland, contrary to the Versailles Treaty, England was unconcerned: Weren't the Germans merely occupying their own territory, and didn't Hitler immediately announce that he had "no territorial claims in Europe"? And in 1938, when the German army marched into Austria, they were greeted, not by the anguished cries of a defeated population, but by enthusiastic mobs, cheering *"Ein Volk! Ein Reich! Ein Führer!"* Everyone hoped that Hitler would be content to stay put, digesting his native country, but they knew that now his eyes were cast upon the three and a half million Sudeten Germans living across the border in Czechoslovakia. Not that anyone really cared if the Sudeten Germans merged with Germany (Nazi enthusiasts, they were roused, like jealous lovers, at the spectacle of the Austrians being united with the fatherland). The problem was that Czechoslovakia, a crazy quilt of nationalities created from the fragments of the Austro-Hungarian Empire (including, besides the Sudetens, Czechs, Slovaks, Poles, Magyars, and—remember them?—the Ruthenians), was an island of democracy in Central Europe—and an

> "It is not my intention to smash Czechoslovakia by military action in the immediate future without provocation."
>
> Adolf Hitler,
> May 20, 1938

ally of France. France was, of course, an ally of England, and both countries touted themselves as great powers of the first rank. They couldn't sit back and do nothing as Germany gobbled up a large chunk of Czech territory, or could they? And to tell the truth, Chamberlain was not sure that Britain and France *could* rescue Czechoslovakia. Although they seemed to fear war more than defeat, it was true that the Germans had been spending 16.6 percent of their gross national product on armaments, while Britain and France had been spending a lackluster 7 percent. Chamberlain was determined to avoid a major conflagration that he was not sure he could win, for the dubious goal of denying national self-determination to pro-Nazi Sudeten Germans. (There was a chorus in the background—led by Churchill—which said that war was certain to come anyway, and the real issue was Hitler's determination to dominate Europe.)

To prevent the Germans from seizing the Sudetenland, Chamberlain came up with a radical solution: Why not just hand it to them? Surely if Hitler were pacified beyond his wildest expectations, he would settle down, and peace would be assured. Chamberlain, enthusiastic, volunteered to come to Germany. "Extra!" yelled the newsboys of Prague: "Read how the mighty head of the British Empire goes begging to Hitler!" Mussolini coolly remarked to his son-in-law: "There will be no war. But this is the liquidation of English prestige."

On September 15, 1938, with the Sudetens threatening to revolt and the Germans threatening to invade, Chamberlain, with the support of most of his nation, flew to Munich. The outcome was predictable: Hitler agreed to be given what he was threatening to seize, but he was dubious of Chamberlain's ability to obtain Czech agreement. Chamberlain flew home to tackle that one sticky problem, the question of getting the Czechs to agree to the voluntary dismemberment of their country. France was the key: If the Czechs were certain that their putatively strong ally would desert them, they'd be forced to agree. France, as reluctant to fight Germany as England was, was willing to apply some "friendly pressure" on the Czechs to cede the Sudetenland, but only if England agreed to guarantee the new borders. England, unwilling to guarantee the original, stronger state, reluctantly agreed to guarantee the truncated nation. Driven to it by France and England, the president of Czechoslovakia agreed to relinquish the Sudetenland.

Chamberlain, relieved and certain that war would now be averted, flew back to Germany on September 21 to discuss details of the transfer. He was shocked to discover that Hitler had upped the ante. Hitler now wanted to send his army into the Sudetenland "forthwith." Ger-

> "You were given the choice between war and dishonor. You have chosen dishonor; you will have war."
>
> Winston Churchill, 1938

mans, he insisted, were being slaughtered on the streets of Czechoslovakia (some people had been killed in violent demonstrations), and he could not discuss diplomatic niceties while Germans were dying. He was adamant and quoted an old German proverb to an astonished Chamberlain: "An end, even with terror, is better than terror without end." Historians are still debating his motives, but his fellow countryman, Sigmund Freud, explained: "You cannot tell what a madman will do. You know, he is an Austrian and lived for years in great misery." With Chamberlain imploring him to postpone the invasion, Hitler agreed to wait, but only until October 1—eight days away.

Chamberlain flew home to a nation newly outraged, their tolerance for Hitler's ultimatums exhausted by his refusal to make even a show of legality. War preparations were begun. Trenches were dug in London parks; the pathetic arsenal of forty-four antiaircraft guns were put into place; thirty-eight million gas masks were distributed. On September 28, the day Hitler had given the Czechs as the deadline for acceptance of his demands, as Chamberlain addressed a tense House of Commons called to special session, a dramatic message arrived from an unexpected savior: Mussolini had persuaded Hitler to postpone the invasion and convene a four-power conference to settle the matter. In an explosion of relief, the M.P.s rose to their feet, cheering. At the airport the following day, Chamberlain quoted Shakespeare: "Out of this nettle, danger, we pluck this flower, safety," and flew off, once again, to Munich.

The four-power conference (England, France, Germany, and Italy—Hitler refused to allow Czechoslovakia to attend) was prepared in haste and begun in chaos, with no agenda, no chairman, and no agreed procedures. It devolved to a clanging of individual speeches, with three of the four heads of state often speaking at once. Finally, Il Duce, the only person present who could speak all four languages (poorly, but never mind) took charge as mediator. He submitted a written proposal on the Sudeten question, which he claimed he'd written—but it had actually been penned by the Germans. With the Czechs sweating it out in a nearby hallway, their fate was sealed in under thirty hours.

THE DEAL: The Czechs would withdraw, in stages, from October 1 to October 10, from the areas of the Sudetenland where there was an undisputed German majority. The German army would come in immediately after them. An international commission, composed of the four powers and the Czechs, would decide where, in cases where the population was very mixed, there would be plebiscites held to deter-

When a fool holds his tongue, he too is thought clever.

Yiddish saying

A wagging tongue bites itself.

French saying

If you can't bite, don't show your teeth.

Yiddish saying

mine which nationality was preferred. Once these plebiscites were held, the commission would designate the final borders. Residents wishing to migrate to the other state would be given six months to do so. France and England agreed to guarantee the new Czech state.

The following morning, Chamberlain presented Hitler with an agreement which read: "We regard the agreement signed last night . . . as symbolic of the desire of our two peoples never to go to war with one another again. We are resolved that the method of consultation shall be the method adopted to deal with any other questions that may concern our two countries." "*Ja, ja!*" Hitler exclaimed, as he read the agreement, but witnesses claim there was a peculiar gleam in his eyes as he signed it.

"I believe it is peace for our time."
Chamberlain, September 30, 1937.

RESULTS: "I believe it is peace for our time," Chamberlain said as he waved the agreement to the cheering crowds that greeted him in London. "I have no more territorial demands to make in Europe," declared Hitler. The Czechs left the Sudetenland and, diminished, Czechoslovakia fell to pieces six months later, with Hungary grabbing a bit and Germany seizing the rest. Hitler himself spent the night of March 15, 1939, at the palace in Prague. His credibility in England was finally destroyed: Here was a dictator who could not be trusted. In spite of the guarantee England and France had given Czechoslovakia, there was nothing they could do by then—Czechoslovakia no longer existed. But by the time Germany attacked Poland on August 31, England and Poland had an alliance. On September 3, as German planes destroyed Warsaw, England and France finally declared war on Germany.

The spasm of horror known as World War II quickly spread across the globe and lasted for six years. Of the 53,477,000 who died, 38,573,000 were civilians, as war conventions were violated on a scale never before experienced.

Hitler committed suicide just before the surrender of the German army. Mussolini was hanged by Italian partisans. History has judged Chamberlain's policy of appeasement very harshly. Germany was divided and has been occupied by the Allies since the end of the war. Czechoslovakia was reestablished and promptly expelled all three million Sudeten Germans living within its borders—settling that question, once and for all.

FDR's "Brand-new" Garden Hose and the Birth of the CIA: Lend-Lease

BACKGROUND: Good politicians are masters at word games. They say what they mean without meaning what they say, and the fate of nations hangs in the balance. And sometimes they even know what they are doing. . . .

On August 25, 1939, Britain signed a mutual assistance treaty with Poland. The following week, Germany invaded Poland, forcing Britain into war on the same day that Churchill regained a place in the cabinet as first lord of the admiralty. Churchill had been branded a warmonger and kept out of the official government by Prime Minister Chamberlain, who believed appeasement of Germany and Hitler was the one way to save Britain, whose army was barely beyond the standard of 1918. There were not even enough revolvers to supply all the officers. The return of Churchill to power marked the end of appeasement as the only response to Hitler. On September 11, with Chamberlain's permission, FDR (code name "Potus"—president of the United States) suggested that he and Churchill (code name "Naval Person") share a confidential exchange of naval information. William Stephenson, the head of British Intelligence (code name "Intrepid") was chosen as personal messenger.

For four hundred years, British Intelligence was the most complex and best coordinated in the world. Americans had no overseas secret service; the FBI was confined to United States borders. FDR was openly committed to Great Britain "in case of war"—and he would lead United States public opinion by defining the economic price America would pay if Hitler conquered Europe. Stephenson delivered to FDR incontestable evidence that Hitler intended to invade and destroy Britain in his plans for the New German Empire. Where would he go from there? FDR immediately set up a meeting between Stephenson and J. Edgar Hoover. The FBI was not in alliance with British Intelligence because the State Department had insisted the prewar friendship be broken due to the U.S. Neutrality Act. Without the knowledge of the State Department, and acting with a Jeffersonian interpretation of the Constitution that "the transaction of business with foreign nations is executive altogether," FDR authorized "the closest possible marriage" between the FBI and British Intelligence while he pressured Congress to change the Neutrality Act. A 1919 statute still in force allowed outdated arms not necessary to United States defense to be sold without permission of the Congress or the secretary of war. FDR began secretly shipping military equipment across the Canadian border to avoid riling the powerful isolationist movements. He was facing a new campaign for his third term as president on a platform of peace and neutrality. He supplied a half million rifles, eighty thousand machine guns, and shells, bombs, and hundreds of thousands of tons of metals for British arsenals.

In September of 1939, he successfully pressed Congress to revise the neutrality laws to a "cash and carry" basis. No credit. No loans. According to the polls, 90 percent of the American public favored such a change, because the existing law was aiding aggressors. As FDR convincingly insisted: "There is far less chance of the United States getting into war if we do all we can now to support the nations defending themselves against attack." Britain placed a $1.33 billion order for military equipment. In May of 1940, Churchill became the new prime minister of England. He informed FDR that cash was becoming a serious problem. They had $1.4 billion more to spend. They had over $2 billion in credits and property in the United States and $8 billion in Canada, but cash—and materials easily converted to cash—was at a premium. If they spent all of it on making war, how could they feed themselves? By July, Britain was armed, and the center of Britain's secret-service operations, British Security Coordination (BSC) was moved to Rockefeller Center in New York City, safe from the Nazis who had just conquered France across the narrow English Channel. Desperate for immediate sea support, Churchill urgently needed fifty or sixty destroyers from FDR. To pay in cash would leave them at this crucial time dangerously short of funds. FDR replied that the navy flatly refused, "in the present anxiety about defense," to part with fifty destroyers. He dared not risk an executive order to circumvent cash and carry, with the election only four months away; and he could not wage a battle with Congress to change the Neutrality Act of 1939 because it would take too long—England might be invaded by then.

THE FIRST DEAL: Churchill and Lord Lothian, Britain's ambassador to the U.S., knew the United States Navy had been pressing England for bases. It was proposed that FDR "transfer" the ships to Britain in exchange for ninety-nine-year leases on bases in Newfoundland, Bermuda, the Bahamas, Saint Lucia, Trinidad, and British Guiana. FDR agreed and gave a press conference announcing negotiations to "acquire" naval and air bases.

RESULTS: With Naval Operations approval, the Justice Department decided this could be done, because "transfer" did not impinge on cash and carry. Even Wendell Willkie, FDR's opponent in the coming election, approved of the transfer, although he did not like the idea that a Senate vote had been circumvented and "the voice of the people" not heard. FDR had newspaper editorials and polls to prove he was not ignoring the voice of the people.

In August, the Battle of Britain began: under Goering's direction, Germany savagely attacked England from the skies. The blitz, or bombing of London and other key cities, commenced in September. Many in Britain, including Lord Halifax, the foreign secretary, wanted Churchill to make peace with Hitle; while in Washington, American Ambassador to England Joseph Kennedy testified before House and Senate committees to condemn Churchill and to swear that Nazi Germany could never be beaten. Churchill swore: "We shall never surrender!"

In November 1940, FDR was triumphantly returned to office. Both parties had promised aid to Britain; both parties had promised continuation of neutrality. By early 1941, Britain needed equipment for ten divisions and twenty-six thousand airplanes. It was a $5 billion order that would put the United States on full wartime production and provide an economic bonanza. FDR's advisers said $250 million had to be paid immediately; it would require over $600 million to prepare United States industry for production. Churchill replied: "We should stand stripped to the bone." FDR got him twenty-six Flying Fortresses, "to test out under combat conditions," but with $10 billion in investments in North America, England had a weak case in claiming

"Our comradeship and our brotherhood in war were unexampled. We stood together and because of that the free world now stands."

Churchill, on being made an honorary citizen of the United States poverty. Then, FDR found "the ways and means" that would not only clear the way for all-out aid to Britain, but also gain for the United States what he believed it most needed (now that the bases were secured) to fight and win the war that he knew could no longer be avoided. He told America he was trying "something brand new."

A NEW DEAL: "To get away from the dollar sign," and derail cash and carry, FDR had the Treasury write H.R. 1776: "An Act To Further Promote The Defense of The United States, And For Other Purposes." It became known as the Lend-Lease Act. It authorized the president, without recourse to Congress, "to sell, transfer title to, exchange, lease, lend, or otherwise dispose of . . . any defense article . . . to any country whose defense the President deems vital to the defense of the United States." Repayment was to be decided by the president, "in kind or property or any other direct or indirect benefit" that he considered satisfactory. The bill became law in March 1941. The "benefit" FDR requested: England was to secretly organize an American intelligence service equal to its own superb BSC.

RESULTS: England's $5 billion equipment order—eventually $31 billion—was converted into a United States order for American industry, then "lent" to Great Britain. FDR compared it to lending a neighbor his garden hose to put out a fire. "I don't want $15—I want my garden hose back after the fire is over." Instead of a garden hose, he got back what would soon evolve into the CIA. By the end of 1941, the United States was paying for England's war and in effect was fighting an undeclared war of its own against Nazi tyranny, a war led by a president with full power to intervene in foreign affairs as he saw fit. "When the war is won," FDR said, "the powers under which I act automatically revert to the people—to whom they belong."

Nevertheless, in 1940, those involved in the resettling of the BSC into Rockefeller Center were sworn to secrecy to protect both the organization and FDR, who could have faced impeachment for his "binding agreements" with Churchill, in violation of a strict reading of the Neutrality Act. William ("Big Bill") Donovan, who had acted for FDR as secret courier the way Stephenson had done for Churchill, and who had been a prime negotiator during the bases-for-warships trade, was appointed FDR's coordinator of information for the newly formed centralized agency: Office of Strategic Services (OSS); it was to report directly to the Joint Chiefs of Staff. Now, no longer would the United States depend upon military attachés and diplomats for scraps of information about foreign nations.

In 1945, after the war, President Truman saw no need for British-American coordinated services; he disbanded the OSS. In 1946, he set up the National Intelligence Authority. In 1947, in response to the Cold War, he created the CIA, "a peacetime foreign intelligence agency." British Intelligence, to this day, firmly believes that in 1940, FDR would not have run for a third term had Churchill not been resolved to fight Hitler and had Churchill not made it clear that he could not succeed without FDR's assistance.

S.C.R.A.M.: The Atomic Energy Commission and Big Business

BACKGROUND: Atoms are miniature solar systems. The nucleus, at the center, is like our sun, with electrons orbiting it like our planets. The nucleus consists of protons and neutrons, its weight determined by their number, its glue nature's most powerful force—nuclear energy. When a nucleus is split by a well-aimed alien neutron, this energy is released. (Uranium was the original choice to "fission," because its nucleus is crammed to bursting and easily shattered.) Rather than

Nuclear power enthusiasts show their support of the industry by jogging with a 12-inch chunk of nuclear fuel rod.

making only explosions when the atom was split, the plan was to produce electricity "too cheap to meter." It seemed simple. So, what went wrong?

In 1946, Congress and Truman established the United States Atomic Energy Commission (AEC), which provided civilian control over nuclear weaponry and energy. It forbad private ownership of nuclear materials. The AEC was to set guidelines for the commercial nuclear-energy industry, deciding what a public utility could do with the atom. It was to encourage the idea of freely developing nuclear energy while, *at the same time*, preaching restraint and respect for this volatile merchandise. No one could stop splitting nuclei once they started, and chain reactions occurred when freed neutrons shot into surrounding nuclei. The process could be *slowed down* by inserting control rods into reactors during fission. These rods absorbed some flying neutrons before they hit a whole nucleus, but it was a bit like protecting an ovum from marauding sperm. (The original nuclear reactor at the University of Chicago had a suspended control rod with an ax to cut the rope: "Safety Control Rod Ax Man" = S.C.R.A.M.) Everyone knew that the most basic problem was safety, but who needed government strictures for an industry that didn't yet exist?

Attention was focused on what nuclear energy could do, *would do*, very soon, if the right industries became interested in development. The AEC's General Advisory Committee was not as eager for development as was the AEC itself. They saw a long road ahead before reactors would be safe and feasible; this was because the top scientists and engineers refused to design the reactors, since all the glamorous work had already been done and all the Nobel Prizes awarded. While the AEC encouraged bigger bombs, people hesitated to invest money in the very dangerous atom. Then along came Admiral Hyman Rickover. He wanted to build a nuclear submarine for the navy, but he needed practical solutions to his queries. He turned to the industries developing mobile power systems.

THE FIRST DEAL: Rickover and the AEC would foot the bill for a lab that Westinghouse Electric Corporation would build at Bettis Airport near Pittsburgh. Westinghouse did not know what it would be doing beyond getting a free ride to develop (and patent) nuclear energy equipment. The contract detailed nothing: It simply guaranteed that both the AEC and Westinghouse would work "in a spirit of partnership and friendly cooperation with maximum effort and common sense in achieving their common goal."

RESULTS: This became the basis upon which companies undertook future business with the AEC. The "partnership" ended the AEC's policing function. By January 1954, Rickover's submarine was a proven success, and interest swelled in nuclear energy. In August, Congress passed a new law giving the AEC unrestricted power to give licenses to *private* industry to build and run power stations. Anyone who applied for a license got one. Detailed plans of projected projects were unnecessary because no one knew exactly how to develop their ideas. Besides, theoretical safety precautions had never actually been tested. Why bother putting restraints on creative endeavor? But the builders promised not to use the plants unless they were safe. "What precisely is *safe*?" wondered the AEC's general advisors. "We'll know when we see it. Trust us," the licensees successfully argued. No mention was made of nuclear waste.

There were about thirty-one references in the new law to the "health and safety of the public," but no one got specific. Then business started to worry about law suits "exceeding available insurance." Who would have to pay if something went wrong? But, hypothetically speaking, what *if*, God forbid!—and Lewis Strauss, chairman of AEC, claimed "Divine Providence" was guiding AEC—*what if* there were an accident? Congress and AEC worked out a solution with company lobbyists.

THE SECOND DEAL: The Price Anderson Act was passed in 1957. In case of an accident at a nuclear reactor, *no one* had a legal claim against the builders or operators or licensors of the plant. No matter what the company's culpability was, it was forever blameless. A money fund of $560 million was started by the AEC and private insurance companies to cover victims; industry was not required to contribute or to pay when the money ran out. To the act was added a plan for tax incentives to any company taking a fling at atomic development, no matter what its ability: free nuclear fuel for seven years, government funding for reactor designing, and free assistance in AEC labs if the companies built the nuclear plants themselves. All profits from sales of plants to utilities belonged to the companies.

RESULTS: Price Anderson effectively repealed every citizen's right to sue for damages caused by someone else's negligence. That year, Rickover, the AEC, Westinghouse, and Duquesne Electrical Power of Pittsburgh built the water-cooled, uranium-fueled Shippingport Nuclear Power Station on the North Ohio River. It worked, but it cost so much to run that it couldn't pay its own bills. (The estimated building cost was $91.5 million; the actual cost was approximately $968 million.) The AEC overlooked these warnings of future fiscal grief.

> Even now, perhaps a majority of our countrymen still believe that science and technics can solve all human problems. They have no suspicion that our runaway science and technics themselves have come to constitute the main problem the human race has to overcome.
>
> Lewis Mumford

Physicist Edward Teller actively preached that safety measures "retarded development" and with Strauss demanded full-steam ahead on water-cooled and "breeder" reactors. (Breeders are so called because their plutonium is wrapped in uranium that "breeds" more plutonium when those neutrons start flying about. A breeder reactor can explode; water-cooled reactors cannot—they overheat and melt. Unstoppable, the core would burn through the earth all the way to China; thus, the "China Syndrome.") The AEC Advisory Committee reported on this. The AEC suppressed the reports. Strauss did not want to frighten the public. There were enough problems already: The United Auto Workers challenged AEC authorization for the Fermi Breeder Reactor within the city limits of Detroit. The UAW lost its suit when the Supreme Court ruled that the AEC could do whatever it pleased.

By 1961, with all roads cleared for a government-subsidized nuclear industry, there were two plants in operation and five under construction. That was it. They cost too much and their generated electricity was 30 to 60 percent more expensive than that from fossil fuel or hydro power. Enter Nobel-Prize Laureate Glenn Seaborg, who had "birthed" the new element plutonium in 1941. His immortality was on the line, and from 1961 to 1971 he unscrupulously pushed nuclear energy with all the authority his scientific honors could bring to the chairmanship of the AEC. He proved to be a master salesperson, and the world was ready to believe him.

By January 1971, fifty-three reactors were under construction. A test of the most popular cooling system (E.C.C.S.) failed to cool the reactor. The AEC announced they would "provide reasonable assurance" that such systems would be effective in the "unlikely event" of an accident. When two members argued with the statement, they were fired. Although hearings were arranged by the AEC to examine the E.C.C.S., the commission ignored all signs of danger and granted more permits.

When James Schlesinger took over the AEC in July 1971, he promised to regulate the industry. He commissioned the "Reactor Safety Study" to quell doubts, but the AEC made Dr. Norman C. Rasmussen of M.I.T. study director. Unequipped for the job and unabashedly pro–nuclear energy, his study found the whole business to be sound and safe. Nevertheless, in 1974, Congress abolished the AEC. The Department of Energy was formed to promote nuclear energy; the Nuclear Regulatory Commission (NRC) was put in charge of safety. But reactors were still built following the AEC's vague regulations, with designs winging it on matters of safety.

"As we look at the status of nuclear energy development, we see something solid. We find that quietly, without fanfare, the thing we have been waiting for has happened: the age of nuclear power has begun."

Glenn Seaborg,
September 1964

By 1970, nuclear energy was producing less than .5 percent of the country's energy. In 1972, the Fermi Atomic Power Plant in Detroit was sealed up forever after a meltdown. On March 28, 1979, one-year-old Three Mile Island near Harrisburg, Pennsylvania, had the first "general emergency" when a meltdown began as the core of the reactor reached three thousand degrees. There was total panic at the collapse of the system. It took fifteen hours, fifty minutes to stabilize it. The "experts" did not believe the instruments because the situation "should never have been that grave." (Some of the alarm signals were on the *back* of the control console and could not be seen by board operators when the water-cooled system failed.) After that, no new orders for nuclear plants were placed with the NRC. Forty-eight were canceled. Seventy-three are still in operation.

But what about the fifty-nine already built and waiting for NRC operating licenses? Since 1979, twenty-seven have gotten the go-ahead, though none of the problems that caused Three Mile Island have been solved. By 1983, nuclear energy was the second largest producer of electricity: 12.5 percent. There was still no permanent system for safe disposal of nuclear waste, but there is a law requiring "safe" evacuation routes. NRC? AEC? There seems to be little difference . . .

The Permanence of the Provisional: The Geneva Conference, 1954

BACKGROUND: The French say, "there is nothing more permanent than the provisional," and in Vietnam, their former colony, that nearly turned out to be the case. Only twenty years of bloody struggle reunited the country, "provisionally" divided for what was to have been a two-year period.

The Vietnamese had established their record of strong national identity back in the year 939 when they successfully fought the Chinese to win their independence. But they were no technological matc for the French, who subjugated them in the nineteenth century. A nationalist movement arose almost immediately, which sought to oust the French (who were there because of an economic interest in raw materials and a market for their goods). The French were temporarily replaced by the Japanese during World War II, but, aided by their British ally, they returned after the war. No one was pleased to see them again, and anti-imperialist forces from all sides of the political spectrum banded together under the popular Ho Chi Minh. That Ho was a Communist did not bother his followers, many of whom were not; they felt that his leadership represented their best chance to eliminate foreign domination. The French trotted out Bao Dai, the French-educated hereditary emperor of Vietnam, but he was a very unpopular and ineffectual leader whom most regarded as nothing more than a French puppet. In 1946, the conflict known as the French Indochina War erupted; Ho established his capital at Hanoi and quickly came to dominate most of the countryside, while the French controlled Saigon and some of the other cities.

By 1950, France, bled dry by this colonial war so far from home (and following so quickly on the heels of World War II), and losing badly, turned to the United States for aid. By 1954, the United States was paying 80 percent of their war bill—about $500 million annually. Critics in the United States said that America was paying for a colonial war which ran counter to the wishes of the native population, but Secretary of State Dean Acheson said that we were contributing to the development of "genuine nationalism." His successor in the Eisenhower administration, John Foster Dulles, hinted broadly that the United States just might resort to the use of nuclear weapons against the Viet Minh (as the anti-imperialist forces were called). But even with vast amounts of American military aid, the French were unable to defeat Ho—in fact, they were still losing badly. When twenty thousand French soldiers were surrounded at Dien Bien Phu, the French requested that America send in troops. Vice-President Nixon floated a trial balloon to the American people: "To avoid further Communist expansion . . . in Indochina, we must take the risk now by putting our boys in." Massive public hostility to this remark caused the Eisenhower administration to back down (Korea was still on everyone's mind). Instead, the French virtually admitted defeat and called a peace conference in Geneva, with delegates from the United States, England, the USSR, France, China, and Vietnam meeting to discuss the future of the embattled country.

THE DEAL: Vietnam would be temporarily divided at the 17th Parallel, with the Bao Dai government controlling the south and the Ho Chi Minh government controlling the north. Viet Minh forces would withdraw from the south, and French Union forces from the north. In July of 1956, free national elections would be held to elect a permanent government for the entire country.

Geneva, 1954.

RESULTS: The unpopular government of South Vietnam, knowing that it could never defeat the popular Ho, refused to participate in national elections, claiming that it had never agreed to the results of the Geneva Conference.

By 1955, the French left Vietnam. America continued to pour millions of dollars in military aid into the south. In 1955, Bao Dai was ousted by the American-backed anti-Communist strongman, Ngo Dinh Diem, in an election so rigged that Diem received more votes than there were registered voters. His autocratic regime, armed to the teeth by the United States, appeared to be stable for a few years; but in 1960, a coalition of the Viet Minh in the north and nationalists in the south began a "National Front for the Liberation of the South," to overthrow Diem and unite the country. America upped the ante and sent in "advisors": In 1962, there were 8,000 Americans working with Diem's army; by 1963, there were 25,000. By 1963, the United States was convinced that Diem was more of a political liability than he was worth, and he was assassinated in a CIA–approved action just three weeks before President John Kennedy was shot. His replacement proved to be no more popular, however, and by 1968, in spite of the presence of 500,000 American combat troops and a war budget of $30 billion a year, it was clear that all the United States had achieved was an "escalating military stalemate." In 1973, a peace treaty between the United States and North Vietnam ended American involvement. The number of Americans who died there was 56,000, and another 303,000 had been wounded. Among the Vietnamese, 1.3 million were killed.

On April 29, 1975, completely overrun by troops from the north, the government in Saigon surrendered. Vietnam, once again, was united.

Princess of a Flower Pot: Grace Kelly and Prince Rainier III

BACKGROUND: Men have done many things to be guaranteed an heir. Few have done it so publicly as Prince Rainier of Monaco, who had more to lose than most.

Monaco is an independent principality of 464 acres—extended from 375 by landfill—on the Mediterranean, an enclave within Alpes-Maritimes departement in southeastern France. It consists of three adjoining sections: La Condamine (the business district); Monte Carlo (the gambling district); and Monaco-Ville (the hilltop capital district). With its natural harbor and mild climate, it is one of the most popular tourist spots on the Riviera. It has a population of about twenty-four thousand, but only about twenty-five hundred are citizens of Monaco (*Monegasques*) and they are forbidden to gamble at the casino.

Monaco has been ruled by the Genovese Grimaldi family since 1297. In 1861, the tiny principality came under French protection, but its crowned head remained an absolute ruler until 1911 when a constitution was promulgated, then redrafted in 1918, giving France powers that were indirectly responsible for the making of an American myth.

THE FRENCH DEAL: Under the new constitution, France has the right of approval on Monaco's successors to the throne. If the throne becomes vacant of a male heir, Monaco becomes an autonomous state under French protection. In return, Monaco has a customs union with France, their currencies are interchangeable, and they receive

French protection in case of war, as well as tax and military exemptions.

RESULTS: Prince Rainier III succeeded his grandfather, Louis II, in 1949. He was in need of a fecund wife. For four years he dated the French actress Gisele Pascal, but not only was she reportedly unable to have children, she also refused to give up her career for a crown.

Enter Grace Kelly of Philadelphia and Hollywood. Born in 1930, she was the daughter of an Irish and German immigrant family—her mother was German—that built a multimillion-dollar masonry empire (and Philly's famous Packard Building). Her father, nearly the city's mayor, had many influential friends, and after Grace graduated from drama school in New York City, they helped her get her career off the ground in television and the movies. Her patrician beauty—though she was far from aristocratic in breeding and had no place on the Main Line circuit—and her strongly comedic acting talent were parlayed into stardom. To moviegoers in the fifties, she projected the image of "ice queen," the antithesis of that *other* blonde, the hot "love goddess" Monroe. It was Grace the Good versus Marilyn the Bad, until Hitchcock gave her a sexual identity on screen when he molded her into the paradigm of his cool-blonde heroine. She made eleven films in barely six years, winning an Oscar for the forgettable *The Country Girl*, defeating the unforgettable Judy Garland in *A Star Is Born*.

Grace met Rainier in 1955. She was filming Hitchcock's *To Catch a Thief* on the Riviera when *Paris-Match* brought them together for a magazine article. At the end of the year, he arranged to be invited to the Kelly home for Christmas Day. Three days later they announced their engagement.

THE AMERICAN DEAL: In return for producing a male heir for his throne, giving up her career, accepting the impossibility of divorce, and adding Hollywood glamor to a moribund gambling town for the decadent rich, she received a title (Her Serene Highness), tax exemption for her multimillion-dollar fortune, a two-hundred-room pink palace, all the perks of royalty, and a role she could never outgrow.

RESULTS: The wedding in 1956 was one of the most flamboyant of the century and made global headlines, giving Monaco a tourism boost unlike anything in its entire history. Princess Grace, Her Serene Highness, was hailed as a fairy-tale figure made manifest, though she said, "that sounds very icky and revolting. I certainly don't think of my life as a fairy tale." She confessed that she married "on instinct," and it turned out to be the smartest career move of her life. She enlarged the Grace-the-Good persona to such a degree that Brigitte Bardot—another French monarch of sorts—dubbed Grace, "Her Majesty the Frigidaire." A male heir was born in 1958.

During her reign, Monaco ran into trouble with France, and in 1963 new fiscal arrangements helped to prevent the French populace from using Monaco as a tax shelter. Four years later, to reclaim its integrity, the government of Monaco bought out shipping magnate Aristotle Onassis, who owned most of the businesses in the principality. In September 1982, Princess Grace was killed in a car accident. The official release was that the fifty-two-year-old Grace suffered a stroke at the wheel, but her body was found in the back seat of the car, while her daughter (unlicensed to drive) was found alive and slightly injured in the front. It had the makings of a wrong turn in a Hitchcock thriller, but the authorities in Monaco insisted that Grace was driving; the promising mystery-movie scenario was shelved as the entire world mourned the loss of Princess Grace. Along with Jackie Onassis [see "How Do I Love Thee? Let Me Count the Ways: Jackie and Ari," page 89] and Elizabeth Taylor [see "When ET Played Cleopatra . . . and Lost: Elizabeth Taylor," page 354] she had, in the words of Newsweek, "maintained a feverish public interest longer than any celebrity in our time."

Nuclear Brinkmanship: The Cuban Missile Crisis

BACKGROUND: The world has never been as close to the brink of nuclear destruction as it was during the Cuban missile crisis in 1962. But just in time, Soviet Premier Nikita Khrushchev packed up his Cuban missile base and sent it home, forestalling Armageddon in exchange for a simple promise from President John F. Kennedy.

It began when, just one year after Kennedy was completely humiliated by the fiasco of the Bay of Pigs invasion, and just weeks before a crucial midterm election that could have cost the Democrats the House, the president learned that the Russians were installing nuclear-missile launching sites in Cuba just ninety miles off the American coast. Not that proximity, in an age of intercontinental missiles, meant that much strategically, but Cold War emotions were running high. Secretary of Defense Robert McNamara explained: "A missile is a missile. It makes no great difference whether you are killed by a missile fired from the Soviet Union or from Cuba." But he added that if the United States allowed a Russian missile base in Cuba, "the political effect in Latin America would be large." Special White House Counsel Theodore Sorensen later wrote: "To be sure, these Cuban missiles alone, in view of all the other megatonnage the Soviets were capable of unleashing upon us, did not substantially alter the strategic balance in fact. . . . But that balance would have been substantially altered in appearance; and in matters of national will and world leadership, as the president later said, such appearances contribute to reality."

With a flair for the dramatic so powerful the world was left stunned, JFK decided to forgo traditional diplomacy and deliver an ultimatum to the Russians on live television. On that Monday evening, October 22, Kennedy declared that he was calling a naval "quarantine" of Cuba (he chose the medical term because "blockades" are banned by international law). All ships coming within five hundred miles of the island would be searched, and if they were found to contain "offensive" weapons, they would be turned back. He would lift the "quarantine" only after the missiles were withdrawn. The United States then encircled the island with 180 ships, including 8 aircraft carriers. United States armed forces were put on war alert and the Strategic Air Command was put on full war footing, just one step away from actual hostilities. Most of the arsenal of B–52 bombers, loaded with nuclear weapons, was kept airborne, and, together with 156 intercontinental missiles in the United States and 105 short-range missiles that America had in Europe, the United States had the nuclear equivalent of 30 billion tons of TNT aimed at the Soviet Union.

On October 23, the day following Kennedy's speech, Khrushchev denounced the blockade as "outright banditry." He ordered Soviet ships to proceed to Cuba—but as they approached the five-hundred-mile zone proscribed by the blockade, they suddenly turned around. The following day, a couple of Russian tankers entered the zone, submitted to being searched, and were allowed to proceed. Reconnaissance photos indicated that the Russians were actually speeding up their construction of the launching sites. The Joint Chiefs of Staff were clamoring to bomb Cuba. Attorney General Robert Kennedy later wrote: "They seemed always ready to assume that a war was in our national interest."

The Soviet Union insisted that the missiles were being put in Cuba solely for defensive purposes, and the Cubans insisted that they had legitimate reasons to bolster their defense: The United States had a long history of invading Cuba, starting in 1898 (that time they stayed seven years) and again as recently as the year before. Russia was merely helping her ally for "humanitarian" reasons.

Robert Kennedy later wrote of those days: "I felt we were on the edge of a precipice with no way off. . . . President Kennedy had initiated the course of events, but he no longer controlled them." The president sent his brother Robert to tell the Russian ambassador "that if they did not remove those bases, we would remove them." Robert Kennedy said that on Saturday, October 27, "the expectation was a military confrontation by Tuesday." "It was a time," wrote Khrushchev, "when the smell of burning was in the air." One whiff was enough for the Soviet premier—he came up with a plan for peace.

THE DEAL: The Soviet Union would dismantle and remove its missile sites (under U.N. supervision), in exchange for a promise that the United States would *never* again invade Cuba.

RESULTS: Castro was furious, and he refused to allow the U.N. in to inspect. The United States had to rely upon reconnaissance photos and sight inspection of Soviet ships carrying off the missiles. Robert Kennedy, in his book about the crisis entitled *Thirteen Days*, wrote of JFK and his closest advisors: "The fourteen people involved were very significant . . . probably the brightest kind of group that you could get together under those circumstances. If six of them had been president of the United States, I think the world might have been blown up." The arms race has more than kept pace with the Cold War, and today the planet bristles with over fifty thousand nuclear warheads, none of them in Cuba.

The Democrats won the November election.

A Tear in the Curtain: The Exchange of East German Political Prisoners

BACKGROUND: In the early 1960s, the East German government discovered it had an abundance of an unusual resource that easily fetched a high price in the affluent West: political prisoners.

In the years before the political boundary known as the iron curtain materialized into the Berlin Wall, hundreds of thousands of East Germans moved to West Germany every year. When the total of those who left exceeded three million and the exodus showed no signs of abating, in 1961 the East Germans, strapped by labor shortages, built the wall to stem the tide. Soon their jails, already crowded with political and religious dissidents, filled with people caught trying to escape and a generous sprinkling of Westerners apprehended for aiding escape attempts, or for the more serious charge of spying.

After the United States and the USSR collaborated in the 1962 exchange of U-2 pilot Frances Powers for the Russian spy Colonel Abel, Willy Brandt, who was mayor of West Berlin at that time, was inspired to explore the possibility of prisoner exchange on a larger scale. A West Berlin lawyer named Jurgen Stange was brought in because of his friendship with a politically well-connected East Berlin lawyer named Dr. Wolfgang Vogel—their offices, in fact, had been just a few minutes apart until the wall added an hour and a half to the trip. Stange asked his friend Vogel to find out if the government of East Germany could be induced, for any reason, to release some of the political prisoners it held. He returned with startling news, exceeding everyone's expectations: Not only were they interested but on a scale far beyond the capacity of the West Berlin municipal government. For ten thousand dollars per head, they would be willing to trade thousands of people. Stange went to Bonn to explain the situation to West German Chancellor Conrad Adenauer, who ultimately agreed, in principle, to ransom prisoners. But he would not consider actually forking over large sums of coveted hard currency to the East Germans, who would then be free to spend it on the open market, where their own currency was fairly worthless and where they might purchase military hardware the West certainly would not like to fund. Perhaps they were interested in something other than cash?

THE DEAL: The East Germans could regard the West as one great big department store, and each prisoner was a charge card with a personal credit limit of ten thousand dollars. Instead of getting cash, the East Germans would be paid in goods of their choosing: coffee, tropical fruits, pharmaceutical products, tractors—things hard to come by in Communist-bloc countries. West Germany got to choose the people they would rescue.

RESULTS: By 1979, fifteen thousand prisoners had been traded. With adjustments for inflation, and the odd prisoner who cost more (highly trained technicians went for double the average), the West Germans paid over $300 million. The elegant Dr. Vogel, one of very few private lawyers still practicing in East Berlin, is thought to have collected a 10-percent commission on these swaps, making him a very rich

"If the serious Western press continues to write about it as 'trade in human flesh' I wouldn't be surprised if one day the government here said 'All right, that's the end of it.'"

East German lawyer,
Wolfgang Vogel

man. He has a big Mercedes, custom-made suits, a lakeside vacation home, a fashionable office with four secretaries—in other words, a lifestyle that is completely anomalous in East Germany. Asked about the morality of his government's "sale" of human beings, Vogel replied: "They have to make good on the damage they have caused the state by their crimes—sabotage, trying to escape, the cost of training them, and so on."

When the usually spartan marketplaces of East Germany are suddenly chock-a-block with consumer goods, few are aware that the presence of these delicacies signals the release of yet another batch of prisoners. And while the super-high-tech border controls now in use have reduced to a mere trickle the number of people who still try to escape, some two hundred people a year manage to do it. Ironically, many of them are border guards.

Dealmaker as Nobel Laureate: Henry Kissinger

"Power is the ultimate aphrodisiac."

Henry Kissinger

Henry Kissinger (born: 1923, Furth, Germany; emigrated to U.S.: 1938) virtually began his professional life with behind-the-scenes maneuvering. During World War II, Kissinger served with U.S. Army Intelligence and later, as a student at Harvard, maintained his ties to military intelligence as a reserve officer. Early in his career, he gave considerable attention to his ambition to establish a power base for himself. He sent hundreds of Christmas cards, with personal notes, to all public figures in Washington and abroad with whom he had any contact. When he was denied a tenure-track position at Harvard after finishing his doctorate there, he spurned a tenure offer from the University of Chicago, preferring instead a temporary job at Harvard. He knew the value of an association with the most prestigious university in the nation. (He was ultimately rewarded with a professorship there.) His academic success and prestige, and his continuing campaign of self-promotion, led to a number of appointments as a consultant to important think tanks, foundations, and government agencies. It was as a consultant to the Rockefeller Brothers Fund that he first met Nelson Rockefeller, with whom he had a long and important association. When Rockefeller worked as Eisenhower's Special Assistant for Cold War Planning (his job was to monitor covert CIA operations), Kissinger was his advisor. When Rockefeller lost that position to Vice-President Richard Nixon in 1955, Kissinger was named as a consultant to the National Security Council. Later, he came to be regarded by the Johnson administration as a "trusted consultant" and was active in the secret talks being held in Paris with the Viet-namese. Having seen his hopes of a high White House appointment thwarted when, in 1964, Rockefeller was booed off the platform at the Republican convention, Kissinger eagerly solicited an appointment with Nixon, who was then correctly regarded as the front-runner in the 1968 election. To prove his mettle, Kissinger volunteered secret information about the Paris peace talks to the Nixon camp. President Johnson was so enraged by these leaks that he called both the CIA and the FBI in to investigate their source—they did not manage to uncover it in time. When the polls began to show the election swinging over to Humphrey, Kissinger was quick to contact him, writing a letter critical of Nixon and offering his services. "It was grotesque," said Ted Van Dyke, an important Humphrey aide. "I remember Kissinger being a both sides of the street kind of guy."

When Nixon was elected president, Kissinger was appointed to the White House staff, ultimately as executive secretary of the National Security Council (NSC), a body established in 1947 and charged with advising the president "with respect to the integration of domestic, foreign and military policies relating to national security." The NSC is not responsible to Congress. Nixon endowed it with greater authority over both the formulation and conduct of foreign policy than it had had in the past. According to Kissinger, writing in his memoirs, Nixon had "very little confidence in the State Department. Its personnel had no loyalty to him: the Foreign Service had disdained him as vice-president. . . . " Foreign policy would be conducted directly by the White House; Kissinger would therefore have "de facto power greater than the de jure constitutional authority of the Secretary of State and Defense," a former Kissinger aide wrote. Kissinger, finally at the seat of power, saw his most important job as that of "handling" the president. According to investigative reporter Seymour M. Hersh, "Coping with Nixon, pleasing him, and trying to find out what he really wanted were the most important priorities to Kissinger. They would become even more important than his own convictions about American foreign policy." Secretary of State William Rogers said that he was "prepared to take a subordinate role." By 1971, Senator Stuart Symington said in a Senate address that Kissinger was "secretary of state in everything but title." Kissinger was after the title as well; it finally became his when Nixon, beleaguered by Watergate, capitulated to Kissinger's threats to resign. Kissinger, nearly the only untarnished member of the administration, had the whip hand.

From this position of extraordinary eminence, Kissinger was able to apply his considerable talents to manipulation on a global scale. His

Idealism is the noble toga that political gentlemen drape over their will to power.

Aldous Huxley

celebrated secret trip to China in 1971 reversed the long-standing American policy that had ignored the existence of eight hundred million Red Chinese. His no-less-renowned "shuttle diplomacy" of early 1974 produced a settlement in the Middle East which did lead to the Camp David accords. Not all of his tactical decisions were successful: He got caught wiretapping the staff of the NSC and some journalists—he had an elaborate system of feeding important reporters "leaks," in exchange for well-placed coverage of his views. (He called this process "feeding the animals.") He wiretapped *them* to find out who else might be leaking information to them. And the bombing and invasion of Cambodia in 1970 did not force a peace settlement on North Vietnam and, in the process of failing, destroyed a nation.

Paradoxically, a striking nonsuccess is also the chef d'oeuvre of Kissinger's career: He was awarded a Nobel Prize (1973) for ending a war which was not over. The Paris Peace Agreement, negotiated by Kissinger and for which he shared the prize, promised North Vietnam $3.25 billion in American reparations payments: Kissinger knew quite well that the American government would not, in fact, provide them. The agreement called for talks to arrange the details of the payment; and though these talks actually began, they permanently ended when, on Kissinger's order, the American team withdrew "for consultations." Eventually, the North Vietnamese realized that the United States was not going to come through, and they launched the 1974–1975 offensive, which won the war. The Ford administration charged that the offensive abrogated the reparations agreement, but in fact the agreement had been abrogated earlier by Kissinger. It was in the interval when the desired simulacrum of peace was in place that the laurels were awarded to Kissinger and to Le Duc Tho, the Vietnamese negotiator.

Since resigning as secretary of state, Kissinger's activities have been more mundane, if more profitable. He functioned as personal consultant to the Shah of Iran [see "The Hostages Had a Friend at Chase Manhattan: U.S. Banks and Iran," page 21] and has served as advisor to a number of corporations, including NBC, the Chase Manhattan Bank, Goldman Sachs & Co., Twentieth Century-Fox, and the General Electric Company of Britain. He has his own company which offers advice on matters international and which is said to command retainer fees of up to $250,000. He lectures often, for fees estimated at up to $25,000, and his memoirs (two volumes so far) are reported likely to make $5 million for him. His role on the international political stage seems far from over. In 1983, President Reagan appointed Kissinger to head a bipartisan commission on Central America.

I Beg Your Pardon: Nixon and Ford

BACKGROUND: When, only one month after becoming president, Gerald Ford pardoned Richard Nixon for all criminal acts Nixon might have perpetrated while president, people charged that Ford had gained the presidency because he promised Nixon the pardon. Actually, Ford's motivation may have been stranger than that.

Nixon, as president, was facing a truly grim situation: The House Judiciary Committee was recommending three articles of impeachment against him (their long list of his offenses included obstruction of justice in the investigation of Watergate, abuse of power through the use of the IRS for political purposes, illegal interference with the CIA, FBI, and Department of Justice, and illegal wiretapping). The Watergate grand jury seemed close to indicting Nixon and bringing him to trial, although Watergate Special Prosecutor Leon Jaworski (chosen by Nixon himself) was still not quite sure that a president *could* be indicted while in office. The secretary of defense, James Schlesinger, was becoming concerned that Nixon might use the armed forces to stay in office: "There are a lot of parliamentary governments that have been overthrown with much less at stake," he told an acquaintance. Secretary of State Henry Kissinger, in his book *Years of Upheaval*, writes of a meeting with Chief of Staff Alexander M. Haig: "He told me that Nixon was digging in his heels . . . it might be necessary to put the 82nd Airborne Division around the White House to protect the president."

With all the scare talk, and the months of *Sturm und Drang*, the nation was relieved when, on August 9, Nixon finally resigned. His

Nixon's enigmatic farewell gesture immediately after his resignation, 1974.

successor, former Congressman Ford, had proven his loyalty to Nixon and to the Republican party. Nixon aide Alexander Butterfield, a former Air Force colonel, said, "Nixon had Ford totally under his thumb. He was the tool of the Nixon administration—like a puppy dog. They used him when they had to—wind him up and he'd go 'Arf, Arf.'"

But once he was in the seat of power, and Nixon was in exile in Southern California, Ford seemed to enjoy the presidency and his own burgeoning popularity. The press and the nation seemed to be giving Ford their strong support. A pardon was bound to change all that. Nixon, growing worried, showed that even out of power he still had some dirty tricks up his sleeve. According to Seymour M. Hersh's article in the *Atlantic Monthly* in August of 1983, Nixon called Ford on September 7 and did what he did so well—he threatened.

THE DEAL: If Ford did not pardon him immediately, Nixon would *immediately* announce that Ford, in exchange for the presidency, had *promised* to pardon him. If Ford did pardon him, Nixon would maintain silence on agreements they had made, or had not made, involving the pardon and the presidency.

RESULTS: Ford pardoned Nixon the following day. The nation was outraged. The pardon was still a big issue in the 1976 campaign, which Ford lost to Jimmy Carter.

Nixon, who has never admitted to any criminal wrongdoing, did share his feelings with the public: "No words can describe the depths of my regret and pain at the anguish my mistakes over Watergate have caused the nation." He now collects a yearly presidential pension of $80,100 (a lifetime annual pension equal to the yearly salary of a cabinet secretary) and an additional $96,000 a year for assistants.

> "When you've got them by the balls, their hearts and minds will follow."
>
> Charles W. Colson, aide to Richard Nixon

"Whatever's in There Is in Us Now!": The Love Canal

BACKGROUND: A needy city government and a prosperous private company joined forces to solve an entire community's economic problems and created a new problem *without* a solution.

In the 1890s, William T. Love had big plans for the city of Niagara Falls. They included building a great industrial canal perpendicular to the Niagara River. The canal was barely started when Love's project collapsed, leaving the city with a huge trench one mile long, ten to forty feet deep, and approximately fifteen yards wide, forever known as Love Canal. Decades later, the scarred land was bought by Hooker Chemical Company, which, like dozens of other chemical companies in the area, thrived on the cheap hydroelectricity generated by Niagara Falls. Besides enormous profits, Hooker's chemical manufacturing produced thousands of tons of "waste" material. From the late 1930s to the early 1940s, Hooker dumped over twenty thousand tons of liquid waste—stored in fifty-five-gallon metal barrels—into Love Canal. To do this, they dug fifty-foot holes into the clay bottom of the canal, then buried the drums, forming, Hooker thought, "a sealed clay vault." But the drums ruptured from the pressure; they rusted and rotted open from the moisture; and they (and their contents) slowly rose to the surface flooding the area and leeching into the earth through underground cracks and crannies for miles in every direction.

By the mid-1950s, homes had been built in a ringed fashion around the "field" that Hooker created by filling Love Canal with industrial debris in 1953. People reported that sometimes the field glowed with a green phosphorescence. In 1953, Hooker deeded Love Canal to the Niagara Falls Board of Education for one dollar; the deed freed Hooker from every liability. When a foundation for an elementary school was dug at what had been the canal's center, scalding, reeking, searing chemicals and gas made it necessary to move the foundation eighty feet away from the actual canal. Nevertheless, the school was quickly completed and immediately occupied. In 1958, several children were burned while playing in puddles in the field. Hooker was informed but did not issue a public warning because they were technically no longer responsible. Besides, the construction had disturbed the burial ground, they claimed: Love Canal was a sealed container.

Homeowners in the area knew that Love Canal was a broken container. By 1959, thick black sludge was seeping through the concrete basement walls of houses directly facing the canal. Hideous smells permeated the air. The homeowners complained to the city but nothing was done. Living and working in a chemical town, the people were used to noxious odors. They assumed their health problems and their children's birth defects were the will of God. Since the earth could not reclaim the more than two hundred chemicals it had not formed, backyards became soggy from the seepage. Trees and shrubs died. Liquids of different colors flowed down the streets. The area was like a sopping, toxic sponge. Unable to sell their houses, the homeowners were trapped. Though informed of the horrors, the city did nothing.

City Manager Donald O'Hara had struggled to get the financially

"I'm telling you we're not backing down to anybody. We're not giving in. My child has a congenital birth defect, and we're going to fight the stinking Hooker chemicals. You can bet on that. We want to live and we're going to fight."

Thomas Heisner,
Love Canal homeowner

ailing Niagara Falls out of the red. He knew the city could not afford to clean Love Canal; nor could it afford the lawsuits. Mayor Michael O'Laughlin agreed. Council meetings refused to recognize the attending homeowners. Hooker refused to comment. In 1976, the New York State Department of Environmental Conservation tested a red syrup found in the sump pumps of several houses. They found deadly PCBs. They did nothing. In 1977, the Environmental Protection Agency's Rochester regional office suggested in an unreleased memo that all the houses affected be bought immediately and the people relocated. Nothing happened.

In 1978, the Hooker Chemical Corporation, a subsidiary of the mammoth Occidental Petroleum Corporation (whose chairman is Armand Hammer), grossed, nationwide, $1.78 billion with a net gain of $3.85 million. The city of Niagara Falls was barely in the black: A huge urban renewal project had failed miserably, while tourism was declining drastically. The *only* hope for economic revival was the chemical industry. Hooker had made its position on Love Canal clear: "No comment!" The city was forced to act accordingly.

THE DEAL: Hooker was negotiating with the city to build a $17 million headquarters. In exchange for this—over three thousand jobs and crucial tax dollars—the city had gratefully given prime land, moving a projected hotel from the site, and had granted lucrative tax and loan incentives. Fearful of causing the "responsible corporate citizen" to move to a more appreciative town, the city council had also kept its collective mouth shut on the subject of Love Canal.

RESULTS: City Councilman Pierre Tangent revealed the truth at a council meeting: A lawsuit against Hooker was not a good idea during the current, desperately important negotiations. Reporter Michael Brown bucked his conservative paper, the *Niagara Gazette*, to pursue the story. Hooker claimed they had no records. Brown persevered. Hooker found the records. It was worse than anyone imagined. Although many of the chemicals were proven to destroy human metabolism and cause cancer in laboratory animals, local politicians and State Senator Lloyd Paterson tried to turn Brown off the story; but Congressman John La Falce, the single exception among the politicians, joined him in his fight.

The county health commissioner, Dr. Francis Clifford, insisted everyone was overreacting, even after Brown made public the 1977 EPA–Rochester report. The state commissioner ordered the exposed chemicals in the field covered, a fence built, and the gas-contaminated basements ventilated. (Clifford installed two fifteen-dollar window fans in the basements with the greatest amount of poison in the air and had a small wooden snow-fence erected around part of the canal.) A health survey was taken by the state. Abnormally high rates of miscarriage (35.3 percent in one age group), birth defects (club feet, deafness, retardation), and cancer (of the lungs, kidney, pancreas, liver; as well as leukemia) forced the state to act. This was the largest problem of chemical pollutants in history.

The school was closed. But what about the homes? The owners could not afford to abandon them, and the banks were not offering to buy them back. The Love Canal Homeowners Association was formed, with Lois Gibbs as president. Under public pressure, much of it generated by Ms. Gibbs, the state put up the money to relocate families from the "first" ring. But the toxins were soon found beyond these homes. Houses blocks away in every direction had deadly chemicals oozing through cinder blocks. In October 1978, a remedial drainage program was begun. (The project was controlled by City Manager O'Hara, who soon quit the city to take a job with the company to whom he had assigned the multimillion-dollar contract.)

Then Brown discovered—in the face of Hooker's denials—dioxin in Love Canal. The killing power of dioxin is "incomparable." Three ounces can annihilate one million people. Love Canal contained 130 pounds! It was the final straw. President Carter declared the area a national emergency site. Eventually more than seven hundred families were evacuated, involving some three thousand individuals. The state, federal, and local governments paid in excess of $800 million for the investigation, the O'Hara remedial drainage, the relocation, and the buying of 423 homes. Hooker excused its behavior as "state of the art" mistakes. In the words of its president, David Baeder: "In our opinion, the company acted responsibly from beginning to end. There is not one incident where we didn't come forward to cooperate fully." Investigations of other Hooker Chemical plants around America revealed similar poisonings of the environment. The conclusions were inevitable: There is no such thing as a chemical "by-product." Industrial "waste" has been redefined as the public has become informed and activated, but the dumping continues; since 1980, however, dumping waste is a felony. Experts say it will take more than ten years and $30 billion to clean up the contaminated sites; and the government charges that fifty million tons of hazardous waste, or 90 percent of the national annual total, are still being dumped illegally.

In May 1982, Hooker Chemical was found guilty in a federal court of polluting a drainage creek from the Niagara River; the cleanup could cost them $50 million. The Love Canal suit against Hooker is

"When you get right down to it, you'd be hard pressed to find any group of people who care as much about the environmental and economical well-being of Niagara Falls as the people at Hooker."

Hooker ad campaign after Love Canal

still pending. The Love Canal Revitalization Agency has been buying back the houses from the government in the outer, "less contaminated" rings. The EPA declared these safe to inhabit, as did the Department of Health and Human Services, until the Office of Technology Assessment—a research arm of Congress—in March 1983 said the EPA had no sound basis for saying the neighborhood was safe [see "Government Gratitude: The Environmental Protection Agency as a 'Sweetheart' Dealmaker," page 209]. Niagara Falls officials are still pushing to resell the houses, and over 130 people have signed up to buy them at bargain prices.

Big Mac—The Saving of an American City: New York City Faces Bankruptcy

BACKGROUND: In 1975, New York City owed $6 billion in short-term loans. The city barely had enough to pay its pension fund and bondholders; and the debt had been incurred to finance housing projects and pay pensions in anticipation of selling more bonds paying 9.25 percent—very high for municipal bonds—to cover it. Mayor Abraham Beame and First Deputy Mayor Cavanagh had "balanced budgets" on the surface and had happily ignored the reality that the financial climate, overextension at banks, and rumors of default had killed all chances of more money until the current $6 billion was repaid.

Governor Hugh Carey formed an advisory committee with Felix Rohatyn as chairman. They formed the Municipal Assistance Corporation (MAC), which they patterned after the New Deal's Reconstruction Finance Corporation; it would direct the city's money. Banks agreed to lend New York City the $280 million due immediately; but Beame settled a sanitation strike on terms the city could not afford, and the banks backed out, fearing their money would be lost in the spiraling costs of running a metropolis as if there were unlimited funds. (MAC's plan to sell long-term bonds, to be paid off from the city's billion-a-year sales tax, also collapsed.) MAC knew that if the city fell, the state would follow, and the entire United States would be affected. The State Legislature formed the Emergency Financial Control Board (EFCB) to take control of the city's budget. The MAC team would raise the money that EFCB would spend *carefully;* the state would put up $750 million, and the city's unions would join the fight.

"As things went on, it became clear to me and to others, outside New York, that what was happening was not just New York. New York was itself too large an entity to be an aberration. It couldn't be that it almost went bankrupt if the same disease was not highly prevalent in the body politic, the body economic, and the body national."

Felix Rohatyn,
from *The New Yorker,*
January 24, 1983

THE UNIONS' DEAL: In return for their jobs, the American Federation of State, County, and Municipal Employees, the Uniformed Sanitationmen's Association, the United Federation of Teachers, and the Teamsters agreed to the following: to defer wage increases until the city's budget was truly balanced and the city's bonds were again salable (in 1981); to assume some of the pension funding that the city had paid alone; and to invest their pension money in MAC bonds.

RESULTS: The banks agreed to sign on, and the first $2.3 billion was raised from unions, the state, and banks, which kept the city from going under. Then the federal government agreed not only to "seasonal" loans in 1975 (to be paid back every year), but also to long-term loans in 1978 for "capital-construction projects" (to be paid back when the project was completed), and to federal loan guarantees.

THE CITY'S DEAL: From 1960 to 1975, the number of civil servants had tripled, reaching three hundred thousand, though the population was declining; through layoffs and attrition, 20 percent were cut. City University charged tuition for the first time in its 129 years. Wages were frozen. The city expenditure was drastically cut (rising less than 10 percent from 1975 to 1980; it had risen 80 percent from 1970 to 1975). The transit fare was increased 40 percent, and non–civil-servant experts were given key jobs in the financial divisions.

RESULTS: By 1981, MAC raised $4.5 billion from the general public, the unions, and the banks, and the short-term loans were paid off. MAC will end in 1984, or when $10 billion worth of bonds are sold.

Dealmaker as Savior: Felix Rohatyn

Felix Rohatyn was born May 29, 1928, in Vienna. In 1935, as anti-Semitism grew fierce, his parents moved to France, then in 1941 to Brazil, and the next year to New York City. He planned on a career in physics but in the summer of 199 took a job at Lazard Frères, a conservative banking firm. By 1955, after two years in the army, he was working contentedly in foreign-exchange transactions, earning $22,000 a year, when he met Samuel Bronfman, the owner of the Seagram Company, who advised him to shift into corporate finance and mergers. The switch meant a $7,000 cut in salary [see "Dealmaker as Corporate Leader: Peter A. Cohen," page 121] and night school to learn accounting. He worked with ITT on acquisitions and mergers involving billions of dollars, including one of the largest in history: ITT and Hartford Fire Insurance Company.

"Putting two big companies together involves just as much political work as financial work. When it comes down to the essentials, you are dealing with greed and power. The greed has to be handled by the financial way that you put these companies together, so that, in the last analysis, everyone's interests are served. The power is a different matter. That requires as much negotiation as the financial side, maybe more. More deals break down on the power side than on the financial. There are valid issues of face, of authority, and of appearance."

Felix Rohatyn,
from *The New Yorker*,
January 24, 1983

In 1970, the chairman of the New York Stock Exchange formed a "crisis committee," with Rohatyn as chairman, to save the exchange. Many firms had lost track of their transactions, but, continuing to buy and sell stock, they had huge capital discrepancies and no idea what they had bought or where the stocks were. Trading was declining and rumors of chaos were leading to panic as customers were withdrawing funds. The committee had the power to suspend member firms, many of whom were merged out of business. They succeeded because they caught the problem in time and "too many people had too much to lose if we failed."

After saving the stock exchange, he was appointed by Governor Carey to an advisory committee facing the problem of saving New York City from imminent bankruptcy. The committee formed the Municipal Assistance Corporation (MAC) and did the deeds that saved the day [see Big Mac—The Saving of an American City: New York Faces Bankruptcy," page 206]. He became the liaison between the committee and the press and became a celebrity. In 1978, he became chairman of MAC; his term expired on December 31, 1983. Still active at Lazard Frères, he sits on the boards of Schlumberger, MCA, Pfizer, American Motors, and Owens-Illinois, as well as two foreign companies.

KEEP ON TRUCKIN'

In 1983, when Congress passed the five-cent gas-tax increase, there was heavy lobbying from the depressed trucking industry. Not only would they be paying higher fuel bills, but their licensing fees for using the roads were also slated to increase from $210 a year to $1,900 by 1987. In return for their not striking in protest, truckers were granted the right to drive "outsize double trailer trucks" on most of the 230,000 miles of "primary" federal and state roads. This would end the "mid-America roadblock" caused by the ban against these vehicles in Arkansas, Missouri, and Illinois. The five-cent increase supposedly will provide $5.5 billion to repair the nation's deteriorating infrastructure of roads and mass transit. The trucks are 75 feet long, 102 inches wide, and weigh 40 tons. When fully loaded, they do more damage to a road than 4,550 cars. (Also, they are not safe because, unless fully loaded, their wheels lift off the ground when the brakes are hit hard.) What the government giveth with one hand . . .

Ronald Reagan, the 40th president of the United States.

Government Gratitude: The Environmental Protection Agency as a "Sweetheart" Dealmaker

THE DEAL: Political favors are always being granted, no matter what the consequences to the electorate. When Ronald Reagan ran for the presidency in 1980, he promised industry that he would "lighten government interference," if they contributed to his campaign fund and voted for him and his conservative platform. They did. He did.

RESULTS: ◆ Reagan's major Environmental Protection Agency (EPA) appointees all had close industrial ties.

Rita Lavelle, in charge of the $1.6 billion "superfund" to clean up toxic-waste dumps, was the former head of public relations for a subsidiary of the Aerojet-General Corporation, a California firm labeled one of the top polluters in the state.

John Daniel, chief of staff, was a lobbyist for the American Paper Institute and the Manville Corporation, the leading asbestos manufacturer that was bankrupted by asbestos-related lawsuits.

Kathleen Bennett, assistant administrator for air, noise, and radiation, was a lobbyist for Crown Zellerbach Corporation, a major paper company.

Robert Perry, general counsel and enforcement chief, was with Exxon.

John A. Todhunter, EPA assistant administrator and chief of the pesticides and toxic-substances program, was a consultant to the American Council on Science and Health, a research and education group largely funded by big business to counter citizens' concerns about pollutants and food additives.

♦ John A. Todhunter, in charge of controlling toxic substances, was accused by his staff of ordering studies on dioxin and formaldehyde altered to appear less dangerous and more closely allied to the chemical industry's position. Deleted were dioxin's possible link to miscarriages and formaldehyde's suspected cancer risk—it was proven carcinogenic in rats. (Soon after, the government bought the entire town of Times Beach, Missouri—eight hundred homes and thirty businesses—for $33 million because of dioxin poisoning. There are twenty-one other poisoned sites in Missouri, two in Illinois, and eighty in other states.)

♦ In 1976 Congress passed the Resources Conservation and Recovery Act (RCRA), directing the EPA to establish safety regulations for landfills, penalties for violators, and a system for tracking hazardous wastes from "cradle to grave." However, the concessions to industry—or loopholes—made business exempt from the rules if they generate less than one ton of toxic waste a month, *or* if the waste is recycled, *or* if it is mixed with other products. (The Times Beach debacle occurred because a waste hauler mixed dioxin with an oil base and sprayed it all over the state—streets, parking lots, farms—to help control dust. With the law as it stands, the polluting of Times Beach could happen again.) It took a threat of court action against the EPA for them to issue the RCRA regulations in 1980. The EPA also fought off the Senate attempt to close the loopholes.

♦ In 1982, the EPA suspended the RCRA requirement that waste generators and haulers file annual reports detailing the "death" of their toxic wastes or where the bodies are buried. The EPA said the requirement was impossible to enforce: There are sixty thousand large "hazardous waste generators" and fifteen thousand haulers.

♦ The EPA's budget was cut by 48 percent in "real dollars" since Reagan took office. The enforcement division was abolished, and the number of pollution cases prosecuted fell 70 to 80 percent.

♦ When Ann Burford resigned as EPA administrator, Reagan nominated John Hernandez for the job. Hernandez, a water-pollution expert, seemed fine until a House subcommittee discovered that he had personally intervened to allow Dow Chemical to edit a July 1981 EPA report about dioxin contamination in two rivers and a bay near Dow's Midland, Michigan, plant. References to dioxin, fertility problems, and birth defects were cut, as well as the report's conclusion: "Dow's discharge represented the major source, if not the only source of contamination." The head of EPA's Midwest regional office, Valdas Adamkus, testified that his staff had been "forced" by the Washington headquarters to strike out the passages. Hernandez did not get the job. Dow refused to give technical data about its toxic emissions and the Justice Department moved in with a suit.

◆ Decline in EPA spending (in millions of dollars):

1980 $1,251.2
1981   1,229.7
1982   1,002.3
1983   826.3 (est.), plus 12-percent cut in personnel

SOME THINGS NEVER CHANGE

We have had in the good cities many struggles of one group against another, as the poor against the rich, or one group of poor against another, when they were unable to agree on a mayor or representative or an attorney.... We see many good cities where the poor and middle citizens have no voice in the administration of the city, but where all the power is held by the rich; because of their money or their lineage, they are the formidable power. It also happens that certain citizens are the mayors, or the aldermen, or the treasurers, and the next year they elect their brothers or their nephews, or some other close relations, such that in ten or twelve years, all the rich men have captured the administration of the town; and when the time comes to audit the town records, they cover themselves by saying that certain of their number have verified the accounts of the rest. Such things must not be tolerated, for the communal finances must not be audited by those who are in charge of administering them.... Many discords are born in the communes due to the royal tax imposed on the city, for it happens often that the rich men who are in charge of the taxation of the citizens pay less than they ought to, and similarly exempt their relatives and the other rich men ... thus, the entire burden of the tax falls upon the poor community. By this means, an injury is done; the poor do not wish to suffer it, but they know no good means to claim their rights but through force; from whence there have been on many occasions a number of killings.

Philippe de Beaumanoir (1250–1296), *Les Coutumes de Beauvoisis*

Dealmaker as Iron Lady:
Margaret Thatcher

Much is made of the fact that Margaret Thatcher was born (as Margaret Roberts) to a grocer and a dressmaker, in an apartment over the store, in the small provincial town of Grantham. Mr. Roberts was also a lay Methodist minister, and that this background implanted in the future prime minister values of thrift and industrious self-reliance is oft-proclaimed by the lady herself. Less noted is the fact that Mr. Roberts was also a local politician and was successively elected alderman, magistrate, and mayor of Grantham. Margaret Roberts participated in the 1935 general election when, at the age of ten, she was a messenger for the local Conservative party.

Margaret Roberts studied hard, and she received a scholarship to Oxford, where she studied chemistry and X-ray crystallography. She was also president of the student Conservative Association. When she went on to a career as a research chemist for a plastics manufacturer, she stayed active in the local Conservative party, running unsuccessfully for Parliament in 1950 and again in 1951.

Following the 1951 election, she married Denis Thatcher, a businessman and fellow Conservative activist. She also began studying law while still working as a chemist, and, in 1954, she was admitted to the Bar, beginning a practice as a specialist in taxation and patent law. She had given birth to twins a year earlier, but this did not stop her political career. In 1959, at age thirty-three, Thatcher was elected to the Parliament from Finchley, an upper-middle-class constituency of North London which she has represented ever since. Her talents as a political thinker and administrator were recognized, and she filled several secondary positions in the Macmillan government.

When the Labor party returned to power after the 1964 election, Thatcher became an important voice of the Conservative party in opposition, holding several "shadow cabinet" positions. When the Heath government came to power in 1970, she was appointed secretary of state for education and science, where she achieved great notoriety for opposing previous Labor party efforts to phase out elite grammar schools. Ironically, given her later emphasis on government cost-cutting, she fiercely resisted such cuts in her own department, although she did institute the cessation of government-purchased milk for secondary-school students, a position which resulted in considerable personal vilification in the media. (It is worth noting that during the first four years of her prime ministry, government expenditure on education has increased, even after inflation, despite cost-cutting elsewhere.)

After the elections of February 1974, the Conservatives were out again, the Heath government having been widely perceived as ineffectual at best; the party also lost badly in another general election in October of that year. Thatcher, by this time the opposition spokesperson for economic affairs, led an intraparty revolt against Heath. She was elected the Conservative party leader in February of 1975. Thus, if the Conservatives won a general election, Margaret Thatcher would become prime minister, the first woman ever to occupy the office.

Thatcher was then and has remained at the right wing of her party. The English magazine *The Economist* observed that although her party tends more to the center than she, she is "enough of an intellectual to assuage the doubts of those in the Tory party whose recurrent nightmare is of falling to a Ronald Reagan style of Conservatism." She is uncompromising on certain issues (such as capital punishment, which she favors) but not particularly doctrinaire across the board. Her prime concern is with economic matters; her aim, described in the *New York Times,* is for "nothing less than the transformation of British society through a dismantling of aspects of the Socialist welfare state that she believes inhibit initiative and self-reliance."

After a turbulent winter of disruptive wildcat strikes in England in 1978–1979, hostility to the unions gave the Conservative party a victory in the general election of May 3, 1979. Thatcher, as prime minister, addressed the problem of inflation with a combination of reduced government spending and a tight-money policy; and inflation did indeed slow down, but only at the cost of very high unemployment and an extraordinary number of bankruptcies. After a few years of Thatcherism, the popularity of the government declined precipitously. A poll in late March 1982, found that a large number of people in England felt Thatcher was the worst prime minister in history.

Then Argentina invaded the Falkland Islands. Thatcher responded with considerable military strength, and the Argentines, unprepared for such a response, crumbled. The British victory galvanized public opinion: Thatcher was hailed as a heroine of high stature. Her traits of pugnaciousness and stubbornness, which had attracted criticism before, became sterling virtues of the sort that had made England great in the days of Drake, or Churchill. The epithet "Iron Lady," which she had borne for years, was now unalloyedly positive. By the summer of 1982, it was apparent that she could call an early election and win, a stratagem that had been unthinkable a few months earlier.

"You can strike your way down, but you have to work your way up."

Prime Minister Thatcher

That election was held on June 9, 1983, and Thatcher's Conservative party won in a landslide of historical proportions. In exchange for the pleasure of feeling a sense of self-reliance and pride last enjoyed in the imperial era, Britain will continue to endure the rigors of Thatcherism.

HEAVY PRESSURE

There is no reason for confusing the people and the legislature; the two, in these later years, are quite distinct. The legislature, like the executive, has ceased, save indirectly, to be even the creature of the people; it is the creature, in the main, of pressure groups, and most of them, it must be manifest, are of dubious wisdom and even more dubious honesty. Laws are no longer made by a rational process of public discussion; they are made by a process of blackmail and intimidation, and they are executed in the same manner. The typical lawmaker of today is a man wholly devoid of principle—a mere counter in a grotesque and knavish game. If the right pressure could be applied to him he would be cheerfully in favor of polygamy, astrology, or cannibalism.

H. L. Mencken
1930

VI

BEYOND THE PALE: RELIGION

Oh, God, if there be a God, save my soul,
if I have a soul!

ANONYMOUS FIELD SOLDIER

Ring around the Rhine:
The Ring of the Niebelungen

BACKGROUND: The time is before time. The price of gold has never been higher—a gold ring brings chaos to heaven and earth—while one woman's love saves the day.

Wotan, king of the gods, has the giants Fasolt and Fafner building a palace, Valhalla, for his divine family. The giants took the job when Wotan offered them Freia, the goddess of youth and beauty. Wotan's wife, Frika, can't believe his stupidity: Without Freia, the gods and goddesses will grow old! But Wotan, ever duplicitous, has used Freia only for bait; he really intends to give the giants a ring that will make them the most powerful earthlings. This ring is made from the mystical Rhine gold hidden in the river and guarded by three aquatic maid-

Siegfried and the Rhine Maidens by
Albert Pinkham Ryder.

ens. Wotan's plan, to "borrow" some, seems foolproof, but Fate introduces Alberich, a Niebelung—that race of ugly gnomes who inhabit the bowels of the earth. On the day Valhalla is completed, Alberich makes a pact that brings about the fall of the gods.

THE DEAL: The ring grants dominion over the entire world and the wealth of the ages and possibly over the love-obsessed gods themselves. *But* the gold brings a cold, dead heart and a loveless life devoid of spiritual beauty. Besides the ring, the Tarn Helmet can be made from the Rhine gold. It has the power to change its wearer into any form or to make him invisible. Grabbing the treasure before the giants can, and making off with it, Alberich shouts: "Love I renounce forever!"

RESULTS: Loge, the god of fire, convinces Fafner and Fasolt that the ring is more desirable than Freia. But, he adds, *alas*, Alberich has just swiped it. Angered, the giants command Wotan to get the gold as they carry Freia off. She is not gone five minutes when the gods begin to age.

Distraught, Wotan and Loge descend to the subterranean Niebelheim. There, everyone slaves for Alberich, amassing a priceless hoard. Alberich's enemy, Mime, warns Wotan and Loge of his master's powers. The visitors feign disbelief of the Helmet's abilities. Alberich offers a demonstration by turning himself into a toad. Loge snatches the Helmet; Wotan seizes Alberich. They carry him home, then demand that he turn over his hoard *and* the ring. He delivers all but the ring, which Wotan rips off his finger. In a rage, Alberich curses the ring *and all who touch it!* He vanishes as the giants return bearing Freia, whose presence rejuvenates her family. Wotan offers the giants Alberich's hoard and the Tarn Helmet. Fasolt demands the ring. Wotan angrily hands it over, knowing that the gold belongs to the Rhine maidens and until it is restored, order will not reign in the world. Immediately, Alberich's curse takes effect: Fafner slays Fasolt for the ring. He takes the treasure and the Tarn Helmet, changing himself into a dragon to guard it. As the gods march over a rainbow bridge into Valhalla, Wotan—condemned for having touched the ring—schemes to free himself from Alberich's curse. He resolves to father a race of heroes, or demigods, called Walsungs. They will destroy the Niebelungs, end the curse, and reclaim the gold for the Rhine maidens.

Decades later on earth, Siegmund, a Walsung and son of Wotan, rescues a maiden from being married against her will, then flees her enraged kin. He has grown up alone in the forest. As a child he survived an attack by an enemy race that killed his family and captured his twin sister. (He does not know that Wotan arranged these trials to strengthen him.) Exhausted, he arrives at a hut where he finds Sieglinde, wife of Hundig. She tends him, offering a place by the fire. Siegmund and Sieglinde sense deep unspoken ties. Hundig returns and discovers that Siegmund is the man who (in his attempt to save the maiden from marriage) murdered his family at the wedding. The laws of hospitality forbid him to deny Siegmund shelter, but in the morning they will fight. Sieglinde administers a sleeping potion to her husband, then tells Siegmund that she was kidnapped as a child and forced to marry Hundig. At her wedding, "an ancient wanderer" thrust a sword, Nothung, into the ash tree that forms the fourth wall of their home. No one has been able to free it. A profound affinity unites them as they realize they are brother and sister. Love overwhelms them. He withdraws the magic sword and the lovers run into the night.

Wotan, worried about his offspring, summons his favorite daughter, Brunnhilde. She and her seven sisters are goddesses known as Valkyries, who carry mortal heroes to Valhalla when they fall in battle. Riding great steeds, they fly through the sky undaunted. Wotan orders her to see that Hundig is killed. A raging Fricka, protectress of the sanctified marriage vow, claims Hundig has been dishonored; *Siegmund* must die! Wotan explains that he needs Siegmund: The ring must be returned immediately to the Rhine maidens by the voluntary act of a hero. Fricka insists Wotan must not shield his Walsung twins. She would be humiliated and the gods disgraced. Wotan sadly agrees. He must lose his beloved children to the vengeance of Hundig. He commands Brunnhilde *not* to protect Siegmund. The curse of the ring has made Wotan the victim of Fate instead of its master.

Obediently, Brunnhilde flies to Siegmund and tells him that he must follow her to Valhalla. He asks if Sieglinde will be there, too. When told no, he refuses. The Valkyrie is so stunned that a hero would surrender his place among the gods for love that she decides to disobey Wotan; but when she tries to save the Walsung, Wotan breaks Nothung and Siegmund is slain. Brunnhilde and Sieglinde fly to a mountain peak, where Sieglinde blesses Brunnhilde and hides in the nearby forest. To punish Brunnhilde's disobedience, Woton decides to put her into a deep sleep upon the mountain peak. The first man to find her will awaken and claim a mortal woman. With the death of Siegmund, Wotan confesses, he has lost all hope for the gods' survival. Then Brunnhilde tells him of Sieglinde and Siegmund's son-to-be, Siegfried: *He* will be the hero! She begs Wotan to surround her with a ring of fire that only a true hero will dare violate. Wotan agrees. She is put into a magic sleep, and with the help of the fire god, Loge, the flames obey Wotan's command.

When Siegfried is born, his mother dies. He and the pieces of Nothung are rescued by the Niebelung Mime, who wants to use him to slay the dragon-form Fafner for the ring. Siegfried mends Nothung, a feat requiring superhuman strength and fearlessness—the prerequisites for a true hero; then he is ready to face the infamous dragon. In slaying it, his hand is splattered with blood. He tastes a drop. Instantly he can understand the birds. One of them tells him about the ring and the helmet. Siegfried grabs the lot. Alberich appears and berates Mime for leading a hero to the ring. Mime decides to poison the Walsung but Siegfried, warned by a bird, kills Mime, much to Alberich's glee. Alone, Siegfried asks the bird to lead him to a friend. The bird leads him to Brunnhilde. Wotan appears, making the passage more difficult, but Nothung breaks his staff. Defeated, the king of the gods renounces his empire of the earth. The era of human love supplants the dynasty of the gods.

Plunging into the flames, Siegfried finds Brunnhilde asleep. His gentle kiss awakens her. Rapturously, Brunnhilde sheds her Valkyrie spirit and surrenders to her own womanly love. Siegfried places the ring on her finger and they rejoice. But soon it is time for the hero to go on his quests. Brunnhilde gives him her horse and he journeys down the Rhine, drawn to the castle of the Gibichungs, where, unbeknownst to him, Alberich's son, Hagen, lives with his half-siblings and pawns, Gunther and Gutrune.

Hagen is prepared for Siegfried. By means of a love potion, he will bind him to Gutrune, but will deny him Gutrune until he delivers Brunnhilde *and her ring* to the pliable Gunther. All goes as planned. Siegfried drinks the potion, obediently dons the helmet, takes Gunther's shape, and enters the ring of fire. Brunnhilde attempts to protect herself against "Gunther" but cannot. He takes the ring off her finger and conquers her. Changing places with the real Gunther, Siegfried returns to wed Gutrune. When Brunnhilde arrives at the castle on Gunther's arm, she sees Siegfried with Gutrune. She also sees the ring on *his* finger—the ring Gunther supposedly took from her—and she knows she has been tricked. Not knowing he is under a spell, she jealously assumes he betrayed her for Gutrune. She asks why he is wearing it, then reveals that Siegfried is wedded to her! Remembering none of it, he denies all of it. She curses him. Shaken by Brunnhilde's passionate distress, Gunther grows suspicious.

Hagen happily obliges Gunther and slays Siegfried, who calls for

Brunnhilde with his dying breath. His body is carried to Gutrune. Crazed with grief, she blames Gunther who blames Hagen who demands the ring as spoils. Gunther refuses; Hagen kills him. When he tries to take the ring, Siegfried's dead arm rises in protest. All fall back. Informed of Hagen's plot by the Rhine maidens, Brunnhilde comes forward. She claims the ring and demands a pyre for her hero. When it is lit, she rides her Valkyrie steed into the flames. The Rhine floods the earth and the Rhine maidens snatch the ring from Brunnhilde's finger. Hagen tries for it and is dragged down. Alberich, his curse, and Niebelheim are drowned. Valhalla is ablaze; the corrupt gods are dead. Brunnhilde's self-sacrifice restores harmony to the universe. The powerful god of human love now rules the earth.

DOUBLE DUTY

In ancient Egypt when a person died, the soul, or psychostasia, traveled across the stretch of country that separated the land of the living from the land of the dead to enter the Hall of Double Justice, or the Hall of Two Truths, the judgment place. This was presided over by Osiris, the god of the dead, the redeemer and the judge, along with forty-two of the most important gods—each corresponding to a province of Egypt—to whom the deceased recited protestations of innocence, proving he had led a holy, pure life. Each god was addressed by name, assuring the gathering that the spirit was fearless and religious. Maat, the goddess of law and truth, placed herself or a feather—her ideogram—onto one of the pans of balance, while the heart of the deceased was placed on the other. If the scale was in perfect equilibrium, the deceased was allowed to mingle freely with the gods and the other spirits of the dead. In return for this entry into heaven, the spirit agreed to cultivate the gods' domain and keep the dykes and canals in good repair. (All unpleasant tasks were performed by "answerers," the little statuettes that were buried with the dead for this purpose.) Maat often appeared at both ends of the judgment hall *at the same time*, doubling justice and giving the hall its name.

You Can't Call That a Meal: The Abduction of Persephone

BACKGROUND: Hades, god of the infernal regions, longed to marry the delightful young Persephone; but the girl's mother, the formidable goddess of agriculture, Demeter, rejected the grim and mournful Hades as a husband for her daughter, a girl of extraordinary beauty. Nevertheless, one day while Persephone was out gathering lilacs, Hades seized her, and in spite of her valiant struggle to free herself, he succeeded in carrying the girl off to his dark underworld kingdom.

When Demeter discovered that her child had disappeared (she had no idea that Hades had abducted her), she was beside herself with grief. Her terrible anguish caused all the plants in the entire world to shrivel and die, as famine spread. It was the first autumn. At last, the fountain Arethusa, moved by Demeter's misery, told her that Hades had dragged the girl off to the underworld. Indignant, Demeter raced off to see Zeus, king of the gods, and demanded that he force Hades to release Persephone. Zeus was in a tight spot: He was not only Persephone's father, he was Hades's brother as well.

THE DEAL: Zeus, squeezed by conflicting loyalties, came up with a plan: If in her stay in the underworld, Persephone had not eaten any food, she would be released. If she had eaten while in the land of the dead, she'd be condemned to stay there as the wife of her ravager.

RESULTS: Sweet Persephone could not lie. Hades had offered her a pomegranate, and while she had not eaten it, she had sucked on the moist pulp of one small seed. "Sorry, Demeter," said Zeus, "the kid stays." "Are you crazy?" screamed the goddess. *"You can't call that a meal!"* A compromise was reached. Persephone would spend half the year with Hades in the underworld while the earth was cold and dark; the light and warmth of spring and summer would mark her return to the world and her adoring mother.

Sing for Your Supper: Orpheus and Eurydice

BACKGROUND: Musicians have been highly honored (with knighthoods, gold and platinum discs), bequeathed to their heirs fabulous sums (John Lennon left over $250 million), driven their fans to appalling extremes (Callas's ashes were swiped from her mausoleum), and they've enthralled the world from the year dot. But only one has ever managed to bring back the dead . . . almost.

Orpheus was the child of Apollo, the Greek god of medicine and music, and of Calliope, the muse of epic poetry. His father taught him to play the lyre with such divine passion and rock-hard technique that all the world swooned. To hear his songs, rivers stopped flowing, scudding clouds halted overhead, and even the sun was seen to pause in its arc. Daily, trees uprooted themselves to follow him, flowers ran to embrace him, and rocks softened their jagged edges when touched by his notes. Animals made fools of themselves to sit by his side. It therefore came as no surprise when the beautiful nymph Eurydice agreed to be his bride.

Hymen, the god of marriage, oversaw the nuptials, but much to everyone's horror, his torch spewed forth black smoke, causing the guests to weep. It was not a propitious beginning to a happy-ever-after affair, and it turned out very soon to be as clear an omen as any god could devise. While walking in a field, Eurydice was rudely propositioned by a shepherd. Pulling herself free, she ran without watching her step, was bitten by a snake, and died. Beyond consolation, Orpheus went after her to the land of the dead, breaching the jaws of hell and entering the pitch-black groves of fear.

Taking up his lyre, he sang for Hades, god of the underworld, and for Mrs. Hades, Persephone. No musician ever played to a tougher house. While he sang, the spirits of the dead felt life flow in their veins again. The three-headed canine doorkeeper, Cerberus, stood with his mouths agape while the Furies wept for the first time and their reptile tresses lay down to slumber in peace. Sisyphus leaned on his rock; Tantalus stopped his stretching. Orpheus begged for his young wife to be returned to him on earth. He sang to hearts that knew not how to answer human prayers, but the purity and magic of his music taught them tenderness.

THE DEAL: Hades would allow Eurydice to return to earth with Orpheus because Persephone wished it. An exceptional gift warranted an exception to the rules. *However,* Orpheus was to leave immediately and not look back until he reached the upper air. He had to trust that Eurydice was following in his steps.

RESULTS: Overcome by love, a mad desire possessed him right at the end of the journey. He looked back. Eurydice was sucked back down into the eternal darkness where she never blamed her beloved for his impatience to look at her. He tried to give a second performance, but the way was barred to him. He grieved and wept and sang his tale until the jealous single nymphs became outraged at his undying love and his refusal to let bygones rest as bygones. High on wine and magic weeds during a nocturnal bacchanal, the Thracian women tore Orpheus limb from limb and tossed his head into the river where it continued to sing: "Eurydice! Eurydice!"

The Muses buried his parts. Zeus set his lyre among the stars. At the entrance to the land of the dead, his beloved wife awaited him. Dead to time, they lived in each other's eyes for all eternity.

Who Is the Fairest of Them All?: Paris and Helen of Troy

The Judgment of Paris *by Lucas Cranach, the Elder.*

BACKGROUND: Traditionally, beauty-contest winners shriek and scream and burst into tears, while the losers weep quietly and selflessly applaud their queen. Not so with the immortal goddesses. Among their many gifts, generosity of spirit was rarely included. But starting a war was a bit much, even for them.

When it was prophesied that Paris, son of King Priam and Queen Hecuba of Troy, would cause the destruction of their city-state, he was abandoned on Mount Ida where he was raised by shepherds. Blessed with extraordinary beauty, he was eventually sought by Zeus (king of the gods) to settle an unpleasant business involving Hera (queen of the gods), Aphrodite (goddess of love and beauty), and Athene (daughter of Zeus, goddess of wisdom, war, and peace). The discord had arisen at the nuptials of Thetis and Peleus. All the immortals had been invited except for Eris (goddess of strife) who, infuriated by the snub, lobbed into the ivory-white hall a golden apple on which she had shrewdly inscribed: "For the Fairest."

No slouch when crossed, Eris caused a ruckus that was soon to erupt into a ten-year war when Hera and Aphrodite and Athene each stepped forward to claim the apple. Zeus quickly intervened, declaring that the handsomest of mortal men should choose the fairest goddess. The royals assented. Guided by Hermes to Mount Ida, the three eager contestants descended upon Paris. After the rules were announced to him, each goddess was presented in all her divine glory. Determined to claim the prize, each shamelessly attempted to influence his decision by offering a heavenly bribe. Horrified by his predicament, he tried to refuse the honor, but Hermes commanded him to bow to the will of Zeus. Paris considered his alternatives.

THE DEAL: Hera told him, "If you award the prize to me, I will make you lord over all men." Athene promised that he would always triumph in battle. Aphrodite, unable to offer scepters or victories, promised Paris the most sublime of mortal women for his very own.

RESULTS: Paris awarded the golden apple to Aphrodite. Hera and Athene were enraged; they swore to avenge themselves cruelly.

The most beautiful of mortal women was Helen, daughter of Zeus and Leda. Unfortunately, she was already married to Menelaus of Sparta who, upon his betrothal to her, had been promised fealty by all her other wooers (of whom there were *many*). With the help of Aphrodite, who was not bothered by Helen's prior commitment, Paris sailed to Sparta and was entertained as a guest of Menelaus. On the tenth day, with the host gone on business, Paris convinced Helen to sail away to Troy with him. When Menelaus returned, he insisted Helen come home, but the Trojans refused to allow it. He then demanded that the insult be borne by all of Greece. Hera and Athene could not have agreed more.

Thus, the Trojan War occurred. After ten years of fighting, the destruction of Troy was accomplished by Paris as foretold in the prophecy—with the help of a wooden horse. Paris, himself, was killed by Philoctetes, one of Helen's original suitors, while she, ever in sympathy with the Greeks, was returned to Menelaus.

"The Wished-for Wind Was Given": Agamemnon Sacrifices His Daughter

BACKGROUND: The Trojans had outraged and humiliated the Greeks when Paris, with the help of Goddess Aphrodite, snatched Helen, the wife of Greek King Menelaus. Menelaus's brother, Agamemnon, as commander-in-chief of the Greek army, was pledged to avenge the honor of the Greeks. In preparation for the Trojan War he had spent two years assembling a huge military force (his officers included the redoubtable Achilles and Ulysses). It was while waiting for his fleet to gather and set sail that Agamemnon boasted that as a hunter, he had no peer: He was better even then Artemis, goddess of the hunt. Artemis was miffed at this mortal's macho boasting, but when Agamemnon went hunting and shot a stag dear to the goddess, she was outraged and retaliatory. She visited pestilence upon the army and calmed the winds they needed to sail off to the war. Only one thing could mollify her.

THE DEAL: A virgin, dear to the heart of Agamemnon, must be sacrificed to the goddess: This meant his daughter, the fair Iphigenia.

Only then would the wind blow fair. Agamemnon sent for his daughter.

RESULTS: "I was cut off from hope in that sad place," said Iphigenia (according to Tennyson); but at the very moment she was to die, the goddess wrapped her in a cloud and spirited her off to the Isle of Tauris, where she became a priestess in Artemis's temple. A deer was sacrificed in the girl's place; "The wished-for wind was given" (according to Wordsworth) and the army set sail for a war they fought for the next ten years—and won.

Father of Many Nations: Abraham and God

BACKGROUND: They were putting other gods and goddesses before Him, but then again, had He really campaigned for glory on the earth He Himself had created? He would offer a covenant to a champion of monotheism, a promoter of the exclusive adoration of one God— Himself. How else would the world resound with His name? He chose Abraham.

THE DEAL: Abraham would serve the Lord with unfailing devotion. He would leave his ancestral country and resettle in a land the Lord would give him. In return, Abraham would be the father of many nations: His seed would be as numerous as the stars.

RESULTS: Abraham didn't complain when the Lord insisted that he and all the male members of his household be circumcised. He just did it. And although he had only one child, Ishmael—son of Hagar, handmaiden to his wife, Sarah—Abraham did not decry the Lord when He said that Sarah would be the mother of nations. Sure enough, at ninety, Sarah conceived: Isaac, the delight of their old age, was born. Is anything too hard for the Lord? When the Lord asked Abraham to present Isaac as a burnt offering, Abraham, unquestioningly and unflinchingly, laid his son upon an altar and was about to slay him when God stayed his hand. "Now I know that thou fearest God," God said. It was the final test.

Abraham outlived Sarah, and died an old man full of years (a hundred three-score and fifteen). Today he is hailed by Judaism and Islam (through Ismael) and Christianity (through Judaism) as Father of the Faithful.

YOU BETTER WATCH OUT!

If you walk in my statutes and observe my commandments and do them, then I will give you your rains in their season, and the land shall yield its increase, and the trees of the field shall yield their fruit. And your threshing shall last to the time of vintage, and the vintage shall last to the time for sowing; and you shall eat your bread to the full, and dwell in your land securely. And I will give peace in the land, and you shall lie down, and none shall make you afraid; and I will remove evil beasts from the land, and the sword shall not go through your land. And you shall chase your enemies, and they shall fall before you by the sword. Five of you shall chase a hundred, and a hundred of you shall chase ten thousand; and your enemies shall fall before you by the sword. And I will have regard for you and make you fruitful and multiply you, and will confirm my covenant with you. . . .

But if you will not harken to me, and will not do all these commandments, if you spurn my statutes, and if your soul abhors my ordinances, so that you will not do all my commandments, but break my covenant, I will do this to you: I will appoint over you sudden terror, consumption, and fever that waste the eyes and cause life to pine away. And you shall sow your seed in vain, for your enemies shall eat it; I will set my face against you, and you shall be smitten before your enemies; those who hate you shall rule over you, and you shall flee when none pursues you.

And if in spite of this you will not harken to me, then I will chastise you again sevenfold for your sins, and I will break the pride of your power, and I will make your heavens like iron and your earth like brass, and your strength shall be spent in vain, for your land shall not yield its increase, and the trees of the land shall not yield their fruit. . . .

And if in spite of this you will not harken to me, but walk contrary to me, then I will walk contrary to you in fury, and chastise you myself sevenfold for your sins. You shall eat the flesh of your sons, and you shall eat the flesh of your daughters. And I will destroy your high places, and cut down your incense altars, and cast your dead bodies upon the dead bodies of your idols, and my soul will abhor you. And I will lay your cities waste, and will make your sanctuaries desolate, and I will not smell your pleasing odors. And I will devastate the land, so that your enemies who settle in it shall be astonished at it. And I will scatter you among the nations, and I will unsheathe the sword after you; and your land shall be a desolation, and your cities shall be a waste. . . .

Leviticus, 26

Dealmaker as Creator:
The Judeo-Christian God

In the beginning, there was God. Eager to become the first and ultimate Dealmaker, God created the universe and the creatures that dwell therein. The Creator's first tenants, Adam and Eve, were immediately dealt a hand: "If you want to remain in the Garden of Eden, you must not eat from the Tree of Knowledge." They agreed, then reneged, and since then, God's row has been hard to hoe. Banished from Eden, facing death and pain, the original two set the stage for the Creator's negotiations with Noah, a just man among the multitudinous sinners: "If you build an ark and do my bidding, the earth's sinful inhabitants will get another chance after the flood." The Creator also promised that "while the earth remaineth . . . day and night shall not cease." Alas, God's new flock soon put aside their burnt offerings for blocks and built the Tower of Babel to reach to heaven. Annoyed by their presumption, God scattered mortals to the far ends of the earth and divided them into separate races with languages of their own. Then God chose Abraham to perpetuate the Divine One's name: "If you obey me, I will make of thee a great nation; I will bless them that bless you, and curse them that curse you." All seemed well between God and the chosen people until they fell into slavery. God selected Moses to liberate them and appeared on earth as a burning bush. This time, there were new demands: the Ten Commandments, yet another maneuver by God to create an ethical, monotheistic world. But God failed to eliminate evil from the human heart; still mortals transgressed. So, some say, a Divine Son was created and the covenant of Sinai was replaced by the covenant in Jesus Christ who died on the cross to make amends to God, his Father, for the sins of humanity. The Creator was appeased: "If humanity keeps the Ten Commandments as well as faith in Christ, I will open the gates of heaven and all the unfulfilled promises in the Bible will come to pass: Evil and death will be eliminated, the dead will rise, the lions will lie down with the lambs—life, in short, will be bliss." Yet again, God's offer has failed to keep humanity on its best behavior. And the promises of the Bible are still unfulfilled. Perhaps, as some say will happen, God will come again, and renegotiate the terms for bringing heaven to earth. We're waiting.

God pictured as an old white man with a white beard from The Visconti Hours.

BVM and the Immaculate Insemination: Mary, the Mother of God

The Holy Family *by Raphael*.

BACKGROUND: The gods have never hesitated to make use of humanity. Myths and legends abound of divine interventions, but few mortals have received the favors bestowed upon "Mary, the Mother of God."

Mary was born in Galilee. Almost nothing is known of her personal history, not even her age or why she was the favored one when God decided to forgive Adam and Eve for their original sin by sending his Son to earth. Unannounced, the angel Gabriel appeared to Mary with the news of her destiny, a destiny that would change the world.

THE DEAL: Mary would conceive in her womb and bring forth a son and would call him Jesus. He would be great and be called the Son of God. The Holy Spirit would come to her and she would be overshadowed by God, who would perform an immaculate insemination without disturbing her virginity. Son Jesus would redeem the world. In return for her services, Mary would be blessed and revered by all generations.

RESULTS: Along with her son, a new religion was born. Since virgin births were common in pagan mythology, the early Christians had little difficulty accepting her divine condition. As Mariology developed into a cult of its own, the premise of Mary's early chastity became a central symbol of purity, encouraging asceticism; sacred birth became a rallying cry for the sanctity of motherhood, locking the church into positions against abortion or contraception and neatly uniting Mary with Eve, who is blamed for all the pain in life. Christianity offered eternal salvation by transcendence, not removal of earthly suffering. In the words of Saint Jerome: "Now that a virgin has conceived in the womb and borne a child . . . now the curse is broken. Death came through Eve, but life has come through Mary."

The total creation of Christian mythology—few facts exist in the sacred texts—Mary inherited the attributes of the Jungian Great Mother, and of Diana and Artemis and Selene. Her son absorbed the symbols of the sun: His birthday is celebrated at the winter solstice; his resurrection at spring equinox. She absorbed the symbols of the moon. In 431, she officially became the Mother of God. In 1854, she was declared an immaculate conception herself, born free of original sin. In 1950, it was decreed that she was bodily assumed into heaven. In 1974, she was placed in "sociocultural contexts" by Pope Paul VI, who unsuccessfully tried to remove the image of submission and make her an active, modern woman for the twentieth century to emulate.

Her major temples, the great European Gothic cathedrals, are among the high points of human achievement. She has inspired the most sublime art and music. Philosophically, she neatly reconciled the opposites of virgin and mother; in a religion that polarizes the spiritual and physical worlds, she became an impossible ideal. She is the most successful image of goodness and purity ever created by man, as well as a perfect symbol of Western man's attitudes toward women.

Head Waitress:
Salome and John the Baptist

BACKGROUND: Herodias was possibly the greatest stage mother of all time. She prompted her talented daughter to display her wares, then negotiated a heady compensation.

Around A.D. 28–30 Rome's administrator, Herod, was the corrupt ruler of Galilee and Perea. He had divorced his wife to marry his niece, Herodias, who had divorced her husband, Herod's half-brother, for him. There was much criticism of this maneuver, but it was John the Baptist's public rebuke of Herodias that had offended her the most. John was a popular Jewish prophet who preached the imminent arrival of the Messiah, Christ. He was the son of Zacharias and Elizabeth, a kinswoman of the Blessed Virgin Mary. According to Luke's gospel, an angel appeared to announce John's birth to his father who, being very old, was struck dumb when he questioned the angel's veracity. It was John who baptized Jesus.

Herodias convinced Herod to arrest John, but Herod needed little prodding: Rumor had it that John was risen from the dead—a feat accomplished about three years later by Jesus, according to the Bible—and Herod feared not only his pointed criticism, but also his immense following and the powers supposedly working within him. But he dared not kill John outright for fear of awakening the wrath of the people and bringing Rome down on his head.

Enter Salome, Herodias's nubile daughter by her first marriage. At a birthday banquet for Herod, Salome used all of her considerable talents to win her mother's revenge on John the Baptist.

THE DEAL: Salome agreed to dance for Herod. In return for this birthday treat, Herod promised under oath to give her *whatever* she fancied—up to half his kingdom.

RESULTS: Salome danced the legendary dance of the seven veils. Herod was overwhelmed. She then asked, with her mother's prompting, for the head of the imprisoned John the Baptist on a platter. Herod, under an oath made before the movers and shakers of Galilee, was forced to oblige.

When Jesus heard of John's death, he went away from Galilee to a private, deserted place, but the multitudes followed from the city. The next day he performed one of his most famous miracles: He fed the entire crowd of five thousand with five loaves and two fishes.

Salome repented and followed Christ. She stood beside BVM and Mary Magdalene at his crucifixion and went with them to anoint his body the day he was discovered risen from the dead.

Herod, on the other hand, was nudged on by Herodias to demand a royal title from Rome. Around A.D. 39, Caligula banished them both from the Roman Empire.

John the Baptist is the only saint—beside BVM—whose birthday is celebrated by the Roman Catholic church as a feast day.

THIRTY PIECES OF SILVER

"And at that time, one of the twelve, he who was called Judas Iscariot, went to the high priests and said: 'What are you willing to give me if I betray him to you?' And they paid him thirty pieces of silver. And from that time he looked for an opportunity to betray him."

Matthew 26:10

And when he was gone forth into the way, there came one running, and kneeled to him, and asked him, Good Master, what shall I do that I may inherit eternal life? And Jesus said unto him, Why callest thou me good? there is none good but one, that is, God. Thou knowest the commandments, Do not commit adultery, Do not kill, Do not steal, Do not bear false witness, Defraud not, Honour thy father and mother. And he answered and said unto him, Master, all these have I observed from my youth. Then Jesus beholding him loved him, and said unto him, One thing thou lackest: go thy way, sell whatsoever thou hast, and give to the poor, and thou shalt have treasure in heaven: and come, take up the cross, and follow me. And he was sad at that saying, and went away grieved: for he had great possessions.

And Jesus looked round about, and saith unto his disciples, How hardly shall they that have riches enter into the kingdom of God! It is easier for a camel to go through the eye of a needle, than for a rich man to enter into the kingdom of God. And they were astonished out of measure, saying among themselves, Who then can be saved? And Jesus looking upon them saith, With men it is impossible, but not with God: for with God all things are possible. Then Peter began to say unto him, Lo, we have left all, and have followed thee. And Jesus answered and said, Verily I say unto you, There is no man that hath left house, or brethren, or sisters, or father, or mother, or wife, or children, or lands, for my sake, and the gospel's, But he shall receive an hundredfold now in this time, houses, and brethren, and sisters, and mothers, and children, and lands, with persecutions; and in the world to come eternal life. But many that are first shall be last; and the last first.

Mark, 10: 17–31

Leave Him to Heaven: Mephistopheles and Goethe's Faust

BACKGROUND: Before you sign anything, read the fine print carefully and don't be too hasty to discuss terms. But even the Devil makes mistakes.

Mephistopheles—a.k.a. the Devil—is convinced that human beings are "far beastlier than any beast." He never tires of reminding the Lord of the failures of mankind. Bored with the routine, the Lord suggests that Mephistopheles examine the exemplary life of Doctor Faust, a good and holy scholar with the highest principles *and* exquisite sensibilities. Ever eager to best the Lord, Mephistopheles bets that "there's a chance to gain" Faust. The Lord well knows that every human is incapable of avoiding error, but he agrees to let the Devil "trap" Faust, because he also knows that man's spiritual instincts eventually lead him to "the one and only way"—salvation. The Devil doubts this eternal optimism. Laughing, he plots his deed. He seeks out Faust who, being human and intellectually rapacious, is a surprisingly easy catch for the cunning Evil One. They quickly come to terms.

THE DEAL: In exchange for his soul, Faust will know the secrets of the universe. The Devil is beguiling:

> Come, bend thyself to prompt indenture,
> And thou mine arts with joy shalt see:
> What no man ever saw, I'll give to thee.

Faust will wield unlimited power on earth, then after death, in hell, will be the Devil's servant. Inflating himself all too high, Faust cannot resist becoming a god, albeit a mortal one. A pact is signed in blood because Mephistopheles insists, "Blood is a juice of rarest quality."

RESULTS: Mephistopheles spreads his cloak and the two fly through the air. Immediately, Faust is doing what no other man has ever done. Then he drinks a witches' brew renewing desires long exhausted by endless work; he lusts for carnal pleasures. The subject of his heated thoughts is a pure, poor virgin, Margaret, who is quickly driven "love mad." The sated Faust, insulted by her brother, kills him in a duel. Frenzied with grief and guilt, she drowns her love child and is sentenced to death; but when Faust attempts to carry her from her punishment, she refuses, repents, accepts her due, and is saved by the Lord.

Moving outside time, Faust learns to control nature and rule the seasons. Returning to earth, he creates an ideal community where justice and truth rule supreme. At a great old age he dies. The Devil claims his soul: A bargain is a bargain. But God holds a different inventory. *He* claims the soul of Doctor Faust. Although the conditions of the contract between Mephistopheles and Faust have been scrupulously met in the realm of the physical, there is another aspect of man's nature that must be taken into account. Although a physical prisoner of the Devil, Faust had done the spiritual work of the Lord. Mephistopheles is forced to concede defeat. The angels soar to heaven bearing the immortal part of Faust: "Who'er aspires unreservedly/Is not beyond redeeming."

ROMAN CATHOLIC BURIAL PRAYERS

Let us pray. O Lord, we implore Thee to grant this mercy to Thy dead servant, that he (she) who held fast to Thy will by his (her) intentions, may not receive punishment in return for his (her) deeds; so that, as the true Faith united him (her) with the throng of the faithful on earth, Thy mercy may unite him (her) with the company of the choirs of angels in heaven. Through Christ our Lord. Amen.

O God, great and omnipotent Judge of the living and the dead, before Whom we are all to appear after this short life, to render an account of our works. Let our hearts, we pray Thee, be deeply moved at the sight of death, and while we consign the body of the deceased to the earth, let us be mindful of our frailty and mortality, that walking always in Thy fear and in the ways of Thy Commandments, we may, after our departure from this world, experience a merciful judgment and rejoice in everlasting happiness. Through Christ our Lord. Amen.

The Soul from Purgatory Springs:
The Catholic Church, Indulgences, and the Reformation

BACKGROUND: The Moslem infidel had seized Palestine in the year 969. When word reached Rome in 1095 that the Church of the Holy Sepulcher had been sacked, Pope Urban II called the faithful to arms. To motivate them, he promised the one thing a God-fearing Christian would find irresistible.

THE DEAL: Crusaders would receive complete remission of the temporal punishment (penance) due them for their sins—plenary indulgence. They would be released from suffering in purgatory, and, on the authority of the pope, could expect to enter heaven immediately after death.

St. Peter's in Rome.

RESULTS: The First Crusade was a success. The Christians took Jerusalem in July 1099, and promptly massacred every last Moslem and Jew they found there. Others were soon clamoring for indulgence: They were terrified of suffering in the world to come for their sins, and penance, at that time, sometimes involved years of hard endeavor. Soon the pope was granting plenary indulgences to anyone who had funded or advised the Crusades. By the end of the thirteenth century, indulgences were granted to secular rulers for political purposes. By 1344, individuals could purchase them at the moment of their death—and they could be purchased for those already deceased, ensuring their release from purgatory. The pope quickly realized that the sale of indulgences was a good way to raise funds, and the church began "commissioning" others, usually Dominican monks, to sell indulgences (a system that allowed ample opportunity for embezzlement). In the sixteenth century, the church decided to replace the thousand-year-old church that stood on the site of Saint Peter's grave—the symbolic center of Christendom since the first century. Special fund-raising efforts had to be made for the grand, sumptuous jewel they had in mind. Resplendent with art treasures, it would be the largest church in the world. Only popes would read mass there.

In 1515, Pope Leo X promulgated a new indulgence to meet the continuing expenses involved in the building of Saint Peter's. This one came at an especially unpropitious time: Anticlerical sentiments, ranging from simple resentment of privilege to proto-Protestant heresy, were rampant, and for some time demands for churchly reform had been heard. In 1517, a particularly unscrupulous Dominican named John Tetzel set himself up as a dealer in indulgences in the German city of Magdeburg. His advertising slogan was: "As soon as coin in coffer rings, the soul from purgatory springs." For Martin Luther, a monk and professor in a nearby town, this was the final straw; Luther didn't believe that anyone could really buy grace for himself or set his relatives free from purgatory. Anyway, the sheer ostentation of the opulent Saint Peter's bothered him. Luther wrote a public statement voicing his objections, and, as was the practice of men in his profession, nailed it to the door of the castle church. Soon the debate became much broader: Luther was excommunicated in 1520; in 1525, the first of 150 years of religious wars commenced. The Protestant Reformation had begun.

The Indulgence of 1515 not only failed in its purpose, it backfired. The Saint Peter's project lay moribund for many years as the energies of the church were absorbed by the outbreak of the Reformation and the religious wars. (Rome was sacked by Protestant troops in 1527.) When Saint Peter's was finally built, its baroque magnificence reflected the extraordinary energy of the Counter-Reformation, a movement that ended the sale of indulgences, once and for all.

> "He may be said to have abolished the charge for admission to heaven."
>
> **George Bernard Shaw on Martin Luther**

INDULGENT PROTEST

As once the German conquerors of Rome had prided themselves on being simpler, purer, than the heirs of Cicero and Virgil, so now Luther set himself up against Michelangelo and Raphael. Even the technical occasion of his breach with Rome was symbolic: he objected to the sale of indulgences in order to raise money for the building of St. Peter's—if it had been for the purpose of massacring German peasants, Luther might never have become a Protestant.

A. J. P. Taylor,
The Course of German History

PASCHAL TIME

In the Latin Missal, Easter is called "Pascha," a name chosen from a Hebrew word meaning "passing over." The Jews celebrated the feast of "Passover" because the destroyer of the first-born of Egypt "passed over" the houses of the Israelites, who had sprinkled the transom and the posts of their doors with the blood of the paschal lamb; and because the Jews were, in that same night, delivered from bondage, "passing over" through the Red Sea into the land of promise (Ex. 12, 11). Since Christians have been redeemed and have "passed over" to the freedom of the children of God, we too call the day of His Resurrection, "Pascha" or "Passover."

Since Christ rose from the dead, we know that He is the Son of God, His doctrine is divine, His Church is true, and we, as members of His Mystical Body, provided we are His true disciples, shall one day rise with glorified bodies.

Saint Joseph Daily Missal
The Official Prayers of the
Catholic Church for the
Celebration of Daily Mass

LANDRAU THE FAT, SHAME ON YOU!

In feudal Europe, itinerant merchants, traveling from marketplace to marketplace, were forced to pay tribute to the local lord in order to obtain the right to trade. Sometimes these fees were exorbitant, and the merchant would appeal to Church authorities. In response to clerical pressure, the feudal lord would sometimes issue a refund and an apology, such as this eleventh-century example:

I, Landrau the Fat, seduced and tempted by the greed that often creeps into the hearts of worldly men, admit that I have stopped the merchants of Langres who passed through my domain. I took their merchandise from them and kept it until the day when the Bishop of Langres and the Abbot of Cluny came to me to demand reparation. I had kept for myself a part of what I had taken and restored the rest. The merchants, to obtain this remainder to be able in the future to cross my land without fear, consented to pay me a certain sum for tribute. This first sin suggested to me the idea of a second, and I undertook to impose and to cause to be imposed by my officers, an exaction called a toll on all those who crossed my territory for business or pilgrimage ...

God Wills It: Venice and the Fourth Crusade

BACKGROUND: They were sworn to rid Jerusalem of the Moslem infidel, but the Fourth Crusade never did get to the holy land: First the Venetians sidetracked them with some dirty work; then looting Christian cities seemed every bit as satisfying.

Transporting Crusaders across the Mediterranean had always been a profitable business for the Venetians, but the Fourth Crusade, called in 1201, promised to be a real bonanza. The Venetians, who lived in a republic built on 118 islets spread across a lagoon, were master shipbuilders, and their strategic location gave them control over the sea trade between the East (of Byzantium and the Moslems) and the West. Their state-owned shipbuilding industry was so efficient that, when pressed, they could turn out a fully equipped warship in less than one day. But as efficient as it was, the shipbuilding industry was also highly vulnerable, since vital raw materials had to be acquired away from the lagoon. So, when the Hungarians seized the city of Zara on the Dalmatian coast (now Yugoslavia), the Venetians were worried: They got the lumber needed to build their ships from the heavily wooded islands near Zara. They feared that the Hungarians, covetous of the Venetian trade with the East, would be able to threaten their empire.

The Venetians attempted to reconquer Zara, and they were still licking their wounds when the pope called the Fourth Crusade. Everyone expected that this would be the largest effort ever made to free the holy land from the Moslems. Experience had already shown that the most expedient method of transporting Crusaders to Jerusalem was by sea (that gave them less opportunity to get sidetracked by plundering along the way; and, anyway, the Byzantine Empire was not what it once was and the old road through Anatolia was barely passable). Since even the greatest of the nobles who took up the cross did not possess a fleet, a Crusader delegation was sent to Venice to "implore the aid of the masters of the sea for the deliverance of Jerusalem." Overly optimistic, the Crusader leadership negotiated with Doge Dandolo, the leader of the Venetians, for the transport of "9,000 esquires, 4,500 knights, and 20,000 footmen with provisions for 9 months." The doge agreed to provide a fleet large enough to accommodate this huge expedition, and their 4,500 horses, for the fabulous sum of 85,000 silver marks of Cologne (some $3 million), which, back in the thirteenth century, was a huge amount. Venice

> Men never do evil so completely and cheerfully, as when they do it from religious conviction.
>
> Pascal, *Pensées*

— 237

also agreed to provide 50 fully armed ships and 6,000 Venetians, at their own expense, in exchange for an equal share in the territories and plunder they would "liberate" with the Crusaders.

When the deadline of June 24, 1202, rolled around, the Venetians had readied every last galley, but the Crusader army was far smaller than its misguided leadership had expected. Responding to the cry of *Dieu le volt!* ("God wills it!") were a mere ten thousand—one-third of the expected force. Worse still, they were able to raise only fifty-one thousand marks—they were short by thirty-four thousand. The clever doge, a man whose devotion to commerce exceeded his piety, threatened that, until the Crusaders met their financial obligations, not one ship would sail. Moreover, he was outraged: Hadn't his shipwrights worked night and day readying the fleet? His threats produced a small trickle of funds, but the Crusaders were still very much in arrears. When the doge was certain that he'd extracted all the gold and silver he could, he thought of something the Crusaders could do for Venice that might induce him to allow the Crusade to proceed.

THE DEAL: If the Crusaders would assist Venice in conquering Zara, the doge would defer payment of the rest of the fee. In fact, he would allow them to pay him from the booty they expected to seize from the Moslem enemy. The Crusaders, eager to start out, agreed.

RESULTS: Although some Crusaders voiced moral objections to attacking the Hungarians, who were, after all, Catholics, most of them joined in. Five hundred ships, personally led by the ninety-three-year-old doge, sailed from Venice. "Far as our gaze could reach, the sea shone with the white sails of ship and galley. Our hearts throbbed with joy and we felt that so noble an armament might achieve conquest of the whole earth," one participant recorded. Within one week, Zara was conquered and sacked. When word reached the pope, he was horrified and quickly excommunicated the entire Fourth Crusade (he later reconsidered when he learned more of the circumstances).

This eager bunch was not destined to face off against the infidel. Leaving Zara, they set sail for Constantinope, the capital of Byzantium. (The Byzantiums were Christians, but they had broken with the pope in 1054.) The marauding army sacked the city, which was then considered to be the most beautiful and most advanced urban society of its day, and raped and murdered thousands. From their share of plunder (estimated at $15 million) the Crusaders repaid the Venetians. The Venetians, ever tasteful, carried off many fine art treasures that today still adorn their city (the bronze chargers that surmount

At that time, Jesus said to His disciples: "If anyone love Me, he will keep My word, and My Father will love him, and We will come to him and make Our abode with him. He who does not love Me, does not keep My words."

John 14: 23

the portal of Saint Mark's Basilica are among the most famous). The Venetians also appropriated a large share of Byzantium territory, including Corfu, Crete, the Cyclades, and an unbroken chain of ports stretching from the Black Sea to Venice. The maritime pre-eminence they therefore achieved gave rise to the rich and powerful city-state that came to be called "La Serenissima"—the Most Serene Republic. Many consider Venice the most beautiful city ever built in the Western world.

Zara is now known as Zadar, and it is a city of a hundred thousand. Italy was forced to cede it to Yugoslavia after World War II.

The Fourth Crusade never did make it to Jerusalem. The holy land never was recovered. Byzantium, seriously weakened by the invasion, fell to the Turks in 1453.

CONTINUAL GUIDANCE

If you take away from the midst of you the yoke,
the pointing of the finger, and speaking wickedness,
if you pour yourself out for the hungry
and satisfy the desire of the afflicted,
then shall your light rise in the darkness
and your gloom be as the noonday.
And the Lord will guide you continually,
and satisfy your desire with good things,
and make your bones strong;
and you shall be like a watered garden,
like a spring of water,
whose waters fail not.

Isaiah 58: 9

"Paris Is Surely Worth a Mass!": Henry of Navarre

BACKGROUND: When the visionary mystic Nostradamus predicted in 1564 that a Protestant would soon wear the crown of Catholic France, he did not supply precise details. Nevertheless, this prophecy turned out to be one of his best.

In spite of intense persecution, the Protestant reform movement founded a Presbyterian church in 1559 in Catholic France. Forty percent of the nobility, tired of Catholicism's control and corruption, joined the new church as "Huguenots." During a tournament that same year, held to celebrate the marriage of his thirteen-year-old daughter to Philip II of Spain, France's King Henry II was mortally wounded in a sporting accident. He and his wife, Catherine de' Medici, had produced four healthy sons, safely securing Catholic succession to the throne. Or so they assumed.

Their first son, married to Mary Stuart, became Francis II under the regency of his mother. The powerful arch-conservative Catholic family de Guise wrested control of the court. After one year, Francis II died of meningitis; he was succeeded by his ten-year-old brother, Charles IX. Mother Catherine, fearful of the de Guise influence, sought allies among the Huguenots; and Antoine de Bourbon of Navarre was appointed the first Protestant Lieutenant of France. In 1562, to the outrage of the Catholics, the January Edict granted Protestants the freedom to worship publicly. De Guise promptly slaughtered a congregation, beginning forty years of religious wars. Plots, intrigues, and assassinations convulsed the French court, while Catherine played both sides to protect the throne.

The king's sister, Margaret de Valois, was engaged to Antoine de Bourbon's son, Henry of Navarre. It was intended to be the first mixed marriage, but the growing powers of the king's Protestant chief advisor, Coligny, made Catherine uneasy. She collaborated in an unsuccessful de Guise plot to assassinate him. Then panicking, realizing the king would discover her treachery, she convinced him that she had uncovered a Huguenot plot against the crown, a plot led by Coligny. On August 24, 1572, Saint Bartholomew's Day and the day after the wedding of Margaret to Henry of Navarre, fifteen thousand Huguenots (including Coligny) were massacred. (Pope Gregory XIII sent his congratulations to France for a job well done.) The newlyweds were held captive at court. Navarre was forced to convert to Catholicism or die.

After two uneasy years, Charles IX died. The third son, Henry III, took the crown. To placate the Huguenots, he issued the Peace of Beaulieu (1576), granting almost complete religious and civil freedom. Navarre renounced Catholicism and became leader of the Protestant faction in France. The de Guise clan formed and armed the reactionary Catholic League, forcing the king to revoke much of Beaulieu. Then the fourth son, the Duke of Anjou, died in 1584. Since Henry III was childless, Protestant Navarre was his legitimate successor by blood and marriage.

The religious wars escalated. Pressure from the Catholic League, a

Papal bull, and Catholic Spain's invincible Armada, forced Henry III's Edict of Alencon (1586): His successor would be a Catholic. The next year, the king's troops were defeated by Navarre's at Coutras, and de Guise revolted against the weakened Henry III, evicting him from Paris with the help of the League and Spain. The king then had Henry de Guise assassinated. The furious and aggressive response of the League forced Henry III into an alliance with Navarre. As the two planned to regain Paris, the king was assassinated in 1589 by a Jacobin friar. With his dying breath, he begged Navarre to become a Catholic. Navarre refused. He was the successor; France would have to accept a Protestant king.

At the pope's urging, King Philip of Spain sent troops to Paris in support of the League, claiming the French throne for his daughter, the niece of Henry III and granddaughter of Henry II. The Duke of Savoy, grandson of Francis I, claimed France. The Duke of Mayenne, brother of de Guise, claimed France, but in 1590 was defeated by Navarre, who then failed to take Paris. The wars raged. Only the popular Navarre, as Henry IV and victor over the de Guise clan, could save France from bloody disintegration. But without the support of Paris, even as the dynastic king he could not claim France. And the regime in Paris would never kneel to a Protestant.

The Triumphal Entry of Henry IV into Paris *by Peter Paul Rubens.*

THE DEAL: If Henry of Navarre converted to Catholicism, the French Parliament and the League would officially elect him king. On July 25, 1593, Navarre proclaimed his rights as Henry IV and officially abjured Protestantism. It is reported that he said to his mistress, Gabrielle d'Estrées: "Paris is surely worth a mass!"

RESULTS: The Huguenots were horrified, the pope skeptical, but the French people happily rallied behind Henry IV, ending forty years of national strife. To eliminate Spanish influence, he declared a successful war on Spain. Then, in 1598, he issued the Edict of Nantes granting religious and civil rights to Protestants—there were, by then, over one million Huguenots—ending the religious wars. He became one of the most popular figures in French history and is called the only king the poor remember. With the help of his great minister Sully, he revived the treasury, promoted agriculture, and sent Samuel de Champlain to Canada, where he founded Quebec. He improved and beautified Paris. He is credited with a reign full of ease and happiness, summed up by his apocryphal promise of a chicken in every pot on Sunday: *"la poule au pot tout les dimanches."* Henry IV died by an assassin's knife on May 14, 1610.

MURDER BY PROXY

I call thee, Evil Spirit, Cruel Spirit, Merciless Spirit; I call thee, who sittest in the cemetery and takest away healing from man. Go and place a knot in ———'s head, in his eyes, in his mouth, in his tongue, in his windpipe, and put poisonous water in his belly. If you do not go and put water in his belly, I shall send against you the evil angels Puziel, Guziel, Psdiel, Prsiel. I call thee and those six knots that you go quickly to ———'s, and put poisonous water in his belly, and kill ——— because I wish it. Amen, Amen. Selah.

A European death incantation from the Middle Ages, from Moses Gaster, *The Sword of Moses*

A Baby Only a Mother Could Love: Rosemary's Baby

BACKGROUND: Becoming a star is hard nowadays, but the plan Guy Woodhouse's rampant ambition devises with the help of a needy Satanic cult is not recommended by any reputable drama school.

Guy and Rosemary are happily married. He's acted small roles on Broadway and in TV plays, and starred in a batch of lucrative TV commercials. He's doing well enough to afford an apartment in the Bramford, a palatial New York City Victorian building. Edward Hutchins, a friend of Rosemary's, warns them that "the black Bramford" is a "danger zone"; heinous things have happened there over the years. But the young couple move in and quickly meet their eccentric neighbors—Minnie and Roman Castevet who have the adjoining apartment and share a common bedroom wall. Though Guy is in a state over losing a role in a new Broadway play, he dines with the "lonely" Castevets to make Rosemary happy. They enchant him by taking an avid interest in his budding career. Guy starts spending time with Roman. Minnie gives Rosemary a gift: a pendant containing some foul-smelling magical herb. Weird chanting comes through the bedroom wall.

THE DEAL: Minnie and Roman are in league with Satan, who wants to bring a flesh-and-blood son into the world, as his chief enemy has already done. In return for stardom, Guy agrees to let Satan use Rosemary as a maturation vessel. Instead of endangering his own soul, he leases Rosemary's body without her knowledge. He is promised she will not be hurt. When the Son of Satan is born, he will be taken by the Castevets. Rosemary will be told her baby died in childbirth. She will never know what has been unleashed upon the world through her womb.

RESULTS: The actor who beat out Guy for the Broadway role goes blind. Guy is cast. The night of the devilish conception, Guy gets Rosemary drunk and she "dreams" she is raped at a ritual gathering by an "unhuman" creature. She awakens marked by deep scratches; Guy claims his jagged nail made them when he pounced on her after she passed out. Rosemary is not amused. But Rosemary *is* pregnant. And Guy is offered a lead in a new TV series: "I'm suddenly very hot!" he crows.

Rosemary's pregnancy is a difficult one. She suffers sharp, clawing pains, as if something horrific is happening inside her. Everyone but Hutchins tells her not to worry; he is convinced something is wrong. Hutchins dies; his dying word to Rosemary is "anagram." She discovers "Roman Castevet" equals "Steven Marcato," the son of a famed Bramford satanist. Catching on, Rosemary shares her suspicions with Guy. He says she's crazy. The doctor says she's mad. But the clues continue to pile up, and Rosemary realizes she and her child are in terrible danger. She flees the Bramford, is recaptured, and immediately gives birth in her bedroom. When she awakens she is told the baby was born dead.

But that night, she hears a baby crying. Locating the secret passage between the apartments, she interrupts the coven's party. Her living, breathing baby is the guest of honor. He's dressed in black inside a black bassinet that bears a swinging silver crucifix tied upside-down. His eyes are golden yellow with vertical, black-slit pupils like the eyes of a cat. He has claws, budding horns, and a tail. She decides to kill him . . . *it*. But he is her son. Perhaps her mother love can save him? *Her baby!* The coven quietly worships: "Hail, Rosemary! Hail, Satan!"

Rosemary's Baby, a novel by Ira Levin

THE FINAL PRAYERS OF THE ROMAN CATHOLIC LATIN MASS

May the tribute of my worship be pleasing to Thee, most holy Trinity, and grant that the sacrifice which I, all unworthy, have offered in the presence of Thy majesty, may be acceptable to Thee, and through Thy mercy obtain forgiveness for me and all for whom I have offered it. Through Christ our Lord. Amen.

VII

BELOW THE BELT: LEGAL AND EXTRALEGAL

Justice is a contract of expediency entered
upon to prevent men harming or being harmed.

EPICURUS

"We Cover the World War II Waterfront": The Mafia Enlists in U.S. Naval Intelligence

Charles "Lucky" Luciano.

BACKGROUND: On March 7, 1942, the navy's Intelligence Office appealed to District Attorney Frank Hogan and Chief Rackets Investigator Murray Gurfein for help in ending Nazi sabotage on East Coast waterfronts. Nazi subs were attacking U.S. ships just off Long Island; the *Normandie* had been the victim of arson in her North River pier the previous month. The enemy was everywhere. Americans were required to unite to fight. C. Radcliffe Haffernden, head of the Naval Intelligence section investigating espionage and sabotage, began the delicate operation of contacting and utilizing the Mafia's powerful waterfront connections. Socks Lanza, a man known to have friendships within the Mafia, was under indictment for conspiracy and extortion. He and his attorney met with Gurfein on a park bench in Manhattan on March 26. Socks convinced Naval Intelligence that the imprisoned Lucky Luciano was their best bet: He knew everyone who mattered.

THE DEAL: In exchange for Mafia cooperation with Naval Intelligence, Lucky Luciano would drop his petition to have his sentence reduced and would think instead of executive clemency—a full pardon. Luciano demanded that his assistance be kept secret. If the Nazis won the war, he wanted to be able to return to Italy without fear of assassination. Naval Intelligence agreed not to tell a soul.

RESULTS: Naval Intelligence men were placed in union jobs as shiploaders, dockworkers, waiters in pier bars, and clerks in hotels all over Manhattan. The island and the surrounding coastal areas were cased by underworld informants. Luciano was transferred to a prison closer to New York City. He worked with his big-shot buddies Frank Costello, John Dunn, and Willie Moretti. (Socks had already brought in Meyer Lansky.) Haffernden claimed that 40 percent of their tips were reliable. Early in 1946, Luciano was dutifully granted executive clemency unquestioningly by New York's Governor Dewey for "rendering wartime service." On February 9, Luciano was deported to Sicily. Rumors abounded that Dewey had sold the pardon for campaign funds. In 1953, he privately requested an exhaustive and secret probe into the exact nature of those "wartime services." In the spring of 1954, after twenty-six hundred pages of testimony and interpretation, Chief of Naval Operations Carl F. Espe confirmed that Luciano's role in the war effort had linked the navy with the underworld. He requested Dewey's silence, however, because the facts might "jeopardize operations of a similar nature" in the future, should they be required. The report was kept with Dewey's private papers and not released until after his death.

Dealmaker as Godfather: Charlie ("Lucky") Luciano

Mafiosi are a particular breed of Sicilian who usually stick together in their endeavors, but Lucky Luciano broke the mold, as well as a few laws.

Born in Sicily in 1897, Salvatore Lucanio traveled in steerage with his family to New York City in 1906. They lived in a tenement on the Lower East Side. Speaking no English, he did poorly in school but came to admire the Jewish children in the neighborhood who worked and made good allies. Hitting the streets at fourteen—after the fifth grade—he became leader of a gang, insisting that each member have a paying job as a front. The gang pooled their money and doled it out by group vote so no one would flash it around and draw suspicion. He accepted Irish as members. Then he teamed up with Francisco Castiglia (Frank Costello), who was a non-Sicilian from Cozenso. The two were arrested in 1915 and sent to jail for one year for possession of a gun and "being prepared to do the work of a gunman." In 1918, he got another year for delivering heroin in the hatbands of the hats that he was legally delivering.

For his second gang, he hooked up with math prodigy Meyer Lansky, the wild and impulsive "Bugsy" Siegel, and Costello. He purposely caught "the clap" to avoid World War I on a medical discharge, and with his three pals he set up a "bank" in which they pooled their funds. "Ever since we was kids, we always knew that people could be bought." Enter 1919 and Prohibition. Luciano recognized the opportunity for organizing crime into a major industry. The four joined up with Joe Adonis and created "Lansky's Law": "If you

"We're bigger than U.S. Steel!"

Meyer Lansky

have a lot of what people want and can't get, then you can supply the demand and shovel in the dough." They sold the best scotch uncut. A fifth cost them $2.50; they sold it for $30.00. Costello bought them political and police protection; Lansky did the bookkeeping; Siegel rode shotgun (with Lansky); and Adonis and Lucky set up the business. New alliances were formed with the garment district through Lepke; in Brooklyn through Scalise and Gambino and Anastasia; in The Bronx through "Dutch" Schultz; in New Jersey through Zillman and Moretti; and in the gambling industry through Rothstein.

By 1923, Lucky was a huge success, courted by the Godfathers of the New York City "families" to give up his independence and join their outfits. But the Godfathers hated Jews, and Lucky hated nobody who had "talent." He joined forces with Nucky Johnson, who ran Atlantic City. In exchange for 10 percent of the booze game, Nucky gave him an exclusive landing right on "his" beach, protection on his territory, and full control of all slot machines. Lucky organized New York City "mom and pop" stores into a mammoth bookmaking/betting machine by guaranteeing each store $150 a week; he grossed over $500,000 a week. In 1925 he made $12 million, tax free, from booze alone. His payroll ran about $1 million for over a thousand people—with over $5 million for protection (most of it to the police) and $2 million in expenses. He netted $4 million in profits per year. He and Lansky invented the numbers' racket, where people bet on a daily winning number; and since the stupendous profits could not be legally invested, they turned to loansharking to individuals, industries, and labor unions—at up to 1,000 percent interest. (If Lucky gave the union leaders bucks, they gave him control of small locals. If businesses couldn't pay back, he got a partnership.)

He *owned* the police department by 1925, eventually paying Commissioners Warren and Whalen twenty thousand dollars a week. He also bought the politicians of both parties: "In my opinion it was a three-party system—them two and us." He helped elect over eighty politicians: "They belonged to me lock, stock, and barrel." In 1927, he became second-in-command to Don Masseria, a Godfather; he gained a family empire *but* kept full control of his liquor industry. He reorganized the "outfit" and merged the country's best bootleggers into a cartel, The Seven Group. In 1928, Governor Al Smith asked Lucky to help him get elected president: If you deliver delegates for me, I'll help you control the whiskey industry *legally* when I repeal prohibition. Smith won the nomination but lost the election to Hoover. It was one of the few times Lucky ever backed a loser.

After the stock-market crash, Lucky backed Moses Annenberg when he started "the racing wire," a national telephone service for bookies that became "the heart of the biggest gambling empire in the world." As the result of a war among the Mafia families—Lucky arranged for the death of his own Don Masseria—five New York families emerged overseen by Don Maranzano and Lucky, who was given the remains of the Masseria clan as family of his own. He quickly orchestrated Maranzano's demise, ending the old-order Sicilian don tradition. Making Lansky his *consigliere,* he refused to be called the Boss of Bosses because it was un-American not to have a majority (of five) rule in New York City. At the end of 1931, with Capone's support in Chicago, he formed the *Unione Siciliano,* a national syndicate of organized crime with himself as uncrowned but openly honored leader.

Governor Franklin D. Roosevelt was running for president. Smith was running again, but Lucky sensed the FDR drift and threw his weight, bucks, and votes to FDR, who promised to muzzle Judge Seabury's investigations into crime. Smith wept, begging Lucky not to trust FDR. After winning the nomination, FDR double-crossed Lucky and built a platform on crushing the underworld. Under Seabury's spotlight, Major Jimmy Walker resigned and Tammany Hall was publicly exposed, while Lucky negotiated the gambling rights to Havana for a guaranteed $3 million a year minimum, after $3 million up front to his Cuban ally Batista. Because "during Prohibition we probably ran the biggest truckin' operation in the United States," Lucky moved into the protection-of-deliveries racket, getting a stronghold on the unions and the fast-food business: If you don't pay up, your bread/meat/milk/fish will spoil. By the end of 1935, he estimated the outfit was "grossin' maybe a couple billion dollars a year."

New York District Attorney Thomas Dewey arrested him on ninety counts of "compulsory prostitution." In 1936, he was sentenced to thirty to fifty years in prison. He still ran the show from prison until "Operation Underworld" sprang him when he cooperated with Dewey and U.S. Naval Intelligence [see " 'We Cover the World War II Waterfront': The Mafia Enlists in U.S. Naval Intelligence," page 246]. Exiled to Italy, he was consulted for advice by his "family" on all matters of importance. In 1952, he offered to settle the narcotics problem for the United States—"at least a fuckin' good part of it"—in return for a United States visa, but he was refused. He received $25,000 a week from the States and the occasional "respect" payment, living a fairly quiet life as a tourist attraction, while keeping himself engaged in the intrigues of his United States clan. He retired in 1959, after

Castro came to power in Cuba and his family was restructured. Lucky died of a heart attack in 1962. He was buried in Queens, New York, with his natal family.

THE CHARTER OF THE CITY OF LONDON, 1130, FROM KING HENRY I

Henry, by the grace of God King of the English, ... sends greetings to all his faithful subjects, both French and English throughout England. Know that I have granted to my citizens of London that they shall hold Middlesex at farm for a composite payment of £300 annually ... with full power to appoint as sheriff whomsoever they please of their own number, and as justice anyone or whomsoever they please of their own number to look after the pleas of my crown and the proceedings to which they give rise; no one else shall be justice over these people of London. And the citizens shall not plead outside the city walls for any plea ... nor shall any of them be forced to prove his innocence at law in a trial by combat. And if any citizen is impleaded in a crown plea, let him assert his standing as a citizen of London by an oath which shall be judged within the city ... and let all men of London and all their goods be free and exempt from payment of any toll, passage ... and other dues throughout the whole of England and in all the seaports ...

Tears Wept by the Sun:
Pizarro and the Incas

BACKGROUND: Pizarro, the Spanish conquistador, could not have arrived in Peru, center of the Inca Empire, at a time more auspicious for his mission of plunder. The Incas were fighting a bitter civil war; their powerful civilization had been undermined because the previous king had, out of his love for the son he'd had with a beautiful Ecuadorian princess, divided his kingdom between that son, Atahualpa, and his rightful heir. In this well-regulated theocracy, the king's power far exceeded that of European rulers. He was emperor, pope, and demigod, both lawmaker and the law—and having two such supreme rulers was confusing to the people. The kingdom they'd inherited was one of the most advanced the world had seen: Aqueducts carried water five hundred miles, flagstone roads up to thirty-two hundred miles long connected all parts of the huge empire, and agrarian laws equally divided all arable land, ensuring that while few were rich, no one starved.

Chief among the Incan arts was goldsmithing. The Peruvian highlands teemed with gold, the "tears wept by the Sun," as the Incas called it, and it was the sun that they worshipped. Their temples were filled with elaborate gold ceremonial objects, and the huge central temple in the capital was literally a gold mine. The walls and the ceiling were gilded and positioned so that when rays of morning light hit the altar, heavenly, golden light was reflected back over the entire structure. It was dazzling. The greedy conquistadores had been lured to the New World by their fantasies of such treasure (they were looking for El Dorado, where "the sands sparkled with gems, and golden pebbles as large as birds eggs were dragged in nets out of rivers") but, so far, great treasure had eluded them. Hearing from the coastal people about the wealthy highland kingdom of the Incas, Pizarro and his intrepid force of 177 men (and their horses) hacked their way through the thick underbrush and, shivering in their clumsy armor, climbed the Andes in search of the Incan leader they were certain could lead them to riches.

In November of 1532, Pizarro found Atahualpa encamped with part of his army outside a deserted city. (A few months before this, Atahualpa had captured the capital and his rival half-brother, whom he eventually had killed.) Establishing camp in the empty city, Pizarro devised a plan that was as perfidious as it was audacious: He would dispense with all diplomatic niceties and simply invite the king over and capture him. With their absolute ruler in bondage, the Incas would do whatever the conquistadores asked. Of course, the Spanish were vastly outnumbered, but they had two things in their favor: They had no scruples, and the Incas had no guns. So, with the unsuspecting Atahualpa coming to meet the exotic white man, two-thirds of the Spaniards hid in surrounding buildings, their guns loaded, awaiting Pizarro's signal. When the Incan king arrived, he was being carried on a throne of solid gold and was bedecked in a huge, gem-encrusted gold headdress. It was enough to make the conquistadores salivate. A priest, unable to restrain himself, immediately rushed up to the stone-faced ruler and, through a severely taxed interpreter, attempted to explain the story of Christ and the Crucifixion. He put special emphasis on the fact that Christ's power had passed, through the Apostle Paul, over to the popes, and that it was the present pope who had commissioned the Spanish king to conquer and convert the New World. Embrace Christ and acknowledge the authority of Emperor Charles IV, cried the priest, thrusting a Bible into the hands of Atahualpa. Atahualpa was very insulted and said, "I am the greatest Prince on Earth. . . . As for the pope, he must be crazy to talk of giving away countries which do not belong to him." With that he threw the Bible on the ground. Pizarro gave the signal, and suddenly death rained down on the confused Incas; never having encountered guns before, they could not understand death coming at them from such a distance. The Spanish killed as many as they could, taking care not to harm Atahualpa, whom they took as a hostage.

THE DEAL: Within only a few days, the Incan King deduced that behind the Spanish show of religious zeal lay an overriding lust for gold. Therefore, he made Pizarro an offer: If I fill this room [it was seventeen feet by twenty-two feet] with gold up to here [9 feet] will you release me? Sure, said Pizarro—if you do it within two months.

RESULTS: Atahualpa's followers, desperate to save their king, dispatched couriers to the capital; they returned bearing the finest gold treasures. Temples were stripped and the famous gold gardens, resplendent with full-scale gold reproductions of plants, animals, birds, even fountains, were dismantled and brought to fill the room. (Most of it was eventually melted down into ingot. The value of the treasure has been put at $800 million in today's terms.) Having fulfilled his part of the bargain, Atahualpa demanded to be released. Liberate the very man who might unite the Incan Empire against us? Unlikely, said Pizarro. You will be burned at the stake—unless you are willing to convert to Christianity, in which case we will execute you in the faster Spanish style of the "garrote"—strangulation by a short noose twisted by a stick. Finally realizing the true moral mettle of the invaders of his doomed kingdom, Atahualpa accepted baptism and was strangled.

With the execution of their supreme ruler following the chaos of the civil war, the Incan Empire quickly fell to pieces. The Spanish were able to step in, establishing political rule over Peru that lasted until 1821. The avaricious conquistadores had trouble deciding among themselves how the Incan plunder was to be divided, and they fell into warring factions. Pizarro had his throat slashed by Spanish assassins in 1541. He left behind a bloody and brutal legacy, and two young children by the daughter of Atahualpa, last of the Incan kings.

America's Inquisition: HUAC versus "The Tinseltown Pinks"

BACKGROUND: "Are you now or have you ever been a member of the Communist party?"

The test of loyalty to Congress's House Committee on Un-American Activities (HUAC) was the willingness of those subpoenaed to inform on their "Commie" friends. They then avoided being savaged by the press "red-baiters"—among the most virulent were Walter Winchell, Hedda Hopper, Victor Riesel, Westbrook Pegler, and George Sokolosky—and being blacklisted (and denied work). HUAC supporters—like the American Legion and the American right-wing public—boycotted programs, sponsors, and artists.

THE DEAL: Those testifying could (A) invoke the First Amendment with its *guarantee* of free speech and association; (B) invoke the Fifth Amendment with its privilege against self-incrimination; or (C) be a "friendly witness," that is, cooperate and inform on friends.

RESULTS: **A.** Go to prison for contempt of Congress and be blacklisted like the "Hollywood Ten": Alvah Bessie, Herbert Biberman, Lester Cole, Edward Dmytryk,* Ring Lardner, Jr., John Howard Lawson, Albert Maltz, Sam Ornitz, Robert Adrian Scott, and Dalton Trumbo.

B. Be blacklisted and not work. This procedure was supported by the New York/Hollywood unions. Those accepting it: Howard da Silva, Gale Sondergaard, Carl Foreman, Paul Robeson, Anne Revere, and Lillian Hellman, among *many* others.

C. Be "patriotic" and inform on your friends, hoping to continue working in the "cooperating" industry. Those accepting it: Jerome Robbins, Budd Schulberg, Elia Kazan, Abe Burrows, Sterling Hayden, Clifford Odets, Artie Shaw, Adolphe Menjou, Lee J. Cobb, Robert Rossen, Robert Taylor, and *many* others.

America was convulsed by frenzied anti-Communist witch hunts that became a national obsession, overriding constitutional rights. Using leverage gained by the Cold War, right-wing extremists and fanatical idealists came into power using the greed of the studio chiefs and corporate sponsors, the fear and cowardice of the contract players and independent talents, the gullibility and ignorance of the American public, and the amorality of the American press in search of a hot issue.

There were exceptions to the results of A, B, and C. Larry Parks chose C but was still hounded by Hedda Hopper, who wrote of him as a "sneaking Commie whelp who, too late, confessed his shame before Congress." John Wayne, Hopper, and others formed the thousand-member Motion Picture Alliance—in its bylaws: "We do not publicly associate with traitors." Parks's $75,000-contract for a picture he had

---

"The Fifth means they can't ask *me*, the First means they can't ask *anybody*."

   Pete Seeger, who took the First

"It will do no good to search for villains or heroes or saints or devils because there were none; there were only victims."

   Dalton Trumbo (A), 1970

"To understand all is not to forgive all."

   Albert Maltz (A), 1978

---

*After prison he joined the C group.

—— 253

started with Columbia Pictures was torn up and his contract bought out. His career was destroyed.

For five years after the hearings, Oscar winners had to swear: "I am not now, nor have I ever been a member of the Communist party." The blacklist ended after three blacklisted writers, working under pseudonyms and selling their scripts on the artistic black market, won the Oscar three years in a row: Dalton Trumbo (A) in 1956 for *The Brave One*; Carl Foreman (A) in 1957 for *The Bridge on the River Kwai* [see "You Can't Take It with You: Bill Holden's Deferred Salary for *Kwai*" page 350]; and Ned Young (B) in 1958 for *The Defiant Ones*. In 1959, the Motion Picture Academy rescinded its bylaw prohibiting awards to those who refused to cooperate with HUAC.

◆ ◆ ◆ ◆

Business as Usual

John Randolph (B), it was announced, would act in a summer-stock production in Chicago soon after he was blacklisted. The theater manager, who did not believe blacklisting was constitutional, was informed by the local American Legion post that its members were planning to picket and close the show if Randolph appeared. The head of the patriotic American Legion post was a florist. The theater manager called a Teamster friend who called the florist: "You picket that show and your trucks don't roll." The American Legion did not picket.

THE FALL FROM GRACE: KLAUS BARBIE AND U.S. ARMY INTELLIGENCE

In 1947, American intelligence officers recruited Klaus Barbie as a paid anti-Communist spy, even though he was listed on a central Allied registry of war criminals as wanted in France for murder. After learning in 1949 that Barbie had been directly responsible for the torture and murder of French patriots and Jews, as well as for the deportation of thousands to death camps, the U.S. Army Intelligence officers continued to use him as a paid informant in occupied Germany.

In December 1950, a memorandum from Captain Walter Unrath of the Army Counter Intelligence Corps recommended that the army dissociate itself from Barbie but noted that sending him to stand trial in France would expose to the world that "this unit has probably used the services of a war criminal and protected such person." Besides, American intelligence secrets known to Barbie might fall into the hands of French Communists and their Soviet allies. In return for Barbie's cooperation, U.S. Army Intelligence lied and said they had lost contact with Barbie. In 1951 they smuggled Barbie and his family out of Europe through an underground railroad called the "rat line," set up for Soviet-bloc defectors and informants. It was operated for them by "a Fascist, war criminal, etc." Croatian priest. Barbie and his family sailed from Genoa to Argentina, then went to Bolivia where he prospered for thirty-two years. He was expelled by the new government that took over in Bolivia in February 1983, to France, where he will stand trial as a war criminal.

In August 1983, the U.S. State Department made a rare official apology to France after the Justice Department released a 218-page report on the arrangement between Barbie and U.S. Army Intelligence officers.

The Affair: Dreyfus

BACKGROUND: World history is riddled with political scandals. Few have dislodged a civilization's cornerstone, brought about a great writer's murder, and haunted four successive presidencies for nearly twenty years. It started with the unjust persecution of one man and became an international cause célèbre, dragging the decadent nineteenth century alive and well into the twentieth.

In 1893, at a time when *la belle France* was in a froth of anti-Semitism—Paris had become a mecca for Jews fleeing pogroms in Central and Slavic Europe—Alfred Dreyfus, a Jewish honor student at the War College in Paris, was assigned as a trainee to the Army General Staff, on which no acknowledged Jew had ever served in the entire history of the French military. Poised, self-confident, apolitical, he boldly marched into this aristocratic, Roman Catholic, "incontrovertably French" stronghold, even though many generals and most of his fellow officers were openly hostile. He worked tirelessly, which annoyed everyone even more, and he seemed destined for a triumphant career.

Not at all like Major Ferdinand Esterhazy who, having finagled a permanent commission in the regular army and the roseate of the Legion of Honor, was going nowhere *fast*. Sick of being hounded for gambling debts, this cunning scoundrel offered himself as a spy to the Imperial German Embassy in Paris. Having no access to classified material, he sold them shoddy goods, including a packet of five items to which he added a hand-written covering note, or *bordereau*, that curtly identified its contents by subject. The German attaché forwarded the packet to Berlin but ripped up the *bordereau* and threw it into his embassy wastepaper basket. The French cleaning woman was a counterintelligence (CI) agent. She dutifully delivered her find to her boss, Major Henry, who handed the proof of treason to his chief, Colonel Sandherr of the Army General Staff, who took it to his boss, General Mercier, the minister of war.

Desperate to avoid a scandal—there had been a string of espionage cases—and eager to steady a shaky political position, Mercier was determined to bag the spy. He had the *bordereau* photographed and distributed to every department of the General Staff. It was immediately decided that only a trainee, moving from department to department, could have access to such varied information. Only one trainee was assumed capable of perfidy—the one they all believed had never belonged among them: Alfred Dreyfus, Jew. And the handwriting matched . . . sort of. Everyone agreed there was good cause for a formal investigation. Five graphologists studied the evidence; it was two for, and three against. Mercier ordered the arrest. The appointed preliminary investigator hesitated: How could he accuse one of the army's young superstars on such weak evidence?

On October 15, 1894, Dreyfus was locked into a military prison. The newspapers went berserk with vicious glee over the jailing of the Jewish officer. Their worst fears were realized; even the revered army had been corrupted by the infidels. Frenzied, CI scurried to strengthen its case. Another scrap from the embassy wastepaper basket referring to a known spy, Duclois, as "D," was slipped into the Dreyfus file. Then Sandherr ordered Henry to doctor an intercepted Italian Intelligence message; an innocuous enquiry about Dreyfus became an instruction to disown him. And some undecipherable shreds were added for dramatic weight. At the court-martial, without informing Dreyfus or his defense attorney, this bogus file was sneaked into the judges. Dreyfus was found guilty of passing secrets. On April 13, 1895, he was sent to Devil's Island, southeast of Venezuela, where he was confined to a small, insect-ridden cage in agonizing heat with minimal food, under constant and sadistic surveillance. Many times he veered toward death. Only his drive to be vindicated and his love for his strong, devoted wife, Lucie, and their two children kept him alive. He wrote in his diary: "I no longer know how I manage to live. My brain is pulverized." His brother, Mathieu, continued the fight to free him.

Upon Sandherr's death, Major Georges Picquart became head of CI. The wastepaper basket at the German Embassy revealed another spy: one Major Esterhazy. A sample of his handwriting—*voila!*—matched the script of the famous *bordereau*. Picquart then discovered that the secret file had been illegally submitted as evidence. Indignant, he went the rounds of the top brass. They all tried to silence him. What did it matter if a little chicanery had sent the Jew to Devil's Island? It was a matter of national security and army morale, which was also a matter of national security. Stunned, Picquart insisted: But the man is innocent! Word of the file, Esterhazy, and the *bordereau* reached the press. Slowly the tide began to turn. The vice-president of the Senate informed Lucie Dreyfus that he believed her husband to be innocent. Reprieve seemed imminent. The army was poised on the edge of disgrace.

THE DEAL: Major Henry, fiddling with the file, forged a new piece of "evidence" that *directly* incriminated Dreyfus. (He even forged a note from the kaiser.) Picquart was shipped to a war zone where the army brass assumed he would be killed; Henry became acting chief of CI. Esterhazy was honorably retired from the army for "temporary infirmity" and in October 1897 was offered immunity from prosecution for spying if he agreed to follow army instructions in all matters relating to "The Affair," as the Dreyfus case was now known around the world. He agreed, threatening to expose everyone if he were not properly protected.

RESULTS: To appease the Dreyfusards, Esterhazy was "investigated" by the army and found innocent of all charges: Henry's "evidence" proved Dreyfus had done it all. Esterhazy claimed that he, himself, and the army were victims of a plot by the Jewish "syndicate." The country became fiercely fragmented between the army, the French Catholic church, the aristocracy, political Conservatives, the anti-Semitic press, Socialist workers, *and* the Liberals, Radicals, and intellectuals. (The outstanding writers, artists, and academics signed a petition, "Manifesto for Intellectuals," and the new word *intellectual* entered the world's dictionaries.) The larger, pro-army faction had a headlock on the nation until Emil Zola wrote *J'Accuse (I Accuse)*. The newspaper that printed it experienced a circulation leap from thirty thousand to three hundred thousand copies. Zola accused *by name* the members of the General Staff of various collusive villainies. He was tried for libel and eventually fled to England. Picquart was dismissed from the army.

After national elections in 1898, a Radical government was formed. However, the new war minister proclaimed: Leave Dreyfus on Devil's Island. Why endanger the army for moral peace? The case

> . . . when the truth is buried underground, it grows, it chokes, it gathers such an explosive force that on the day when it bursts out, it blows everything up with it.
>
> Zola, *J'Accuse*

Captain Dreyfus after being convicted in Rennes, France, 1899.

was reopened, the file reexamined—it was now fluffed up to over three hundred items—and the forgery discovered. Henry confessed before committing suicide. Lucie Dreyfus petitioned the government for a revision of the army's judgment. In 1899, after four years, two months, five days of imprisonment, Dreyfus was retried at Rennes, France, by a military court. Again, the army found him guilty! "A thrill of horror and shame ran through the whole civilized world," said the London *Times* editorial. Only the Catholic and anti-Semitic presses gloated. A month later, Dreyfus was pardoned. Though not vindicated, he was a free man. Physically and emotionally devastated by his ordeal, he acquiesced, wanting only to be left in peace. For the Dreyfusards, amnesty was not enough.

In 1902, Zola, also pardoned, was murdered by anti-Dreyfus masons who sealed his chimney while they worked on a nearby roof; he died of carbon-monoxide poisoning. Two years later, after constant pressure from the Dreyfusards "for the honor of France," Dreyfus was decreed innocent of all charges and reinstated into the army as a major. He was also inducted into the Legion of Honor. No one on the General Staff was prosecuted; each player in The Affair remained a hero to some faction.

The vehement anti-Semitism abated somewhat, but a new government formed by a Radical and Socialist coalition turned for revenge on the Catholics and their aristocratic co-conspirators. By October 1903, a small revolution had closed sixteen thousand Catholic institutions. On December 9, 1905, separation of church and state became law in France. After two thousand years, Rome's oldest daughter would go it alone. Picquart was reinstated to the General Staff and became minister of war under Clemenceau in 1906. Esterhazy lived comfortably, self-exiled to England where he claimed to have been a misunderstood double-agent who had been working for the army all the while. Dreyfus died in Paris in 1935.

BEE'S WAX

Law did not exist in Europe as a profession until the thirteenth century when the lawmaking function of the people began to be displaced by a specially trained class of professional initiates. From the beginning, lawyers were not popular with the laboring classes, who felt that lawyers served only the interests of the rich elite. One thirteenth-century exception, a man who devoted himself to mediating on behalf of the poor, was made a saint, and a popular ditty about him stated:

> Saint Yves is from Brittany
> A lawyer but not a thief
> Such a thing is beyond belief!

A few centuries later, Shakespeare wrote about a landlord-tenant dispute in *Henry IV, Part II*:

DICK: The first thing we do, let's kill all the lawyers.
CADE: Nay, that I mean to do. Is this not a lamentable thing, that of the skin of an innocent lamb, should be made parchment? That parchment, being scribbl'd o'er, should undo a man? Some say the bee stings; but I say, 'tis the bee's wax; for I did but seal once to a thing, and I was never mine own man since.

The Fourth Man: Communists in the British Upper Crust

Four little boys from school are we
Pert as a school-boy well can be
Filled to the brim with radical glee
Four little boys from school.

BACKGROUND: The entire "Fourth Man" affair has the air of a perverse Gilbert and Sullivan operetta, complete with knights, high art, the old-boy syndrome, and high treason: the triumph of British upper-class morality over honor and duty. Not very cricket . . .

During the 1930s, Anthony Blunt was a brilliant young don at Cambridge University. His despair over Prime Minister Chamberlain's appeasement of Hitler at Munich forced him to choose "conscience over country." As he explained: "In the mid-1930s, it seemed to me and to many of my contemporaries that the Communist Party and Russia constituted the only firm bulwark against Fascism, since the Western democracies were taking an uncertain, compromising attitude towards Germany." All over the world, anti-Fascist intellectuals agreed with him. (In America, their commitment to the Communist party would later haunt them when Senator McCarthy ran amock with his congressional witch hunts [see "America's Inquisition: HUAC versus 'The Tinseltown Pinks,' " page 252].) But rather than join the Communist party and fight Chamberlain openly from within the system, Blunt became a Soviet "mole," or spy. As a central figure in the Apostles, a university club whose members, mostly drawn from the privileged upper class, saw themselves as "the leading intellectuals of revolution," Blunt secretly recruited three spies for the Soviet Union: Guy Burgess, Donald Maclean, and Harold ("Kim") Philby. In 1937, he approached an American, Michael Straight, but was rejected.

During World War II, Blunt admitted: "My loyalty was with Moscow." He and the other three eased themselves into government intelligence. Blunt became a high-ranking officer in MI5—the British FBI concerned with internal counterintelligence: searching for spies in England—while the three infiltrated the foreign service (MI6). Blunt resigned from MI5 in 1945. Two years later, he became director of the Courtauld Institute of Art in London; by 1956 he had won for the institute recognition as one of the finest art-history schools in the world. He was knighted for his achievement, and became, as Surveyor of the Queen's Pictures, the curator of the royal art, which is one of the truly great collections.

Then, in 1963, Kim Philby's cover was blown and he was revealed to be a double agent under contract to MI6 but actually working for Russia. Amid tremendous publicity, he fled to the Soviet Union, joining Maclean and Burgess, who had defected in 1951 just as they were about to be exposed. It was known that someone "in high places" had assisted them; when Philby convincingly denied playing that role, it became clear that a "fourth man" was still lurking about. Over the years, Sir Anthony, due to his associations with the Trinity College radicals (especially Maclean, Burgess, and Philby) and his

MI5 info, was interrogated eleven times by British Intelligence, but he consistently and successfully denied his guilt. Until Michael Straight resurfaced in America.

Straight had edited *The New Republic*, a strongly liberal magazine. Under clearance examination by the FBI for a job in the Kennedy administration, he revealed his contact with Blunt; the FBI alerted their British counterparts. It was an undeniable, substantive account of Sir Anthony's espionage. Confronted with Straight's allegations, Blunt cracked. "He sat in silence for a while. He got up, looked out the window, poured himself a drink and after a few minutes confessed."

THE DEAL: Sir Anthony Blunt categorically denied any present connection with the espionage business, but he was respectfully offered immunity in exchange for continued cooperation with British Intelligence. He apologized for his "appalling mistake," claiming that he had not caused loss of life directly or compromised military operations. His apology was politely accepted. He also agreed to give information on the defected three who were out of commission and comfortably settled in USSR.

RESULTS: For having committed high treason during wartime, Sir Anthony Blunt received *no* punishment. His impeccable reputation in art circles and all honors remained intact, his *very* high social standing was not tarnished, and his custodial job and directorship continued; *no one was embarrassed*—not he, or the queen, or her intelligence officers, or any of their well-heeled friends. Blunt would have died with his secret on ice but for a "leak" from an unknown source to the British press in 1979. It caused an uproar throughout England. Prime Minister Margaret Thatcher was forced to publicly strip Blunt of his knighthood, he resigned from the British Academy, and the scandal was denounced in Parliament as proof of Britain's double standard of justice: The old-boy network of powerful, influential friends can maneuver forgiveness for *any* crime. Though he said that he "bitterly regretted" his behavior, he always justified his right to choose conscience over country, like E. M. Forster, and said, simply: "I could not denounce my friends."

Blunt died in his home in London in March 1983. Burgess died in 1963. Maclean died in February 1983. Philby is the lone survivor of the infamous four.

The only nagging question remaining about the Fourth Man? Who'll play Blunt in the Masterpiece Theater production?

Not a Good-Neighbor Policy:
Butch Cassidy and the
Governor of Wyoming

BACKGROUND: It is said that some people can charm the birds from the trees. It is a rarer bird that can charm responsible people out of their trees.

Butch Cassidy was the leader of the largest, most successful, last great "gang"—the Wild Bunch. He was possibly the most charismatic of his breed in United States history, and the American public adored him. He killed only once in his life when, for a brief period, he went "straight" and was working as a payroll guard. In the beginning of his career, he was arrested and jailed in Wyoming. When he came up for parole before the governor of the state, he struck a bargain unique in the annals of criminal justice.

THE DEAL: The governor asked him to go straight. Butch, being honest, said he couldn't, but, if freed, he would never commit a crime in Wyoming again.

RESULTS: The convict's proposal was accepted by the governor of Wyoming. Butch kept his word. If his gang went across the border into Wyoming to pull off a job, he sat that caper out.

Cassidy and the Sundance Kid left the United States for the safer pastures of Bolivia. There they became known as *bandidos Yanquis* and in true outlaw style died in a shower of bullets.

ONE VIEW OF PLEA BARGAINING

Sometimes I've got to make deals with sinners to catch devils. If I have a weak case I have to have *some* testimony. And why should a guy testify for me for nothing? If everybody kept his mouth shut, they'd all go free. Sometimes I'm not fighting with both hands. I've got one hand tied behind my back. So I have to make deals. People will say, "But all of them are guilty of murder." The fact is sometimes bad people get deals and go free. It's a practical world.

Ralph N. Greene III,
ex–chief assistant state attorney,
Duval County, Florida

Stick It to Her: The Wizard of Oz

BACKGROUND: A witch needs a wand to do her stuff, but during persecutions, a wand around the house is a dead giveaway, so witches turn to the ubiquitous broom. It takes a lot to separate a working witch from her broom—sometimes, it takes murder!

Dorothy Gale, gentle and sweet, lives on a Kansas prairie in a small wooden house with her dog, Toto, her Aunt Emily, and her Uncle Henry. Dorothy longs for the magical day when she can travel out of Kansas over the rainbow where the dreams that she dares to dream really will come true. A cyclone traps her in the house with Toto and a shattered window knocks her out. When she comes to, she and her house are up *inside* the wind funnel. It drops her into the Munchkin Country of the Land of Oz, on top of the Wicked Witch of the East.

The joyful Munchkins and their friend Glinda, the Good Witch of the North, rejoice that the Wicked Witch is dead, until her evil sister, the Wicked Witch of the West, appears. If she owns her sister's ruby slippers, she will have a monopoly on all the evil in Oz. Magically, Glinda transports the slippers onto Dorothy's feet because their power will protect her; they can't be taken by force, since the wearer commands them. Horrified at having the Wicked Witch for an enemy, and longing for dull Kansas, Dorothy begs for help. Only the great and powerful Wizard of Oz can help her now. Where does he live? In the Emerald City. How does one get there? Via the Yellow Brick Road.

Dorothy Gale, and her little dog, too, set off to see the Wizard. Not far along, they meet a straw scarecrow who needs—he thinks—a brain. Then they meet a tin woodman who needs—he thinks—a heart. And finally, they meet a cowardly lion who needs—he thinks—some courage. The Wicked Witch tries to keep them from Oz, but Glinda intercedes and the Emerald City is quickly reached. The wondrous and all-wise Oz sets a hard bargain.

THE DEAL: If Dorothy and her three friends *kill* the irksome Witch of the West, bringing back her broomstick as proof, the Wizard will grant their wishes. The four agree to try.

RESULTS: They head for the Country of the Winkies to the west of the Emerald City. The Witch sends her Winged Monkeys to capture Dorothy, Toto, and the slippers. The three distraught friends sneak into her castle where Dorothy is a prisoner, staunchly refusing to hand over the ruby goods. The Tin Woodman chops down her locked door, and Dorothy leads the chase, but the Wicked Witch corners the crew. Lighting the broomstick, she torches the Scarecrow. Quickly, Dorothy grabs a pail of water and douses the fire, soaking the Witch, who promptly melts, screaming: "Who would have thought a good little girl like you could destroy my beautiful wickedness? What a world! What a world!"

Triumphant, the four return to Oz bearing their charred trophy. Though the great Oz is revealed as a humbug (a refugee from "Bailum and Barney's" Circus), he teaches the adventurers that within themselves are the very things they sought: the Cowardly Lion was always brave, the Scarecrow shrewd, and the Tin Woodman loving. He promises to take Dorothy back to Kansas in a balloon but accidently departs from Oz alone, leaving Glinda to teach Dorothy that she, too, always had the power she sought: the ruby slippers tapped together three times will transport her home. Dorothy awakens in Kansas: "There's no place like home, Auntie Em," she cries. "There's no place like home!"

Survival of the Fittest with a Little Help from His Friends: Darwin *and* Wallace Create "Evolution"

BACKGROUND: When the old-boy network banded together to protect their chum Darwin's right of priority with the newfangled theory of evolution, they had no idea that they were erasing another genius from history. But, in effect, that is precisely what they did.

Alfred Russel Wallace was born in England in 1823, the eighth of nine children, and raised in poverty. At fourteen he was forced to leave school and home to become a surveyor with his migratory-carpenter brother. Constantly outdoors, he found nature "more and more the solace and delight" of his lonely life. In 1841 he bought a botany book and discovered the order in the plant kingdom. By literally saving pennies, he bought other books and devoted all his free time to collecting specimens and building an herbarium. Three years later, he took a job as an English teacher; in the local library he met Henry Walter Bates. Bates adored insects, particularly coleoptera (the Latin name for the order of insects known as beetles, chafers, weevils, fireflies, and ladybugs). Wallace became enthralled. Unlike dogs, cats, horses, birds, or other commonly observed species whose varieties are instantly recognizable, beetle families have as many as thirty thousand species, some with only minute differences whose boundaries cannot be determined. Why? Why so many? And where did they come from?

The idea of evolution was not new. Aristotle wrote of it. The Roman Lucretius had imagined that man was evolved by a natural law from an early beastlike form. Jean Baptiste Lamarck, the great eighteenth-century zoologist, had conjectured, "Everything passes by insensible shades into something else." Logically it made sense—nature is full of endless similarities and overlappings—but not one of the theorists had delivered any evidence on which to base a hypothesis. And in the mid-nineteenth century, the idea that species were not fixed eternally was comparable to a belief in alchemy. In fact, the most renowned scientists, bound by religious beliefs, taught that each species was individually created by God.

In 1848, Wallace and Bates bravely set off for the uncharted Amazon, where both could study the teeming natural world while earning their livings by sending back to England specimens of insects (at one penny each) and small mammals for British naturalists and institutions. While Wallace gathered specimens, he assembled evidence and began drawing conclusions by scrupulous adherence to the results of observation, conclusions that he reduced to general laws. In 1854, he went to the Malay archipelago. During his first two years, he collected thirty thousand specimens. In September 1855, *Annals*, the British journal of natural history, published his paper, "On the Law which has Regulated the Introduction of New Species," which he wrote in Sarawak, Borneo. It was concerned with the distribution of animals as an indication of "the way in which species have come into existence," changing by natural succession and descent from one into another. He did not suggest how or why this happened, but he offered cogent examples to prove his point.

Tucked away on his island, he was not aware of the response his Sarawak Law generated in England, because nothing appeared in print. However, Sir Charles Lyell, the father of scientific geology and an avid champion of the fixity of species, was so shaken by the logic of Wallace's paper that he immediately visited his close friend, Charles Darwin, whom he knew to be deeply engrossed in the species question. He urged Darwin to write out his views "pretty fully" before Wallace stole his thunder and ranked in history as the source of his theory.

Darwin, in 1855, was Britain's foremost naturalist, a leading geologist, and a prominent zoologist. He was an honored member of every prestigious society for scientific endeavor. He had published ground-

> "I rather hate the idea of writing for priority, yet I certainly should be vexed if anyone were to publish my doctrine before me."
>
> Charles Darwin, May 3, 1856

265

breaking books and monographs in each of his disciplines. In 1837, in his private "Notebook on Transmutation of Species," he had discarded the theory of fixed species; in 1844, he jotted down notes on "natural selection," the theory that Herbert Spencer dubbed "survival of the fittest."

But in 1855, when the Sarawak Law appeared, Darwin had published nothing on evolution. Heeding Lyell's warning about Wallace, Darwin worked furiously. He knew that natural selection explained *why* life was a series of adaptations to environment—some forms lived to improve the race while inferior forms died. But the question of how it all started, how so many species came from a few—"divergence"—was still unanswered. He wanted no part of controversial fragments; he wanted the whole theory completed, even if it meant waiting and writing a book. Then Wallace wrote a letter to Darwin. Completely isolated, he had chosen the famous naturalist as a correspondent because of similar passions. Darwin answered cordially and encouragingly that "they had come to similar conclusions."

In February 1858, Wallace finished a twelve-page essay, "On the Tendency of Varieties to Depart Indefinitely from the Original Type." He mailed it to Darwin from the small island of Ternate on March 9, the same day he mailed a letter to Bates's brother, also in England. In those days, mail took approximately three months to travel that route. Frederick Bates received Wallace's letter on June 3. Darwin claimed not to have received Wallace's letter and essay until June 18. However, on June 8, he wrote Hooker that he had finally—after nearly twenty-five years work—completed his theory of how species *continually* diverged in nature, calling his new theory "the keystone of my book." Coincidentally, Wallace's Ternate paper concludes, "there appears no reason to assign any definite limits" to the progression of certain varieties away from their parent species. In other words, there could be unlimited, random change in unlimited random directions on to infinity, possibly having begun from *one* primary organism, the strongest creations surviving by natural selection.

On June 18, when Darwin forwarded the Ternate paper to Lyell (at Wallace's suggestion, if Darwin thought it "sufficiently important"), he wrote: "Your words have come true with a vengeance that I should be forestalled . . . [and] all my originality smashed." Honorably, he suggested the essay be sent to a journal for publication immediately, although his own 1844 sketch contained, he claimed, all the same data—minus, he neglected to mention, a theory of divergence. And also, he wrote, he had a statement in a letter that he'd written in 1856 to the American botanist Asa Gray: "I come to the heterodox conclusion that there are no such things as independently-created species—that species are only strongly defined varieties," which, though an echo of Lamarck and written *after* the publication of the Sarawak Law, supposedly proved it was *his* theory. Both Hooker and Lyell felt Wallace's prior findings to be a great tragedy for their cherished friend and esteemed associate. In science, as in all competitive fields, the question of priority is paramount.

What to do? Wallace was no problem. He was far away in the Malay archipelago. Had the great Darwin, a great leader of the scientific establishment, devoted his life to this business of evolution only to be bested by an ungentlemanlike "bug-catcher" with no true education or serious credentials? Darwin confessed to beginning "half a letter to Wallace to give up all priority to him," when Lyell and Hooker rushed to his aid. "I have received your letter," he wrote Hooker on June 29, " . . . you have acted with more kindness, and so has Lyell, even than I could have expected." The much-vaunted code of Victorian England's rectitude honoring "reputation" above all else was about to be broken as Lyell and Hooker and Darwin arranged to steal Wallace's fame.

THE DEAL: If Wallace's Ternate paper were published, it would be the first exposition of a complete theory of the mechanics of evolution. Natural selection and continual divergence would be forever known as Wallaceism because Darwin was not ready to publish anything for at least two years. So Lyell and Hooker changed the agenda of the upcoming (July 1, 1858) meeting of the mighty Linnean Society, of which they (and Darwin) were prized members. Wallace's *complete* Ternate paper was read *after* extracts from Darwin's 1844 sketch and part of his letter to Asa Gray. The billing order of Darwin-Wallace was stressed and the society was told that Darwin-Wallace had "independently and unknown to one another conceived the same very ingenious theory." The society was also told that neither had published his views before. No mention was made of the Sarawak Law. The date 1844 insured priority for Darwin. Lyell and Hooker had the great satisfaction of exhibiting their power—not many members of the Linnean Society had the clout to change the agenda—and the tremendous honor of gaining immortality for one of their own.

RESULTS: Hooker described the meeting: "The interest excited was intense but the subject was too ominous for the old school to enter the lists before armoring. After the meeting it was talked over with bated breath: Lyell's approval and perhaps in a small way mine, as his lieutenant in the affair, rather overawed the Fellows, who would oth-

"You have no idea of the intrigues that go on in this blessed world of science. Science is, I fear, no purer than any other region of human activity, though it should be. Merit alone is very little good; it must be backed by tact and knowledge of the world to do very much."

Thomas Henry Huxley (1825–1895), the principal nineteenth-century exponent of Darwinism

erwise have flown out against the doctrine." Darwin wrote to Hooker: "You must let me once again tell you how deeply I feel your generous kindness and Lyell's on this occasion; but in truth it shames me." And he imagined what Wallace would say: "You did not intend publishing an abstract of your views till you received my communication. Is it fair to take advantage of my having freely, though unasked, communicated to you my ideas and thus prevent my forestalling you?"

Wallace and Darwin became "codiscoverers" of the theory known as Darwinism; but the enormous success of Darwin's book *Origin of Species,* published in 1859—the first edition of 1,250 copies sold out the first day—brought the word "Darwinism" into the language, aided by Wallace himself, who called his own book *Darwinism* in 1889. (When Herbert Spencer chided him for confirming "the erroneous concept universally current" that Darwin had no copilot, Wallace humorously replied: "Some of my critics declare that I am more Darwinian than Darwin himself and in this, I admit, they are not far wrong.") *Origin* originally contained no acknowledgments or source citations—the "error" was minimally amended with a "Historical Sketch" added to the third edition—and though Wallace received nine textual references for his work as a naturalist, he was not mentioned as "codiscoverer" in the original summary until Lyell pointed out the omission.

When the Linnean Society published its minutes, Darwin considerably rewrote his "abstract," while the Ternate paper appeared as it was read, printed without Wallace's knowledge or consent. (Darwin had Hooker write a letter to Wallace explaining what had been done.) There was little published response to the minutes. However, S. H. Haughton, president of the Royal Geological Society of Ireland, reviewed Darwin's paper on natural selection: "To this there can be no objection, except that of want of novelty." He then wrote of Wallace that he "adopts the same line of reasoning, and carries it one step further." Haughton, at least, had noticed that Wallace was second to no man.

Wallace lived on the edge of poverty because there was no money in science then—most of the noted scientists were wealthy gentlemen for this reason—but his fame as a naturalist and "codiscoverer" brought him access to all the great minds of the day. In 1881, Darwin petitioned Queen Victoria to grant Wallace a yearly pension; the two hundred pounds, less than Darwin's yearly butcher bill, kept the Wallace family comfortable. In 1892, he was elected to the Royal Society of London. Over the decades, Wallace published books and monographs on many subjects. He died in 1913.

A Pound of What?:
The Merchant of Venice

BACKGROUND: If you can't meet your payments, the bank forecloses or the Mafia loanshark fits you out in cement boots, but no forfeit is as famous as the one demanded by Shylock in his quest for a wild revenge.

Bassanio loves the wealthy Portia and needs money to pursue her in style. He asks his dearest friend, Antonio, for a loan, but Antonio's funds are all tied up in ships at sea carrying goods from port to port. Yet, for his true friend, Antonio agrees to lower himself and do what he abhors: borrow money from a man whom he detests—Shylock, a usurer.

Knowing that he is hated for being a usurer as well as for being a Jew, Shylock agrees to lend the money, although he loathes Antonio for his prejudice and for his being a Christian: "To buy his favour I extend this friendship."

THE DEAL: Shylock will lend Antonio whatever sum he wishes *interest free*, but, upon the due date, if the money is not returned, an exact pound of Antonio's "fair flesh" is to be cut off from whatever part of the body that Shylock wishes. Antonio agrees to this "merry sport" and goes off to the notary to seal the bond.

RESULTS: When all Antonio's ventures fail, he misses the due date. Shylock demands that the bond be honored to feed his revenge. Of what other use is a pound of human flesh? Antonio accepts his fate: No one can deny the course of the law. Bassanio, who has wooed and won Portia, offers Shylock twice the original sum. He is rejected. When the adversaries meet in court, the Duke of Venice introduces a young Doctor of Law to decide the case. Unbeknownst to everyone, it is Portia disguised as a man. She pleads for mercy. Shylock will not be budged. He wants his pound of flesh. Portia awards it to him: one exact pound, not an ounce more or less, from Antonio's breast, *but* Shylock must take it without spilling one drop of blood because, "The bond doth give thee here no jot of blood." If Shylock takes too much or too little flesh, or if blood is drawn, he must die. Portia also explains that it is against the la for an alien—and Shylock, being a Jew, is legally an alien—to seek the life of a Venetian—and Antonio, the Christian merchant, is a citizen of Venice. For this crime, Shylock must give Antonio half his goods; the other half must be given to the state. Shylock is ruined by his inability to know pity and to understand forgiveness. Antonio, *somewhat* tempered by his experience, forgives Shylock by accepting half the property in Shylock's daughter's name and by asking the duke to leave Shylock the other half until death, when it will go to the daughter's husband. Then he insists, as a final humiliation, that Shylock be forced to become a Christian. The duke agrees. Shylock leaves the court in abject despair. All the Christians rejoice.

He Did It His Way: Frank Sinatra Breaks a Contract

BACKGROUND: Young Frank Sinatra, a virtually unknown singer from Hoboken, New Jersey, was certainly friendly enough when he signed an exclusive contract with Tommy Dorsey, leader of a very well-known dance band. A few years later, it was "friendly pressure" that

NYC *police protect young "Blue Eyes" from the Bobby-Sox Brigade, 1944.*

released Sinatra from the contract: Somebody allegedly menaced Dorsey with a gun.

In 1940, when the twenty-five-year-old singer signed on with Dorsey, Sinatra's fame had not extended too far beyond the patrons of the New Jersey club where he'd been a singing waiter. Dorsey started Sinatra at a hundred dollars a week. After two years, it was clear that the skinny young man had the touch: His mysterious sexual allure drove women wild and he upstaged even Dorsey. This was his moment; the young singer had to go out on his own. But he had that contract with Dorsey. Freedom can be costly.

THE FIRST DEAL: Sinatra could walk away from the band that had launched him, but Dorsey would collect $33\frac{1}{3}$ percent of all his future earnings—and Dorsey's manager would get another 10 percent.

RESULTS: Sinatra was *hot.* The bobbysoxers swooned and squealed and grew hysterical (the boys were off fighting World War II—Sinatra was 4-F). A critic from the *New York Herald Tribune* wrote that Sinatra was "an amazing phenomenon, more revealing sociologically than from a musical standpoint." As his fame snowballed, so did his income, quickly rising from a weekly $750 to $1,750 to $2,500, at the

5,000-seat Paramount Theater in New York. He made the cover of *Life*. Columbia Records offered him a $360,000 advance to cut records for them. Suddenly Dorsey's cut seemed outrageous.

THE SECOND DEAL: "Somebody put a gun in Tommy's mouth and asked him whether he'd let Frank go. Under the circumstances, Tommy naturally said he would," according to speculation in Earl Wilson's biography, *Sinatra*.

RESULTS: Sinatra was a man with many well-placed friends. (Lucky Luciano [see "Dealmaker as Godfather: Charlie ('Lucky') Luciano," page 247] carried a gold cigarette case inscribed, "To my dear pal Lucky Luciano from his friend Frank Sinatra"; and in 1972, Sinatra was called to testify to the House Select Committee on Crime.) He went from crooning in the clubs of New York to clowning and crooning in Hollywood (in *Anchors Aweigh*), to some serious performing (winning the Oscar for Best Supporting Actor in *From Here to Eternity*), to earning $60,000 a night for casino performances in Las Vegas, to over $100,000 for one concert. He's invested in casinos in Vegas and Lake Tahoe and his records are perennial best-sellers (fourteen of them gold). He's now reported to be worth over $50 million. That's life!

THE POPE'S HIT MAN: MEHMET ALI AGCA

Mehmet Ali Agca, born in Turkey in 1958, shot Pope John Paul II on May 13, 1981. Agca claims he was paid $1.7 million for the hit by a fast-talking Turk who randomly approached him in the Hotel Vitosha in Sofia, a hotbed of Balkan intrigue. If he killed the pope, they'd pay him well for his work *in cash* and help him escape from Italy; and if he got caught, they'd rescue him somehow.

The Italian Defense Minister Lelio Lagoria told Parliament: "Ali Agca's attack on the Pope is to be considered as a real act of war in a time of peace, a precautionary and alternative solution to the invasion of Poland." The Vatican is convinced the Soviet KGB paid Agca the $1.7 million, using the Bulgarian secret police (DS) to do the recruiting. Agca was immediately tried, convicted, and sentenced to life in prison. It is not known whether dealmaker Agca thought he was working for the Turkish underground or the DS or the KGB. It *is* certain that he will never spend his $1.7 million, which is one of the risks of the world's most vicious profession.

The Watergate of the Art World: Mark Rothko's Estate and the Marlborough Gallery

BACKGROUND: Mark Rothko was a founder of the New York School of painting; in the late 1940s and 1950s they created Abstract Expressionism, the first world art movement to originate in America. In 1955, *Fortune* described art as an international currency: "gilt edge" equals Old Masters; "blue chip" equals Impressionists and Picasso; "venture capital" equals the New York School. Fifteen years later, an unscrupulous accountant with a taste for art fed the $32 million Rothko estate to the world's largest art cartel, but the artist's daughter proved a strong opponent.

Bernard J. Reis was a shrewd accountant. Working with artists, he frequently traded his services for art. Traditionally nonmaterialistic, the artists were grateful and loyal to him. When Frank K. Lloyd decided in the early 1960s to open a New York branch of his Marlborough art cartel (Lloyd/MNY), Reis was the man with access to the now "blue chip" work of the New York School: Rothko, Pollock, de Kooning, Motherwell, Gottlieb, and others. Even Rothko, who had struggled to maintain his artistic independence, fell for the Lloyd/MNY glamor. Concerned with the fate of his work after his death, he (with Reis's help) formed a charitable foundation to protect his "artistic remains" from disappearing into corporations, Swiss warehouses, and bank "art funds." His will left his unsold work—798 pieces—to this foundation. Reis, Theodoros Stamos (a minor painter), and Morton Levine (an anthropology professor) were his executors. Reis was not only a director of the foundation, but also a director and secretary-treasurer of Lloyd/MNY.

On February 25, 1970, Mark Rothko committed suicide. The initial value of his estate was $5 million. (The paintings alone were later valued at $32 million.) Under New York State law, children are entitled to one-half a parent's estate left to a charity; and with 798 paintings, there seemed no cause to deny the children their due. Then Lloyd/MNY removed 13 pieces from the studio "for safekeeping." The widow demanded their immediate return. True, on Reis's advice, Rothko—hideously depressed from prescribed-drug and alcohol abuse—had signed an "exclusive" contract with Lloyd/MNY, but they had already taken all the work due them. Where did they get off taking 13 more? In a few months, the widow was dead. Reis informed Rothko's other two executors (Stamos and Levine) that "hundreds of thousands" were needed by the foundation for upkeep on the paintings, to pay huge tax bills, and to cover legal fees. It was decided that 100 paintings were to be sold. Rothko was contractually bound to Lloyd/MNY, who needed the works to maintain Rothko's international market value. (In fact, the contract did not cover the United States.) Reis also said the sale was "estate business" and the foundation, as "chief beneficiary," did not need notification. The stage was set.

THE DEAL: Though the contract bound Lloyd/MNY to buy four Rothkos a year at the current market value, which was then $50,000 each, the executors sold the 100 paintings to Lloyd/MNY for $1,800,000, or $18,000 each, payable over twelve years *without interest*. The remaining 698 canvases were given to Lloyd/MNY "on consignment" for twelve years with a 40 to 50 percent commission, though 30 percent is standard. No minimum prices were stipulated that would avoid fake low sales and covert higher "resales." In return for this compliance with Lloyd/MNY, Stamos was signed for a one-man show, for which Abrams, the art-book publisher, announced a book tie-in; Levine, having illegally borrowed $5,000 from the estate, was given another $5,000; and Reis solidified his position with the Lloyd cartel and eventually sold his private collection for over $1 million.

RESULTS: When Kate Rothko claimed her paintings—approximately 150 after taxes, she precipitated a scandal known as the "Watergate of the art world." Lloyd/MNY publicly sold some Rothkos for six to ten times their cost. Kate pressed for her paintings. Upon discovering that Lloyd/MNY had them all, she decided to fight Lloyd for her father's art and "his way of looking at things." Her filed petition charged that the three executors had "entered into a conspiracy with Marlborough Gallery . . . to defraud the estate of Mark Rothko."

The art world expected the mighty, corporate Lloyd/MNY to squash the child. But Assistant Attorney General Harrow became involved, representing "the public" defrauded along with the charitable foundation. The judge ordered Lloyd to stop selling Rothkos: "It is clear that the issue of self-dealing pervades the proceedings." Lloyd ignored the injunction and attempted a cover-up. When the gallery's stock book was finally presented, it was as tampered with as Nixon's tapes: pages were missing, dates were altered, slips documenting paintings were incomplete.

The trial finally began in 1974. There were sixteen attorneys involved. Reis, claiming illness, never appeared. *In absentia,* he blamed his own lawyer for misinforming him about Rothko's Lloyd/MNY contract; he blamed Rothko for asking him to be an accountant, an executor, and a director of the foundation. Stamos and Levine said they thought $1,800,000 for 100 paintings was a "good deal." Levine announced he had paid back the $10,000 loan with interest as soon as he'd found out it was illegal for an executor to borrow from the estate. Lloyd stonewalled it up to the end, then offered to return 658 pictures and $1 million (104 were "gone," he said—"sold in bulk"—while 36 were sold for $2,474,250). It was not an acceptable solution: Kate assumed the 104 unaccountables were probably parked somewhere waiting to be merchandised by Lloyd/MNY once she was out of the way.

After eight months and over $2 million in legal fees (over half of which was Kate's), she won. The three executors were removed, 658 paintings were returned, and $9,252,000 in damages were awarded (including a fine of $3,875,000 against Lloyd for breaking the injunction). Reis was found in "serious conflict of interest"; Stamos was found to "curry favor with MNY"; Levine was found "to have followed their leadership" and to have failed "to exercise ordinary prudence." Lloyd was accused of perjury and collusion. (No one was judged guilty because it was "unnecessary to this decision.") Kate was victorious, but not yet paid.

From his home in the Bahamas, Lloyd tried to ship his assets ($30 million retail) to Switzerland via Canada, but Harrow intercepted them and put a lock on the goods until the bond for Kate's money was posted. Lloyd offered 19 of the so-called "sold 104" for credit of $90,000 each and eventually turned over 43 by the time the bond was posted. Lloyd/MNY was expelled from the Art Dealers Association. Unfortunately, most in the art world believed that Lloyd, like Nixon, was "guilty" only for getting caught. Some of the major estates—Pollock and Gottlieb—decamped from the gallery, but it prospered, as did Reis. (The damages were paid by Lloyd because Reis, Stamos, and Levine pleaded poverty.)

On March 8, 1977, Lloyd was indicted for tampering with evidence; a warrant was issued for his arrest. Living in the Bahamas, he was declared "a fugitive from American justice" until January 1981 when he returned to be tried. He was found guilty, but rather than being sent to jail, he was ordered to set up—for New York City high-school students—a scholarship fund, private showings of each new exhibit in his disgraced gallery, and an art lecture series. There are still no laws regulating the art world. International practices remain the same as those exposed by Kate Rothko, and another *Matter of Rothko* may simply be a matter of time.

Dealmaker as the Grand Acquisitor:
Francis K. Lloyd

BACKGROUND: Franz Kurt Levai was born in Austria on July 13, 1911. In 1940, he fled the Nazis to England. Both his parents died in Auschwitz. He changed his name to Francis Kenneth Lloyd (in honor of Lloyds of London—a solid, classy establishment), and joined forces with Harry Fischer (a rare-book expert from Vienna) to open Marlborough Fine Arts (named after the duke—a solid, classy establishment). Then, in 1950, they hired David Somerset, the son of the Duke of Beaufort, who not only added class-in-the-flesh but also brought in cash investors. After the war, the aristocracy was sorely in need of money for death duties and for estate upkeep; their castles and stately homes were crammed with Old Masters that they wished to sell discreetly. By 1960, Lloyd had set up holding companies in Liechtenstein to funnel the flowing funds into Swiss banks. But how many Old Masters were there? He needed an endless supply of something, *anything*: "If it sells, it's art." The problem with successful, living artists was easy public access to their work and an endless supply of it. *However,* if the flow could be stemmed and fiercely controlled, each work could then be hailed as "important"—a small supply creates a huge demand. Almost single-handedly, he created the "big-bucks scene" in contemporary art.

THE DEAL: Lloyd promised established artists shows in his galleries around the world, lavish color catalogues, reviews by major critics, monographs with "historical perspectives," placement in major collections and museums, gifts of materials, tax-free Swiss bank accounts, press agents, tie-ins (posters, books, documentary films), and anything else they could think of. In return, they signed "exclusively" with him and accepted his premise that small supply made big demand, which meant no unauthorized selling. The artists gave him a third of every sale price.

RESULTS: By investing vast sums to merchandise art, using modern media techniques, the international Lloyd/Marlborough art cartel was born. Established artists flocked to him. He soon operated twenty-one legal entities, most of them Swiss trusts. The beneficiaries were himself and his family. "I collect money not art." He held total control of his empire, making all decisions. He started a "wholesale business," buying the paintings of his artists in undifferentiated blocs through his Liechtenstein office in order to eliminate taxes almost entirely, then

reselling them one at a time at market value, which he manipulated
in a dozen different ways: He would send the pictures to public auction and buy them himself at higher than established prices; he would
arrange with museum curators—most notably from the Metropolitan
in New York City—to give his artists prestigious "retrospectives" with
much of the displayed work for sale through his galleries; he would use
the Art Dealers Association of America (ADAA) to make appraisals
for the IRS that guaranteed the "value" of his (and the other dealers')
artists' work as tax-deductible gifts to museums. By 1975, Lloyd's personal assets in the United States alone were estimated at $30 million.

In 1971, he and the executors of the Mark Rothko estate were accused of conspiracy and conflict of interest in selling and consigning
Rothko's works, resulting in the most spectacular and complex litigation (eleven years) in the history of modern art. Lloyd was convicted
of evidence-tampering and sentenced in 1982 to make social restitu-
tion. He is currently planning to do for the Bahamas what he did for
art—merchandise it out of this world.

"Dearest Cucumber": Senator McClellan versus Drew Pearson

BACKGROUND: Blackmail is against the law, but the head of a Senate
subcommittee had a way with stolen words that made a world-famous
journalist look the other way.

County Attorney Thomas Ratliff was running for lieutenant governor of Kentucky in 1967 and he needed some hot publicity to prove
his law and order credentials. He was also a rich and successful owner
of coal properties that were being stirred up by the antipoverty workers organizing miners to fight black-lung disease. Forming a posse, he
got a warrant for the arrest of a young activist couple, Margaret and
Alan McSurely, charging them with sedition. On August 11, 1967,
he raided their home, taking everything in sight: books, papers, and
even clothes. He then arrested them (they were soon freed by a federal tribunal).

Meanwhile, Senator John McClellan of Arkansas was heading a
Senate committee investigating the April 1967 black riots in Nashville. Local hero Ratliff's raid may have turned up something to tie
the McSurelys into the troubles in Nashville, too. McClellan sent an
aide to sift through the McSurely property. A love letter with the sal-

utation "Dearest Cucumber" was discovered among Margaret McSurely's papers. Though it was written to her before her marriage, its value was inestimable to McClellan.

THE DEAL: The letter was from Drew Pearson, a respected journalist and one of McClellan's most outspoken critics. McClellan let the married Pearson know he had the letter. Pearson, according to his former partner Jack Anderson, knew the letter was genuine.

RESULTS: Fearing blackmail by McClellan, Pearson never wrote about him again in his syndicated column.

In January 1983, after fifteen and a half years of litigation, the McSurelys won $1.6 million in damages—against Ratliff ($1,102,000), McClellan's estate ($218,260), and three of McClellan's aides ($189,255)—for violations of their First and Fourth Amendment rights to free speech and protection from illegal search and seizure.

GROSS, UNPLEASANT, AND CRUDE, BUT NOT WORTH $26 MILLION

Kim Pring, Miss Wyoming of 1978, looked like a big winner again in 1980 when a jury awarded her $26.5 million in a suit against *Penthouse* magazine. A story they ran about a sexually wild Miss Wyoming was libelous, Ms. Pring maintained. *Penthouse* appealed. A federal district court judge reduced the judgment to a still-fabulous $12.5 million. *Penthouse* appealed again. Finally, the U.S. Court of Appeals ruled that the story was "gross, unpleasant and crude," but it was "clearly a complete fantasy. No living person was being described." Ms. Pring would get nothing.

The story was written by Phillip Croffari, a professor at William Paterson College in New Jersey.

Danny Boy: The Murder of Harvey Milk and Mayor Moscone

BACKGROUND: Politics makes strange bedfellows. But no matter what your sexual preference, death is the strangest bedfellow of all. Especially when death wears the guise of an ex-cop with a penchant for Twinkies.

Harvey Milk was born in May 1930. In the navy, he proved himself a superb sailor but was dishonorably discharged for being gay. He moved to San Francisco (S.F.) in 1972 with no job and no plan of attack. S.F. was a hotbed of gay activism, greatly upsetting the mainly Irish-Catholic police department (SFPD). They had done their best to quash it over the years—"We enforce God's laws as well as the city's!"—but by the early 1970s they faced a fight: The gay community had united to become a political force, winning the support of many politicians. Harassment continued, its severity depending upon who was in power.

Milk opened a camera shop in March 1973. By September, he was running for S.F.'s Board of Supervisors. As a political activist and populist Democrat, he aligned himself against the real-estate barons, against the corporate forces, and against the moral crusaders with their tourism barons. He was a great, charismatic speaker but he had trouble forming a coalition with liberals and moderates, gay or straight. He was impatient with the political process of compromise; but, like all successful politicians, Milk had a way with the press. He came in tenth out of thirty-two in the election.

Harvey Milk, newly elected to San Francisco's Board of Supervisors, 1977.

His camera store became a gathering place on Castro Street. He tackled police brutality as a spokesperson for the gay community. He formed a liaison with the Teamsters on the successful gay boycott of Coors beer, and won their respect and their endorsement when he ran for supervisor in 1975. He also won the Fire Department's endorsement. Still, the moderates of all persuasions cursed him as a maverick while the radicals hated his affiliations. He lost the race but won an appointment as a commissioner from the newly elected mayor, the liberal George Moscone. As state senate majority leader, Moscone had shepherded the bill to repeal the antisodomy laws in California. Though Moscone vowed to wipe out prejudice against *all* minorities, SFPD Captain William O'Connor was publicly against having gay cops on his force, even though gays comprised up to 20 percent of the population. He was replaced by Charles Gain, who was prominority, to the disgust of the SFPD.

At forty-six, Milk was the first acknowledged gay city commissioner in the United States. After five weeks, he surrendered his seat to run for State Assembly; he lost. Around America, Anita Bryant successfully raged against gays, yet in 1977 Milk was again elected to the Board of Supervisors—along with Daniel James White, a conservative Irish Catholic ex-cop. Milk was determined to "educate" White away from his real-estate and cop cronies; but only White voted against the gay rights' bill. Their public feud was on.

Suddenly, White officially resigned from the board because he

"The Blacks did not win their rights by sitting quietly in the back of the bus. They got off! Gay people will not win their rights by staying quietly in our closets.... We are coming out! We are coming out to fight the lies, the myths. We are coming out to tell the truth about gays! ... History says that, like all groups seeking their rights, sooner or later we will win."

Harvey Milk
SF Gay Freedom Day
Parade, June 28, 1978

The grieving family at a memorial service for George Moscone, San Francisco's mayor slain by the "Twinkies Killer."

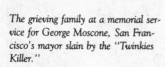
couldn't support his family on $9,600 a year. His leaving broke the six-to-five conservative majority on the board. Milk was ecstatic. Now he might succeed with his rent-control bill, and the mayor might convince the board to force SFPD to hire and promote more minorities. Ten days later, White wanted back on the board. He had met with officials from the Board of Realtors (BOR) and with the Police Officers Association (POA). They had changed his mind. Mayor Moscone said okay: "A man has a right to change his mind." Milk had reasons to believe the mayor might change his own mind.

THE DEAL: White was the only city politico who was publicly antigay. The mayor was up for reelection in a year. The gay vote was powerful. If Moscone reappointed White without a reelection in his district, which was the legal procedure, Moscone would lose the gay vote if Milk had anything to say about it. (White was unpopular with his blue-collar constituents; Milk knew he would never win reelection.) Afraid of losing the gay vote, the mayor agreed to withdraw his offer to White, citing the city charter.

RESULTS: Enraged, White held a press conference. At his side were not his district leaders, but officers from the BOR and POA. Someone scrawled graffiti in a cop's john: "Who's going to get the mayor?"

On November 27, 1978, Daniel White went to City Hall to confirm that he would not automatically be reappointed. He sneaked in a window to avoid the metal detectors. Corralling Moscone and Milk, he shot them both dead, then fled. He turned himself in to his friend who was the vice-president of the POA. His trial began on May 1, 1979. The jury was mainly comprised of white working-class ethnic Catholics. All gays had been rejected as biased. White was presented as "idealistic," the image of "American values, family, and home," driven temporarily crazy by a "vile biochemical change" in his body caused by the Twinkies, potato chips, and Cokes that he'd stuffed into himself the sleepless night before the shootings. The prosecutor behaved as if the case spoke for itself, while five psychiatrists insisted that White's "exemplary life" ruled out premeditated murder. On May 21, the jury found White guilty of voluntary manslaughter. He was sentenced to seven years, eight months. Though he was eligible for parole in January 1984, the governor requested he not be allowed to return to San Francisco.

Dianne Finestein, the new mayor, said to the press: "As I look at the law it was two murders." One reporter noted: "Sara Jane Moore got life for *missing* Gerald Ford." The SFPD dispatcher broadcast the verdict, then burst into a chorus of "Danny Boy." Five thousand gays rioted. Milk has become the first martyr of the gay rights' movement.

White was released from prison in January 1984. Thousands marched in protest carrying a huge banner: "He got away with murder."

OUT OF COURT AND INTO PRINT

Literary agent Aaron Priest took offense at literary agent Bill Adler's characterization of him in a 1983 book: "I once had some dealings with Aaron Priest, the agent who represents, among others, Erma Bombeck, and once was enough." Agent versus Agent led to an out-of-court settlement that seemed to amuse the publishing community. Adler was forced to print a one-third-page statement in *Publishers Weekly,* the industry magazine, which read: "I regret that there may have been some misinterpretation of the remarks I made about Aaron Priest in my book. . . . Aaron Priest is a very tough and honest negotiator, and what I meant was that I would not want to be on the outside of a deal with him too often."

Porn's Pawn: Linda Lovelace Stars in *Deep Throat*

BACKGROUND: Linda Lovelace now claims that all she ever got out of her starring role in *Deep Throat* was notoriety. The movie's made hundreds of millions of dollars, so even for Lovelace, that's pretty hard to swallow.

Lovelace says that she lived in constant terror of her gun-toting husband, Chuck Traynor. She claims that he brutalized her physically and emotionally, and when she attempted to return to her family, he

Anatomically incorrect.

threatened to murder them all. It was Traynor who taught Lovelace the exotic sex trick that made her world-famous: By relaxing her throat muscles, in the manner of sword swallowers, Lovelace perfected the art of "deep throating."

Lovelace says that Traynor worked as a pimp, forcing her to service his more kinky customers (sadists, urine freaks, groups). She claims that his sweet talk on their wedding night was, "now you'll never be able to testify against me." When the couple moved from Florida to New York, Lovelace began performing in trashy 8mm. porn films; her male co-star in one of these was a German shepherd dog. She was "discovered" by porn director Gerard Damiano, and her unique skill aroused his creativity. Why not team Lovelace with the formidable Harry Reems (described as "a hard act to follow") and make a film about a woman whose clitoris is in her throat? Damiano's financial backer, Lou Peraino, was opposed to casting Lovelace, insisting that the star be "a blonde with big boobs." Forget plot; Peraino contended that the formula was simple: "Big tits sell tickets." Lovelace says that Traynor forced her to give Peraino a demonstration of her specialty. If he liked it, perhaps the movie-going public would appreciate her too. The tryout took only two or three minutes, as Lovelace recalls. The part was hers.

THE DEAL: Traynor would receive $100 a day for his wife's services as the star of *Deep Throat*. Lovelace alleges that she was functioning under Traynor's reign of terror: She obeyed his order to appear in the film to avoid being beaten, perhaps even murdered.

RESULTS: Shot at a cost of $40,000, *Deep Throat* has earned its creators over $600 million (Traynor was paid $1,200 for Lovelace's contribution). Damiano went on to direct the highly successful porn film *The Devil in Miss Jones*. Lovelace became an internationally known celebrity, and while in Hollywood preparing a live act, she finally escaped from Traynor and went into hiding. Lovelace says Traynor told her friends that "if they tried to hide me or help me, he would kill them. He would also kill their wives and children. . . . Several of them got a court order barring Chuck Traynor from ever talking to them." Their marriage ended in divorce. Chuck then married the former Ivory Snow girl, porn star Marilyn Chambers. Lovelace married a childhood friend and retired to raise two children in a tiny suburban house outside of New York. Hard times have forced the couple to supplement their income with welfare, but Lovelace, who says she has turned down offers of $3 million to make another porn film, insists, "I wouldn't do any of that again even if I could get $50 million."

VIII

AMONG THE MUSES: THE ARTS

In Hollywood, the deal is the art form.

JOAN DIDION

Roll Over, Beethoven: Beethoven Finds Financial Freedom

BACKGROUND: Back in the days before large concert halls and recording contracts, even the best composers were always hustling noble patrons for support. The great Beethoven gained his financial and, therefore, his artistic freedom, only when he threatened to pack his bags and move his act elsewhere.

Beethoven had been living in Vienna, the music capital of the Western world, for sixteen years, ever since he moved there to study with Haydn. He was already forty years old, and he was tired of having to please noble patrons with his work in order to pay his bills. Composers and musicians would dedicate their works to noble patrons who, with rare exceptions, would tolerate little deviation from standard musical form. And a musician would then have to be available to perform at the command of his patron; in the glory days of the Hapsburg Empire, aristocrats kept their own orchestras and even opera companies, but hard times had reduced them to chamber ensembles or soloists. Mozart had rebelled against this system and died, impoverished, at thirty-five. Haydn was the official court music director (*Kapellmeister*) to a prince for thirty years, which caused a contemporary to describe him as "nothing more than the court conductor of a Hungarian magnate."

Beethoven longed to be free of the demands of aristocratic patronage. An early supporter of his, Prince Lichnowsky, had compelled him to make changes in *Fidelio* and had insisted that Beethoven perform for guests at his country estate. Beethoven regarded such performances as "menial labor," and when forced to perform them, insisted on playing in a room adjoining the audience so that he could be heard but not seen. To remain free of any one patron, Beethoven was supporting himself by selling dedications to his new works to avid aristocrats who would then get exclusive performance rights for a few months, along with the dedication. It was the nineteenth-century equivalent of being the only one in town with the latest hot LP: Everyone wanted to be invited to your house to listen. But although he

"Keep your eye on him; the World will hear from that young one."

Mozart, after hearing Beethoven play in 1787

was making money, Beethoven was forced to give the people what they wanted, and he was growing tired of writing minuets. (Not that he had no time left for his "real" work; by 1809 he had written, besides *Fidelio*, his only opera, the First and Second Symphonies, the *Eroica*, the *Pathétique*, the *Moonlight Sonata*, and much more.)

When Napoleon made his twenty-three-year-old brother Jerome the king of Westphalia (northwest Germany), the young monarch, who has been described as a "prodigal and effeminate young satrap," lost no time in attempting to establish his kingdom as an arts center. Ludwig van Beethoven, the greatest composer of the day, would add luster to his court as few others would. To lure Beethoven to his kingdom, King Jerome offered him a fabulous salary with virtually no strings attached. Beethoven told his friends in Vienna that he would be forced to accept Jerome's offer, because: "I have to do nothing except conduct the King's concerts which are short and not numerous— I am not even bound to conduct any opera . . . I can devote myself wholly to the most important purpose of my art, to compose works of magnitude—and also have an orchestra at my disposal."

When word began to circulate in Vienna that the undisputed great genius of the day was leaving, three concerned young nobles got together to see if they could stop him: His Imperial Highness, the Archduke Rudolph, son of the emperor and the Princes Lobkowitz and Kinsky made Beethoven an offer that left king Jerome singing the blues.

THE DEAL: Beethoven promised to make his home permanently in Vienna or "one of the other hereditary countries of His Austrian Imperial Majesty" and to conduct one charity concert a year, or else contribute a new work for such a concert. He would receive the very generous fixed sum of four thousand florins a year (allowing him to live very well, keep two servants, and leave town for the summer). The nobles stated in the agreement that, "as it has been demonstrated that only one who is free from care as possible can devote himself to a single department of activity and create works of magnitude which are exalted and enoble art, the undersigned have decided to place Herr Beethoven in a position where the necessaries of life shall not cause him embarrassment or clog his powerful genius."

RESULTS: It wasn't all easy street after that, in spite of the agreement. Four years later, the devaluation of Austrian currency reduced the real value of his annuity by 60 percent. Then Kinsky died and Lobkowitz went bankrupt, but ultimately Beethoven won generous settlements against their estates. And although he was never entirely free of hav-

> "There ought to be in the world a market for art where the artist would only have to bring his works and take as much money as he needed."
>
> Beethoven

ing to hustle music sales and concert tickets (public concerts of soloists were just catching on), he was the first major composer to spend most of his creative life free of the restrictions of a single patron. And with that freedom, he was able to move music beyond the formal conventions of the past, establishing a new era, and with it, some of the most sublime music ever created. When he died in Vienna in 1827, thirty thousand mourners lined the streets to witness the funeral procession.

He Should Have Known Better: Brian Epstein Mismanages the Beatles

BACKGROUND: Brian Epstein certainly proved his prophetic genius when he "discovered" the Beatles, became their first manager, and convinced EMI to record them; but the licensing arrangements he was subsequently responsible for can only be described as giveaways. Epstein regretted them until the day he died.

Brian Epstein, a year before he died, with the lads he discovered in a Liverpool basement club.

Epstein, the twenty-seven-year-old son of a prosperous Liverpool merchant, was managing the record department of the family department store when, in 1961, he went to a small basement club to check out a local group he'd been hearing about. The Beatles, four young men done up in black leather, were popular with local kids, but they were nearly unknown outside of Liverpool. Epstein immediately became obsessed with them; a month after they first met, the "lads" signed him on as their manager—he would get 25 percent of everything. He insisted that they abandon their punk-style leathers for the identical suits that became their early trademark, and then he stormed the London record companies, finally negotiating a contract with EMI. The Beatles would get one penny for every single they sold. "Love Me Do," written by Paul when he was sixteen, and "P.S. I Love You," with John playing a harmonica he'd shoplifted (he was too poor to buy it), was their first release. It quickly climbed to number seventeen on the English charts. When their next single, "Please Please Me," became number one overnight, the Beatles were rushed into a recording studio to cut an album. They sold over $10 million in records in the United Kingdom alone that first year. "I Want to Hold Your Hand," released in December of 1963, sold 1.5 million copies in five days. The Beatles appeared on "The Ed Sullivan Show" in the United States; they were paid a total of $3,500 for the appearance, and had to pay their own air fares to New York. Their concerts were breaking all previous records; they were the hottest group the music world had *ever* seen. Epstein was besieged by licensing offers from both sides of the Atlantic. Manufacturers were eager to peddle all sorts of paraphernalia bearing the image of those irresistible mop-tops: clothing, toys, household goods, posters, food—even Beatle wigs. With international tours and record contracts to worry about (and the careers of other Epstein discoveries like Cilla Black and Gerry and the Pacemakers, who were, at the time, enjoying huge successes as well), Epstein decided to delegate responsibility for merchandising to the legal advisor he had chosen: flamboyant, English celebrity attorney David Jacobs. But Jacobs soon found his busy office overrun with Beatle knickknacks and suggested to Epstein that they establish a completely separate company just to handle licensing. In fact, Jacobs knew a man who would be glad to take the merchandising business off their hands: Nicky Byrne.

THE DEAL: Byrne now says that he was only kidding when he asked Jacobs for 90 percent of all merchandising arrangements and was completely stunned when Jacobs agreed, saying "10 percent is better than nothing." The new company was called Stramsact in the United Kingdom and Seltaeb (Beatles backwards) in the United States.

RESULTS: In the first year, more than $50 million worth of Beatle products were sold in the United States alone. One million Beatle T-shirts were sold the first three days they were marketed. When Epstein realized how much the licensing arrangements were costing the Beatles, he was mortified and insisted that Byrne renegotiate. Byrne quickly agreed to up the Beatles' percentage by 36 percent. Epstein still wasn't happy and began to issue United States licenses himself. Byrne sued; Epstein hired Louis Nizer and sued Byrne. Finally, in the summer of 1967, Epstein wrested control of merchandising back from Byrne. But meanwhile, the Beatles had lost out on about $100 million.

A few weeks later, Epstein, age thirty-three, died of a drug overdose. The Beatles split up in 1970. They were the biggest moneymakers in the history of music. Today, Paul McCartney earns $40 million a year; Yoko Ono, widow of John Lennon, controls a fortune worth $250 million. *Imagine.*

UNHEARD-OF SALARIES

Horowitz receives the highest fee of any pianist in history: 80 percent of the gross.

Pavarotti receives the highest fee of any classical concert artist in history: $100,000 a recital.

"See the Music and Hear the Dancing!": Balanchine, Kirstein, and the New York City Ballet

BACKGROUND: Born in Saint Petersburg, Russia, in 1904, Georgi Maletonvitch Balanchivadze—simplified for Western ears to "George Balanchine" by Diaghilev in 1924—studied at the Maryinsky Theater's ballet school from 1910 to 1921, then studied music at the Petrograd Conservatory for three years before becoming ballet master at Petrograd's Malay Theater. When a small group of dancers, including Balanchine, were allowed to tour the West, they all defected and were hired by Diaghilev's famed Ballet Russe with Nijinsky. By 1929, when Diaghilev died, Balanchine had created ten ballets for the company (including *Apollo*, with Stravinsky), and had achieved international fame as an innovative choreographer in the classical tradition.

He wanted to settle in London, but the British government refused him a residence permit. In 1933, he formed his own company in Paris, where the wealthy Lincoln Kirstein came under the spell of his genius. Ballet in America was practically nonexistent, but Kirstein had a vision that he shared with Balanchine of creating a great new company in the New World, a place eager for the excitement and beauty of modern creative energy in dance. Kirstein then convinced the director of Wadsworth Atheneum, a museum in Hartford, Connecticut, to offer institutional sponsorship to Balanchine's school. The way seemed clear for Mr. B., as he was soon known to his students, to immigrate and bless this continent with his art. However, Mr. B. had a more practical grasp of the obstacles ahead.

THE DEAL: Hartford was out of the question. He knew that a major company, the likes of which they envisioned, had a hard climb ahead and needed a major metropolis to support it. If Kirstein wanted America to have a company of international stature, it had to be based in the largest, richest, and most cosmopolitan city: New York. If New York City was not possible, Mr. B. preferred to stay in Europe where dance already had an audience, one slowly coming to value his innovative, plotless works.

RESULTS: On January 2, 1934, the School of American Ballet, financed by Kirstein who had yet to inherit the bulk of his family fortune, opened its classrooms in Manhattan on East Fifty-ninth Street and Madison Avenue. The Kirstein-Balanchine company was christened American Ballet in 1935; its first ballet was the masterpiece *Serenade*. They gave a triumphant Stravinsky festival in 1937, but the Depression defeated them at the box office. To survive, they joined the Metropolitan Opera Company until 1938, when Mr. B. fled, unable to stand their "conservatism and philistinism." He choreographed on Broadway (*On Your Toes* and *Where's Charley?*), in Hollywood (*The Goldwyn Follies*), and abroad until Kirstein, now independently wealthy, established a new organization for him called Ballet Society in 1946. The new company became a constituent of City Center and in 1948 changed its name to the now-legendary New York City Ballet. Low on funds, his ballets were often staged without scenery or costumes—the dancers performing in simple practice clothing—giving his pure-dance works a heightened sense of the avant-garde that mass audiences were slow to appreciate. His absolute, one-of-a-kind genius revolutionized dance as totally as Jackson Pollock's did art [see "The Second American Revolution: Jackson Pollock and Peggy Guggenheim," page 307].

As with Pollock, by the mid-1950s Mr. B. began to achieve public recognition. The company produced a new breed of dancer: fast, mobile, energetic, distinctly American, and among the finest in the world. Many of Balanchine's ballets have taken their place as sublime achievements of the twentieth century. At his death on April 30, 1983, he left a legacy of nearly two hundred ballets. The New York City Ballet is now jointly run by former dancer/choreographer Peter Martins and choreographer Jerome Robbins [see "America's Inquisition: HUAC versus 'The Tinseltown Pinks,'" page 252].

NUMBER-ONE MEATHEAD

"All in the Family" was first offered to ABC–TV by Norman Lear, its producer, in 1968. They turned it down. Based on a British BBC hit, " 'Til Death Do Us Part," the show was again offered to ABC in 1969. Again, they said no thanks. In 1970, Lear went to CBS. Executives there loved it, bought it, then ran up against William Paley, the chairman, who hated it. Paley agreed to carry the controversial program—it broke a catalogue of TV taboos—but only if the promotion were kept to a minimum (so as not to throw good money after bad), if it were scheduled for 9:30 P.M. on Tuesdays (where it could do little damage to CBS's weekly line-up), and if a warning was broadcast before each episode: "The program you are about to see is 'All in the Family.' It seeks to throw a humorous spotlight on our frailties, prejudices, and concerns. By making them a source of laughter, we hope to show—in a mature fashion—

just how absurd they are." By the seventh episode the show had doubled its ratings; by the next fall, it was number one in the ratings. It played for thirteen seasons on CBS (both as "All in the Family" and "Archie Bunker's Place"), leaving prime-time in May 1983, when it was twenty-third in the national ratings.

Desilu Loves Lucy, Too:
Desi Arnaz Saves "I Love Lucy"

BACKGROUND: It was a variation on the tried-and-true dumb blonde and hot-tempered Latino, but the comic redhead and her innovative husband changed the way TV functioned and fixed it forever in their own image. They had the last laugh all the way to immortality . . . not to mention the bank.

In January 1950, Lucille Ball was starring in "My Favorite Husband" on CBS radio. It was a big hit and CBS decided to transfer it to TV, which was still in its infancy. Broadcasting live, several TV cameras would shoot the action simultaneously from different positions on the studio floor, while in a control room the director would choose which images reached the home sets. There was no cable connecting the East Coast with the West; programs were broadcast live from New York City to the Mid-Atlantic states; then poor-quality kinescopes—a process not unlike tape recording—were shipped to California for eventual viewing by the rest of the country. New York City was the center of TV action because there were more viewers in its broadcasting area.

Lucy agreed to do "Husband" on TV, but only if her real husband, Desi Arnaz, played the Husband. She had been married to Desi for ten years and was tired of their separate careers which held her in California doing radio shows and movies while he toured the country as a singer and orchestra leader. CBS paused. Desi was a handsome Cuban; the Husband was a WASP. Everyone finally agreed it would not work but Lucy and Desi craved a show for themselves. They put together comedy routines and hit the road as a team. (In those days, the big movie theaters still had live acts between screenings.) Audiences loved Lucy. Audiences loved Desi. Audiences loved Lucy *and* Desi even more.

Early in 1951, CBS agreed to do a comedy pilot with them. The pilot would be used to find a sponsor. The series was to be about the

real Lucille Ball married to the real Desi Arnaz and all the complications in two successful careers. Immediately, Lucy and Desi knew the format was too narrow, too "in show-biz." They scaled it down to earth by changing Desi, successful orchestra leader, to Ricky Ricardo, struggling orchestra leader; and Lucille became Lucy Ricardo, his bumbling, mischievous wife. In the second episode they planned to add two neighbors: Fred and Ethel Mertz. The pilot was broadcast live from California, and the kinescope was sent to CBS in New York City. Within forty-eight hours, Philip Morris was the sponsor. The budget was set at $19,500 per episode for thirty-nine episodes. CBS would own 50 percent of the show, and the newly formed Desilu Productions would own 50 percent. If the budget ran over, CBS would pick up the tab. All was settled. CBS told Lucy and Desi that as soon as the two moved to New York City, work would begin.

Move to New York City? The whole point of "I Love Lucy" was to allow the couple (and their soon-to-be-delivered first child) to live happily ever after in California. Move to New York City? CBS insisted: They could not possibly show kinescopes to the largest portion of their audience. There seemed no way out until Desi announced they would *film* the show—then east and west would have the same quality picture. Film? Film was used in movies only, in a one-camera process that required hundreds of individual shots painstakingly assembled like a giant jigsaw puzzle. Film? Who had time for film? This was one-show-a-week TV. And what about the audience? CBS insisted Lucy work in front of a live audience because her work was always best that way. What audience could sit forever waiting for the movie camera to be moved from one shot to the next? Improvising madly, Desi explained: He would film the show with three cameras at once in front of a live audience as if it were a play. It had never been done before, but he would find a way. How much would the film cost? Desi estimated arbitrarily ("Who knew?"): $5,000 more per episode, raising the cost from $19,500 to $24,500. Philip Morris agreed to come up with $2,000 more. CBS matched them. Lucille Ball and Desi Arnaz and Desilu Productions took a gamble that eventually would earn them hundreds of millions of dollars.

THE DEAL: From the original $19,500 budget, Lucy and Desi together were to receive a salary of $5,000 with 50 percent of the profits (if there were any). To meet the new $24,500 budget, they took a salary cut of $1,000 per episode, but in exchange they received the other 50 percent—or full ownership—of the thirty-nine original "I Love Lucy" episodes in the 1951–1952 season, as well as full ownership of all future episodes in all future seasons (if there were any). CBS went along with the plan, convinced the show could not be filmed satisfactorily and doubly convinced the stars would soon be in New York City for business as usual, or live and kinescope broadcasting from Manhattan. CBS was also not concerned about giving away their 50 percent of "I Love Lucy." What was 50 percent of nothing? Once a show was aired, who needed it?

RESULTS: The total salary cut for Lucy and Desi that first season was $39,000 ($1,000 for each of the thirty-nine shows); but in their tax bracket, they would have kept only $5,000 of that lost $39,000. The two joked that they bought the other 50 percent of the "Lucy" films for $5,000. (In 1957, when reruns had become a staple of TV, CBS would pay Desilu $4.5 million in cash for the rights to 179 "Lucy" episodes, a neat return on a $5,000 investment.)

To produce that first weekly season, Desi demonstrated an inventive and administrative genius that gave birth to a new order: the filmed situation comedy, now the core of American TV. First, he converted a small studio to hold an audience in accordance with zoning and fire laws; the first of its kind for a multiset production and the beginning of a TV empire. He hired Karl Freund, a master cinematographer who had invented the light meter. Freund quickly solved the most demanding technical problems, including how to light a set for close-up, medium shot, and long distance all at the same time, so three cameras could simultaneously shoot the scene in 35mm. Then Desi had an editing machine built with three screens to show the film from the three cameras at the same time, all synchronized to the soundtrack. This allowed him to edit as if he were sitting in a control room with the action live in front of him. What equipment Desilu was not inventing, they bought outright instead of renting. The first show cost $95,000 to produce—$70,500 over budget! The second was $85,000; the third was $75,000; and the fourth $60,000, making "Lucy" $220,000 over budget. CBS howled. Desi assured them prices would fall when everything fit together. Soon some episodes were brought in for $12,000, and all thirty-nine averaged only $9,500 over budget. Since the equipment was bought with "Lucy" money, Desilu claimed they owned it. CBS agreed. And since Desilu was the only studio in the world equipped to film shows with three cameras in front of a live audience, CBS contracted with them to film other shows— "Our Miss Brooks," Loretta Young's "Letters to Loretta," "The Danny Thomas Show"—and CBS had to pay rental fees on the equipment Desilu had acquired with CBS money. (The editing machine alone grossed over $300,000.) By the end of the first season, "I Love Lucy" was the hottest show on TV, and it became the first to reach 10 million homes (10.6 million, to be exact, on April 7, 1952).

For the second season, CBS raised the budget to $30,000 per episode; but any overrun was to be borne by Desilu. CBS also bought 25 percent of Desilu Productions for $1 million. By the end of 1953, Desilu was producing 299 half-hour shows, the equivalent of 80 movies a year; by 1957, the output had increased to 691. Then Desi wanted out of "Lucy." Playing Ricky for six years and running Desilu was too much. He wanted to quit while "Lucy" was still number one. So in 1958, the weekly half-hour "Lucy" became five "specials": "Lucy-Desi Comedy Hour." That same year, Desilu bought RKO studios for $6,150,000, making it the biggest television-movie facility in the world, with 35 sound stages and a back lot of 40 acres for filming outdoor sequences. In 1959, when the last "Lucy-Desi Comedy Hour" was aired, and the real-life Lucille Ball divorced the real-life Desi Arnaz, Desilu Productions grossed $20,400,000. "I Love Lucy" had become part of American mythology.

IN HIS PRIME TIME

Mike Wallace on "60 Minutes" has signed with CBS for the next five years. The show makes $50 million in profits a year, and Wallace, in the fifth year of his new contract (1988), will be earning $1 million a year. He'll be sixty-nine years old.

Final shot, January 14, 1983.

S*M*A*S*H Goes F*L*U*S*H:
The Licensing of "M*A*S*H"

BACKGROUND: TV, TV on the wall, what's your hottest game of all? Pac-Man? Atari? "Name That Tune"? Wrong! It's rerun syndication of network shows on local stations. *Oh*, you say? *Easy*, you say? Then how did Twentieth Century-Fox manage to drop the ball (for tens of millions) with a show that *Newsweek* called "the most original, courageous and successful enterprise in the annals of television"?

In 1970, Robert Altman filmed a novel called *MASH*. Fox had paid one hundred thousand dollars for the rights to the book that had been turned down by seventeen publishing houses. M*A*S*H (the asterisks added by Fox) became a sleeper smash, touching the American nerve endings already rubbed raw by the antiwar movement.

Fox's TV department decided to go for a series. They offered the book's authors a thousand dollars for each produced episode and were hoping for your basic yuk-a-minute sit-com. Gene Reynolds, a successful producer, agreed to work on the project. He, in turn, convinced Alan Alda that together they could do something very special in the twenty-four minutes and forty seconds of air time alloted them each week: They could create TV's first black comedy. Larry Gelbart agreed to write the scripts if they could keep the anarchic quality of the movie but be less "smart ass."

On Sunday, September 17, 1972, the first "incoming wounded" alert sounded on 4077th's loudspeaker on CBS. America got its first dose of what Gelbart called "the Marx Brothers in *All Quiet on the Western Front*." CBS had tried to lighten the emphasis on war; Fox had tried to get Reynolds to shoot on videotape in two and a half days before a live audience. Both failed. Reynolds shot what Gelbart wrote as if it were a film, out of sequence, with a full day's rehearsal, on a set with no audience. The only compromise Reynolds made was adding laughter to scenes not set in the operating room. The first few scripts were unfocused and rocky, until the eighth, which dealt directly with death, then "M*A*S*H" found its footing and flew. The critics were mostly favorable. When the show finished its first season of twenty-four episodes, it was forty-sixth in the year-end ratings. Instead of killing it, CBS read the reviews, took a risk, extended it a season, and slotted it on Saturdays between "All in the Family" and "The Mary Tyler Moore Show." By the end of its second year, "M*A*S*H" was a smash.

Fox, desperately in need of cash, was ecstatic. "M*A*S*H" was its *only* TV hit and was jokingly referred to as "Fox's television division." Producing a TV series is a very risky business. There are only three outlets for the product—ABC, CBS, and NBC—and production costs make it rare for a show to run in the black until two full seasons have passed, and then the big bucks of syndication aren't available until a show has at least five years in the can. Only then are there enough different episodes—at twenty-four a season—for it to be shown five days a week, off-peak, on the local stations.

In 1975, at the end of the third successful season, with only seventy-two episodes in the "M*A*S*H" library, a hungry Fox made an offer to the local stations for syndication of reruns. It was very early in the show's run, two of the stars were checking out (McClean Stevenson and Wayne Rogers), and the ratings were slipping (albeit temporarily, but nobody was certain of that). And to top it off, there was a catch that made all the prospective buyers pause.

THE DEAL: The sale was on a "futures" basis. Seven seasons of "M*A*S*H" were on the block, and no one could buy unless they promised not to start airing the episodes until October 1979. Fox made no guarantees that the unorthodox show would have an audience by then, but they wanted all the money up front . . . and none of it was refundable if "M*A*S*H" took a permanent nose-dive in the public's affections. At approximately $13,000 an episode for the largest stations, it was a pretty piece of change to risk since frequently huge hits like "Six Million Dollar Man," "Marcus Welby, M.D.," "Mission Impossible," and even "All in the Family" did poorly during the main time slots for syndication: 4:00 to 6:00 P.M. and 7:30. However, everyone knew the prices for hit shows were rising fast. If "M*A*S*H" kept spinning, it would be a bargain at Fox's asking price.

RESULTS: Fox raised about $25 million in total sales. They were satisfied, or so they thought. The following year, syndication prices went through the ceiling. WPIX in New York City paid $35,000 an episode for 123 "Happy Days." And a record was set when each episode of "Laverne and Shirley" earned $54,000. Fox was bemused, but the worst was yet to come. In 1979, when "M*A*S*H" appeared in reruns, it turned out to be the strongest syndicated show in the field. The stations had a gold mine. No matter what its time slot, it knocked all the competition off the map. Many nonnetwork stations, including UHF, were showing it as often as three times a day, frequently in prime time, earning the stations enough money in local advertising to pay the boom prices for the high rollers like "Happy Days." "M*A*S*H" became the second most successful TV property ever produced, each episode has grossed over $1 million. ("I Love Lucy" is first; it had a twenty-year head start.)

The final original episode of "M*A*S*H" was aired Monday, February 28, 1983, to an estimated 125 million people. It was a special two-and-a-half-hour good-bye, and CBS charged $450,000 for a half-minute commercial, $50,000 more than NBC dared ask for the previous month's Super Bowl telecast. The show pulled the highest ratings in TV history: 77 percent of televisionland watched, knocking the 1980 episode of "Dallas" ("Who Shot JR?") into second place. And another record was set: At 11:03 P.M., the water usage in New York City rose by an unprecedented 300 million gallons, as about one million people flushed their toilets at once!

After eleven years, two hundred and fifty episodes, fourteen Emmys, seven different time slots, seventeen writers, and a loss of more than half the original cast, the stars voted to end it while they were still on top. (The penultimate week, the show was number five in the Nielson ratings.) Now Fox is preparing the second package of "M*A*S*H" episodes for syndication to begin screening in 1985. With "After M*A*S*H" one of the few hits of the 1983 fall season, Fox is set for a killing. The asking price for each episode has quintupled since the 1975 go-round. They expect to gross $125 million, with an operating profit for themselves and $50 million for actors' residuals and profit participants like Alda, Gelbart, and others. (Alda received approximately $5 million from the 1975 syndication; he stands to make $25 million on the current sale. None of the other actors share directly in the profits, but they were all extremely well paid.) In the words of Robert Morm, Fox's senior vice-president for syndication: "We'll get prices in the second syndication that no one will ever get again. We'll make up this time for not getting enough the first time around."

Hawkeye and Margaret would happily scarf down a martini to *that*!

◆ ◆ ◆ ◆

"M*A*S*H" Cash: What the Actors Made

Alan Alda (Hawkeye Pierce): $150,000 per episode
Loretta Swit (Margaret "Hot Lips" Houlihan): $40,000
Mike Farrell (Hunnicut): $35,000
Harry Morgan (Colonel Potter): $35,000
Jamie Farr (Corporal Klinger): $25,000
William Christopher (Father Mulcahy): $25,000
David Ogden Stiers (Charles Winchester): $20,000

HOW TO

"If you want to make a deal, get the other guys into *your* office, and keep them there, until they begin to feel 'My God, let's get this thing done and out of the way.' Very often, you can get people to sign by suggesting both sides are so far apart that the meeting ought to be postponed for a week. For guys with heavy schedules, that's a frightening thought. They start thinking of what they've got on their calendars for the next week, and suddenly the deal doesn't look so bad after all."

An observer of Fred Silverman's style, as reported in Michael Korda's book *Success*. Silverman was head of ABC programming, having been lured away from the same job at CBS at age thirty-eight for $250,000 a year and a $750,000 paid-up life-insurance policy.

"I always think I'll just listen to that song of Judy's and then go about my business," Margaret Hamilton, the Wicked Witch of the West, said in 1983. "But I never can. I cry always. Eternally, the movie moves me."

MGM's *The Wizard of Oz* was made for the immense sum (in 1939) of $2,777,000. (The average MGM extravaganza at that time cost $1.5 million.) It was not a success and took twenty years to earn back its money at the box office, eventually grossing $6 million. In 1956, CBS wanted to lease *Gone with the Wind*. They offered MGM $1 million. Turned down, they opted for *Oz* at $225,000. It was an amazing success with the viewers and quickly became an American institution. For the next twenty-seven years, it was shown twenty-four times (sixteen on CBS; eight on NBC), netting $15 million for MGM and only once failing to make the Neilsen Top Twenty. No other movie ever made the list the second time around except *Gone with the Wind*. The first nine years, *Oz* captured an average 49 percent of the TV audience each time it was shown and is estimated to have enchanted 383 million homes. No other program has been rerun so often. In 1976, CBS paid $800,000 for each year of a five-year contract; then in 1981 they paid $1 million for the privilege. Their option runs through 1985. *Oz* is currently one of the top ten best-sellers on video cassette.

One Raider Less on the Gold-plated Ark: Tom Selleck and "Magnum, P.I."

BACKGROUND: An actor's life can be very difficult. Take Tom Selleck. In the beginning, his career consisted of struggle. When his big break came, it was a mixed blessing: a CBS contract for a magnum opus that might miss the spot, and a surefire hit (about the Lost Ark) that was sailing away.

Selleck was born in Detroit on January 29, 1945, but moved to Los Angeles when he was four. In high school, he was captain of the basketball team and won a sports scholarship to the University of Southern California, where he majored in business administration until some extra-credit, "easy" theater courses changed his life. His first

America's #1 Pin-up Boy, cast as the lead in Raiders of the Lost Ark, *was legally prevented from playing Indiana Jones.*

role was in an Air Force training film that got him into the Screen Actors Guild. Then he scored a success in a Pepsi commercial, playing (with conviction) a basketball player. During a 1967 shot at "The Dating Game," a talent scout spotted him. He went through Twentieth Century-Fox's acting school and for over a year did bits, frequently playing volleyball. His bits included the role of "the stud" in *Myra Breckenridge* with Mae West and Raquel Welch and a corpse in *Coma* (1978). He leaped into soapdom on "The Young and the Restless," but never made it to the front lines of emotional warfare.

Recognition, of sorts, came with his green eyes colored blue as he graced Salem cigarette billboards across the United States for four years—the silent, unnamed symbol of mentholated man's country. He scored in TV commercials, including a stint as the Chaz cologne model. Being a famous "face" makes it hard to get acting roles because producers and directors aren't amused when the audience is distracted during a show by the entrance of "The Chaz Man! Oooooooooooohh!" but Selleck continued to audition and continued to win good TV roles, including *six* pilot shows for series that weren't bought by networks.

Enter James Garner. Star of CBS's successful "Rockford Files" (produced by Universal), he liked Selleck when a guest shot on the show brought the two actors together. Unthreatened by Selleck's height, looks, and style, Garner encouraged him to share the screen and Selleck was brought back "by popular demand" for another segment, making both CBS and Universal very happy with him. Obviously, the kid had what it takes. Soon after, Garner claimed he was too sick to work from an ulcer and bruises and injuries sustained while playing Rockford for eleven episodes short of six full seasons. Universal sued him for $1.5 million for breach of contract. Garner countersued and, natch, the show was dead. But the detective format was decidedly alive in the ratings.

THE DEAL: Saying bye-bye to "Rockford" and "Hawaii-Five-O" (also canceled, after twelve hit sleuthing seasons) meant that CBS had two bullet holes in its 1980 fall line-up, as well as an empty television studio in Diamond Head, Hawaii. CBS made it clear to Universal that a "new" detective format with mucho macho action, a Hawaiian locale, and the relatively unknown Selleck—big stars like Garner were too much of a hassle—could seduce them into buying it and prime-timing it into the Thursday slot being vacated by the retiring "Waltons." "?" had to start production in July 1980.

RESULTS: Universal dragged out an old idea: "Magnum, P.I." It was an hour-long show revolving around the adventures of Thomas Magnum, private investigator, Vietnam vet, and 007 type. The pilot was completed, screened, and hated by the brass at Universal. Selleck suggested Magnum be made more human, not get the girl *every* time, make a few mistakes: on a scale of 007, be a 004½. The pilot was reworked, reshot, and submitted to CBS.

Then the actor's dream became the actor's nightmare—not the one about being on stage naked or with all the lines forgotten, but two sensational jobs at once. Steven Spielberg and George Lucas cast him in *Raiders of the Lost Ark*. They wanted a new face. They asked CBS to postpone "Magnum" from the fall to a midseason winter debut, perhaps as a replacement for one of the new shows that would invariably bomb. "All in the Family" and "Dallas" had been midseason subs; it was no disgrace. Or CBS could put the new P.I. on ice for a year. *Ark* would most likely make Selleck a superstar, a big plus for any aspiring TV series. Selleck held his breath when he wasn't praying.

CBS refused, fearful of losing the already announced "Magnum" idea to a competitor and worried about the demands superstars make. The two jobs conflicted and Selleck belonged to CBS. He packed for Hawaii. As it happened, an actors' strike delayed production three months. *Raiders*, shooting abroad, was exempt. "I could have gone to Europe and Africa," Selleck said with a sigh, "done *Raiders*, then come back to Hawaii to do 'Magnum.' "

"Magnum, P.I." became one of the most successful shows of the 1980 TV season. In 1981, Selleck won the People's Choice Award, as well as a nomination for an Emmy as best actor in a dramatic series. His new eight-year "Magnum" contract is for a record-setting $7 million. He made his starring debut in a movie in the $20-million bomb, *High Road to China*, in 1983. It was the top picture in the marketplace for three days until lousy word of mouth dropped attendance by 50 percent. His second effort, *Lassiter*, was moderately successful. Selleck keeps seaching for his lost *Ark*, wanting to be more than last year's rich pin-up boy at forty.

Clean-a-Masterpiece Theater: Japan and the Sistine Chapel

BACKGROUND: Japan is one of the world's greatest civilizations. For centuries, it has produced the most exquisite visual and literary art, and despite its isolation well into the middle of the last century, it has come to treasure Western art as highly as its own. Add that to the Japanese penchant for taking pictures, and we have the answer to the Vatican's prayers.

Michelangelo Buonarroti (1475–1564) was a sculptor, painter, architect, and poet, and a towering figure in Renaissance, mannerist, and baroque art. Pope Julius II commissioned him to decorate the Sistine Chapel, the private chapel of the popes. The frescoes across the ceiling, on the principal themes of the Bible, were executed between 1508 and 1512; those of The Last Judgment on the altar wall were done between 1534 and 1541.

Michelangelo considered himself primarily a sculptor; modern theorists of art have based their opinions of his color sense on the frescoes he completed, most notably the ones in the Sistine Chapel. The dark and somber, almost muted hues, were ascribed by many to the influence of the fanatical monk Savonarola's apocalyptic visions. They had greatly impressed the artist, adding immeasurably to the tragic sense of human destiny expressed in his art, poetry, and letters. Subsequently, he was never considered much of a colorist by the experts.

Over the centuries, soot and grime have caked on the walls of the chapel. Frescoes by the other artists were cleaned and restored, but the idea of touching Michelangelo's images verged on the sacrilegious. In fact, when the neighboring art was renewed, it was all kept relatively muted—the Renaissance painters adored bright colors—so the famed masterworks wouldn't look pale and faded by comparison. Then a new cleaning solvent was invented that drew encrusted dirt off the plaster surface without altering the paint. It was tested on other sixteenth-century works and was declared safe. Master restorer Gianluigi Colalucci estimated that the job of cleaning Michelangelo's frescoes would require twelve years and $3 million. The Vatican couldn't pick up the tab [see "Art Product, 54.7 Gross Tons: The Vatican Show," page 322], and only one sponsor was willing to take on the task. Ever able to combine their sense of history and beauty with day-to-day practicality, the Japanese came up with an outrageously ingenious offer.

THE DEAL: In return for staking the entire $3 million, enabling a total restoration of the Michelangelo frescoes, the Japanese will fil every inch of the work, perched on the scaffolding beside the restorers.

RESULTS: Japan's Nippon TV network will broadcast thirty documentaries culled from their projected twelve years of filming. They will also control complete world rights to the film, parts of which will inevitably be sold to every civilized country and studied in universities forever. At first the bright studio lights disturbed the restorers, but they soon adjusted to their working companions, who, Colalucci says, "are so discreet and so intensely interested themselves that it has become a pleasure to have them."

The cleaned portions are a "revelation," displaying colors as exuberant as any Fauvist would be proud to claim. The Vatican Museum director exclaimed: "It will be necessary to completely revise much of what has been written for hundreds of years on the person and pictures of Michelangelo." The master has been revealed as one "whose colors are of a beauty, subtlety, and skill that are entirely unexpected." The only people not surprised are probably the Japanese with their genius for common sense: Michelangelo was the most influential artist of his time; if he had used dark and muted colors, surely others would have followed suit.

DRAWING INTEREST

"What's it like to be Picasso?" a young American admirer once asked the great artist. Picasso asked him for a dollar bill, pinned it to an easel, drew some characteristic strokes, signed it with a pen, and returned it to the speechless youth. "Now your dollar bill is priceless," said the amused Picasso: "That's what it is like to be Picasso."

Picasso's Patrimony: *Guernica* Is Given to Spain

BACKGROUND: Civil war was raging in Spain his native country, when Picasso was asked by the anti-Fascist Spanish Republic to do a painting for their pavilion at the 1937 Paris World's Fair. When word reached the artist that the Fascist forces of Generalissimo Francisco Franco had savagely bombed the Basque town of Guernica, Picasso was grieved and outraged. The antiwar masterpiece *Guernica*, a twenty-five-foot-long mural considered to be one of the great works of the twentieth century, was the result. The painting was sent to New York in 1939 on a tour to benefit the Spanish Refugee Relief Committee; when World War II broke out, Picasso asked that *Guernica* and a number of his other works be held at New York's Museum of Modern Art (MOMA) on extended loan. With the war's end, and Franco's

Fascist dictatorship in control of Spain, Picasso asked MOMA to house *Guernica*—until things changed in Spain.

THE DEAL: *Guernica* would be given to Spain only after the death of Franco and "the re-establishment of public liberties" in Spain.

RESULTS: Franco's dictatorship did not end until his death in 1975. Two days later, the five-hundred-year-old monarchy was restored, with Juan Carlos de Borbón proclaimed king. He immediately promised "profound improvements" in political conditions. In 1977, for the first time in forty-one years, free elections were held in Spain. The new government pardoned more than half the nation's political prisoners, loosened restrictions on the press, granted the right to assembly, and legalized the Communist party. By 1981, lawyers for the Picasso estate (the artist had died in 1973) determined that public liberties were sufficiently reestablished in Spain: *Guernica*, valued for insurance purposes at $40 million, could go to the birthplace of its creator.

The Spanish minister of culture, at the official transfer ceremony, said that the painting would "enrich the national patrimony of Spain." William Rubin, director of painting and sculpture at MOMA said that for Spain the painting "could be a symbol of a kind of national reconciliation, since it might be seen as the final act in the closing of the Civil War."

With the end of Fascism in Spain, Picasso's antiwar masterpiece ended a forty-two-year stay in America.

Dealmaker as Artist-Diplomat:
Peter Paul Rubens

Peter Paul Rubens (1577–1640) was not only the premier painter of his day, he was also a distinguished diplomat, called upon to intervene in the political affairs of war-torn Europe. His undisputed charm was inherited from his remarkable parents. Rubens's father, a brilliant and handsome magistrate, had nearly gotten himself beheaded when his passionate, clandestine affair with the young Anna, Princess of Orange, led to her pregnancy during a long absence of the prince. It was only the tireless efforts of the devoted and astute Mrs. Rubens that won his release after twenty-six months of imprisonment. She was a forgiving woman as well: Peter Paul was born four years later.

Rubens was late in displaying any artistic genius, but he showed, early on, a fierce desire to be an artist. A prodigious worker, he would thrive, throughout his life, on exceptionally long hours of labor. By the age of twenty-one, he was accepted as a master painter by the painters' guild of Antwerp. In 1599, the same year that the Habsburg rulers Archduke Albert and his Spanish wife, the Infanta Isabella, came to rule the Spanish Netherlands (including Antwerp and the rest of Belgium), Rubens left for Italy, the art capital of Europe. In service to an Italian duke, Rubens was sent all over Italy to copy great masterpieces, including those of Raphael, Titian, and Correggio. Having assimilated the Renaissance, in 1608 Rubens returned to Antwerp to become one of the giants of the Baroque.

Appointed the official court painter by the archduke, Rubens insisted upon maintaining his own studio in Antwerp (the court was in Brussels). Soon commissions from the Catholic church and the nobility were pouring in from all over Europe. Rubens worked quickly, but there were far too many commissions for one artist to handle on his own; he was soon employing a large group of helpers. Young apprentices prepared canvases. More experienced artists painted from designs provided by Rubens, who himself added the finishing touches.

When Marie de' Medici, widow of Henry IV of France and mother of Louis XIII, decided to build herself a magnificent new home—the Luxembourg Palace—and invite twenty of Europe's greatest artists to decorate it for her with paintings illuminating the career of her late husband, Rubens raced to Paris to convince the Queen Mother that only one living artist was worthy of her project: Rubens, of course. By arguing that the paintings should actually highlight the life of Her Majesty (and in the most flattering way), Rubens won the largest commission ever before given to a painter. In the course of the three years Rubens spent painting for Marie (the paintings are now in the Louvre), the two developed a close relationship, paving the way for a liaison between Marie and the court in Brussels. The paintings themselves caused quite a sensation, and even more commissions poured in from nobles everywhere; a list of Rubens's portraits reads like a *Who's Who* of his day. Of particular importance among these were the portraits he did of the Duke of Buckingham, England's principal minister in France. Two years later, Buckingham sent a secret emissary to Rubens, asking him to travel to Madrid to propose an armistice in the war that was raging between Spain and England. Rubens's Spanish sojourn ultimately led to his being appointed as the ambassador of the Spanish court in England. While not conducting complicated negotiations—and sometimes while negotiating—Rubens painted royal portraits. He so thoroughly endeared himself to King Charles I (who had him paint the ceiling of the banqueting hall in Whitehall) that the king made him a baronet—Sir Peter Paul. Upon his return to the Netherlands, the Archduchess Isabella rewarded him with the post of secretary of the Privy Council, a post that required no work, paid three thousand gold crowns a year, and could be inherited by Rubens's son.

In 1631, Marie de' Medici was placed under house arrest (in Luxembourg Palace) by Cardinal Richelieu, the man who ruled her son—and France. Despite her constant guard of musketeers, the Queen Mother managed to smuggle out a letter to the Archduchess Isabella, asking for asylum in Brussels. Marie requested that all arrangements for her departure be made by Rubens. Rubens lost no time in traveling to Paris where he held two weeks of intensive negotiations with Richelieu, who was under extreme pressure from the Vatican, Spain, and others to release the Queen Mother. When Marie and Rubens arrived in Brussels, the entire city turned out to cheer. One month later, the grateful Marie came to Rubens's house to thank him with generous amounts of gold and diamonds, even staying overnight—an enormous honor, since Rubens was a mere commoner.

Rubens, who died in 1640, left behind a legacy of over a thousand paintings, many of them a testimony to the beauty of female flesh, in abundance. His popularity has not diminished, even in these thin times.

The Second American Revolution: Jackson Pollock and Peggy Guggenheim

BACKGROUND: Cast your bread upon the waters and it comes back as sandwiches. Especially if you're superrich and the waters are the floods of genius.

Paul Jackson Pollock was born on January 28, 1912, on a sheep ranch in Cody, Wyoming. He was the youngest of five sons born to Stella May McClure, an Irishwoman, and LeRoy McCoy Pollock, a Scotch-Irishman who was adopted by the Pollock family. In 1930, desiring to be "an artist of some kind," Pollock traveled to New York City to study with Thomas Hart Benton at the Art Students League. He worked as a stonecutter restoring public monuments to supplement his scholarship. From 1935 to 1942 he worked on the WPA's Art Project, and during this period he broke away totally from pictorial realism to paint his "interior landscape." Also during this period, his battle with the disease of alcoholism began in earnest.

In 1942, Pollock showed a painting, *Birth*, at the McMillan Gallery in New York City. It brought him to the attention of Peggy Guggenheim's advisors. Ms. G., a copper heiress with a penchant for modern art and artists (she married Max Ernst), had recently opened her gallery, Art of This Century, to display her own formidable collection as well as to sell avant-garde work. Pollock was invited to show collages in her 1943 Spring Salon for Young Artists. He was working at odd jobs in New York City: doing window displays with Lee Krassner (eventually his wife), painting neckties, and doing custodial work at the Museum of Non-Objective Painting (now the Guggenheim Museum—Solomon's, not Peggy's).

Attending to her advisors, and against her better judgment (she later confessed: "It was always difficult for me to accept Pollock's greatness"), Ms. G. advanced him $150 a month against sales, with an evening-up if more than $2,700 worth of work was sold, allowing one third commission to the gallery. If less than $2,700 was earned, she would take what he owed her in paintings. At his first one-man show in November 1943, the catalogue declared: "Pollock's talent is volcanic. It has fire." And the influential critic Clement Greenberg became a champion: "I cannot find strong enough words of praise." Then, on May 2, 1944, the Museum of Modern Art bought *The She Wolf* for $650; it was the first Pollock to grace a museum. The follow-

> "I want to express my feelings rather than illustrate them."
>
> Jackson Pollock

ing year, Pollock married Krassner; they decided to move to East Hampton, Long Island. She and W. N. M. Davis, a collector, convinced Ms. G. to make it possible . . . and stupendously worth her own while.

THE DEAL: The East Hampton farmhouse, five acres of land, and a large barn cost $5,000. Ms. G. loaned $2,000 for the down payment and raised Pollock's stipend to $300 a month for two years: 1946 to 1948. The $2,000 was to be repaid from the $300 at $50 a month. In exchange, Ms. G. received Pollock's *total output* minus one painting a year.

RESULTS: Ms. G. came to call this arrangement "my most honorable achievement." It was the biggest strike in the business since grandpa fell into his first mine. "Each age finds its own techniques," Pollock stated, and by 1943–1944 he had begun to synthesize all the previous work by dripping and pouring paint onto his canvas: "This is akin to the method of the Indian sandpainters of the West." By 1947, with the canvas unstretched on the floor, he was walking around it and working from all four sides. During the next three years he produced the seminal works of what Robert Coates in *The New Yorker* christened Abstract Expressionism. These particular paintings brought the movement instant international recognition and shifted the world center of "advanced painting" from Paris to New York. "They broke the ice for us," de Kooning said.

But in 1947, Ms. G. gave up her gallery and returned to Europe. Betty Parsons agreed to represent Pollock. Collector Davis bought a painting and financed Pollock's next show. Most critics found his art disorganized and violent despite its superhuman control of form, and the public did not buy it. In 1948 he was in a terrible money bind—once trading a work on paper for food—but in 1949 he met the artist and sugar heir Alphonso Ossorio, who purchased his work and encouraged him. Pollock's reputation grew by leaps and swirls. Even *Life* magazine in August 1949 was forced to ask: "Jackson Pollock: Is He the Greatest Living Painter in the U.S.?"

In 1950, while Ms. G. tried and failed to arrange a show in Paris— a feat Ossorio managed in 1952—three of his works were shown at the Venice Biennale, causing violent arguments pro and con. (*Time* magazine labeled him, in pure Luce-ite prose, "Jack the Dripper.") At the same time as the Biennale, Ms. G. showed all twenty of her Pollocks—two she had given to the Stedelijk Museum in Amsterdam—at Piazzo San Marco in Venice. She had the largest collection of work by the man quickly becoming the most important painter on earth.

"All profoundly original art looks ugly at first."

Clement Greenberg, art critic

Pollock died in a car accident at 10:15 .. on August 11, 1956, a victim of alcoholism. At his death his income was under $3,000 a year. Ms. G., disturbed by her diminishing role in his history—one catalogue for MOMA described her as his "first dealer"—wrote her autobiography to set the record straight. But she had her canvases stored in the cellar of her Venetian Palace: "and as the cellar was very damp, I began giving away pictures, including Pollock, which I now very much regret." When in 1960 the Tate of London paid $100,000 for a Pollock, her regret grew into frustration. She had previously noticed that some drawings, paintings, and other works dated during the period when his "total output" belonged to her, were being shown. She sued Lee Krassner Pollock for $122,000. Four years later, in 1965, she retracted "all charges of wrongdoing on the part of the defendant." She was given a pair of small Pollocks worth $400.

Pollock is the only major artist of his generation whose work is frequently forged. Many attempt, in his own words, "to splash a Pollock out." However, the failure to replicate Pollock's unique line and color harmonies makes the forgeries easily detectable by art detectives. In 1976, *Lavender Mist*, a 1950 oil bought by Ossorio for under $5,000, was sold to the National Gallery in Washington D.C. [see "Neo-Classical Tax Dodge: Andrew Mellon Creates the National Gallery," page 309] for $2.3 million. On today's real-estate market, the Pollock property on Long Island is worth in excess of $500,000.

> "When I am painting I have a general notion as to what I am about. I *can* control the flow of paint; there is no accident, just as there is no beginning and no end."
>
> Jackson Pollock

Neo-classical Tax Dodge: Andrew Mellon Creates the National Gallery

BACKGROUND: Andrew W. Mellon, one of the world's wealthiest men, had ridden roughshod over the American economy as secretary of the treasury (1921–1932), but when Franklin D. Roosevelt became president in 1933, Mellon was in deep trouble. Roosevelt had called him "the mastermind among the malefactors of great wealth," and was attempting to have him convicted of tax fraud. But Mellon countered with beneficence so bedazzling that even crusty FDR was blinded by what the billionaire promised to bestow: a National Gallery of Art, brimming with an exquisite collection of masterpieces.

Mellon had become one of the world's richest people when he changed the loan policy of the Pittsburgh bank he'd inherited from his father: Rather than loan new businesses money at the traditional fixed rate of interest, he would take a share in the enterprise instead. He soon owned large shares of several profitable corporations, including the Aluminum Company of America and Gulf Oil. By the time he went to Washington (where he served under two presidents, lowered income taxes, and devised financial policies that helped lead to the crash of 1929) he was worth hundreds of millions of dollars. Notoriously shy, he was happiest surrounded by Old Masters, which he collected with avidity. With the death of J. P. Morgan, he was America's foremost collector. When the impoverished Soviet government offered to sell twenty-one masterpieces from the Hermitage, Mellon was the only bidder, snapping them up at $7 million. The purchase was kept a secret because the United States still did not recognize the Communist government, and, as Mellon's assistant later put it: "It probably would not have been good politics for the Secretary of the Treasury publically to spend millions for rare paintings at a time when the government was swamped with unemployment, bank failures and general distress."

When the Democrats swept into office in 1933, FDR seemed determined to discredit the former treasury secretary, seen by some as the ringleader of the Depression. FDR sent hoards of federal investigators swarming in on Mellon, and in 1934, the attorney general announced he had evidence that Mellon had committed tax fraud on his 1931 return and that he owed the government just over $3 million in back taxes and penalties. Mellon counterattacked: He had, in fact, *overpaid* his taxes that year by $139,000—and he insisted on a hearing to clear himself of charges of fraud. At this hearing, Mellon's central argument emerged: He had given millions of dollars in paintings over to a foundation he'd established to found a National Gallery. *Yes,* the paintings were still hanging in his house, and *no,* he had not previously announced his intentions publicly, but his defense lawyer insisted that, "it is impossible to conceive of a man planning such benefactions as these and at the same time plotting and scheming to defraud the government."

THE DEAL: Mellon would donate his entire collection of art (value: $50 million) to the nation; and he would build a marble palace ($16 million) in which to exhibit these works; and he would leave a permanent endowment fund; and he would insist that the institution *not* be named after him, but that it be called The National Gallery of Art. The government would exonerate him on charges of fraud and would donate a site, just below Capitol Hill, on the mall.

RESULTS: FDR sent Mellon a thank-you letter which read, in part: "I was not only completely taken by surprise but was delighted by your very wonderful offer . . . for many years I have felt the need for a national gallery of art in the Capital." When the beautiful neo-classical gallery opened in 1941, Mellon was not there to see it: He died in 1937. But it was his hope that the splendor of the building would attract other collections, since if it housed only his there would be a scant twenty-four works of art per acre. Sky-high inheritance taxes conspiring with the human desire for immortality soon swelled the National Gallery's holdings with the renowned Widener, Kress, Dale, and Rosenwald Collections. By the 1960s, the National Gallery had run out of exhibition space. Paul Mellon, Andrew's son and himself an important art collector, announced his willingness to fund a new building, and Congress voted to provide an adjoining site on the mall. Today, the graceful, modern East Building, paid for by Paul, sits opposite the neo-classical West Building, paid for by his father. Both structures are made of pink Tennessee marble and are joined underground. Inside, some five million visitors a year marvel at the finest collection of Botticellis, Rubens, Raphaels, da Vincis, Rembrandts, and many other masters in the new world.

The Odor of Sanctity:
The Lasting Results of Expert
Dealmaking

"He did not perfume his avarice with the odor of sanctity—affect the role of friend to man, build churches or libraries, endow a university

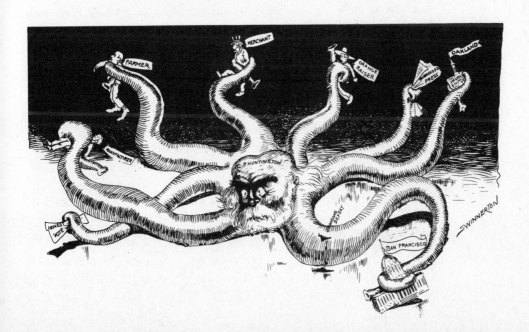

or give away bright new dimes," said one observer about the railroad baron Collis P. Huntington. But many other artful dealmakers and their heirs (including Huntington's own nephew, Henry), having acquired vast wealth, hoped that by creating great public institutions they could implant in the public imagination a lasting image of themselves as benefactors of the human race, munificent and noble. Long after memories of restraint-of-trade cases, union busting, child-labor abuses, stock fraud, or other acrimonious scandals had faded, the culprits would endure in "living history" by their splendid good works. Here was a deal with posterity. (According to *Standard and Poor's*, multiply by eleven to calculate today's prices in relation to the 1890s.)

♦ Rockefeller: John D. Rockefeller (1839–1937) was the founder of Standard Oil [see "If You Have To Ask How Much It Costs, You Can't Afford It: J. P. Morgan Puts Together U.S. Steel," page 10, and "Dealmaker as Patriarch: John Davison Rockefeller," page 18]. By the time of his death, he had given away a much-publicized $500 million. In 1901 he founded the Rockefeller Institute for Medical Research, a prestigious post-graduate school in New York City, now called Rockefeller University. In 1910, the Rockefeller Foundation was endowed with $100 million, "to promote the well-being of mankind throughout the world"; its current endowment is $1,014,354,292. (Since its founding, the foundation has helped mankind to the tune of $1,594,000,000.) He virtually funded the University of Chicago—originally a Baptist theological seminary—with gifts amounting to $45 million. Among the many works of his progeny are New York City's Museum of Modern Art and The Cloisters, Virginia's town of Colonial Williamsburg ($50 million) with the Abby Aldrich Rockefeller Folk Art Collection, Maine's Acadia National Park, and Fredonia's Michael C. Rockefeller Arts Center. The Rockefeller dynasty lives on.

♦ Carnegie: Andrew Carnegie (1835–1919) was the founder of Carnegie Steel Company [see "If You Have to Ask How Much It Costs, You Can't Afford It: J. P. Morgan Puts Together U.S. Steel," page 10, and "Dealmaker as Industrialist: Andrew Carnegie," page 33]. During his lifetime, he gave away $350 million—90 percent of his fortune, the largest of his day. In 1895, he created the Carnegie Institute, "a cultural palace—for the people," that includes a library, an art gallery, a museum of natural history, and a vast music hall; it bills itself as "Pittsburgh's prime symbol of culture." In 1900, he funded the Carnegie Institute of Technology in Pittsburgh, now Carnegie-Mellon University. In 1911, he endowed the Carnegie Corporation of

Philanthropy is almost the only virtue which is sufficiently appreciated by mankind.

Thoreau

Charity shall cover a multitude of sins.

Peter 1: 8

New York with $125 million; its current endowment is $380 million. The foundation's priorities are "the prevention of damage to children, avoiding nuclear war, and giving aid to developing countries." (Since its founding, the corporation has dished out approximately $600 million.) Other Carnegie foundations include the Carnegie Endowment for International Peace (1910) and the Carnegie Institution of Washington, D.C. (1902). Besides being the founding patron of New York City's internationally renowned Carnegie Hall, he funded over three thousand libraries around the world. There is no Carnegie dynasty in the limelight today.

♦ Vanderbilt: Cornelius Vanderbilt (1794–1877), the "Commodore," was an American railroad magnate who amassed the largest fortune of his day. He funded Vanderbilt University in Nashville, Tennessee. It was opened in 1875 and was run under the auspices of the Methodist Church until 1914. Two great residences, now national shrines to the age of opulence, were built to house his progeny. The Breakers, in Newport, Rhode Island, was completed in 1895 at a cost of $2.5 million (excluding the furnishings); it was the summer "cottage" of Cornelius Vanderbilt, Jr. Biltmore House, in Asheville, North Carolina, was also completed in 1895, at a cost of $11 million (excluding furnishings). This 255-room house was originally set on a 125,000-acre plot; 250 acres were landscaped and 112,000 acres became Pisgaw National Forest. Gertrude Vanderbilt Whitney founded New York City's Whitney Museum. And Little Gloria is happy, at last.

Biltmore House.

Blue Boy.

♦ Stanford: Leland Stanford (1824–1893), a U.S. railroad baron, founded Palo Alto's Stanford University after declaring to his wife, upon the death of their only child at age fifteen, that "the children of California shall be our children." The campus was designed by Frederick Law Olmsted (of New York City's Central Park fame); the first student to enroll was Herbert Hoover. The Stanford University Museum of Art houses a large collection, ranging from pre-Columbian to contemporary, with numerous pieces of sculpture by Rodin.

♦ Guggenheim: The fortune was made in mining and smelting by Meyer (1828–1905) and the eldest of his six sons, Daniel (1856–1930) Guggenheim. Son Solomon (1861–1949) founded the Guggenheim Museum in New York City, housing his vast collection of contemporary art in a controversial building designed by Frank Lloyd Wright. Son Simon (1867–1941) set up the John Simon Guggenheim Memorial Foundation, in memory of his son, to give fellowships to writers, scholars, and artists.

♦ Flagler: Henry Flagler (1830–1913) was one of John D. Rockefeller's original partners in the oil-refining business (the company was called Rockefeller, Andrews, and Flagler until it was changed to Standard Oil). He was *the* developer of the entire east coast of Florida—from Jacksonville to Key West, along the route of his railroad—and the founder of Saint Augustine, Daytona, Palm Beach, and Miami. His palatial Palm Beach home, "Whitehall," is now the Henry Morrison Flagler Museum, displaying the nineteenth- and twentieth-century megabucks sensibility in the decorative arts.

♦ Morgan: John Pierpont Morgan (1837–1913), the most powerful American financier, gained control of many of the nation's railroads and founded United States Steel Corporation and many other trusts [see "If You Have To Ask How Much It Costs, You Can't Afford It: J. P. Morgan Puts Together U.S. Steel," page 10, and "Dealmaker as Financial Titan: John Pierpont Morgan," page 14]. The Pierpont Morgan Library in New York City was formerly his Renaissance-style marble home. It houses his extraordinary collection of illuminated medieval and Renaissance manuscripts, rare books, and Old Master drawings.

♦ Frick: Henry Clay Frick (1849–1919) was a steel and coke industrialist, and a partner of Andrew Carnegie. The Frick Collection is in his Fifth Avenue mansion in New York City. The outstanding collection of Renoirs, Fragonards, Vermeers, El Grecos, Gainsboroughs, and others, is displayed in the fabulously furnished rooms.

♦ Huntington: Henry Huntington (1850–1927) was the nephew and business associate of Collis P. Huntington, the railroad baron; in 1913 he married his uncle's widow, Arabella. The Henry Huntington Library and Art Gallery in San Marino, California, was built in the tradition of a nineteenth-century British manor house and is surrounded by a 207-acre garden. This collection is particularly outstanding for its eighteenth- and nineteenth-century British art, including Gainsborough's famous *Blue Boy*, as well as its huge library of the rarest manuscripts and first editions.

♦ du Pont: Henry Francis du Pont (1880–1969) was one of the scions of the gunpowder and chemical dynasty. In "Winterthur," a large estate once owned by his great-uncle and aunt, H. F. du Pont gathered American antiques: furniture and decorative accessories including paneling and woodwork taken from houses built between 1640 and 1840 along the eastern seaboard. In 1930, the house—expanded to over 100 rooms—and 960 acres of Maryland were turned over to the Winterthur Corporation, a nonprofit educational organization endowed with $70 million. In 1951, the Henry Francis du Pont Winterthur Museum was opened to the public. The Louise du Pont Crowninshield Research Building, named for the founder's sister, houses the library, scientific labs, and conservation facilities.

♦ Getty: J. Paul Getty (1892–1976) inherited his father's relatively small oil business and engineered its growth into the large and profitable corporation it is today. He became the richest man in the world, personally worth some $3 billion. The J. Paul Getty Museum in Ma-

The J. Paul Getty Museum.

libu, California, is a re-creation of a first-century Roman villa; it was built as a showcase for Getty's collection of Greek and Roman art. The endowment is now worth some $1.6 billion, making it the richest museum in the world; and since current federal tax laws require a museum to spend 4.25 percent of its endowment's current market value every year—in the case of the Getty that comes to $60 million annually—the museum has announced plans to build the Center of the History of Art and the Humanities on a 162-acre site in Brentwood, California.

A Library of the Works of God:
The Glass Flowers of Harvard

BACKGROUND: If necessity is the mother of invention, it all too infrequently stimulates something both practical and magically beautiful. Why, when it happens, does humankind then let it self-destruct?

In 1846, when Swiss-born scientist Louis Agassiz arrived in America he was already an international institution, famous for his studies of fossil fishes and glacial movements. Five thousand Bostonians flocked to hear him deliver the Lowell Lecture at Harvard. Rather than return to Europe, he accepted a professorship in zoology and geology at the school in 1847 because his ambitious plans for creating a museum of natural history—"a library of the works of God"—were greeted with excited approval. An ardent collector of specimens, Agassiz was also a great teacher who strongly influenced the growth of science at the university and throughout the United States. His lectures, in the words of Henry Adams (class of 1858), "had more influence on [my] curiosity than the rest of the college instructions altogether." His plant specimens inspired the brilliant botanist Asa Gray to set up the Museum of Vegetable Products at Harvard in 1858; not only was it a research tool for their students and colleagues, but it was also a means of instructing the public, who were encouraged to visit its carefully organized displays. A zoology museum was soon added, as well as ones for geology, mineralogy, and botany.

Dr. George Goodale was the first director of the Harvard Botanical Museum. As he went about the task of collecting specimens for his exhibits, he realized that dried or preserved plants and plant parts looked, well, *dead*. And wax or papier-mâché replicas weren't much better; besides not being very accurate, they aged quickly and badly.

To cultivate an actual garden was not practical, because blooms bloom when they bloom and not when students (or the public) want to see them. He knew how hard it is to stimulate interest in the beauty of plants and flowers when the proffered model is not even attractive. The problem was solved for Dr. Goodale when he visited the Museum of Comparative Zoology.

Glass replicas of marine invertebrates were astoundingly successful. They were made by a father-and-son team in Dresden, Germany, Leopold and Rudolf Blaschka, who supplied museums around the world with them. In 1886, when Dr. Goodale visited their studio/home, the two glass-artisans were less than keen about flowers. They were making a fine living with the invertebrates. Leopold had once dabbled in plants for his own amusement; they had proved difficult and not very rewarding financially when sold to a local museum. In fact, there were still several orchids left from the experiment. Dr. Goodale took one look and knew his problem was solved: They were exquisitely lifelike and perfect in every detail.

The Blaschkas, after much discussion, agreed to make a few glass models. *Only a few.* When these eventually arrived at Harvard, they were a mass of broken bits: New York customs had clumsily mishandled them. Yet everyone who studied the fragments was astounded by their beauty. Among the viewers, Elizabeth C. Ware and her daughter Mary Lee were so excited by the Blaschka's art that they offered to finance the project. Letters were exchanged with the Dresden studio, and the two men agreed to spend half their time on Harvard's flowers. Dr. Goodale drew up lists, including as many orders, genera, and species as possible. Some plants had to be shipped to Dresden for cultivation and reference in their garden; others were tracked down in the royal gardens and greenhouses of the castle in nearby Pillnitz, where the Blaschkas received special permission to view and sketch.

The first shipment of twenty glass plants arrived at Harvard in 1887. A customs official traveled to Massachusetts so the carefully packed and crated works of art could be correctly unwrapped. They were magnificent treasures as well as sublime teaching aides—they also very quickly took the public's fancy. For the next three years shipments arrived, but then the entire project faltered. The Blaschkas no longer wished to do *both* invertebrates and flowers. One group had to go.

THE DEAL: On April 16, 1890, the Wares offered—as a memorial to Dr. Charles Eliot Ware (class of 1834)—8,800 marks payable in half-yearly installments for ten years in the name of the Botanical Department of Harvard University. The Blaschkas were to make *only* glass models of plants, flowers, and botanical details for those ten years. The Wares agreed to pay freight, consular certificates, and insurance, and to provide for proper exhibition. The Blaschkas agreed to refuse all other commissions and to complete the lists that had been submitted to them.

RESULTS: In 1892, Rudolf Blaschka journeyed to the Caribbean and throughout the United States to examine and sketch, making detailed color notes of several plants under their natural conditions. A second field trip was canceled in 1895 when his father, Leopold, died; he continued alone for nearly half a century until retiring in 1936.

The Ware Collection consists of approximately 847 lifesize models representing 780 species and varieties of plants in 164 families, with over 3,000 detailed models of enlarged flowers, anatomical sections of various floral and vegetative parts of the plants, plus three special exhibits: a large group of "lower plants," or Cryptogramma, illustrating the complex life histories of fungi, bryophytes, and ferns; 64 models showing fungal diseases; and several insects and plants illustrating pollination. The plants are exhibited by family in order of evolution, from the simplest to the most complex.

The Blaschkas had no special process to produce their marvels. Ordinary pincers and tweezers were used to twist and mold the shapes. In Leonard's words: "We have tact. My son Rudolf has more than I have, because he is my son, and tact increases in every generation." The models are made entirely of clear or colored glass, with wire used to support and strengthen the heavier structures or hanging fruits. The clear glass was finished by "cold painting," a process eventually replaced by a system Rudolf created of fusing colored, powdered glass to a molded surface. Eventually, all the glass used was "self-prepared" in studio furnaces; evenings, weekends, and holidays were devoted to experimenting with various glass formulas to manufacture the highest-quality, most resilient materials.

Over the years the fame of the collection has grown. Some plants were sent to the Paris International Exposition in 1900, six went to St. Louis for the Louisiana Purchase Exposition in 1904, and six were destroyed in a flood that devastated the Corning Glass Museum in 1959; but in 1974, three went to Tokyo as part of the Harvardiana exhibit. The collection is housed in two rooms on the third floor of the Botanical Museum. It draws over a hundred thousand visitors a year, making it the largest public attraction at Harvard. It is also the sight of more endangered species per square foot than anyplace else on earth. Due to unstable humidity, the color layer fused to the molded glass has begun to detach. The condition is not reversible, but it can be stabilized. In the mid-1970s, a fund-raising drive failed; and Harvard University, for all its wealth, cannot find the necessary monies to air-condition the two halls and save this national treasure that has been described as "an artistic marvel in the field of science and a scientific marvel in the field of art." It seems a betrayal of the Wares and of Louis Agassiz. And of the rest of the human race.

Fooling a Rockefeller in Oils: Diego Rivera and Rockefeller Center

BACKGROUND: Later it would be called "radical chic," but in the 1930s, when the Rockefellers commissioned a Communist artist and found Lenin up against the wall in Rockefeller Center, people called it foolishness. "Lenin's off the wall!" insisted Nelson, while a chorus yelled "Property is theft!"

Many people expected trouble when, back in 1932, the Rockefeller family announced that they had commissioned the great Mexican artist Diego Rivera to paint a large mural in the entrance hall of the tallest building in the recently constructed Rockefeller Center. The flamboyant, three-hundred-pound artist was nearly as well-known for his politics as he was for his art, and he was also known for behavior

The central section of Diego Rivera's mural re-created in Mexico City with the offending portrait of Lenin at the right.

so insolent that he'd been ousted from the Mexican Communist party, a group he'd helped to found. He believed in art as propaganda, and his stay in Moscow in 1927–1928 had helped him to clarify his views: Art, he believed, "should respond to the new order of things . . . and the logical place for this art, belonging to the populace, was on the walls of buildings." He was famous for the monumental murals he'd created in Mexico depicting social problems, but in the United States, among the walls he'd decorated were those of Mrs. John D. Rockefeller, Jr., who'd hired him to do portraits of her grandchildren. Other family members collected his work, and the Rockefeller-founded and -funded Museum of Modern Art gave Rivera the second solo show in their history.

When the art-conscious clan decided to virtually redo midtown Manhattan and build the twenty-two-acre Rockefeller Center, it was natural that they should turn to their favorite artists for help. With young Nelson, fresh from college, at the helm of the new enterprise, a great emphasis was put on the choice of mural art for the center of the Center, the seventy-story R.C.A. building. It was Nelson who came up with the idea of a competition open only to three family favorites: Picasso, Matisse, and Rivera. Each would be given detailed specifications elaborating color scheme (white, black, and gray) and theme ("Man at the Crossroads looking with Hope and High Vision to the choosing of a new and better future"), and for $300, they would be asked to submit sketches. Picasso refused even to meet with family representatives; Matisse demured, explaining that he could not work with that color scheme or theme. Only Rivera was interested at all, but not in competing with other artists or in working with those colors. "Suppose," he asked Nelson, "some ill-disposed persons should chance upon such a nickname as 'Undertaker's Palace'?" When Nelson agreed to the use of color, Rivera agreed to submit sketches, and both the family and the artist generated elaborate verbal descriptions. The family told Rivera: "The philosophical or spiritual quality should dominate. . . . We hope these paintings may stimulate not only a material but above all a spiritual awakening." The artist told the family: " . . . my panel will show the Workers arriving at a true understanding of their rights regarding the means of production, which has resulted in the planning of the liquidation of Tyranny, personified by a crumbling statue of Caesar, whose head has fallen to the ground. It will show the Workers of the cities and the country inheriting the Earth." The family, ever pleased with the bit of the earth they'd inherited, wired Rivera: "Sketch approved . . . can go right ahead with larger scale."

THE DEAL: Rivera would execute a 1,071-square-foot fresco (a painting made by applying color directly onto prepared plaster) based on the sketches he'd submitted to the Rockefellers and on the copious verbal descriptions they'd exchanged. The family would pay Rivera $21,000, and out of this fee Rivera would pay for all supplies and assistants.

RESULTS: It was expected that, as Rivera transformed his small sketches into a large mural, there would be changes; as an artist, Rivera said he "thought with his hands." But as the mural neared completion, the unexpected features of Lenin became unmistakably clear as the face on the "worker's leader" anonymously portrayed in the sketches. A heroic portrait of the Supreme Commander of the Soviet Revolution in the expensively embellished showplace of the Supreme Capitalist Dynasty? The family thought not. Nelson, ever polite, wrote to Rivera: "While I was in the number one building at Rockefeller Center yesterday viewing the progress of your thrilling mural, I noticed that in the most recent portion of the painting you had included a portrait of Lenin. The piece is beautifully painted but it seems to me that his portrait, appearing in this mural, might very easily offend a great many people. If it were in a private house it would be one thing, but this is a public building and the situation is therefore quite different. As much as I dislike to do so I am afraid that we must ask you to substitute the face of some unknown man where Lenin's face now appears."

Absolutely not, said the indignant Rivera; that would "mutilate the concept." But he was willing to compromise by painting "in perfect balance with the Lenin portion, a figure of some great American historical leader such as Lincoln . . ." No, the family thought not, and delivered an ultimatum along with payment in full: Either Lenin is taken off the wall, or you are taken off the job. Rivera and his assistants painted on until Nelson sent in a small squadron of Rockefeller Center guards, who covered up the mural and closed off the entrance to the building, "the skyscraper menaced by the portrait of Lenin." The Battle of Rockefeller Center was on, as Rivera supporters rallied, holding huge demonstrations in support of the artist. Rivera went on the radio and asked, "Let us take as an example an American millionaire who buys the Sistine Chapel, which contains the work of Michelangelo. . . . Would that millionaire have the right to destroy the Sistine Chapel?" Among the family supporters was the cowboy philosopher, Will Rogers, who said in a radio broadcast: "This artist was selling some art and sneaking in some propaganda. . . . Rockefeller

Just as the monks of the Middle Ages, through ignorance, it is true, erased antique literary productions from parchments . . . just so Rockefeller's lackeys, but this time maliciously, covered the frescoes of the talented Mexican with their decorative banalities. This recent palimpset will conclusively show future generations the fate of art degraded in a decaying bourgeois society.

Trotsky

had ordered a plain ham sandwich, but the cook put some onions on it. Rockefeller says, 'I will pay you for it, but I won't eat the onions.' Now the above is said in no disparagement of the Mexican artist, for he is the best in the world, but you should never try to fool a Rockefeller in oils.''

Although Nelson had promised that the mural would never be destroyed, it was pulverized on his order after being kept draped for six months. The wall was blank for many years until José Maria Sert was commissioned to paint a black, white, and gray replacement. Informed that his work had been destroyed, Rivera was outraged and recreated it at the Palace of Fine Art in Mexico. This time, Lenin was joined by both Marx and Trotsky, and John D. Rockefeller was depicted very near to the germs of venereal disease.

Rivera, who was married to the great artist Frida Kahlo, died in 1957. His critical reputation as a master of monumental expressionism has survived. Nelson remained a director of Rockefeller Center until his 1958 election as governor of New York. Rockefeller Center, now a great tourist attraction and daily home to sixty-five thousand workers, is one of the most successful real-estate ventures in history, currently generating about $250 million in yearly income for the family. Lenin, permanently removed from the wall of Rockefeller Center, is himself a big tourist attraction in Red Square, Moscow.

Art Product, 54.7 Gross Tons: The Vatican Show

BACKGROUND: For centuries, buying and selling art has been big business. It wasn't until the late twentieth century that "traveling" art—shipped and exhibited from continent to continent, from coast to coast—entered the big bucks sweepstakes. It hit its apex with Egypt's young King Tutankhamen, who died sometime in January, in 1343

King Tut's fifty-five treasures—fifty-five pieces out of nearly five thousand, chosen to honor the fifty-fifth anniversary of Howard Carter's excavation in November 1922—traveled to six American museums in 1978. One hundred percent of the profits from the catalogue, cards, and reproductions went to Egypt's Cairo Museum, a decrepit tomb desperately in need of repair if the treasures are to survive into the twenty-first century. After expenses, Egypt cleared over $7 million on the merchandise alone. (It is estimated that "unofficial" *objets* and merchandise grossed over $1 billion.) The host museums fared well, too. Chicago's Field Museum sold 1.3 million tickets, tripled its membership, filled its cafeteria, jammed its parking lot, and sold out Tut items in its bookstore/giftshop. It was a bonanza in this era of slashed federal funding for the arts. Big, lavish production numbers were clearly the answer to a museum director's cash crunch.

The Vatican exhibit, though another story, is a beat of the same fiscal heart. In the middle 1970s, the idea for a group of the Vatican's treasures to travel came from the Friends of American Art in Religion, a national committee formed to advise the Vatican on purchasing American religious art. New York's Cardinal Cooke was its head as well as a trustee of the Metropolitan Museum of Art. In 1979, Phillipe de Montebello, director of the Met, asked Cooke to approach Pope John Paul II through official channels, and the show began to take shape.

The Met has not only one of the world's great collections, but also one of the most successful security systems. The Tut exhibit went without a hitch, much to the satisfaction of the professionals involved. There was not one unpleasant incident for any of the artifacts, although upward of ten million people swarmed around them. Ultrasonic detectors, microtransmitters and receivers inside the display cases, together with five hundred (out of fifteen hundred) employees on the security watch created an impeccable public record. The Vatican was impressed. Pope John Paul II was delighted with the idea. The Vatican exchequer was also thrilled. On paper, the Vatican is worth billions; but in practice it barely operates in the black. Its holdings (stock portfolio and real estate) produce an income approximating that of Harvard University's, around $90 million, which is also its yearly budget. But unlike Harvard, it is disorganized, badly overstructured, and cloaked in secrecy: They are constantly robbing Peter to pay John Paul's administrative staff of three thousand, and they are free of all public accountability on how they run their operation. Since the Vatican is one of history's greatest art patrons and collectors, the whole enterprise seemed divinely ordained . . . with the assistance of calculators.

THE DEAL: The Met would act as agent for the Vatican and be in charge of the entire parade, which would last no longer than fourteen months and make no more than three stops. The Vatican received a $580,000 restoration grant, plus a 10 percent royalty on merchandise (catalogue, cards, posters, reproductions, and so forth). The Met would pay *all* expenses (freight, shipping, insurance, and such), produce the merchandise, and sell it wholesale to the other two museums involved (chosen by the Met). The Met would keep *all* its gate and "support-services" monies.

RESULTS: The show was budgeted at $8 million, making it the most expensive in history. Of that sum, $3 million would be shared by the other two museums: The Art Institute of Chicago and the M. H. de Young Memorial Museum in San Francisco. (They were chosen for geographical reasons and curatorial ones: each had expert staff to care for the various types of artifacts.) Curators of seven different Met departments compiled a "wish list" that was eventually altered and trimmed by the Vatican—for reasons varying from size to fragility—to 237 items. Then money had to be raised by the Met. The catalogue rights were auctioned off to the highest bidder. The publisher Harry N. Abrams paid $600,000 for these, plus the right to do an oversized art book based on the show. The Book-of-the-Month Club snatched up both (the Tut catalogue had been a national best-seller for months). Pan Am contributed the $500,000 transportation. Phillip Morris gave $3 million, the largest corporate gift ever made to a single (tax-deductible) event. Insurance—$50 million worth—was taken by the Federal Council on the Arts and Humanities; the works had to be shipped secretly in eleven batches, each at the $10 million maximum allowed by law—54.7 gross tons in the cargo holds of 747s. The $1 million installation cost—plus $1 million in "miscellaneous necessities"—was donated by sponsors who had their names listed with pride in the catalogue, received tax write-offs, and didn't have to stand in line to see the show.

Nearly all the art was restored, some so totally that new photos had to be taken. The famed *Apollo Belvedere,* a Roman marble copy of a Greek bronze, was dismantled, cleaned, repaired, and realigned, making it able to stand unaided for the first time in 407 years. Seventeen centuries of art, crated in handmade boxes within boxes, were competing to break records set by one frail king's burial hoard. They did not. Of the 855,000 attending, 596,000 paid four dollars each—264,000 freebies went to VIPs, trustees, sponsors, critics, and so forth. (Over 1.2 million saw Tut; nearly 1 million paid.) All the Tut tickets sold out in five days; Vatican tickets were available each day of its four-month stay.

What next for the art merchants who run our major museums as if to supply their lucrative gift shops with classy items? In August 1983, Turkey's military rulers approved a law that allowed national art treasures to be temporarily exhibited abroad. The last time pieces traveled to the United States, some were stolen. But the public-relations value of huge shows, the financial rewards, and flawless security has enabled "The Ottomans," a broad sweep of art history from the twelfth to the twentieth centuries, to be planned. The Met in New York City is first in line, of course. Its president, William B. Macomber, is a former ambassador to Turkey. Coincidence, or dealmaker masterstroke?

If that fails in 1985, how about the Louvre? All of it!

WHITE HOUSE MESS!

Although the White House counsel cleared the project, the Office of Government Ethics questioned it, wondering whether it violated the 1965 executive order that prohibits government employees from "using public office for private gain." Gain? The whole thing started when Michael Deaver, deputy chief of staff at the White House, actually *lost* thirty pounds and sold his diet and exercise book to Morrow for $60,000. Mr. Deaver promised to defer accepting royalties until he returned to the private sector. William Safire, himself a former White House aide, was outraged, and wrote in the *New York Times:* "The payoff will be considerable. Make a reasonable assumption that Mr. Deaver's White House diet book sells for about $15 a copy; that would mean more than $150,000 for him.... Newspaper syndication ... and foreign sales are hard to predict, but the royalty package before agent and ghostwriter's fee could easily top $300,000." But does he know Nancy's diet secret?

Dealmaker as Best-selling Author: Jacqueline Susann

Jacqueline Susann seemed born to attract attention: At fifteen she won the "Most Beautiful Girl in Philadelphia" contest; at sixteen she moved to New York, determined to have a career on stage, and immediately landed a role in Clare Booth Luce's hit play *The Women.* In 1937, a young Broadway press agent named Irving Mansfield spotted the seventeen-year-old Miss Susann at the soda fountain of a drugstore. He was smitten on the spot, and the two were married shortly afterward. Minor roles in other plays followed, and while Miss Susann was rarely out of work long, she was not having the success she craved. In 1946, she and a girlfriend wrote a play called *Lovely Me.* Produced on Broadway, it opened to mixed reviews (one critic called

it a "rowdy, bawdy farce"; Walter Winchell called it "feeble") and had a fairly short run. She teamed up with her friend once again, this time to write a novel entitled *Underneath the Pancake*. It was never published. A radio situation-comedy which she wrote, called "There's Always Albert," was more successful, running on CBS for a while. In the late 1940s Miss Susann began to do television appearances. A sketch on the "Milton Berle Show" led to a part on a soap opera called "Hearts in Harmony." She was next cast as Lola, the cigarette girl on the "Morey Amsterdam Show." Although she ultimately hosted her own talk shows on local TV stations, her television career also frustrated her; Miss Susann longed to become an internationally famous celebrity. Another novel, this one a science-fiction work entitled *Yargo*, failed to find a publisher (it was about a beauty-contest winner who is kidnapped onto a UFO and falls in love with a handsome creature from another planet). In 1962, an ode written to her French poodle, *Every Night, Josephine!*, proved to be a moderate commercial success; but with its publication, Miss Susann discovered her true métier—promotion. Her years of show-biz training, and experience as a talk-show hostess herself, had left her a most accomplished television-show guest. Miss Susann had pizazz, and determination. She prowled the media, shunning no exposure, however small the station or inconsequential its location. But it was with her next published book that she really hit her stride; in fact, she revolutionized the entire publishing industry.

Valley of the Dolls, which is about pill-popping among glamorous women in show biz, was published in 1966. Miss Susann received a $3,000 advance for the book, which ultimately sold 350,000 copies in hardcover, was number one on the *New York Times* best-seller list for twenty-eight weeks, and stayed on that list for nearly one and a half years. Miss Susann conducted so successful a media blitz that her publisher remarked that in those days, "the only thing you could turn on without getting Jacqueline Susann was the water faucet." TV show hosts, usually reluctant to invite novelists for fear they would merely recite the plots of their books, were delighted with her performances. She didn't talk plot, she talked real-life scandal; and with great charm and wit she *denied* that the characters in her book were based on real-life actresses. Paperback rights were sold for $200,000. A whopping 22 million copies were sold in paperback. Movie rights went for $200,000. When Miss Susann saw the film, she wept: "The picture is a piece of shit," she said, unsentimentally. The critics agreed, but the public didn't care: The film grossed $80 million.

For Miss Susann's next novel, *The Love Machine* (1969), she received a handsome $250,000 advance, a $200,000 advertising guarantee, and limos and hotel suites paid for by the publisher while she was on the road promoting the book. *The Love Machine* (the title alludes to both television—about which Miss Susann said, "You turn it on and it loves you endlessly"—and television executives) hit number one on the *New York Times* best-seller list in five weeks. It sold 60,000 copies a day in paperback, as Miss Susann streaked across America in a private Grumman jet that had "Love Machine" emblazoned on each side. Movie rights sold for $1.5 million.

Once Is Not Enough, Miss Susann's last book, was finished just before she discovered that she was fatally ill with cancer. But neither the disease nor daily chemotherapy treatments prevented her from embarking on a book tour. *Once* became number one on the *Times* list in under a month. Movie rights were sold to Paramount for 10 percent of the gross. Miss Susann died in 1974 before the film was released. At her funeral she was eulogized by a friend: "She was a total professional who achieved unparalleled success in our industry and made contributions that were pioneering and massive. She had more imitators in concept and style than any writer I know . . . but she had no equals."

A Marriage Made in a Pressure Cooker: Library Chemists and DEZ Gas

"What is a book?
Everything or nothing. The
eye that sees it is all."

Ralph Waldo Emerson

BACKGROUND: Substances in nature working together can get specific tasks done, but it is often up to scientists to mix and match as well as to handle the tricky negotiations.

Library chemists George Kelley, Jr., and John Williams at the Library of Congress in Washington, D.C., have been experimenting with books since 1974 to try to neutralize the acid in their paper. Originally paper was made from cotton and linen rags. Wood pulp is cheaper and more plentiful—its introduction revolutionized book publishing—but alum (aluminum sulphate) has to be added to make pulp less absorbent and to prevent the ink from running. However, this additive combines with the natural moisture in the paper to form sulphuric acid; it breaks down cellulose fibers, causing the paper to crumble. Everything printed in the past century—three-fourths of the Library of Congress's twenty million books—is decomposing.

The library has a staff of thirty conservators. Each book has to be taken apart and immersed, sprayed, or brushed with an alkaline solution to neutralize the acids; the process costs hundreds of dollars a volume and takes days to complete. (Only twenty-three thousand a year can be microfilmed.) Recently, Kelley and Williams came upon DEZ (diethyl zinc gas), a substance used in the production of plastics. DEZ binds the molecules of the cellulose fibers. *But,* it bursts into flames when exposed to air and explodes on contact with water. In spite of the dangers, the two men persevered because, being a gas, DEZ doesn't warp the pages or cause the ink to smear. If the chemists could negotiate with the gas, it would work the miracle and end the self-destruction of the books.

THE DEAL: For six days, seven books were locked in a vacuum, a lab container that "looked like a pressure cooker." DEZ gas was allowed to impregnate the pages. When water vapor and carbon dioxide were then *slowly* admitted to the chamber by the chemists, the DEZ gas safely transformed itself into zinc carbonate, an alkali.

RESULTS: The books were saved. Not only were the molecules bound by the DEZ gas, but the zinc carbonate, being an alkali, prevents the paper from turning acidic again for five hundred years. Kelley and Williams were triumphant, but at seven books a time they had a problem. Even if they filled the entire Library of Congress with pressure cookers, the project would take three eternities.

Enter NASA. Scientists at the space agency's nearby Goddard Space Flight Center in Maryland adapted one of their immense vacuum chambers designed to simulate the intense solar radiation encountered in space. It held five thousand volumes. It worked splendidly. The Library of Congress plans to have a vacuum of its own by 1985 and will be treating fifteen to twenty thousand books every two weeks at a cost of less than five dollars a volume. Not only is the process foolproof, but it also can be repeated time and again, every five hundred years, if humans are still around by then . . .

"G——n": Thomas Nelson Instructs a Subsidiary

BACKGROUND: One of the fears of a corporation takeover (one company absorbing the world like the 1950's sci-fi thriller *The Blob*) has been that each subsidiary will lose its autonomy. For publishing houses, this could mean receiving from "headquarters" guidelines that could border on the violation of constitutional rights.

In April 1982, Thomas Nelson, Inc., of Nashville, bought Dodd, Mead & Company in New York City for $4.5 million. Nelson is the world's largest Bible publisher, with 80 percent of their $40 million annual sales coming from the sacred text; they also produce books marketed in Christian bookstores, with any strong words printed using the modest dash system; that is, "g——n" for "goddamn." Dodd, Mead was a small, faltering publishing house with a varied and valuable backlist. The acquisition seemed made in heaven until Nashville executives took a close look at some of 1983 Dodd, Mead titles, whereupon a hue and cry arose. Three of the books had "offensive" language in them, which might give Nelson's Bible-publishing competitors some ammunition to use against them, damaging their reputation with Christian booksellers. Guidelines were imposed. Writers and editors in New York City must not imperil Bible sales in the United States.

THE DEAL: In exchange for authors refraining from "offensive" language, "language that takes God's name in vain," Dodd, Mead will publish, distribute, and market their work. "God," "Christ," or "Jesus" cannot be used as expletives; "fuck" is out, "shit" is in, and "damn" is okay, while "goddamn" is forbidden, along with excessive savagery and sexual matters "not within the nature of the book."

RESULTS: Agents submitting manuscripts were instructed via the press. The three books were stopped in their tracks: Two novels were just set in type, but one poetry anthology, ranging from John Donne to Cole Porter, was already bound and waiting in the warehouse for shipping, after having received a sheaf of favorable reviews from major publications across the United States. Dodd, Mead insisted that Nelson was "not personally censorious," but "is in a difficult position. It has to maintain its reputation in an ultraconservative world."

All three authors refused to change their books. Novelist William Murray, a *New Yorker* writer, said it would be a "betrayal" of his fellow authors: ". . . it's the ethics and morality of forcing changes that's wrong—no writer should put up with it. Of course, it's censorship." Anthologist Richard Coniff rejected Nelson's suggestion of "scissoring out" one Ezra Pound and one Hugh MacDiarmid poem. And novelist Thomas Henege sided with his fellow "sinners": "When the accountants or salesmen who head conglomerates can tell an editor of a publishing subsidiary what he cannot accept for publication because the book might interfere with the stream of revenues from another part of his business—cigarettes, say, or food additives—then I fear for the future of independent thought in the United States. . . . To suggest that I might change the offending diction for the privilege of being published by a subsidiary of Thomas Nelson is an insult."

Dodd, Mead agreed to turn over the type and graphic designs of the three books to the authors, who were allowed to keep their advances. At the time of the acquisition, Dodd, Mead was hoping to increase its annual sales by building a strong new line of first-rate modern fiction. Instead, Dodd, Mead agreed to toe a tight Christian line in the futue and is hoping to find first-rate "nonoffensive" fiction that even Bible sellers will be able to read without blanching.

> "When I was first told that all I had to do was change 20 words, I said, 'Let me sleep on it.' But then I thought: 20 words today, tomorrow a chapter. Who are these people to censor my book?"
>
> William Murray

◆ ◆ ◆ ◆

Other Conglomerate-owned Publishing Houses

Publisher	Owner
Bantam	Bertlesmann
E.P. Dutton	JSD (Dyson-Kissner-Moran)
Holt, Rinehart & Winston	CBS
Little, Brown	Time/Life
Charles E. Merrill	Bell and Howell

Morrow/Avon/Arbor House	Hearst
Putnam/Coward-McCann/	
Seaview/Grosset & Dunlap/	
Ace/Berkeley/Jove	MCA
Random House/Knopf/Pantheon/	
Fawcett/Ballantine/Vintage/	
Del Ray	Newhouse
Simon & Schuster/Summit/	
Linden/Touchstone/	
Fireside/Frommer/Pocket/	Gulf and Western
Allyn and Bacon	
Van Nostrand Reinhold	Litton Industries
Viking/Penguin	Pearson-Longman

The 1936 Epidemic of Scarlett Fever: The Buying of the *Gone with the Wind* Manuscript

BACKGROUND: Publishing has not changed much over the decades. The game plan for a best-selling novel is to stick with a winning formula until it becomes unprofitable, then find a new setup and stick with that trend, and so on. The boffo hit of 1934 *and* 1935 was the immense period piece *Anthony Adverse;* clearly Depression America would spring for a long, historical read. Also in 1934, *Lamb in His Bosom* and *So Red the Rose,* two hits about the Old South, proved that the subject had mass appeal. So what the Macmillan Co., Publishers, wanted seemed clear: a long novel about the Old South, preferably by an unpublished writer who wouldn't ask too much money for a manuscript. They wondered if they should search it out or think about it tomorrow . . .

Harold Latham, an editor at Macmillan, was in the business of finding books to publish. Early in 1935, he set off on a scouting trip to, of course, the Deep South. His associate, Lois Cole, had trained in the Atlanta office; she tipped him off to an old friend of hers, Peggy Marsh, who had been working on a book, a long book about the Civil War, a subject she knew well. Her father, Eugene Mitchell, was a founder of the Atlanta Historical Society and had raised Peggy to be at home with facts and figures of the past. When working as a journalist she had done a successful series on Confederate generals for the Atlanta *Journal*. Peggy had written stories and plays from the year dot,

Does Rhett return to Scarlett? Only Margaret Mitchell knew, and she refused to tell.

and when Lois asked before she left for New York City how the book was going, Peggy had said with a snort, "It stinks!" which meant it was still going and should be gone after. Latham agreed.

A literary luncheon was set up in Atlanta. Peggy corralled all her friends who had dreams of a literary life and encouraged them to speak with Latham. When he spoke to her, she told him flat out, "I have nothing to show you." She was lying. From 1926 to 1929, while bedridden with a broken arthritic ankle, Peggy Marsh had written all but three chapters of a story about a southern woman named Pansy O'Hara, "a girl who was somewhat like Atlanta, part of the Old South, part of the new South; how she rose with Atlanta and fell with it and rose again; what Atlanta did to her, what she did to Atlanta and the man who was more than a match for her." She had written the last chapter first because she knew her characters' fates and she found it easier to work on scenes that stirred her imagination rather than dully writing in sequence. The finished sections were put in manila envelopes, then stored in the closet or under the bed or used to prop up a sagging couch. Her husband, John, had read along, discussed the plot, and encouraged her to finish the book; but once on her feet, she put it aside to resume her busy life, overstocked with family and friends.

On the way home from the literary lunch, a young, would-be author chided Peggy for not fessing up, concluding with: "You know you don't take life seriously enough to be a novelist." Peggy was not amused. Once home, she lugged all the envelopes out of their hiding places—forgetting the ones under the bed and the ones in the pot-and-pan closet—and carted them to Latham's hotel. He was packing to leave Atlanta when her call arrived from the lobby. "I'm downstairs," she said nervously. "Can I see you for a minute?" There she was, in Latham's words: "a tiny woman sitting on a divan, and beside her the biggest manuscript I have ever seen towering in two stacks almost up to her shoulders." She explained in a rush that it was not completed yet, was unrevised, was quite a mess really, with several versions of some chapters. She hadn't intended anyone to read it but she had given her word to Lois Cole that if anyone ever did see it, Macmillan would have first refusal. He could have it if he really wanted it. He really wanted it. He bought a suitcase in which to carry it away.

The following day in New Orleans, Latham received a telegram: "Please send manuscript back I've changed my mind." It was too late. He had begun browsing and was intrigued by the barely literate, green-eyed, "turbulent, willful, lusty-with-life" unsympathetic heroine and her love for her ancestral home, Tara. The untitled mammoth mound of a working draft was one helluva read. By July he had made sense out of it—she'd accidently included a draft of a novella—and had sent to him the remaining envelopes. He wrote her to offer a publishing contract. But there was a nagging question. Could Pansy O'Hara be all put together for a 1936 spring debut before the public taste changed?

THE DEAL: Macmillan would give Margaret Mitchell Marsh a $500.00 advance against royalties for her untitled, unfinished manuscript, plus 10 percent of the projected retail price of $2.50 for each book sold up to ten thousand copies, escalating to 15 percent of each copy thereafter, if there was a thereafter. The publication date was set for April 21, 1936. The completed manuscript—cut, shaped, fact-checked, titled—was due in twenty weeks. On August 6, 1935, Peggy Marsh took a deep breath and signed on the dotted line, knowing exactly what she was up against. If she did finish it, who outside of Atlanta would buy it? Did Macmillan plan to advertise it? Yes, they promised, and because of that expense would she surrender the escalation clause? She accepted a flat 10 percent.

RESULTS: She slaved away in a disciplined frenzy. A first chapter was written and rewritten seventeen times. Even though she knew that the history in her tale was as waterproof and airtight as ten years of study and a lifetime of listening to participants could make it, she verified every historical detail in her local library, convinced she would die of shame if Atlanta found her lacking. By September, "Pansy" was not a strong enough name for the heroine of a novel about survival. On what was to become page 420 of the published text, she had written: "The O'Haras did not take charity. . . . There were the Scarletts who had fought with the Irish Volunteers for a free Ireland . . . and the O'Haras who died at the Boyne, battling to the end for what was theirs." And so it was: Katie Scarlett O'Hara, called Katie Scarlett only by her beloved father. Mean-spirited and selfish, constantly battling and fighting, Scarlett was an American cousin to Thackeray's Becky Sharp, and a far cry from the usually meek leading-lady types in popular fiction.

By December, Peggy was suffering from eyestrain and eczema of the scalp, but she was on schedule. And in the first line of the third verse of a poem by Ernest Dowson, she had found her title. The lyric poem is called *"Non sum qualis"*; its title, in turn, was taken from *The Odes of Horace*, Book IV. It is known by most as *Cynara*. The full line is: "I have forgot much, Cynara! gone with the wind." She wrote the title

Gone with the Wind, which is how it appears on every page of the Macmillan edition as a running head; but over the decades the title has become the all-time winner of persistent misprintings by everyone else—*Gone With the Wind* (uppercasing the first *W*) being the most popular goof, even appearing throughout the published version of Margaret Mitchell's letters.

The book was delivered on time. However, the publication date was changed to May 5. The first 10,000 copies were printed with "Published May 1936" on the copyright page, and these are the only ones considered true first editions. The price was $2.75. The publisher sent 1,000 copies to reviewers around America. Then, the Book-of-the-Month Club astounded Macmillan by making *GWTW* a full selection for July; 40,000 more copies were printed and the publication date was changed to June 30. To the further delight of Peggy Marsh, Macmillan reinstated the escalating clause. Meanwhile, the 9,000 copies remaining from the May printing were distributed to bookstores and were *instantly* sold; reorders were mounting fast. Clearly, word of mouth was sensational. Macmillan reprinted 10,000 more ("Published June 1936"—price $3.00). Again, they were snapped up. Macmillan printed 20,000 more, then, two weeks later, 20,000 more. By the official publication date, there were 100,000 copies in print. By July 13, there were 40,000 more; July 20 brought 36,000 more; July 23 saw a total of 201,000 copies in print. By late September, the seventeenth printing, there were 450,000 copies; by Christmas, the twenty-eighth printing, 1 million copies were in print. It was the fastest-selling book in history. On its first birthday, it had sold over 1.25 million copies.

The *New York Times Book Review* gave it a front-page rave on Sunday, July 5, 1936. "This is beyond a doubt one of the most remarkable first novels produced by an American writer . . . it is, in narrative power, surpassed by nothing in American fiction," wrote J. Donald Adams. "Let me end by saying that although this is not a great novel, not one with any profound reading of life, it is nevertheless a book of uncommon quality, a superb piece of story-telling which nobody who finds pleasure in the art of fiction can afford to neglect." Nobody did. It remained on best-seller lists until March of 1938.

Bookstore windows were broken and copies stolen. (This would not happen again until *Roots.*) In 1937, it won the Pulitzer Prize. Critics complained about its indifferent prose, its repetitions, its sentimentality, its stereotypical characters, its racism, its condoning of marital rape, its battle-of-the-sexes mentality—but the phenomenon blazed unabated. It has been translated into twenty-seven languages with printings in thirty-seven countries. If its value as literature has been questioned by the literati, no one can argue with its value as myth: Scarlett and Rhett, Ashley and Melanie are firmly established in our dreams. What more could any author desire?

Peggy Marsh was traumatized by the enormity of her success: "This period of my life has been the unhappiest one." She swore she would never write another book. In 1949, she was killed by a drunk driver who ran her down while she was crossing an Atlanta street on her way to the movies with her husband.

Gone with the Wind continues to sell. As of December 1983, nearly 5.5 million hardcover sales made it the champion seller, second only to the Bible. Each year it sells over 100,000 hardcover copies and 250,000 paperbacks, more than most current best-sellers.

Selznick Nearly Goes Gone with the Wind: The Buying of the Movie Rights

BACKGROUND: David O. Selznick, for all his smarts, nearly lost the most famous property of his career. Movie history would be very different if he hadn't surrounded himself with people in the know.

Before publication of *Gone with the Wind* (*GWTW*), agent Annie

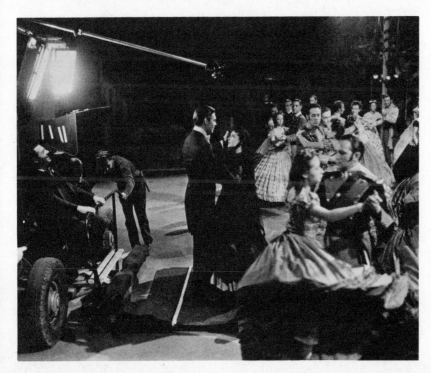

GWTW's first director, George Cukor (left), *before he was fired.*

Laurie Williams set the price for movie rights at $100,000, an enormous sum then (and now) for a first novel by an unknown writer. Kay Brown of Selznick International teletyped her boss from New York City: "This is an absolutely magnificent story . . . we must have it . . . drop everything and buy it!" Selznick, absorbed in his production of *Garden of Allah,* did not respond. Charles Rogers of Universal Pictures wired his enthusiastic scout: "I told you no costume pictures!" Darryl Zanuck at Twentieth Century-Fox nixed it: "too expensive." Jack Warner offered it to his feuding star, Bette Davis; when she refused, fearing he would co-cast Errol Flynn, Warner lost interest. Paramount's recent Civil War epic, *So Red the Rose,* was a bomb; they swore that "boring war" was not box office. MGM toyed with it as a vehicle for Norma Shearer but decided the "immoral" heroine was not good for her image. RKO found Scarlett "unsympathetic," the plot too involved, and the project "too costly"; but Katharine Hepburn, their brightest star, wanted it *madly.*

Kay Brown badgered Selznick. Zanuck offered $35,000 which, to Margaret Mitchell's horror, Annie Williams refused. Brown sent daily telegrams, teletypes, and memos to her boss. The asking price was now $65,000. Selznick finally read the synopsis: "Think it a fine story . . . if we had under contract a woman ideally suited to the lead I would probably be more inclined to buy it . . . I do not feel we can take such a gamble." Kay Brown howled. Katie forced RKO to open negotiations with Annie Williams. The reviews were appearing for *GWTW*; a publishing phenomenon was being born: nearly four thousand copies were sold each day for months. Selznick wavered: He did owe Ronald Coleman one more picture. Brown, frantic about Hepburn's clout and brains at RKO, forced Selznick's hand.

THE DEAL: If Selznick refused to buy *GWTW*, Brown would get Jock Whitney, chairman of Selznick International Pictures, Inc., to buy it for him. Selznick offered $50,000 with no percentage of the box office. Mitchell accepted; she had liked his production of *David Copperfield.* RKO then offered $55,000, Hepburn, and a big-budget production. Mitchell refused. She said she came from a long line of people who believed that once you gave your word, you kept it. She doubted the 1,037-page *GWTW* could be made into a film, but if Selznick was willing to try, okay. But she stipulated that she would have nothing to do with the movie: "All parts of the film job are on their hands and not on mine."

RESULTS: George Cukor was signed to direct. He wanted Hepburn;

they'd worked together on *Bill of Divorcement*. Selznick said no. He wanted a new face: a feminine, seductive girl-woman with the beauty and sex appeal that would make Rhett Butler's twelve-year pursuit believable to moviegoers. *GWTW* was cast with a few hitches. Nearly three years later, Selznick started shooting after having spent $1,081,465 on preproduction. *GWTW* cost $4,250,000, not including prints and advertising.

Selznick oversaw the script, personally adding "Frankly" to Mitchell's "My dear, I don't give a damn," and he fought like hell to get "damn" through the Hollywood censors. The film won ten Oscars and by July 1941 had grossed $32 million. (*Snow White* was the second-biggest money-maker, with $8 million.) It remained the highest-grossing film until *The Sound of Music* in 1965. It is still the film seen by most people around the globe.

In the early forties, Selznick and Whitney liquidated Selznick, Inc., selling MGM their 50 percent of *GWTW* to avoid the heavy taxes. In the end, MGM reaped the lion's share of profits as the film went on and on to become a perennial money-maker. In October 1967, it began its seventh tour of United States theaters with stereophonic sound in 70mm. on a reserved-seat basis; though the images were horribly cropped for the process, it was a top-grossing film of the year, playing in New York City's Rivoli Theater for nearly twelve months. When it was shown on TV for the first time on November 7 and 8, 1976, it was the highest-rated show in history, with 79 percent of the American viewing public watching Scarlett swearing: "If I have to cheat, steal, or kill, as God is my witness, I'll never be hungry again!"

Frankly, My Dears, They *All* Gave a Damn!: The Buying of Gable and Leigh

BACKGROUND: The year 1936 was one of national elections. Europe was on the brink of war. But America had a more pressing concern: Who would play Rhett and Scarlett when Selznick brought *Gone with the Wind* to the screen?

All the world wanted Rhett to be Gable. At a time when many stars were personalities rather than actors, he was the biggest thing in movies. His image was unique: a tough, honest guy with a heart; a butch, devilish sweetie with a sense of humor; and your basic tall-dark-and-handsome type, with stability, promising to be "the ideal husband" with a firm but gentle hand—in short, a paragon of the 1930s in the arena of sexual politics. There was no one like him. Spencer Tracy came close but he was short and not traditionally handsome. John Wayne wasn't a superstar. Gary Cooper was too "beautiful," too all-American boy, but he was close; in fact he was Selznick's second choice for Rhett. Errol Flynn, though too caddish, was third. But as far as the press and the fans were concerned—letters *poured* into Selznick's office—only Gable could tame the shrew that was Scarlett O'Hara.

Unfortunately, there were several big obstacles. For starters, Gable belonged to MGM. He was a contract player earning $4,000 a week. Selznick was the son-in-law of Louis B. Mayer, but there all ties ended. When Mayer decided not to buy *GWTW*, he had no idea the world was going to go berserk over it. Now if Gable could be involved . . . but he wouldn't come cheap, and Selznick's studio was far from rich. And, on top of that, Gable wasn't interested. Ever uncertain of his acting abilities, the King of Hollywood knew the *GWTW* craze sweeping America had his name on it; he said a flat out No! to one and all, as he later recalled: "I was scared stiff. Rhett was simply too big an order."

There was also another major hitch. Selznick produced films, but he had no distribution. The larger studios owned theater chains across the country where their films were showcased; Selznick had a contract with United Artists through 1938 to handle his films, which is why Gary Cooper was a reasonable second choice: He was under contract to Sam Goldwyn, another independent producer, who also used United Artists as a distributor. Always conscious of the public's desires—in this case lust for Gable's Rhett—Selznick dragged his feet over their common ground during negotiations with Goldwyn for Cooper. Gable *was* Rhett Butler. As for the "wholesomely beautiful satyr" Flynn—Warners owned him. They were amenable to lending Flynn, and Bette Davis for Scarlett, if they could wrest distribution rights away from United Artists. Davis wanted nothing to do with the package, even though she knew Scarlett could have been written for her: "The thought of Mr. Flynn as Rhett Butler appalled me."

By May 1938, the film's preproduction was nearing completion. Rumor had it that Selznick was running out of money. (In fact, John "Jock" Whitney, a chairman of Selznick, Inc., and his family had co-signed loans at the bank.) Mayer offered to buy *GWTW* from Selz-

Gable signs. Clockwise, David O. Selznick, E.J. Mannix, Al Lichtman, and Louis B. Mayer.

nick while allowing him to remain as its producer. MGM dangled the essential Gable in front of his eyes, as well as others from the stable: Joan Crawford as Scarlett, Maureen O'Sullivan as Melanie, and Melvyn Douglas as Ashley. Selznick said no, but they all knew Gable was crucial to the success of *GWTW*. Finally, in August, free of United Artists, Selznick was ready to net his Rhett.

THE DEAL FOR RHETT: MGM would lend the thirty-eight-year-old Gable to Selznick for $4,500 per week (with MGM keeping the extra $500 above Gable's contract salary) and a bonus to Gable of $16,666 upon completion. MGM would put up half the estimated $2.5 million budget and would arrange a divorce for Gable so he could marry Carole Lombard. Selznick would give MGM 50 percent of the *GWTW* profits for seven years. MGM would receive the distribution rights to *GWTW* through Lowe's, the MGM chain, and an additional 15 percent of the gross receipts of *GWTW* off the top to Loew's. Principal shooting had to start "no later than January 5, 1939," or Gable was out. Also, MGM was absolved from all liability "if the artist refuses to perform."

RESULTS: All attention could be turned to casting Scarlett. With the world made happy by Gable's signing, Selznick would follow his original plan and cast a newcomer who would inevitably be made a star by

GWTW. He knew that every established diva had a fan club eager to denounce any other winner of the coveted role. Outrage was unavoidable if he took the loan-out route. Besides, why not make one of his very own contract "slave" players a star, one he could loan out or use in future Selznick vehicles? She would have to be a professionally trained actress because the role of Scarlett would require reporting to the set at 7:00 .. and working six days a week, frequently until midnight, for over six months. She would also have to display every conceivable emotion, appearing as she did in almost every one of the 90 sequences and in nearly three-fourths of the 692 scenes. It was an epic role in an epic film. It was far from child's play.

Since it would take two years for preproduction, Selznick realized there was nothing better than a talent search to keep America *GWTW* mad. And so it began. George Cukor, the signed director, was sent scurrying southward to scout locations, but also, supposedly, to check out high-school plays for ingenues. Selznick invested $50,000 in his publicity gimmick; the rewards were monumental. The country was in the grip of Scarlett fever. To keep the game of who-will-play-her alive, every female willing to don a long gown was tested; most of the tests were simple readings, though a few did face a black-and-white camera and each shared her dream with the columnists.

Then, in January 1937, Kay Brown discovered the thirty-four-year-old Vivien Leigh in *Fire Over England*, a British costume film produced by Alexander Korda. Leigh was Irish and French (like Scarlett). After studying at the Royal Academy of Dramatic Art, her extraordinary beauty and talent immediately took her into films and plays. By 1937, she was a rising star in England under exclusive contract to Korda. She was also in love with Laurence Olivier, whose Hollywood agent was Myron Selznick, David's brother. Things happened quickly. MGM signed her to appear in its first English production, *A Yank at Oxford*, with Robert Taylor. It was a small part, but when Selznick saw it in February of 1938 he bought a print for private use. He screened her other films. She became his "dark horse." In public (and in not-so-private memos), he claimed Scarlett was *almost* Paulette Goddard *or* Jean Arthur *or* Tallulah *or maybe* Joan Bennett or, *most probably*, You-Name-Her. The entire business worked like a charm. Selznick approached Korda about Leigh. They would all have to be very clever about this. How would America take to the notion of a foreigner playing one of the most famous women in American literature? Being in the business of manufacturing fairy tales, the moguls knew how much everyone loved a Cinderella story.

Leigh signs. Clockwise, David O. Selznick, Leslie Howard, and Olivia de Havilland.

THE DEAL FOR SCARLETT: In August, when Gable was signed, Leigh was planning a divorce so she could marry Olivier, who was planning a divorce so he could marry her. They agreed to postpone legal action to avoid scandal. (Superstud Gable could do as he pleased; "virginal" Vivien had to keep her nose clean.) She traveled to Hollywood, pretending to be optimistic (if anyone asked) about "replacing" Merle Oberon in *Wuthering Heights*, currently shooting at MGM. In fact, she had refsed a part in the picture to be free for *GWTW*. (Olivier was starring as Heathcliffe, but she couldn't say she was visiting him because they were supposed to be "just friends," if anyone asked.) A short stopover in New York City was arranged to coincide with Selznick's passing through on his way from Bermuda. If anyone asked, she was to lie and say she had not seen him (or anyone else) in New York City. He liked her. She got the part and $30,000. Korda, in exchange for Leigh's loan-out, was to be mentioned prominently in all casting announcements and was to alternate employing her with Selznick. In addition, William Cameron Menzies, a Selznick contract art director, was lent to Korda for *Thief of Bagdad*.

RESULTS: On December 10, 1938, the old *King Kong* and *Garden of Allah* sets were burned in the guise of the Atlanta ammunition depot.

The famous meeting of Selznick and Leigh with the flames glowing on her face *never happened* except in Hollywood legend created from Selznick's public-relations releases, "private" memos, and his revisionist autobiographical sketches. Myron, a little drunk, arrived too late to play the scene as they had planned, so the two were "introduced" after the sets had collapsed, the flames had been extinguished, and the cameras had stopped rolling.

Leigh was "tested" three times to make it all look legit. America *loved* the English rose—Irish and French just like Scarlett—who was as beautiful as they all secretly wanted the screen Scarlett to be, although the first words of *GWTW* are "Scarlett O'Hara was not beautiful . . ." She spent four hours a day working on the correct Southern accent before actual shooting began on January 20, 1939, and she was the only lead performer to conquer it. (Leslie Howard as the whimp Ashley and Olivia de Havilland as the sainted Melanie seem on an extended, one-note visit from the Hollywood Hills. Gable sounds just like Gable.) She worked furiously with George Cukor in the beginning until he was fired—among other reasons, because Gable feared she was getting too much attention—and then she worked tirelessly with Victor Fleming (and with Cukor secretly on Sundays). Her funny and ultimately very touching Scarlett is the one consistent timeless touch of genius in the film. As it should do, it holds the thing together. (Hattie McDaniel's Mammy is the other totally conceived and achieved performance. Amazingly, both deserving women won the Oscar for their work.) Gable is Gable. But the world was right: Gable *is* Rhett Butler. When he takes Leigh in his arms, there is true movie magic. And there will be forever.

Dealmaker as Independent Producer: David O. Selznick

David Selznick was born in Pittsburgh in 1902. His father, Lewis Zelenick, born in Kiev, was a jeweler who, in 1910, moved the family to New York City to open "The World's Largest Jewelry Store." It was a bust. At the time, New York City was the financial and production center for silent movies. All one needed was a camera to be a producer. Learning that "it takes less brains to be successful in the film business than in any other," Lewis formed Selznick Pictures. David, fourteen, worked in the advertising and publicity department designing posters and the eight huge Broadway electric signs that his shrewd father soon owned. He learned by experience each phase of the picture business ("except as a cutter"). He and his brother, Myron, attended every business meeting with their father. By eighteen, he was running the publicity department and producing a biweekly newsreel. The family lived in a seventeen-room, fully staffed Park Avenue apartment, and had a fleet of Rolls-Royces.

Then, in 1923, Selznick Pictures went bankrupt. Lewis had overspent, and Adolph Zukor and William Fox, two studio heads who controlled many theaters, hated him and blocked the distribution of his movies. For a time, David toyed with becoming a writer, but movies were his heartbeat. By 1924 he was hustling to produce shorts—one of Valentino judging a beauty contest earned him a $15,000 profit.

In 1926, David went to California to help his father and brother set up a distribution company that folded. He wanted back into making movies. Adding an O to his name for distinction, he got a job at MGM in October by promising to "make good in two weeks." He was a reader in the story department; fourteen days later, his drive and his sense of what "worked" on the screen impressed Irving Thalberg, who was in charge of all creative aspects of MGM production. David O. Selznick became manager of the writers' department; fourteen days later his salary was doubled. By April 1927, he was an assistant producer, but a disagreement with Thalberg got him fired in November as sound was making its dialogue debut with *The Jazz Singer*.

He became an assistant producer at Paramount, then took over the writing department. He graduated to being chief assistant to Ben Schulberg, Thalberg's opposite number at Paramount. Selznick struggled to merge silent techniques with sound. In April 1930, he married Irene Mayer, Louis B.'s daughter, even though her father warned her: "Keep away from that schnook! He'll end up a bum just like his old man." The 1929 crash slashed into Paramount's profits, and rather than take a salary cut, Selznick moved to RKO in charge of production.

At George Cukor's insistence, he cast Katharine Hepburn for *Bill of Divorcemet;* and he gave his full energy to *King Kong*, which saved the studio from bankruptcy. But working on a shoestring at RKO exhausted him. In 1933, he went back to Thalberg and his father-in-law at MGM, which was the apex of the moviemaking world, the one studio that worked without tight budgets. His first project was *Dinner at Eight.* Then *Dancing Lady* with Gable, Crawford, and Astaire was a smash. As a staff producer, he originated projects and assembled and oversaw the studio talent, molding them to suit his vision—but he still needed okays from Thalberg. His *David Copperfield* was

MGM's biggest hit in years. He made Garbo's *Anna Karenina* and *A Tale of Two Cities* before leaving in 1935 to form his own company, Selznick International Pictures, Inc. Thalberg invested $200,000 in the new company, but the bulk of funds came from John Hay ("Jock") Whitney.

He signed an unknown named Ingrid Bergman for *Intermezzo* (1939); and until Selznick International was liquidated in 1940 to avoid losing all the stupendous profits from *GWTW* (1939) to taxes, he produced ten films, including Hitchcock's first American film, *Rebecca* (1940). He was the only independent producer to win the Oscar for Best Picture two years running: 1940 (*GWTW*) and 1941 (*Rebecca*). He wrote 80 percent of his scripts and was involved with everything in his films.

From 1940 to 1948 he ran David O. Selznick Productions and created six films of his own, as well as developing packages which he sold to other studios. He was a genius at tradeoffs: "MGM, I'll give you Ingrid for *Gaslight* if you give me Robert Walker for *Since You Went Away*." He also made a fortune from loaning Hitchcock out, as well as from the half of Gregory Peck that he owned. But by 1948, television was devouring the movie audience. His last four features were coproductions. His only TV production was telecast on all three networks on October 24, 1954—a variety program celebrating the seventy-fifth anniversary of Edison's inventing the lightbulb.

In semiretirement he continued to market his films through subdistributors, keeping an eye on his monument, *GWTW*. When MGM switched from Technicolor printing to their own inferior Metrocolor, a process that fades with time, he waged a losing battle with them. He died June 22, 1965.

TO THE POINT

In 1920, D. W. Griffith wanted to film *Romance*, the story of an Italian opera star's affair with an English clergyman. The work was written by Edward Sheldon in 1913, but it was owned by the popular actress Doris Keane and her husband, Basil Sidney, who had great success on the stage with it in England. D. W. creatively offered the Keanes $150,000 up front, with 50 percent of the picture's gross over $1 million. This huge advance and "points" have become the standard way of purchasing a desirable property in today's movie industry.

Love at First Sound:
The Birth of the Talkies

BACKGROUND: The word *cinema* comes from the Greek word for motion, *kinema*. So how does sound work into the act? That's what the silent-movie czars were asking in 1926 as their empires tottered. Up until then, only money talked to them, but four hungry brothers gave them an earful that changed the world.

The Warner brothers—Jack, Albert, Sam, and Harry—were movie distributors who, with the profits from their first feature film and hefty help from a banker (Hollywood was in hock to the banks even then), built a small studio in 1919. Lacking a theater chain for their product, they scrambled like the other small independents to fill in the blanks on the theater screens of the "Big Five." (The Big Five were actually six studios: Carl Laemmle's Universal, Adolph "Creepy" Zukor's Paramount, Producers Distribution Corporation [PDC], William Fox's Fox Film Company, Louis B. Mayer's MGM, and First National.) The four brothers quickly branched out into radio (KFWB), a new phenomenon that by 1927 was generating $425 million in income a year. The brothers used radio to advertise their films, forcing theater owners to show them by creating public demand. The four found out through a radio pal that A.T.&T.'s Bell Labs were experimenting with synchronizing sound on discs to movies. Silent films were a thriving industry. Nearly the entire population, 110 million people, went to the movies *each week*. By 1926, Hollywood was producing over four hundred feature films a year at a cost of $120 million, with box-office receipts of over $360 million. Why kill a good thing?

The hustling Warners needed to keep up with the competition. Sound was a novelty item that could draw crowds for a while—who knew how long? But look at radio! Why not take a risk? There were drawbacks. Silents could communicate with anyone on earth: foreign money made up 40 percent of a film's total revenues; Hollywood supplied 82 percent of the world's market. How many countries spoke English? How many *stars* spoke English well enough? (Warners' biggest star was Rin-Tin-Tin. Everyone could understand him! Their other star was John Barrymore, one of the world's great talkers. What did they have to lose?) But talking wasn't what sound was about . . . in the beginning.

In 1926, Warners signed an exclusive contract with Western Electric to develop Vitaphone. All ritzy theaters had live orchestras; Warners now offered everyone "modern" synchronized orchestral music on discs, and filmed "synched" vaudeville acts as curtain raisers. Technically, their moviemaking had to be extensively revamped if they were to deliver the musical shorts without the camera's whirr and the lights' sizzle—horrors to the sound-recording technicians. The camera was locked into a stationary box—good-bye to Griffith's fluid camera work—and movie lights were invented. In many ways, it was back to square one. But the square sang!

Warners bought a theater in New York City, named it for themselves, and wired it for sound. On August 6, 1926, John Barrymore and Mary Astor opened in *Don Juan,* a silent feature with a prerecorded score. On screen, Will Hays, president of the Motion Picture Producers Association, *spoke,* introducing the evening; then filmed musical artists played and sang. The audience was stunned into silence. Vitaphone was a smash. It did the highest single-week's business in the history of the movies. Warners' stock value increased 600 percent. Meanwhile, the other studios were in a tight bind. Warners *owned* Vitaphone. If the others started using it, Warners would make leasing-money from *them!* It cost from $16,000 to $25,000 to wire a large theater for sound, plus $2,000 up front to A.T.&T. In five years, the equipment reverted to A.T.&T. and had to be leased. It all added up to a huge risk for the theater (that is, the studios) given that talkies may have gone kaput with the easily bored public. The moguls crunched hard on their cigars and made an airtight pact, or so they thought. . .

THE DEAL: MGM, Universal, Paramount, First National, PDC, and Fox made a secret agreement in December 1926 not to touch sound for one year. They would then develop a shared system, rather than put more gold in Warners' coffers. If sound died, only Warners would lose, which would serve them right for being so clever. Fox, however, with his cronies on hold, developed and patented an optical sound system called *Movietone.* He signed a contract with Warners, sharing sound systems, but all he wanted was access to the Western Electric amplification units, which he smoothly got.

RESULTS: Warners was no longer alone. There was competition, but also another company to share the risk. By May 1927, Fox had a wildly successful talking newsreel. Only two hundred theaters were wired for sound, but the worst sound program (weak vaudeville acts and dumb silent features) outdrew the best silent features that played alone. Warners had over two hundred sound shorts when *The Jazz Singer,* starring Al Jolson, opened on October 6, 1927, changing the course of movie history. It was the first feature film with several spo-

"... I had scripts and a contract that gave me no choice in the parts I played. That was the difficult side of the contract system. The great side of the contract system was the constant work and the investment by the studio to further your career."

Bette Davis,
a contract player
with Warner Brothers
for eighteen years

ken-dialogue sequences. It cost Warners $500,000 to make and showed a profit of over $3 million. When it went on the road, its success could not be ignored by the resistant movie moguls, because many of the box offices taking in the money were owned by them.

When a new sound system appeared, the other studios grabbed it. "Photophone" sound sequences were inserted like so many talking shorts into many of their completed films, a process mockingly labeled "goat glanding." In 1928, the industry was worth $2.5 billion and faced an instant revolution, which *Fortune* magazine described in October 1930 as "beyond comparison the fastest and most amazing in the whole history of industrial revolutions." The studios literally had to be rebuilt, wooden buildings replaced by soundproof structures. (Some went on night schedules to avoid street noises until the sound stages were completed.) All-new equipment was needed to free the camera from its prison and the actors from the rigidity imposed by the stationary mike. Actors had to be taught to speak naturally; not with fancy elocution but "as if they were being overheard." Many never learned. The myth of the supremacy of the New York stage-trained actor took hold and ruled until the forties when screen acting was again appreciated as a unique art.

All of it had to be done *fast*. By 1928, there were four hundred theaters wired for sound. People were clamoring for "the talkers." In June of that year, the first "all talkie" arrived: Warners' *The Lights of New York*, a gangster film that gave the world its first movie catch phrase, "Take him for a ride."

Some people balked. Their silent dream images were quickly becoming a thing of the past. However, with the Great Depression, the chatting and singing movies ruled supreme as the opiate of the desperate masses willingly held spellbound in darkness for a few hours. "Forget your troubles, come on, get happy . . . "

When She Was Good: Gloria Swanson and the Hays Office

BACKGROUND: Gloria Swanson, America's most glamorous movie star, hadn't really done anything wrong, but in the repressive early days of the Hays office, just being accused (as she was) by her husband of having committed adultery with no less than fourteen different men could have meant the ruin of her career. Just before word of the divorce suit leaked out to the press, the feisty Swanson told her incredulous boss, studio head Jesse Lasky, and director Cecil B. De Mille, that she intended to fight her husband on the ridiculous charges rather than buy him off.

Swanson was fifteen when she made her first film in 1914, earning $13.25 a week. By 1921 she was a famous star; and like the other Hollywood greats, she was used to living exactly as she pleased. But that was before the sordid sex-drug-murder scandals of the early 1920s, which rocked the industry and led studio heads, fearful of government censorship, to band together to form a "dictatorship of virtue." They invited the fearsome Presbyterian elder and former postmaster general Will Hays to establish an agency that would enforce moral standards not just for films but for actors as well. From then on, a star's life was expected to be as flawless as her complexion.

Swanson's love life had been as rocky as her career was smooth. At seventeen she married co-star Wallace Beery, but finding him sexually revolting, she left him after only six weeks. At twenty, she married Herbert Somborn, an unsuccessful film distributor (and later founder of the Brown Derby Restaurant in Los Angeles), who was old enough to be her father. They had a daughter together before she left him and he slapped her with the divorce suit which charged her with adultery with a small legion of men. Swanson was at the pinnacle of her career; she was one of the most highly paid women in America; she got ten thousand fan letters a week and fans threw orchids at her. Would she risk it all for the pleasure of fighting a hustler? De Mille presented her with a telegram which indicated that the news of her husband's charges might endanger the entire film industry. The telegram was signed Will Hays. Swanson capitulated.

The men in Swanson's life: Joseph Kennedy (left), the father of JFK, and the Marquis de la Falaise de la Coudraye on the Riviera.

THE DEAL: Swanson would pay her husband $150,000, and he would quietly divorce her. She would promise to stay out of trouble in the future: A "morals" clause was added to her contract which forbade her to indulge in "adulterous conduct or immoral relations with men other than her husband." Her salary would be increased to $1,000 a day—if she was good.

RESULTS: Swanson was furious when, months later, she discovered that the telegram was faked. Fed up with Hollywood, she took her children (she had adopted a son on her own) and moved to New York, where she revived an old studio. In France, in 1924, for the filming of the legendary *Madame Sans-Gene*, Swanson met the dazzling Marquis de la Falaise de la Coudraye. He was as handsome as he was impoverished, but oh, did he have class! Gloria, who was known as the ultimate clothes horse ("Is there anyone who can flaunt a superb wardrobe with more dash?" asked one journalist) later wrote: "he wore well-chosen suede gloves and carried a walking stick as if it were second nature to do so." Who could resist? Not Swanson, and one month before her divorce from Somborn was finalized, she found herself two months' pregnant. And although she was planning to marry the marquis and desperately wanted the baby, having it six months after the wedding could mean the end of her career. "By having Henri's child," she later wrote, "I would forfeit the chance to become one of the highest paid performers in history." In fact, she continued, "if the press didn't destroy my career, Mr. Lasky could." Painfully, and with regret that lasted throughout her life, on the day following her wedding she had an abortion that nearly killed her.

Returning to Hollywood as the first titled movie star (they called her "the Marquise de la Etcetera"), her marriage to Henri remained childless and ultimately broke up (he then married Constance Bennett) because of her long affair with Joseph Kennedy (father of JFK). Walking away from a million-dollar-a-year contract with Paramount, she became an independent producer of her own films (although she was nearly ruined following the business advice of the very aggressive Kennedy). In the 1930s she retired from films for many years, returning to star in the classic *Sunset Boulevard*. "You were a big star once," William Holden says to her in that film. "I'm still big," she replies: "It's the pictures that got small." Swanson's last film was *Airport '75*, in which she played herself. She died in 1983.

DO NOT APPLY

It's all too obvious that I don't possess
The virtues necessary for success.
My one great talent is for speaking plain;
I've never learned to flatter or to feign.

Molière, *The Misanthrope*

MOVIE DEALS THAT DIDN'T GEL
or
NO ACTOR IS IRREPLACEABLE UNTIL *AFTER* THE FACT

Picture Shirley Temple tapping down the Yellow Brick Road.
Picture Ronald Reagan being misquoted: "Play it again, Sam."
Picture Claudette Colbert saying, snappingly: "Fasten your seatbelts; it's going to be a bumpy night."

The Movie	First Choice	Cast
The Wizard of Oz	Shirley Temple	Judy Garland*
The Wizard of Oz	W. C. Fields	Frank Morgan
The Wizard of Oz	Gale Sondergaard	Margaret Hamilton
Casablanca	Ronald Reagan/ Ann Sheridan	Humphrey Bogart/ Ingrid Bergman
All About Eve	Claudette Colbert	Bette Davis†
Lawrence of Arabia	Albert Finney	Peter O'Toole*
Cat Ballou	Kirk Douglas	Lee Marvin*
East of Eden	Montgomery Clift	James Dean
On the Waterfront	Frank Sinatra	Marlon Brando*
Sunset Boulevard	Montgomery Clift	William Holden
High Sierra	George Raft	Humphrey Bogart
Maltese Falcon	George Raft	Humphrey Bogart
10	George Segal	Dudley Moore
Raiders of the Lost Ark	Tom Selleck	Harrison Ford
It Happened One Night	Myrna Loy	Claudette Colbert*
From Here to Eternity	Eli Wallach	Frank Sinatra*
Three Faces of Eve	Eva Marie Saint	Joanne Woodward*
Ben Hur	Burt Lancaster	Charlton Heston*
My Fair Lady	James Cagney	Stanley Holloway†
The Graduate	Robert Redford	Dustin Hoffman†
Bonnie and Clyde	Jane Fonda	Faye Dunaway†
A Star Is Born (III)	Elvis Presley	Kris Kristofferson
Kramer vs. Kramer	Kate Jackson	Meryl Streep*

*Won Oscar for the performance.
†Nominated for Oscar for the performance.

You Can't Take It with You: Bill Holden's Deferred Salary for *Kwai*

BACKGROUND: Oscar winner William Holden (Best Actor, 1953: *STALAG 17*) was already a rich man when he made *The Bridge on the River Kwai* in 1957, but paying taxes bothered him inordinately.

When it came to negotiating his contract with Columbia Pictures for *Kwai*, Holden made an arrangement that he thought would be very personally advantageous; but because the film became a blockbuster, the real winner may have been the studio.

THE DEAL: Holden would be paid $250,000 plus 10 percent of the gross, but Columbia had to spread out his payments in yearly installments of $50,000. Columbia was free to collect the interest on these deferred earnings.

RESULTS: *Kwai* was a huge international hit, grossing, by the early 1960s, $30 million—it had only cost $2.7 million to make. Holden's share came to $3 million, or sixty years of $50,000 payments: He would have been ninety-nine when he collected the last one. As it happened, Holden, who ultimately established residence in Switzerland to avoid United States taxes, died of alcoholism in 1981. The money was left to the Motion Picture and TV Fund. They'll be cashing those checks until sometime in the twenty-first century.

Columbia hit the jackpot on Holden's deferred payments. The $50,000-a-year payment represents far less than they'd have to pay to borrow an equivalent amount. In fact, Holden has really been paid out of interest earnings—the studio got him for free. But then again, it was Alec Guinness who won the Oscar for *Kwai*.

Sparkle, Shirley, Sparkle: Shirley Temple and Twentieth Century-Fox

BACKGROUND: Their million-dollar baby was signed to a seven-year contract at a salary as small as she was, when her parents decided that America's favorite star would retire to kindergarten unless the studio upped the ante. In a democracy, it's hard to force a five-year-old to work.

Little Shirley Temple, born in Santa Monica, California, in 1928, was only two years old when, according to her mother, Gertrude, "she began to display a rare sense of rhythm and would keep time with her feet to the music on the radio." Her mother enrolled her in dancing school when she was just three, although the fifty-cent weekly tuition put a strain on the family budget (it was the Depression) and there were two other children to support. The sacrifice quickly paid off when a talent scout cruised the school and chose Shirley for a series of one-reel shorts called The Baby Burlesks, at $10 a day. Encouraged by her daughter's success in these films, Gertrude took her on the rounds of the major studios, where she landed several bit parts and ultimately a show-stopping singing role in the 1934 film *Stand Up and Cheer*. Fox signed her for a seven-year contract at $150 a week, and although her fan mail was beginning to pour in, Fox immediately "loaned" her to Paramount for $1,000 a week. Her first feature at Paramount was *Little Miss Marker* (1934), which quickly grossed $1 million and established Shirley as a star. It was also the first of her films that Shirley was allowed to see and it delighted her: She clapped for herself throughout the screening.

Fox, impressed with the Paramount grosses on Shirley's film, came up with a star vehicle for her in 1934 called *Baby, Take a Bow*. She was now one of America's most popular stars, but her salary, relative to her fame, was tiny; and to make matters worse, her seven-year contract would end at the same time as her childhood—she'd be thirteen, a child star no longer. Her parents did some quick arithmetic and announced that their Shirley would be enrolled in kindergarten, full time, unless Fox adjusted her contract. The studio knew that some day the bloom would fade from their little rose, and that every day she stayed home meant she was one day older. They hastily agreed to new terms.

THE DEAL: Shirley would be paid $1,250 a week while filming, and her mom would earn $250 a week as her daughter's hairdresser and coach. A cozy ten-room cottage on the studio lot was renovated into a "kiddie haven" as soon as Gloria Swanson cleared out. Meals were brought to her at the cottage; she was forbidden to eat in the commissary to avoid her being "petted and pampered." Her parents could retire her at any time if they felt that her film career was having a deleterious effect on her personality. Fox got to play beat-the-clock with America's hottest and smallest actress.

RESULTS: Shirley's next film, *Bright Eyes* (1934), introduced the song "On the Good Ship Lollipop," cost $190,000 to make, and earned back its costs in three weeks. Shirley outpolled every other star in Hollywood as America's favorite (her competition included Clark Gable, Mae West, Janet Gaynor, and Greta Garbo). Shirley would shake her golden curls, put little finger to dimpled cheek and exclaim "Oh, my goodness!" and the nation would sigh with delight, forgetting, for just a moment, its Depression woes. Informed that Shirley earned more money than he did, President Roosevelt said, "She deserves it."

In 1935, Fox raised her salary to $4,000 a week, with a $20,000

"If the day ever comes when I feel that Shirley is becoming self-conscious or too aware of her screen importance, I shall cancel her contract immediately and let her grow up to a normal girlhood, far from Hollywood and its studios."

Gertrude Temple

per-picture bonus, plus $500 a week for mom. Shirley's name and image were licensed to fifteen firms manufacturing all sorts of things: dolls, soap, hair ribbons, kitchenware, undies, hats, dresses. These arrangements yielded her over $1,000 a week (plus $100 to Mom as style consultant) for years. She was so popular that on her eighth birthday, 135,000 birthday gifts were sent to her by fans all over the world.

She did have her detractors. A critic in the *New York Times* sourly called her "an assault on the nation's maternal instinct," and another one asked, "Why they bother with titles, or with plots either is beyond me." But David Butler, the director who worked with her in four films, said, "she got into fairyland, she believed it herself and that's why you believed it." Her mother would stand on the sidelines yelling, *"Sparkle, Shirley, sparkle!"* But the sparkle was tarnishing with age. Alan Dwan, the director of *Rebecca of Sunnybrook Farm* (1938), said: "It was sad that the spark lasted only to a certain age. But if Shirley Temple was only a moment in movie history, it was a great moment." After her two 1940 films flopped, Shirley's parents bought out her contract and took her home to wait out her "awkward age" away from the cameras. She was a has-been at twelve and a veteran of twenty-nine films. A comeback she attempted as a teenager was met with a lukewarm response, and she was relegated to "B"-type movies. At sixteen, she became engaged to tall, blond, and handsome John Agar. She married him at seventeen; at nineteen she had a little girl of her own (David Selznick attempted to sign her baby to a movie contract before it was even born); and, at twenty-one, she was divorced. In that same year, 1949, Shirley retired permanently from the screen. In 1950 she married Charles Black, one of the richest men in California (he was dropped from the Social Register for marrying an actress). They had two children. In 1974, after many years of service to the Republican party, including an unsuccessful congressional race in 1967, Shirley Temple Black was appointed United States Ambassador to Ghana. The press had a hard time relating to Ambassador Black as a diplomat; she would forever be a "former child star." She complained: "Dr. Kissinger was a former child, Jerry Ford was a former child, even FDR was a former child. I retired from the movies in 1949, but I'm still a former child." In 1976, President Ford appointed her United States Chief of Protocol, which carried the rank of assistant secretary of state.

Once asked to sing "On the Good Ship Lollipop" at a political event, she refused, insisting: "Nothing could be sadder than a forty-nine-year-old woman singing a child's song. I don't even do that at home."

```
┌─────────────────────────────────────────────────────────────┐
│              HOW DO MOVIES MAKE MONEY?                        │
│                                                               │
│  The average movie costs $10 million to produce and $6       │
│  million to market. The average movie earns, over several    │
│  years, $17 million, or $1 million profit. Here's how it     │
│  breaks down:                                                 │
│                                                               │
│  $8 million from North American rentals                       │
│    6 million from overseas rentals                            │
│    2 million from videocassettes and discs                    │
│    1 million from pay TV and TV                               │
│  Total: $17 million, or $1 million profit                     │
│                                                               │
│  This does not include soundtrack recordings or spin-off      │
│  licensed merchandise.                                        │
└─────────────────────────────────────────────────────────────┘
```

When ET Played Cleopatra . . . and Lost: Elizabeth Taylor and *Cleopatra*

BACKGROUND: If beauty is only skin deep, then Elizabeth Taylor (ET) has gained more mileage from her shallow assets than any woman in the twentieth century. From child star to foxy dame capsizing a studio on a Roman Nile, she led a charmed life . . . up to a point.

Born February 27, 1932, in England, she moved with her parents to the chic heart of movie execdom, Pacific Palisades, where she hobnobbed with the "royal" tots, was spotted in a dancing class by an exec's wife, and was whisked to MGM. Magically pretty, ET (with her stage-mom's help) thrived on the constant exposure and blossomed at fifteen into the publicity machine's "most beautiful woman in the world," earning $30,000 a year, plus $10,000 for mom as duenna. Extremely photogenic and shamelessly ambitious, she was marketed so fabulously well she never took the time away from the camera for acting or vocal lessons, though her shrill, little-girl voice would have driven a serious actress to night school. She played conceited, artificial, vapid rich girls to perfection; it was *all* she played. MGM knew a bankable item, using her patrician beauty like a placid mask while churning out countless publicity stories of her generous heart matched in regal grandeur only by her violet (sort of) eyes.

Husband followed husband and lover followed lover as scandal followed scandal with illness guaranteeing headline attention when husband/lover/scandal waned. Legally, Nicky Hilton (1950) was replaced by Michael Wilding (1952) who was replaced by Mike Todd (1957) who died (1958) and was immediately replaced by Eddie Fisher (1959) without Debbie Reynold's approval. Her MGM contract was coming to an end; she longed to go free-lance and garner big bucks from her notoriety, but she feared losing MGM's stellar packaging. Over the years she had gone from one forgettable box-office smash to another—she was the number-one star in the world. In 1959, on loan to Columbia, she commanded $500,000 for the disappointing *Suddenly, Last Summer*, becoming *the* highest paid superstar. When Walter Wanger, a producer at Twentieth Century-Fox, asked her to play Cleopatra, she agreed. The studio was in trouble and ET would save the day. She had one more MGM commitment—*Butterfield 8*—at her standard $100,000; then she set her sights on making film history. And she did, but not exactly as she planned.

THE FIRST DEAL: Elizabeth Taylor would play Cleopatra for $1 million for sixty-four days' work. She would also get her own hairstylist, two penthouse suites in London's ritzy Dorchester Hotel, a Rolls-Royce to and from work, $3,500 a week for living expenses, $1,500 a week for hubby Fisher to squire her around, first-class tickets to London for six (herself/her agent/three kids/and Fisher), and the first two days of each menstrual period off. Todd-A-O would be used instead of the planned Cinemascope so she could get royalties. Rouben Mamoulian would direct. Peter Finch (Caesar) and Stephen Boyd (Mark Antony) were cast. The budget was $5 million. The production would be shot in England.

RESULTS: First a sore throat then a fever then a cold then an abscessed tooth then maybe meningitis kept her off the set for two weeks at a cost of $121,428 a day. (Lloyds of London paid out $2 million and demanded that Marilyn Monroe or Kim Novak or Shirley MacLaine replace her. Wanger refused.) Two months later, the diva was ready to work, but the script was in its fifth shaky revision and the director quit after having seen $7 million spent on twelve minutes of a lousy movie that he swore would never hit the screen. Joe Mankiewicz was hired to write a new script and direct (for a reported $3 million), and ET was put on hold for $50,000 a week in salary, plus $3,500 expenses. Then her Asian flu developed into staphylococcus pneumonia and she nearly died while all the world watched in petrified attention. (Even Debbie sent a get-well message.) She lived, re-

turning to health more famous and beloved than any woman since Mary Pickford. She took six months off to recuperate. Hollywood gave her the 1960 Oscar for *Butterfield 8* for not dying. But what about *Cleo?*

THE SECOND DEAL: ET would get a *second* million to resume the totally overhauled project in Rome. This time her doctor would get $25,000 for six weeks of temperature-taking on location. She retained all the other perks of the first agreement. Roddy McDowell was bought out of *Camelot* to play Octavius; Rex Harrison (Caesar) and Richard Burton (Mark Antony) were cast.

RESULTS: Sixty new sets were built, and Fox wrote off $5 million on the $7 million spent (minus Lloyds's $2 million). The studio sold 260 acres of back lot to pay its bills. Mankiewicz, defeated by strikes, fights, corporate dementia, and amphetamines, was fired as costs jumped to $500,000 a week—$50,000 going to ET for overtime pay. Meanwhile, Fisher was very publicly displaced by Burton, and ET's adultery, censured by the Vatican, became the hottest news on the planet as Wanger was fired. Then Spyros Skouras, president of Fox, was fired. The film cost $40 million. ET spent 215 days pretending to be Cleopatra. She should have stayed in "beds."

The most expensive movie ever made was a disaster. The critical response was savage; ET became hysterical over her scathing reviews and had to be sedated. Fox went bankrupt. Burton's *Cleo* salary of $250,000 quadrupled for his next picture; ET went on to free-lance nine pictures for $1 million each through 1970 until celluloid turkeys gobbled up her box-office appeal and the ticket-buyer lines that had once sustained her career were replaced by the headlines in the *National Enquirer* and the *Star*. Driven from excess to excess the Burtons became a public spectacle. They married twice (1964, 1975) and ran an open private life that made the world feel implicated: ". . . we live out for the benefit of the mob the sort of idiocies they've come to expect." Her judgment clouded by alcohol and pills, eager for any attention, played court jester to the multitudes. In 1970, no longer bankable after a series of bombs, her salary plummeted, while Burton's career was also ravaged by bombs, heavy drinking, and prescribed medications. Except for *Winter Kills* (1979), in which she does a silent cameo, her last twelve films were all duds. But ever the consummate celebrity, her Broadway debut in *The Little Foxes* (1981) got *very* mixed reviews and made $286,000 a week.

Twenty years after *Cleopatra*, the divorced Burtons were reunited on Broadway at $75,000 a week each, plus a cut of the gross, in *Private Lives*. The reviews were as bad as any she earned for their first appearance together. All told, they made eleven movies as a team (nine as the Burtons), and earned and gained through investments $50 million, which is neatly stashed in Swiss accounts to be enjoyed in monarchical style, tax-free. In the immortal words of Joan Rivers: "When Elizabeth Taylor had her ears pierced, gravy ran out." ET has paid her dues.

◆ ◆ ◆ ◆

"If I didn't rate it, I wouldn't get it because there's never been a producer in the history of the world that has ever given an actor anything that he didn't have to give him."

Lauren Bacall, commenting on her $2,800 a week limo-service perk for *Woman of the Year*

Elizabeth Taylor's Million-Dollar Movies
(plus 10 percent of the gross, plus $4,000 in weekly expenses)

The VIPs (1963)
The Sandpiper (1965)
Who's Afraid of Virginia Woolf? (1966; $1.1 million, no expenses)
The Taming of the Shrew (1967)
Reflections in a Golden Eye (1967)
The Comedians (1967)
Boom! (1968)
Secret Ceremony (1968)
The Only Game in Town (1970)

NIFTY SWIFTY

Irving ("Swifty") Lazar, the legendary literary and theatrical agent, was given his nickname by Humphrey Bogart after negotiating five deals for Bogart in five hours.

What's Four Million Dollars between Friends?: Streisand and Sue Mengers

Barbra did it for $4 million: All Night Long.

BACKGROUND: When two divas plotted to "save" a project dear to one of them, all seemed made in Hollywood heaven for everyone at the top. But all was not exactly as it seemed.

Sue Mengers, at age forty-four, was the most powerful female super-agent in the history of movies. Oz-like, she maneuvered her clients ingeniously to create knockout "packages." Her judgment in backing winning material was considered unerring. Queen of a fiefdom within International Creative Management (ICM), a most formidable talent agency, she had risen through the office ranks by negotiating headline-grabbing contracts that soon attracted some of the world's greatest stars into her orbit, including Ms. Bankable Streisand.

At thirty-eight, the Brooklyn-born Barbra was reported to be a $50-million-a-year international industry all by her unique self. Like Sue, she had a genius for marketing her natural gifts; in four short years, she shot from a small nightclub stage (the Bon Soir), to a small part in a Broadway hit (Miss Marmelstein in *I Can Get It for You Wholesale*), to a hit album (*The Barbra Streisand Album*), and on to TV ("My Name Is Barbra") and a *huge* Broadway smash (*Funny Girl*), the same role that won her an Oscar when her screen-debut Fanny Brice shared the award with Katharine Hepburn's Eleanor of Aquitaine (*Lion in Winter*). Along the way (respectively), Barbra's other first efforts collected the New York Drama Critics' Circle Award, the Grammy, the Emmy, and the Tony to keep her Oscar company.

In 1980, Sue's Belgian-born husband, Jean-Claude Tramont, started directing his first American film. It was a small-budget film starring Gene Hackman and Lisa Eichhorn, who was fresh from her success in *Yanks*. Suddenly, early in production of *All Night Long*, Eichhorn was fired when Streisand agreed to replace her as the soft-spoken, passive, laid-back California blonde, Cheryl Gibbons. "The part was too much of a stretch for Lisa," Tramont explained after the firing. "It's no reflection on her acting ability." The part was diametrically opposed to every detail of the Streisand persona, but the street-kid-turned-superstar was thought capable of stretching to the moon, taking the box-office receipts with her.

THE DEAL: Streisand signed on the dotted line for $4 million up front (Eichhorn was earning $250,000), 15 percent of the profits, and the unprecedented right, as a supporting player in a secondary role, to final cut, which gave her complete control over the film as released for distribution. Tramont received tremendous publicity for his American debut and his budget was upped from $2.5 million to $11 million as the film jumped from the small-film category to major event with La Streisand aboard. Sue Mengers, negotiating the terms for Barbra, expected to earn her usual 10 percent, or $400,000, and the satisfaction of "saving" her hubby's movie from Eichhorn-disaster.

RESULTS: Streisand's name appeared in the ads underneath Gene Hackman's, a second-billing status she had never known (and would probably never know again) in her film career. Universal Studios, the film's producer/distributor, said she took the unlikely role—money aside—because "Barbra is continually looking for new challenges," and Tramont assured her baffled fans that she had not needed cajoling by the mighty Mengers because, "no one can get Barbra to do what Barbra does not want to do!"

All seemed well until Barbra called for her paycheck. Upon discovering that Mengers had deducted a 10 percent commission, she called Sue and demanded a refund. She said she had taken the role—money aside—as a "personal favor" to Sue (and hubby) and personal favors do not warrant an agent's fee. Mengers apologized, claiming the ubiquitous "misunderstanding," and returned the $400,000 to Streisand, who promptly fired her. (For Sue, 1981 was a bad year. She not only lost La Barbra, but also Burt Reynolds, Ali McGraw—who said Sue made her feel she needed a face-lift—and Diana Ross. The stunned industry conjectured that she was secretly planning to take over Columbia or MGM and had cleverly sprung the megabucks' crew to avoid later conflicts-of-interest criticism.)

Streisand strenuously exercised her right to final cut, but *All Night Long* got mixed-to-vicious reviews and bad word of mouth. Usually scolded (and ridiculed) for hogging center screen, Barbra was lambasted for being falsely modest and unconvincing, doing a poor imitation of Monroelike innocence, while her fans squirmed at her attempts to change her image and give a truly inventive performance. The movie bombed. Tramont returned to France to work. Streisand, no longer considered invincible by the movie moguls, was forced to make a taped audition to win backing for *Yentl*, which she also directed, winning the Golden Globe Award for Best Director in January 1984. (It also won for Best Musical film.) Mengers announced at the time that she planned "to keep a low profile."

"I think they should consider giving Oscars for meetings: Best Meeting of the Year, Best Supporting Meeting, Best Meeting Based on Material from Another Meeting."

William Goldman, from *Adventures in the Screen Trade*; screenwriter of *Butch Cassidy and the Sundance Kid, All The President's Men*

Dealmaker as Horatio Alger: Daniel Melnick and David Geffen

It all started in the mail room . . .

Daniel Melnick, age fifty, is a major movie producer. He lists on his résumé *Network, Straw Dogs, Close Encounters, All That Jazz,* and *Altered States,* to name a few of the biggies. He started in the CBS mail room. Over the years, he worked his way into programming and eventually headed the department for ABC. A shift into movies made him production chief at MGM, then president of Columbia Pictures from

June through October of 1978. When his friend Alan J. Hirschfield took over Twentieth Century-Fox in 1980, Melnick turned down the presidency for the role of independent producer allied with Fox. His contract has never been equaled: It ran for ten years (five as producer and five as consultant) and included a retainer of approximately $500,000 a year, a producer's fee for each film (several hundred thousand dollars), access to a million-dollar fund for salaries and overhead, 10 percent of each movie's *gross profits* (ten cents on every dollar entering the studio's coffers, even before costs are met), the right to make three films without studio okay, and his "IndieProd" suite supplied by Fox.

In 1981, when Fox was bought for $703 million by the Denver-based wildcat oil magnate Marvin Davis—he had failed to buy the Oakland A's—Melnick's arrangement with Hirschfield was not acceptable to Davis. Davis had his own ideas about how to run a studio: He had placed Henry Kissinger and Gerald Ford on the Fox board— two great movie wizards?—and Melnick's first IndieProd movie was the gay love story *Making Love,* a dull flop. If Melnick's contract was not outrageous enough, *gay* was not good to Davis; it was the final blow. He blocked Melnick's $1 million overhead fund by claiming IndieProd had never paid for the lavish decoration of its suite, then bought out the contract for $2.5 million after intense negotiations. Melnick moved off the Fox lot and set up an office, intending to produce for other studios.

◆ ◆ ◆ ◆

David Geffen, age forty, says, "I am driven. But I'm not Sammy Glick. I've never killed anyone. I don't have to. I'm too talented." Born in Brooklyn, New York, Geffen flunked out of college and got a job in the mail room at the William Morris Agency (WMA) in 1964. When he discovered that the agency was checking résumés—he had claimed a B.A. from UCLA—he intercepted the letter from the university and changed the facts to suit himself: "I just don't believe in taking no for an answer." Based in the mail room, he sallied forth and signed Laura Nero and other talents to WMA. Then he moved to Ashley Famous Agency (AFA) in 1968 and helped make its music department the second largest in the business. From AFA he went to Creative Management Associates (CMA); then with his proven flawless feel for talent, he started his own agency: "I don't believe in market surveys or target audiences. If I'm an expert, I'm an expert at my

"In Hollywood, a contract lays out the terms for the divorce."

Daniel Melnick

He's a truly entrepreneurial personality with a great agility.

Ted Ashley, Ashley Famous Agency

own taste. I figure, if I enjoy something, others will, too. I run on instinct."

When Atlantic Records wouldn't record an artist he believed in, Geffen started Asylum Records. He became a major creative force in the industry, creating hit after hit and group after group. In 1972 he sold Asylum Records to Warner Communications for $7 million. Warners retained him to run Asylum (merged with Elektra): "I dropped 90 percent of their artists, made new deals, and out of 40 record releases 38 were hits." He crossed over to Warners' movie division to oversee *Oh, God!, Greased Lightning,* and *The Late Show,* but he was naive in the politics of working with other people and could not survive working as part of a group.

When his movie dream collapsed, his doctor announced in 1976 that he had a terminal illness. Geffen retired to die. (He invested that $7 million from Asylum in California real estate and turned it into $23 million.) The doctor was wrong. He didn't die. In 1980, he returned to work backed by Steve Ross, head of Warner Communications: "It's not a question of clout; it's a question of backing," Geffen believes. With a reported $100 million support, he created a new record label, Geffen Records (whose gross profit in 1982 was $50 to $60 million), co-produced Broadway plays (*Cats* had the largest advance sale in Broadway history—$6 million), and produced movies. "I'm Billy the Kid, the fastest draw. It's not arrogance. It's the truth. I'm good at deciding what people like. I'm gifted at knowing what will be a success before it's a success."

GOOD DEAL, BAD DEAL

Well. Let me put it this way: I think I forgot trigonometry a very long time ago. But I can certainly negotiate a deal. I know where the numbers are, what all the effects are on interest rates, and so on. I don't think the cleverness comes from being able to negotiate a good deal—that is to say, the best terms or whatever. I think the *smart* in making a deal is picking the correct *material,* the correct *artist.*

There are *no* bargains in life. I've never seen any. And I'm *not* looking to make a bargain. Because a deal in which somebody else is unhappy or I'm unhappy is a bad deal. It's gonna break somewhere. If I see that a deal can't be made comfortably for everybody, I just pass. Because I know that my life will be shit from this deal.

David Geffen,
New York Magazine, May 17, 1982

The Geffen Goodies

Records (25 million albums sold since October 1980); major releases:
Double Fantasy, by John Lennon and Yoko Ono
Quarterflash, by Quarterflash
Asia, by Asia
Donna Summer, by Donna Summer
Jump Up, by Elton John
Peter Gabriel, by Peter Gabriel
Wild Things Run Fast, by Joni Mitchell
Trans, by Neil Young
Simon & Garfunkel, The Concert in Central Park
Dreamgirls, original cast recording

Movies:
Personal Best: $14 million budget
Risky Business: $5.7 million budget
Man Trouble: $9.5 million budget

Broadway Shows (with percentage ownership):
Dreamgirls: 33%
Little Shop of Horrors: 50%
Cats: 33%
Master Harold: 20%
Good: 20%

Real-Estate Holdings:
Six-floor office building on Santa Monica Blvd. in Beverly Hills
Land and buildings on Hollywood's Sunset Blvd.
Two-hundred-unit apartment complex in Palm Springs, California
Shopping Center in Sylmar, California

ROCKY ROAD

Rocky was a sensational hit. Made for around $1 million, it earned about $100 million. Stallone then made *F.I.S.T.* (a bomb) and *Paradise Alley* (a superbomb). *Rocky II* was a sensational hit. It earned about $150 million. Stallone then made *Nighthawks* (a bomb) and *Victory* (a superduperbomb). To write, direct, and star in *Rocky III*—a sensational hit that earned $63.5 million—Stallone was paid $10 million, the largest up-front salary in the history of movies. Stallone then made *Staying Alive,* or what the wags dubbed, *Staying Awake.* Thanks to Travolta, it made pots of money. What fresh disaster/megabomb before *Rocky IV?*

Sylvester Stallone, 5'7½", presents an 8'6" statue of Rocky Balboa to Philadelphia, the city of his birth.

Celluloid Wildcatting:
Investing in Movies

BACKGROUND: There's no business like show business, they've been singing for years, but only one in every ten movies makes a profit. Still, the first two *Star Wars* earned $1 billion so far, and that's enough to keep hope in the magic alive.

Movies are expensive to make. Studios need all the help they can get to keep afloat. With bank interest at 14 percent, the way to finance productions has become varied and very creative. Brokerage houses are getting into the act, playing with movies the way they play with oil- and gas-drilling ventures.

THE DEAL: Clusters of small investors (as many as three thousand) form a limited partnership (LP). To avoid putting all their eggs in one fragile basket, the LP invests in half-a-dozen films from one studio, and the studio approached agrees to finance no more than half of any one film with the LP's money. None of the profits is distributed until *all* the agreed-upon films are released. The partners collect a yearly fee for having assembled "the package," as well as interest-payment write-offs, investment tax credits,* and deferred income.

RESULTS: SLM Entertainment was born. In 1981, they entered into a "joint venture" with MGM. Three thousand investors came up with $40 million. MGM agreed not to use more than $7.5 million on any one of the six films selected: *Pennies from Heaven, Rich and Famous, Whose Life Is It Anyway?, All the Marbles, Poltergeist,* and *Rocky III.* Only the last two made money, but they made *big* money: $36 million and $63.5 million respectively. However, the big flops erased the big hits, and SLM barely broke even. Nonetheless, SLM II was formed: ten investors with $25 million for Twentieth Century-Fox (distributor of *Star Wars*).

Another example is Delphi Film Associates. The LP was offering units at $5,000. They raised $51 million, which Columbia will use for 40 percent of twelve to sixteen projects. And there's nothing to stop these LPs from investing in countries offering tax shelters and incentives, countries like Australia and Canada and New Zealand.

---

*Up until 1976, investors could deduct four times their film investment. The IRS ended that "incentive."

CHECKING INTO *THE WHITE HOTEL*

Dealmaker Keith Barrish made a fortune in real estate before turning his attention to the movies. He bought the rights to *Sophie's Choice* for $750,000, then produced *Endless Love* and *Misunderstood* before forming his own film company—Keith Barrish Productions—which he hooked up with Twentieth Century-Fox. But instead of the usual producer-studio arrangement, like Ray Stark's with Columbia or Alan Ladd's with Warners where the studio is co-financier, Barrish will use his own $100 million for nine films and Fox will distribute *only,* as they do for *Star Wars* [see "Dealmaker as Filmmaker: George Lucas," page 367]. One of his projects is *The White Hotel* with Barbra Streisand [see "What's Four Million Dollars between Friends?: Streisand and Sue Mengers," page 358], who may finally get her wish to play an opera singer. He has already arranged for the sale of cable rights to his non-existent movies to HBO.

THE HOLLYWOOD LAWYER

The talent are making greater demands upon their lawyers. A lot of writers, not too long ago, just weren't interested in the ramifications of a deal—all they wanted to know was, "How much money do I get paid for this?"

Dick Weston, head of business affairs, Paramount TV

... the old-style Hollywood lawyer representing talent acted in a mostly preventive capacity: after a deal had been cut between an agent and a studio, the lawyer would be called in to draw up a contract that codified the deal, and to anticipate any problems that might arise. Lawyers were primarily concerned with the question, as agent Jeff Berg of ICM poses it, What happens if the parties fall out of love? Today, it's not at all unusual for the lawyers [by virtue of whom they represent] to be at the cutting edge of the deal-making process, dictating the terms to the studios and assisted by the agents, rather than vice versa.

Agents still serve an important function as a "creative sounding board" for their clients (which script will best advance Robert Redford's career?). And they're still the ones who make The Contract, which determines who is negotiating with whom—they set up the chessboard. But this only highlights the centrality of the entertainment lawyer's role. He's the one answering the Hollywood Quiz Question that makes and breaks deals: Who Gets the Money?

Paul Attanasio, *Esquire*, April 1983

Dealmaker as Filmmaker:
George Lucas

George Lucas, who has made more money than any other contemporary filmmaker (and did so before his fortieth birthday), was born in 1944 to a middle-class family in Modesto, California. His father, who was very strict with his children, owned a fairly successful stationery store. The family did not own a television set until 1954; before then, Lucas spent his spare time glued to a neighbor's set. In 1956, when Disneyland opened, Lucas was one of the first in line: "I loved Disneyland." Lucas remembers: "I was in heaven." Lucas was a mediocre high-school student, his grades qualifying him only for admission to the local junior college. When he graduated, a friend mentioned that the film school at the University of Southern California in Los Angeles was very easy to get into. Lucas applied, was accepted, and found his life transformed: "Suddenly my whole life was film—every waking hour." He made a student film that became legendary and won first prize in the National Student Film Festival; he was rewarded with a six-month apprenticeship at Warner Brothers.

As luck would have it, Francis Ford Coppola, the twenty-seven-year-old *wunderkind* of the film industry, was then at Warner's making *Finian's Rainbow.* Lucas became his assistant; Coppola became Lucas's mentor. His work so impressed Coppola that he helped Lucas raise

George Lucas (right) *and Alec Guiness on the set of* Star Wars.

the money to do his first feature, an extended version of his student film. *THX 1138* was made for $777,000—Lucas was paid $15,000 to direct it—and even with a post–*Star Wars* release, the film barely broke even. But in 1972, again with the help of Coppola, Lucas managed to raise the money for his next feature, which turned out to be one of the most profitable movies ever made. *American Graffiti* cost under $1 million to make and has grossed over $115 million. Lucas earned $7 million as director and co-author of the screenplay. Before *Graffiti* opened, Lucas tried to get funding for his next project, *Star Wars*, and had been turned down at Universal. Twentieth Century-Fox agreed to do the film, but they were unenthusiastic. Lucas was willing to write and direct the film for $150,000 and 40 percent of the profits, but he insisted upon holding onto a good share in what are generally considered to be the "garbage provisions" of a film contract: merchandising, publishing, and music rights to the film. Tom Pollock, Lucas's lawyer, says: "Every single deal we've done has been a trade-off of dollars for control, because that's what George has always wanted. The whole history of the *Star Wars* negotiations was dollars versus control." *Star Wars* cost $10 million to make and has grossed $524 million. Lucas's share was $30 million; he was thirty-three years old. And *Star Wars* spawned a merchandising empire that has generated nearly $2 billion in retail sales. Fox thought so little of the financial potential in the licensing that they sold the rights to *Star Wars* toys to General Mills (through Kenner Toys) in perpetuity. In his original arrangement, Lucas split the licensing profits with Fox, fifty-fifty, after the studio deducted a 15 percent licensing fee. This arrangement was revised for *The Empire Strikes Back:* Lucasfilms now receives 90 percent, but Fox will receive 10 percent of all licensing revenues for all future *Star Wars* films. Lucasfilms generally gets a royalty of 1 to 7 percent on *Star Wars* merchandise, although that can be as high as 50 percent in the case of T-shirts.

With the enormous profits from *Star Wars*, Lucas was able to finance *The Empire Strikes Back* himself, making it the most expensive independently produced film ever made. Fox paid for all distribution costs (mostly prints and advertising), and has made over $40 million. The film, which cost $33 million to make, has grossed $365 million. Lucas has earned $51 million.

Lucas was able to "liberate" himself from film directing with the enormous success of *Star Wars*. He finds directing an onerous task and prefers to "mastermind" films and then let other people actualize his concepts. "George didn't think directing was that much fun. He didn't want to be the general anymore. He wanted the sergeants to take over," said an associate. He hired Irvin Kershner to direct *Empire*. His buddy Steven (*E.T.*) Spielberg directed *Raiders of the Lost Ark*, which cost $22 million to make, grossed $335 million, and has earned Lucas, as executive producer, some $25.5 million, and $23 million for Spielberg.

Lucas, who was said to have been personally worth $100 million before his 1983 divorce from his wife, has put a huge amount of money into Skywalker Ranch, his three-thousand-acre Marin County headquarters. Conceived of as a film think tank, over three hundred people are employed there by Lucas. Skywalker Ranch has its own roads (i.e., Lucas Valley Road), its own fire department (two vintage 1950s engines), and guest houses for visiting filmmakers. Lucas enterprises at the ranch include his computer company, Sprocket, which is working on special uses of computers in the classroom, and Industrial Light and Magic, Lucas's special-effects company (they did *Star Trek II* and *E.T.*, as well as the *Star Wars* films). "This is where the future is made," says ILM manager Tom Smith. That future will include six more *Star Wars* films.

Yoda tells us: "Try not. Do. Do or do not. There is no try." Lucas tells us: "The door to your cage is open. All you have to do is walk out, if you dare."

SUCK WIND

"The reason that negotiations take so long in Hollywood—it is common for contracts not to be signed until long after the picture is in release—is that the negotiation establishes the channel of power, the chain of command. Making an individual back down over money in the negotiation process is one quick and clear way to establish that power, to show who is boss. The production company can do this because it has one unassailable advantage: Everyone wants to make a movie. The line is long, the chosen are few, and the chosen learn to suck wind—or someone else is chosen."

John Gregory Dunne,
Esquire, August 1983

ACKNOWLEDGMENTS

CHERYL MOCH: I wish to acknowledge the contribution to this project of my father, Edward Moch, who taught me that words could be play; my mother, Ethel Moch, who convinced me that life could be interesting; and my sisters, Madeline and Judith, who so lovingly and patiently indulge me. Special thanks to: my very special partner, Vincent Virga; my editor, Barbara Grossman, and her assistant, David Groff; my agent, Elaine Markson; and to the following sources of encouragement and creative inspiration: Laine Whitcomb, Liza Solomon, Holly Gewandter, Carole De Saram, Raymond Erickson, Judith Waldman, Nicolle Freni, Diane Gelon, Chuck Boyce, Fabienne Rawley, Ilka Scobie, Ellen Gould, Elliott Forte, Roy Phelps, Sonia Simon, and Marion Weisberg.

◆ ◆ ◆ ◆

Both authors wish to thank Nat Andriani of United Press International and our super dealmaker lawyer, Phillip Taubman, who made this possible.

◆ ◆ ◆ ◆

CHERYL MOCH was born and raised in Brooklyn, New York, equidistant from Coney Island and Greenwich Village, and now lives in lower Manhattan. She has worked as a photo editor and visual researcher on dozens of books and films. She is now writing a book about childhood.

VINCENT VIRGA is the author of two novels, *Gaywyck* and *A Comfortable Corner*, and is currently finishing a third, *Vadriel Vail*. He is also a free-lance picture editor; his most recent clients include Mayor Ed Koch, Ken Follett, Joan Collins, and Jane Fonda.